SPINOZA'S RELIGI

Spinoza's Religion

A NEW READING OF THE *ETHICS*

Clare Carlisle

PRINCETON UNIVERSITY PRESS
PRINCETON & OXFORD

Copyright © 2021 by Princeton University Press

Princeton University Press is committed to the protection of copyright and the intellectual property our authors entrust to us. Copyright promotes the progress and integrity of knowledge. Thank you for supporting free speech and the global exchange of ideas by purchasing an authorized edition of this book. If you wish to reproduce or distribute any part of it in any form, please obtain permission.

Requests for permission to reproduce material from this work
should be sent to permissions@press.princeton.edu

Published by Princeton University Press
41 William Street, Princeton, New Jersey 08540
99 Banbury Road, Oxford OX2 6JX

press.princeton.edu

All Rights Reserved

Library of Congress Control Number 2021939527
First paperback printing, 2023
Paperback ISBN 978-0-691-22419-0
Cloth ISBN 978-0-691-17659-8
ISBN (ebook) 978-0-691-22420-6

British Library Cataloging-in-Publication Data is available

Editorial: Ben Tate and Josh Drake
Production Editorial: Debbie Tegarden
Jacket/Cover Design: Karl Spurzem
Production: Danielle Amatucci
Publicity: Alyssa Sanford and Amy Stewart
Copyeditor: Francis Eaves

This book has been composed in Classic Miller

To my family: Johnny, Joseph, Katy

inquietum est cor nostrum, donec requiescat in te

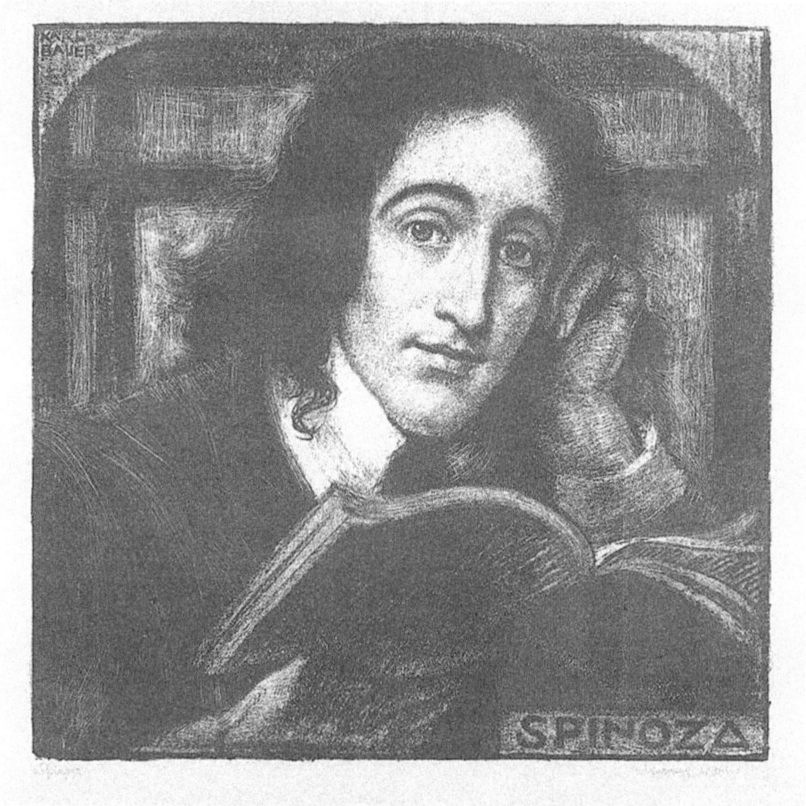
KARL BAUER
SPINOZA

CONTENTS

	Introduction: The Question of Religion	1
CHAPTER 1	Philosophy and Devotion	18
CHAPTER 2	What Is the *Ethics*?	35
CHAPTER 3	Being-in-God	56
CHAPTER 4	Whatever We Desire and Do	79
CHAPTER 5	Participating in Divine Nature	92
CHAPTER 6	*Acquiescentia*	112
CHAPTER 7	How to Love God	134
CHAPTER 8	Eternal Life	148
CHAPTER 9	Spinoza's Religion	164
	Afterword: 'The path to these things'	184

Acknowledgements · 189
Notes · 191
Works Cited · 243
Index · 257

SPINOZA'S RELIGION

INTRODUCTION

The Question of Religion

BENEDICT DE SPINOZA did not have a religion—at least not in the usual sense of the word. He was brought up and educated within Amsterdam's Jewish community, from which he was cast out in 1656, at the age of twenty-three. As far as we know, he made no effort to reconcile with this community: leaving it was, it seems, a welcome intellectual liberation.[1] For the remaining twenty years of his life he pursued his philosophical enquiries in conversation with Christians of various sorts, while refusing to convert to Christianity.[2] In the seventeenth century Spinoza was unusual, perhaps even unique, in engaging closely and deeply with theological questions as a free thinker, deliberately occupying a perspective outside any religious tradition. His masterpiece the *Ethics* (1677) shines out even amongst the philosophical works of his most original contemporaries— Descartes and Leibniz, for example—as a metaphysical and ethical vision unconstrained by the demands of doctrinal orthodoxy.

About a year before his death, while he was completing the *Ethics*, Spinoza wrote a letter to Albert Burgh, a young man who had just converted from Calvinism to Catholicism. Here Spinoza discussed Judaism, Christianity and Islam, and made plain his rejection of dogmatic, sectarian religion. He explained that he knew the truth of his own philosophy 'in the same way you know that the three angles of a triangle are equal to two right angles . . . for the true is the indicator both of itself and of the false'.[3] He asked Burgh, who naturally thought his religion superior to any other,

> How do you know that [your teachers] are the best among those who have ever taught other Religions, still teach them, or will teach them in the future? Have you examined all those religions, both ancient and modern, which are taught here, and in India, and everywhere

throughout the globe? And even if you had examined them properly, how do you know you have chosen the best?[4]

These are good questions, and they are only partly rhetorical. Mocking the pride and competitiveness that often characterise religious sectarianism, Spinoza granted that 'the organization of the Roman Church ... is well-designed politically, and profitable for many. I do not believe there is any order more suitable for deceiving ordinary people and controlling men's minds, unless it would be the order of the Mahommedan Church.' Yet his irreverence towards sectarian claims to spiritual pre-eminence also went in more tolerant, more conciliatory directions. 'In every Church there are many very honourable men, who worship God with justice and loving kindness,' he reminded Burgh, 'for we know many men of this kind among the Lutherans, the Reformed, the Mennonites, and the Enthusiasts. So you ought to concede that holiness of life is not peculiar to the Roman Church, but is common to all.' Spinoza closed his letter by counselling the eager young convert to 'recognize the reason God has given you, and cultivate it'.[5] In his *Theologico-Political Treatise* (1670), he had made similar arguments about Judaism, challenging the idea that the Hebrews were God's chosen people. 'God is equally beneficent, compassionate, etc. to all,' Spinoza argued, adding that as far as 'intellect and true virtue' are concerned, 'no nation is distinguished from any other'.[6]

Given Spinoza's resistance to what commonly passes for religion, the title of this book contains an irony, and perhaps for some a provocation. At the same time, it is entirely in earnest. The book offers a new interpretation of Spinoza's *Ethics* which takes seriously the question of its religious and theological import. At the same time—as I argue in detail in my final chapter—it suggests that understanding Spinoza's religion forces us to rethink the concept of religion itself. And this is no coincidence, since our modern category of religion, structured by notions of belief and belonging, ideology and identity, rose to prominence during Spinoza's century. Thanks in part to Jonathan Israel's pioneering history of the 'Radical Enlightenment', Spinoza is now recognised as an architect of modernity—but was his vision of human beings and their place in the cosmos radically secular, or radically religious?[7] And does this very distinction between 'religious' and 'secular' rest on a distinctively modern concept of religion, which Spinoza challenged in its infancy? How might the *Ethics* lead us to rethink our assumptions about what religion is, and what it means to be religious?

Raising these questions leads to a new appreciation of Spinoza's significance. He is rightly seen as a decisively modern thinker: like other forward-looking philosophers of his century, he turned his back on medieval cosmology and scholastic theology in favour of a more streamlined metaphysics, and took a keen interest in new scientific discoveries. He criticised superstitious religion, and sought to liberate philosophy from the still-powerful churches. Yet look a little closer, and we see that Spinoza challenged some of the defining features of modernity. In place of the increasing separation of God from nature, he argued that everything is in God, and even proposed 'Nature' as an alternative name for God. In place of modern individualism, with its ideals of autonomy and free choice, he regarded human beings as entirely dependent on God, interdependent on one another, and embedded in a complex ecosystem of causes: he understood the self to be deeply impressionable and porous, constituted by its relations with other things, and he rejected the idea of free choice as a kind of superstition, akin to belief in miracles.[8] While an ethic of restless striving and relentless industry shaped, from Francis Bacon onwards, the modern pursuit of scientific knowledge, Spinoza balanced his own emphasis on effort and activity with an ideal of intellectual rest—an intuitive knowing that brings peace of mind—which echoes the ideal of contemplation cherished by pre-modern philosophers, monks and scholars.[9] Indeed, he argued that resting in God is the highest human good. And while modern capitalist culture spurs a race for productivity and profit, fuelled by anxieties which, as Max Weber argued in 1905, can be traced to the sixteenth century's Protestant theologies, Spinoza insisted that our deepest happiness is found not in production, wealth or competitive success, but in knowledge.[10] A wise person, he writes at the end of the *Ethics*, is 'conscious of himself, and of God, and of things, and always possesses true peace of mind' (E5p42s). His own way of life bears witness to this ideal: he lived humbly and modestly, devoted to his philosophical enquiries.

Spinoza thus resisted deep tendencies of modern thought, which had begun to shape his own century and would produce the world we inhabit today. He did so not by drifting back into pre-modern science and religion, but by forging an alternative modernity that preserved or developed some of the profound insights of his ancient and medieval forebears, by setting them on new philosophical foundations. For example, the *Ethics* affirms the traditional theological view that we are thoroughly dependent beings, not by appealing to a Jewish or Christian doctrine of creation, but by arguing that we are modes, which are by definition 'in another', rather than substances, which are self-sufficient, 'in themselves'. To offer just one further example (as we shall see, there are more), Spinoza echoes Plato's insistence that virtue is synonymous with inner happiness—a view challenged first by superstitious beliefs in posthumous rewards and punishments, and later by the means—end thinking of utilitarianism. Yet his defence of virtue's intrinsic value dismantles the idea of final causes that had structured medieval thought.

As its title indicates, the *Ethics* is primarily a book about how to live a good human life. Like a stripped-down *Summa Theologiae*, it begins and ends with God. For Spinoza, we work out how to live well by understanding our relation to God, to other people, and also, crucially, to ourselves. The core principle of his philosophy, governing his ontology and epistemology as well as his ethics, is that 'whatever is, is in God' (E1p15). I call this principle 'being-in-God', and regard it as Spinoza's deepest thought. He argues that the highest, most truthful kind of human life is fully conscious of being-in-God—and conscious, too, that every other creature and thing is also a being-in-God. We will be able to say much more about what Spinoza's religion consists in once we have considered what it means, both conceptually and existentially, to 'be in God'.

In his *Theologico-Political Treatise* Spinoza drew a decisive distinction between 'superstition' and 'true religion'. This distinction was emphasised by early modern writers as diverse as Calvin, Montaigne, Bacon, Hobbes and Bayle. For all these thinkers superstition was, as Bacon put it, 'a deformation of religion'.[11] For Spinoza, it meant a form of religious life based on ignorance rather than wisdom, and motivated more by fear of punishment than by love of truth and goodness. He put this point bluntly in his letter to Albert Burgh, where he wrote that 'having become a slave of [the Roman] Church, you have been guided not so much by the love of God as by fear of hell, the only cause of superstition'.[12]

Spinoza spent all his life in the Dutch Republic, which had a Reformed state church. He had ample opportunity to observe how the Calvinists' emphasis on the stark polarities of salvation and damnation gave rise to unstable emotions—'fluctuations of the soul' (*animi fluctuationes*), and particularly oscillations between hope and fear, confidence and anxiety—which caused turbulence both within and between individuals, and within and between religious communities.[13] For Spinoza, superstitious faith typically involved belief in miracles, and practices of worship that approached God anthropomorphically—as if God were a capricious prince demanding flattery in return for favours, or a vindictive despot who had to be placated by submission and adoration. He criticised the anthropomorphic imagination of 'the common people, who suppose that God is male, not female'.[14] He would have been no happier with a feminine image of God: when grammatical requirements force us to refer to God by pronouns such as 'he', 'him' and 'himself'—which are unnecessary in Spinoza's Latin text—we should bear in mind that these pronouns are merely a linguistic convention, and do not ascribe a personal or gendered nature to God.

Spinoza's critique of certain images of God, and certain forms of religious life, leaves open the question of what a Spinozist 'true religion' would be like.[15] In 1671, he outlined a response to this question in reply to a critique of his newly published *Theologico-Political Treatise* by Lambert van Velthuysen, the governor of Utrecht and a Calvinist Christian influenced by the philosophies of Descartes and Hobbes. Velthuysen had complained that Spinoza, 'to avoid being faulted for superstition, [seems] to have cast off all religion'.[16] Spinoza wondered what conception of religion could have led Velthuysen to make this claim:

> Has someone who maintains that God must be recognized as the highest good, and should be freely loved as such, cast off all religion? Is someone who holds that our greatest happiness and freedom consist only in this [love of God] irreligious? Or that the reward of virtue is virtue itself, whereas the punishment of folly and weakness is folly itself? And finally, that each person ought to love his neighbour and obey the commands of the supreme power? Not only have I explicitly said these things, I have also proven them by the strongest arguments.[17]

These views are indeed defended in Spinoza's *Theologico-Political Treatise*, and they receive an intricate metaphysical elucidation in the *Ethics*. Nevertheless, the question of Spinoza's religion has remained in dispute ever since he wrote this letter. Despite his insistence that 'God must be recognised as the highest good', many of his contemporaries accused him of atheism. In September 1677, a few months after his death, a manuscript of the *Ethics* that Spinoza's young disciple Tschirnhaus had taken with him to Rome was confiscated by Vatican authorities and added to the Index of prohibited books.[18]

Successive generations of readers have repeated the charge of atheism—though during the last century this has increasingly been meant as a compliment, as secularist readers championed Spinoza as an early pioneer of their own worldview. An alternative interpretation of Spinoza emerged towards the end of the eighteenth century, when certain radical thinkers, particularly in Germany, read him as a deeply religious thinker. In 1787,

Herder's *God: Some Conversations* put forward a Christianised Spinozism, setting the scene for Novalis to claim Spinoza as a 'God-intoxicated man'.[19]

While we can admire Spinoza's Romantic readers for their creativity and expansive spirit, their representations of his philosophy are often unreliable. As J. A. Froude wrote in a clear-eyed introduction to Spinozism, published in the *Westminster Review* in 1855,

> The Herder and Schleiermacher school have claimed him as a Christian—a position which no little disguise was necessary to make tenable; the orthodox Protestants and Catholics have called him an Atheist—which is still more extravagant; and even a man like Novalis . . . could find no better name for him than a *Gott trunkner Mann*—a God intoxicated man. . . . With due allowance for exaggeration, such a name would describe tolerably the Transcendental mystics; but with what justice can it be applied to the cautious, methodical Spinoza, who carried his thoughts about with him for twenty years, deliberately shaping them, and who gave them at last to the world in a form more severe than had ever been attempted before with such subjects? With him, as with all great men, there was no effort after sublime emotions. He was a plain, practical person.[20]

In reading Spinoza as a religious thinker, I take a different path from the various interpretations summarised here by Froude. Pursuing the *question* of religion in his thought, I expect this pursuit to be most productive if we treat Spinoza's religion as a genuinely open question, rather than a matter of deciding whether to classify it as Christian, Jewish or Buddhist; pantheist, atheist or secular. All these labels have been applied to Spinozism, but none of them is quite right—not only because Spinoza's religious vision is so original that it eludes ready-made categories, but also because his work calls into question the very *concept* of religion that underlies such classifications. It is, in fact, simplistic to say that the question of Spinoza's religion has been disputed, because the question itself has been so entangled in what Bruno Latour describes as a 'cascade of category mistakes' about the concept of religion.[21] Investigating Spinoza's religion provides an opportunity to confront these mistakes, or confusions, and to think again—yet again—about what 'religion' means.

When the word *religio* occurs in the *Ethics*, it almost always signifies a kind of virtue, and is associated with other virtues. This echoes Thomas Aquinas's discussion of *religio* within the section of the *Summa Theologiae* known as the 'Treatise on Justice and Prudence'. In the *Ethics*, *religio* is never treated as a matter of belief or doctrine. (In the *Theologico-Political Treatise*, religion *is* associated with certain 'tenets [*dogmata*] of universal faith', but there Spinoza makes it clear that religion consists not in adherence to these doctrines, nor in specific practices of worship, but in a way of life characterised by justice and loving-kindness.[22]) Treating *religio* as a virtue might seem to preserve the medieval notion of religion—yet Spinoza understood virtue itself in a new way. My final chapter considers Spinoza's concept of religion in the context of a historical shift that happened during his lifetime, towards an objectifying representation of religion—as both a system of propositional beliefs, and a social reality—so that it became possible to speak of 'a religion', or 'the Christian religion', in the way we do today.

After a long career translating Spinoza, and thereby gaining an unparalleled familiarity with the full range of his writings, Edwin Curley offered the following judgement on Spinoza's religion:

> The question, I think, is whether the advocates of organized religion are entitled to insist that anyone who does not accept their conception of God does not believe in God. Spinoza's God does have a number of the properties traditional religions ascribe to God. It's an immutable first cause of all things, active everywhere in the universe, uncaused by anything else. It's also, Spinoza would argue, a being humans can love. He thinks the love of God is our greatest good. His God does not issue commands, or perform miracles, or reveal itself to man the way the God of the monotheistic religions is supposed to do. It is not the sort of God you can pray to for help in times of trouble. I can understand thinking that belief in so different a God makes for a different kind of religion. But I also think the ethical importance Spinoza attached to this belief weighs heavily in favour of regarding his view as a genuine, if eccentric, form of religious belief.[23]

This book develops an interpretation of Spinoza's *Ethics* which broadly accords with Curley's view—though the extent and orientation of the text's religious 'eccentricity' is one of the questions to be addressed here. Curley is right, I think, to suggest that Spinoza offers a 'different kind of religion' from what we late-moderns are used to. But what kind of religion is it? Framing this question in terms of the familiar notions of 'belief in God' or 'religious belief' will lead us in the wrong direction, and obscure the way Spinoza interrogates the very concept of religion.

Spinoza's own definition of religion as 'whatever we desire and do insofar as we know God' (E4p37s) offers a much more promising formula for philosophical thinking about religion, Spinozist or otherwise. This definition helps us to follow a direction indicated by Susan James in her 2012 book *Spinoza on Religion, Politics and Philosophy*, which offers a reading of the *Theologico-Political Treatise*. James argues that while 'philosophy progressively engulfs theology', philosophy itself 'becomes a form of religion, sharing its capacity to bind, and transforming devotion to the divine law into rational piety. Rather than focusing on a goal external to true religion, this kind of philosophy [cultivates] the same end.'[24]

Most studies of Spinoza's view of religion focus, as James's book does, on the *Theologico-Political Treatise*. But with her remarks about the relation between philosophy and religion in mind, I ask how the *Ethics* illuminates what, precisely, is religious about Spinoza's thought. Responding to this question will involve putting forward interpretations, some of them quite new, of concepts and arguments familiar to readers of the *Ethics*: the metaphysics of substance and mode; the three kinds of knowledge; the critique of free will; the doctrine of *conatus*, or striving for self-preservation; the nature of the affects, particularly desire, joy, love and fear; the intellectual love of God; and the eternity of the human mind. I will also, in my first two chapters, reflect on the nature of philosophy, as Spinoza practised it, and discuss the distinctive literary form of the *Ethics*.

Spinoza's principle of being-in-God makes philosophy inseparable from theology—though he would not himself have put it this way. The word 'theology', though not quite so open-ended as 'religion', isn't straightforward either. Spinoza's rather negative remarks about theology and theologians are an obstacle to appreciating the close connection between philosophy and theology in the *Ethics*, and we need to overcome this obstacle by distinguishing between two senses of 'theology': one broad and literal, and the other much narrower and more culturally specific.

When I talk about Spinoza's theology, I am using 'theology' in its broad and literal sense, meaning a discourse on God, and on things in their relation to God. While the *Ethics*—which provides a definition of God on its first page—is quite evidently concerned with theology in this sense, Spinoza used the word 'theology' more narrowly, to signify a confessional intellectual practice based on scriptural and ecclesial authority, and tied closely to obedience and faith. In Spinoza's hands, this culturally specific sense of 'theology', which was deeply embedded in seventeenth-century debates, became virtually a term of abuse, implying dogmatic sectarianism and even fanaticism. He helped cement a cornerstone of Enlightenment thought by contesting the view, widespread among his Christian contemporaries, that 'reason ought to be the handmaid of theology'.[25] At the end of his *Theologico-Political Treatise*, he declared that he had 'shown how Philosophy is to be separated from Theology . . . and that neither should be the handmaid of the other, but that each has charge of its own domain without any conflict with the other'.[26] In other words, Spinoza argued that philosophy should be emancipated from strictures on religious belief and practice that were enforced by churches and underpinned by belief in the supernatural authority of the Bible—described by Calvin, the supreme religious authority in the Dutch Republic, as 'a declaration of the word of God', and 'the testimony which God has been pleased to deliver concerning himself'.[27] If we were to adopt Spinoza's own conception of theology, we would have to say that he offers a philosophy of God without theology.

Since the word 'theology' comes from the Greek *theos*, meaning God, it is perhaps self-evident that theology, in both its broader and its narrower senses, is a form of discourse or enquiry which takes 'God' as its starting-point. 'God' is given in theology, and it is this givenness that distinguishes theology from philosophy. If God is given through scriptures mediated by an exegetical and ecclesial tradition, then we have theology in the narrow sense, which Spinoza eschewed. Yet God might be given to human thoughtfulness in many different ways: as a question to explore, as a problem to wrestle with, as a mystery to contemplate, as a belief to justify, as a hypothesis to prove, as a desire to pursue, as a doctrine to expound, for example. We have seen that God is given, or defined, in the first few lines of the *Ethics*, but to say that the text is engaged in theology does not commit us in advance to any specific mode of theological engagement—let alone to any specific image of God.

Today, philosophy and theology are distinct and often separate academic disciplines. Because Spinoza tends to be read more by philosophers than by theologians, the theological significance of his thought is rarely discussed by those best equipped to appreciate it. Philosophers little acquainted with theological concepts—such as divine transcendence—or with theological debates concerning the relationship between divine and human agency, tend not to consider how Spinoza contributes to these questions. Theologians, accepting philosophers' judgements that Spinoza is a pantheist or an atheist, usually assume that he simply rejects their conception of God, and do not expect the *Ethics* to reward close reading. I wish to challenge all these assumptions, and show how philosophy and theology are intertwined in Spinoza's metaphysics and ethics. This allows us to draw from the *Ethics* a distinctive account of religion that is, I believe, profound, truthful and compelling.

Philosophers need not be persuaded of Spinoza's importance: his most radical ideas have reinvigorated contemporary metaphysics, and he is recognised as a brilliant theorist of emotion and embodiment. In many intellectual contexts, Spinoza now rivals Kant and Descartes as both the compass and the watershed of modern philosophy.[28] For theologians he remains a more marginal figure, yet he brings to theology both critical and constructive insights that should not be ignored. The *Ethics* articulates a philosophy of being-in-God that does not require the conceptual architecture of a pre-modern age. It thus shows theologians that they need not choose between seeing human beings (and nature as a whole) as grounded in God, and inhabiting the world explored by their scientific colleagues. For while the *Ethics* anticipates the critiques of modernity voiced by many humanities scholars—and not least by theologians—it refuses to indulge in nostalgia for a bygone cosmology. For this reason, it equips us philosophically to confront specifically modern issues, such as religious diversity, nihilism, and ecological collapse. It also outlines a compelling philosophy of religious life, rooted in Spinoza's principle of being-in-God: a philosophy of desire, affect and practice; of restlessness and rest; of living well and facing death. This is not to suggest that theologians will find only a mirror of their own views in the *Ethics*: like any readers, they can expect to have some of their commitments and assumptions challenged. But they may find Spinoza's alternative modernity surprisingly conducive to their sense of the proper orientation of a human life.

When seventeenth-century readers accused Spinoza of atheism, they usually meant that he challenged doctrinal orthodoxy, particularly on moral issues, and not that he denied God's existence. However, when contemporary scholars interpret Spinoza as an atheist, they are concerned chiefly with his metaphysical position.[29] Given Spinoza's extensive treatment of God's existence, nature and productive power in Part One of the *Ethics*, entitled *De Deo* (On God)—and his insistence in Part Five that human 'blessedness' consists in knowledge and love of God—any argument that attributes to Spinoza the kind of atheism espoused by many moderns can proceed only by reading the text with a strategically suspicious eye. Some such interpreters insist that Spinoza was deceiving his readers about what he really thought to keep himself out of trouble. Others argue that his concept of God is so vacuous that he might as well not have used the word *Deus*—and, given that he did use this word, he must have done so for purely pragmatic purposes.[30]

These kinds of argument tend to delve behind the text to access the author's intentions, even to unmask his 'real views'. This is a rather questionable enterprise, and I want to approach the *Ethics* as something more than a representation, more or less trustworthy and sincere, of its author's ideas—for the *Ethics* is also a literary work of art, and a philosophical instrument, that is designed to have certain cognitive and ethical effects on its readers. At the same time, we should avoid overlooking the author, either on account of a structuralist literary theory, or as a consequence of imagining that philosophical texts are merely vehicles for the arguments to be elicited or reconstructed from them. To overlook Spinoza himself would risk abstracting the text from the work that produced and shaped it: the durational, devotional labour of studying, thinking, writing and rewriting over the days, weeks, months, years of its author's remarkable life. Reading the *Ethics* requires us to hold these concerns in delicate balance. While we are letting the text speak for itself—rather than treating it as a window onto Spinoza's hidden intentions, or reading it through the lens of those imagined intentions—we want to do so in a way that does not estrange the product from the means of its production.

With these methodological issues in mind, there are at least two good reasons to challenge the view that Spinoza was a covert atheist. First, the suspicious reading cannot be proven correct or incorrect, leaving an undecidable question: what if Spinoza *did* mean everything that he said about God? And second, regardless of whether or not he meant it sincerely and unequivocally, what kind of religion emerges from the *Ethics* itself? If we simply dismiss these questions, we risk overlooking the theological issues that are quite palpably addressed in the text.

Instead of a hermeneutic of suspicion, I propose a hermeneutic of credulity.[31] Let's accept what the text says, and let's assume its author's sincerity, unless his works themselves demand otherwise. This interpretative strategy does not deny the possibility that Spinoza was deceiving his readers, to some undetermined (and indeterminable) extent, but it does not pursue this line of argument. It certainly does not deny that Spinoza is a subtle writer, capable of irony and rhetorical sophistication.[32] Indeed, we must acknowledge the possibility that the *Ethics* is positively, irresolvably ambiguous, lending itself to two equally plausible, equally coherent interpretations: *either* as a religious philosophy *or* as a secular philosophy. Perhaps Spinoza's famous phrase *Deus sive Natura*, 'God or Nature', signals precisely this ambiguity—not a problem to be solved, a matter to be decided, but an affirmative gesture that opens up the concept of God beyond some of its traditional connotations, turning it into a productive question rather than a divisive dogma.

It is worth considering that a willingness to abide with and explore ambiguity may be one distinctive feature of a religious reading of the *Ethics*. What if ambiguity *must* belong to any human conception of God? A long tradition of apophatic theology—which denies that God can be fully defined or grasped—suggests that God is neither a thing (and so neither an object nor a subject), nor nothing. How, then, should we expect such a God to show up to mark, unambiguously, the difference between a religious worldview and a secular one? It is not as if a religiously conceived universe contains one extra item, which distinguishes it from the atheistically conceived universe.[33]

Reading and re-reading the *Ethics* with the question of religion in mind, we find ourselves drawn into a circular path of thinking. Reading Part One, we ask whether the concept of God outlined there is religious; in order to answer this, we turn to Parts Four and Five to find out how this conception of God figures in Spinoza's account of our highest good and our ethical life. There we read that our highest good consists in knowledge and love of God. To what extent does this signify something religious? It depends on what Spinoza means by God, which takes us back to Part One. Following this theoretical circle does not seem to draw us any nearer to an answer. I went around it several times, rather confusedly, before I recalled Kierkegaard's insight that religiousness must be a matter of *how*, rather than *what*, and that this *how* is located in a human being's 'inwardness'. This immediately brings us closer to Spinoza's conception of religion as a kind of virtue, and begins to disentangle us from the objectifying, speculative notion of religion which Kierkegaard was explicitly resisting in the nineteenth century—and which Spinoza was confronting as it crystallised during his own lifetime.[34] As readers of Spinoza, we must exercise caution in objectifying *his* religion, and even in objectifying the forms of religion he reflected on and criticised.

All this raises questions about *how* we move into and through the interpretative circle of the *Ethics*: how we read the text, how we interpret its philosophical gestures—and how we might appropriate and live out Spinoza's ideas once we have interpreted them. Grasping Spinoza's religion is a question of how we understand 'God', and how we understand ourselves and others as 'in God'; it is a question of how we think, feel and act, and how we orient and order our desire. It may be frustrating to find that Spinoza leaves these questions open for us, but it might turn out to be thought provoking, liberating and also peculiarly binding to spend time in this open space. Even granting the legitimacy of a suspicious, atheist reading of the *Ethics*, a credulous religious reading will draw out aspects of Spinoza's thought that would otherwise be occluded. This promises to enrich our understanding of the text and expand its semantic range.

To what extent can we situate Spinoza's philosophy within a recognisably religious tradition? The autobiographical reflections which begin his early *Treatise on the Emendation of the Intellect*, discussed in my first chapter, call to mind similar remarks in Descartes's *Meditations* and *Discourse on Method*. These works bear witness to the intellectual eclecticism of the seventeenth century: they reveal the influence of Ignatian spiritual exercises of self-examination and mental purification which Descartes encountered in his intellectual formation, alongside Stoic texts recovered during the Renaissance and widely disseminated in early modern Europe.[35] Spinoza's own formation included at least traces of these influences, since after his excommunication in 1656 he studied with Franciscus van den Enden, a poet, art dealer and humanist philosopher who had spent fourteen years as a Jesuit novice before being dismissed from the order in 1633. Prior to 1656, Spinoza's intellectual and spiritual formation was, of course, intensely Jewish.

There is no doubt that Spinoza's philosophy developed in dialogue with both Judaism and Christianity. His critique of religion in the *Theologico-Political Treatise* is aimed at these two traditions, but he also drew in constructive ways on their scriptural and philosophical resources. According to Warren Zev Harvey, Spinoza anticipated the twentieth-century concept of a 'Judeo-Christian tradition' and held that 'Christianity cannot be understood apart from the Hebrew or Jewish tradition'; conversely, he grew up in a Jewish community shaped by complex relations to Christianity.[36] Spinoza cited the New Testament writings of Paul, a Jewish Christian, in support of his own claim that 'God is the God of all nations'.[37] Nevertheless, the specialised character of modern scholarship tends more to separation than to integration, and some scholars have situated Spinoza in an exclusively Jewish intellectual context, identifying Maimonides in particular as both an influence and an opponent.[38] Fewer have explored Spinoza's engagement with Christian thought, and those who do so have tended to focus on the *Theologico-Political Treatise* rather than the *Ethics*, and therefore on political and historical issues rather than ontological and existential questions.[39] As Spinoza's biographer Steven Nadler has argued, 'there is no reason not to be ecumenical here. There are many contexts required for the interpretation of Spinoza's thought, as well as his influence. Research into Spinoza's intellectual sources can only benefit from looking at the variety of backgrounds that make him and his thought so fascinating.'[40]

Some of the chapters in this book seek to supplement the extensive literature on Spinoza's critical and constructive engagements with Judaism by exploring how the theological interventions of the *Ethics* come into focus within a broadly Christian milieu. While acknowledging Spinoza's deep debt to Jewish texts and practices of reading, we can find good reasons for locating the *Ethics* within the Latinate lineage of Christian thought. After he left his Jewish community, he pursued his intellectual work in this Christian context. Writing his most significant works in Latin—the literary language of Augustine, Aquinas and Calvin—he situated his philosophy in the rich intertextuality of western Christianity. His critique of superstitious religion was aimed particularly at the Calvinist doctrines and policies of the Dutch Reformed Church, while his metaphysics developed in opposition to the ambiguously Christian philosophy of Descartes, which was shaped by Catholic scholasticism even as it sought to move beyond it. In Leiden, Spinoza encountered the Protestant neo-scholasticism of Francis Burgersdijck and Adriaan Heereboord.[41] Spinoza's neighbours, friends and correspondents were Christians: some Protestants, some Catholics, others of a nonconformist bent.[42] In his *Theologico-Political Treatise* he approached what Christians call 'the Bible' as a complete text, comprising the Hebrew Scriptures and the New Testament, and though he read these scriptures with a precociously critical eye he quoted approvingly, if very selectively, from the letters of Paul and John. He owned several books on Christian theology and ecclesial history, by authors such as Augustine, Calvin and Hugo Grotius.[43] He commented on Christian teachings about the Incarnation, the Resurrection and the Holy Spirit. And after his death, Spinoza was, so to speak, assumed into the Christian tradition, often as a curiously magnetic danger zone from which thinkers had to distance themselves, as if at risk of contamination, but also as a spur to theological thinking—for the *Ethics* quickly established him as a major thinker of the western philosophical canon, a discourse in which Christian theology remained inseparable from philosophy for at least two centuries. Spinoza deeply influenced Leibniz, Kant, Schelling, Schleiermacher, Hegel, Feuerbach and George Eliot, all of them Christian thinkers in more or less unconventional ways.

However, placing Spinoza in this theological tradition brings problems of its own. Spinoza lived and worked in a Christian context while refusing to become a Christian. His life might have been much easier if he had given in to his friends' entreaties to convert to Christianity, and he chose not to do so. He believed that remaining outside any Church (or university) allowed him greater freedom to philosophise. Assimilating Spinoza either to Jewish religious thought or to Christian theology would deny him the productive and liberating position of intellectual outsider, which he maintained throughout his philosophical career. This outsider perspective was not simply a contingent historical circumstance, but fundamental to his thought.[44] On the other hand, situating Spinoza within modern secularism—with its objectification of 'religion'—would be an equally forced assimilation, suppressing the theological orientation of his work.

If we locate Spinoza in a religious tradition, then, we may follow the example he set in his own life, by placing him in dialogue with Christian theologians without attempting to convert his philosophy to Christianity. It is true that as this dialogue unfolds, surprising affinities may emerge between mainstream Christian thought and Spinozism, but my aim in this book is not to compare Spinoza with Christian thinkers. It is not clear what this comparison would accomplish, and pointing out similarities and divergences between thinkers tends to be a rather superficial exercise. Nor am I setting out a historical argument about the sources of the *Ethics*: establishing the extent of Spinoza's engagement with, say, Augustine or Aquinas would involve detailed philological work which would be unlikely, in the end, to yield definite conclusions. Rather, my purpose in situating the *Ethics* in a theological milieu is to open up a shared conceptual space, inhabited by thinkers of different religious traditions, or of different moments within the same tradition. This opening brings into view the distinctive philosophical task, the distinctive concept of religion, and the distinctive sequence of questions that follow from the principle of being-in-God. My purpose is to see more clearly how Spinoza undertakes this task, how he explores this concept, and how he addresses these questions.

I should probably confess that the interpretation of Spinoza offered in this book reflects, in some respects, my own religious orientation. I grew up without a religion, and while I am drawn again and again to the philosophical question of God and find my inner life shaped by religious ideas, art, exemplars and practices—particularly from Indian traditions and from the more contemplative strands of Catholic thought—I do not fit easily into any religious category. I have come to think that religion, for me, is not a matter of identity at all.

So I wonder whether, in refusing to categorise Spinoza's religion, I am any different from other scholars who interpret Spinoza in their own image. But I do not take myself to be reading Spinoza through the lens of pre-established and firmly held opinions or beliefs. On the contrary: although I have studied and taught philosophy and theology for more than twenty years, and should perhaps be expected to have formed opinions about religious questions, I have until quite recently felt rather tentative and uncertain about my relationship to these questions. My experience did not match the ready-made images of religion I saw around me, and so I wondered whether I was getting something wrong. For example, the questions 'Does God exist?' and 'Do you believe in God?' confused me. Neither 'yes' nor 'no' feels like the right answer, and this is not because I am agnostic, but because the wording of these questions seems somehow to lead away from what *is* meaningful and important to me. 'Are you religious?' is, similarly, a perplexing question, to which the best answer I can offer is a not-very-illuminating 'yes and no'. Reading Spinoza more deeply and pursuing the question of *his* religion has helped me to think more clearly and confidently about my own religious inclinations—and to understand my resistance to the ways religion is usually represented and discussed.

Finally, let me say a few words about the book's structure. Setting out to write chapters that would advance a cumulative argument, I found that the subject-matter resisted me. Perhaps this was partly due to my own limitations, but I suspect it also has something to do with Spinoza's thought, which does not seem to lend itself to linear exposition (an issue I explore in Chapter 2, on the literary form of the *Ethics*). George Eliot, who produced the first English translation of the *Ethics* in the 1850s, and whose fiction evinces the text's deep influence on her intellectual formation, wrote of her novel *Daniel Deronda* that 'I meant everything in the book to be related to everything else there'.[45] Spinoza might well have said the same thing about the *Ethics*. The key elements of his thought considered in this book—the nature of human thinking and knowing; the metaphysical distinction between substance and modes, and the relation between God and human beings; human striving and desire; our participation in divine nature; the distinctive affect named *acquiescentia in se ipso*, which in its highest form means both resting in God and loving God; the eternity of the mind; and the concept of *religio* itself—cannot be divided neatly between chapters.

For this reason, my chapters are rather essayistic: each is relatively self-contained, with its own centre of gravity; what is peripheral in one chapter becomes central in another. One advantage of this form is, I hope, that readers who find one or two of the chapters too demanding—and some of them are more challenging than others—can skip these without giving up on the rest of the book. Perhaps some readers will think it a disadvantage that the areas of convergence between the chapters give rise to occasional repetitions. Yet, as I suggest in Chapter 2, repetition can be a productive force within a text, just as it can be a productive force in life—and perhaps especially in religious life, which so often involves returning, again and again, to a truth we already know.[46]

CHAPTER ONE

Philosophy and Devotion

He felt so strong an inclination to enquire after truth, that he renounced the world in a manner, the better to succeed in that enquiry. Not contented to free himself from all manner of business, he also left Amsterdam, because the visits of his friends too much interrupted his speculations, and retired into the country, where he meditated without any hindrance, and made Microscopes and Telescopes. He was so well pleased with meditating, and putting his meditations into order, and communicating them to his friends, that he spent very little time in any recreation, and was sometimes three whole months without stepping out of doors.

Though he lived a very retired life, his name and his reputation flew everywhere. Free-thinkers resorted to him from all parts. The Palatine court desired to have him, and offered him a professorship of Philosophy at Heidelberg. But he refused it, as being little consistent with his great desire of inquiring into truth without any interruption.[1]

Pierre Bayle wrote this description of Spinoza around 1700, two decades after the philosopher's death in 1677. The passage begins and ends with his longing for truth, which brought him fame yet caused him to retreat from the world. Bayle tells us very little here about what Spinoza was actually doing. We learn what he was resolutely *not* doing: living in a city, receiving visits, going out, taking up a professorship. Instead, he was 'meditating' and 'enquiring'. But what did this task consist in? Was Spinoza just sitting there, in his quiet, modest rooms? If a human being has a 'great desire for truth', how does he follow this desire?

Perhaps with this deep, urgent question hanging in the air, Bayle was as interested in Spinoza's life as in his unorthodox philosophical views. The biographical synopsis in Bayle's entry on Spinoza in his monumental *Dictionnaire historique et critique* includes some dramatic turning-points: an affecting encounter with a 'young woman who taught Spinoza Latin'; the *cherem*, or ban, imposed by Amsterdam's Jewish community in 1656, when Spinoza was twenty-three; an assassination attempt. Yet Bayle seems more fascinated by the contradiction between Spinoza's reputation as a peace-loving, righteous man, and the 'monstrous scheme' contained in the philosopher's works. He is especially indignant about 'the horrid ideas which Spinoza gives us of God', and finds it 'strange' that 'those who were acquainted with him ... agree in saying, that he was a man of a social disposition, affable, honest, obliging, and very regular in his morals'. But after all, Bayle adds, 'we ought not to be more surprised at it, than to see people who live an irregular life, though they are fully persuaded of the truth of the Gospel'.[2]

Bayle denounced the 'Atheism' he discerned in Spinoza's *Theologico-Political Treatise*—'a pernicious and execrable book'—and *Opera posthuma* (1677), which included the *Ethics*.[3] Yet he also found in these works echoes of various religious teachings: Persian 'sufism' and 'cabalism'; some ancient Indian doctrines; the contemplative practices of a Chinese sect named *Foe Kiao*, founded around the same time as Christianity. Bayle explained that these Chinese 'quietists' practised extreme stillness: 'It was not sufficient to continue several hours without any motion of the body; the soul must likewise be immoveable, and lose its thought.' The *Foe Kiao* believed that 'after a man has arrived at the state of quietude, he may follow the ordinary course of life outwardly, and teach others the commonly received doctrine. It is only in private and inwardly that he ought to practise the contemplative exercise of Beatitude.'[4] Spinoza, too, lived harmoniously amongst his ordinary Christian neighbours, and encouraged them to abide by 'the commonly received doctrine'—and Bayle may well have wondered whether this notorious philosopher's predilection for a quiet life had anything in common with the spiritual exercises of these exotic mystics.

The first full biography of Spinoza was published in 1706 by Johannes Colerus, a Lutheran minister of the parish in the Hague where Spinoza spent his last seven years. Colerus moved to the parish in the 1690s, and never met Spinoza. He heard about him from several acquaintances, including his former landlady, who remembered him fondly:

> If he was very frugal in his way of living, his Conversation was also very sweet and easy.... He was, besides, very courteous and obliging, he would very often discourse with his Landlady, especially when she lay in, and with the people of the House, when they happened to be sick

or afflicted; he never failed then to comfort them, and exhort them to bear with Patience those Evils, which God assigned to them as a lot. He put the Children in mind of going often to Church, and taught them to be obedient and dutiful to their Parents. When the People of the House came from Church, he would often ask them what they had learned, and what they could remember of the Sermon. He had a great esteem for Dr. Cordes, my Predecessor; who was a learned and good natured Man, and of an exemplary Life, which gave occasion to Spinoza to praise him very often. Nay, he went sometimes to hear him preach, and he esteemed particularly his learned way of explaining the Scripture, and the solid applications he made of it. He advised at the same time his Landlord and the People of the House, not to miss any Sermon of so excellent a Preacher.

It happened one day, that his Landlady asked him, whether he believed, she could be saved in the religion she professed: He answered, *Your religion is a good one, you need not look for another, nor doubt that you may be saved in it, provided, whilst you apply yourself to Piety, you live at the same time a peaceable and quiet Life.*

When he stayed at home, he was troublesome to no Body; he spent the greatest part of his time quietly in his own Chamber. When he happened to be tired by having applied himself too much to his Philosophical Meditations, he went downstairs to refresh himself, and discoursed with the people of the House about any thing, that might afford Matter for an ordinary Conversation, and even about trifles. He also took pleasure in smoking a Pipe of Tobacco.[5]

Colerus, like Bayle, describes a man who spent most of his time 'quietly in his own Chamber', devoted to his 'Philosophical Meditations'. Though Spinoza seemed to move easily between these solitary meditations and commonplace social intercourse, Colerus also suggests that he was unworldly, caring little for external signs of success and status. He was not only 'frugal', but scruffy: 'As for his clothes, he was very careless of them. . . . One of the most eminent Councellors of State went to see him, and found him in a very slovenly Morning-Gown, whereupon the Councellor blamed him for it, and offered him another. Spinoza answered him, that a Man was never the better for having a finer Gown. To which he added, *It is unreasonable to wrap up things of little or no value in a precious Cover.*'[6]

More recent biographers have shown that there was a worldly side to Spinoza: while he lived in Rijnsburg he met frequently with several close friends, and often travelled to neighbouring cities; as a young man he was fond of the theatre.[7] Perhaps he became single-minded only during his last years, when he wanted to secure his reputation by completing the *Ethics*.

The modern critical eye looks unkindly on naivety, and it would no doubt be naive to treat early sources like Bayle and Colerus as authoritative because of their proximity to people who knew Spinoza personally. But it would also be unwise to dismiss the questions raised by their accounts of Spinoza's way of life—questions that are particularly pertinent to a philosopher who gave the title of *Ethica* to his great work, the fruit of twenty years of intellectual labour. All those hours spent 'meditating'— whatever this means—were, to state the obvious, part of Spinoza's life: he chose to spend most of his time on philosophy and organised the rest of his life around this occupation. We can treat the literary portraits by Colerus and Bayle as an invitation to consider the ascetic, contemplative and devotional elements within Spinoza's philosophical labour.

Devotion need not be an expression of blind faith. It can be animated by desire blended with cognition: in the first place, recognition of a deep, lasting value and importance that is non-negotiable, irreplaceable, perhaps even unconditional. When we are devoted to something, we give ourselves—our time, our attention, our resources—to it freely, though also with a feeling that this is something we *must* attend to. Devotion apprehends its object as necessary: not logically necessary, nor causally necessary, but spiritually necessary.[8]

This is 'a necessity that we feel, that we undergo', as Étienne Souriau put it in his remarkable 1956 lecture 'On the Mode of Existence of the Work to be Made [*oeuvre à faire*]'.[9] Its apprehension is not merely theoretical, but entails a repeated response, is moved to express itself again and again. Though devotion may frequently lapse in distraction, doubt or fatigue, the devotee will sooner or later be drawn back to what she knows, however inarticulately, to be her highest good. The Latin word *religio*, a binding, touches on this quality: the bonds of religious devotion can be an existential anchor as well as a servitude. The steadfastness of a devout life contrasts with the instability of *animi fluctuationes*—the anxious soul's lurching between hope and fear—that Spinoza diagnosed within superstitious faith.

Though he was never in the grip of such a faith, Spinoza hinted that he, too, suffered from *animi fluctuationes*, and that his philosophical labours sought a remedy that would bring him lasting peace. The opening sentence of his unfinished *Treatise on the Emendation of the Intellect* reads as follows:

After experience had taught me that all the things which regularly occur in ordinary life are empty and futile, and I saw that all the things which were the cause or object of my fear had nothing of good or bad in themselves, except insofar as [my] mind was moved by them, I resolved at last to try to find out whether there was anything that would be the true good, capable of communicating itself, and which alone would affect the mind, all others being rejected—whether there was something which, once found and acquired, would continuously give me the greatest joy, to eternity.[10]

Here Spinoza suggests that his philosophical quest was motivated not only by a longing for goodness, joy (*laetitia*) and happiness (*felicitas*), but also by his experience of painful emotions. Indeed, he first writes of fear, emptiness and futility, before announcing his search for 'the true good'. It seems that Spinoza's desire for what he calls his 'new goal' was at least inseparable from, and possibly shaped by, his troubling affects—and particularly his fears.

The opening to the *Treatise on the Emendation of the Intellect* is written in an autobiographical voice that calls to mind Descartes's *Meditations* and Augustine's *Confessions*, texts shaped by Christian contemplative practice, while its form reflects the exercises of classical rhetoric, particularly in Cicero and Seneca.[11] Though its date of composition is uncertain, this is probably Spinoza's earliest known philosophical work. Its translator Edwin Curley argues that it was written before September 1661, when Spinoza was nearly thirty years old: not an old man, but far enough past his youth to look back on a phase of his adult life.[12] Before Spinoza pursues the epistemological questions that are the focus of the *Treatise*, he devotes a few pages to a broader discussion of his philosophical task, which offers a fascinating introduction to his philosophical work as a whole.

In Curley's translation, forms of the verb 'to devote' recur a few times in this text. This does not translate the Latin *devotio*, which comes from the verb *devovere*, meaning to vow, to offer, to dedicate, and is found nowhere in the *Treatise*.[13] Rather, 'devote' translates *dare operam*, a common idiom meaning 'give attention to'. *Dare* means to give or to offer; *operam* is the accusative form of *opera*, a noun meaning work, labour, exertion, effort, and often implying taking trouble or pains over something. The notion of attention expressed in the idiom makes it clear that the labour in question is not primarily physical: it is an offering of consciousness, or thoughtfulness, along with time and effort.

When Spinoza uses this phrase *dare operam* to describe his investment in his philosophical task, he is talking about devoting himself to his pursuit of truth, because he finds it both difficult and important. Devotion in this sense is not necessarily an overtly reverential attitude. It is, rather, the act of registering the value of something by paying whatever costs of energy, time, effort and attention—the basic resources of one's life—it requires.[14]

Souriau's description of the 'tremendous labours' of artistic and intellectual creation certainly captures Spinoza's devotion to his 'work to be made', the *Ethics*—the kind of work that 'does not exist without ceaselessly demanding, over the course of [one's] vital journey, a thousand efforts of fidelity, a thousand painful acceptances of all that this [work] seeks to obtain through the world, and a thousand costly rejections of all that is not compatible with it'.[15] We should be a little wary, however, of the way modern writers tend to associate ascetic discipline so closely with labour and exertion, even a kind of spiritual athleticism, implying relentless industriousness and productivity: this risks overlooking Spinoza's view that the highest human good is a form of striving that involves deep rest.[16]

For Souriau, there is something in the not-yet-completed *oeuvre à faire* that 'seems to deserve the gift of a soul and at times of a life', requiring the maker to 'renounce himself' for the sake of the work.[17] He describes this work or making as 'spiritual', and this is echoed in Michel Foucault's remarks about 'philosophy' and 'spirituality' in his 1982 lecture course on 'The Hermeneutics of the Subject'. In his introductory lecture, Foucault argued that philosophy and spirituality belonged together in ancient thought— from Socrates, the Stoics and the Cynics to medieval Christian asceticism— and were separated in modern philosophy, from Descartes onwards.[18] Perhaps this historical thesis was challenged by his audience, for in his second lecture Foucault admitted that it was 'completely arbitrary' to locate the break between philosophy and spirituality in a 'Cartesian moment', and revised his thesis to suggest that it was the scholastic (that is, Aristotelian) theology epitomised by Aquinas's writings that initiated the break with spirituality.[19] Though Foucault did not reflect on the spiritual elements within Descartes's writings, he suggested that 'the first nine paragraphs' of Spinoza's *Treatise on the Emendation of the Intellect* 'linked the problem [of access to the truth] to a series of requirements concerning the subject's very being', posing the question, 'How must I transform my being?'[20]

It is no coincidence, then, that Foucault's definition of 'spirituality' expresses something important about the kind of philosophical work Spinoza was engaged in:

> We will call 'philosophy' the form of thought which asks what it is that enables the subject to have access to the truth, and which attempts to determine the conditions and limits of the subject's access to the truth.

If we call this 'philosophy', then I think we would call 'spirituality' the search, practice and experience through which the subject carries out the necessary transformations on himself in order to have access to the truth. We will call 'spirituality', then, the set [*l'ensemble*] of these researches, practices, and experiences, which may be purifications, ascetic exercises, renunciations, conversions of looking, modifications of existence, etc., which are . . . , for the subject's very being, the price to be paid [*le prix à payer*] for access to the truth.[21]

What Foucault here calls *spiritualité* resembles the account of devotion that emerges from the opening of Spinoza's *Treatise on the Emendation of the Intellect*. Just as Souriau's 'spiritual' *oeuvre à faire* demands 'costly' renunciations, so Foucault's *spiritualité* involves the requirement to 'pay a price' for the truth—a price that may take the form of various kinds of 'researches, practices and experiences', yet will always consist of an actual quantity of time, effort and attention. This economic requirement is nicely expressed in English idioms such as 'spend time' and 'pay attention'. Foucault emphasises the existential investment demanded by *spiritualité*: 'Spirituality postulates that the truth is never given to the subject by right, [but only] at a price that brings the subject's being into play. For as he is, the subject is not capable of truth. . . . There can be no truth without a conversion or transformation of the subject.'[22] Devotion is never abstract; it always has duration, and it must leave its mark, whether outwardly or inwardly, on the devotee.

{⸻⸻}

Over the first few pages of the *Treatise on the Emendation of the Intellect* Spinoza describes his slow conversion from one way of life to another. As Pierre-François Moreau has shown, it is a first-person narrative of a conversion, an inward 'journey', that echoes Augustine's *Confessions*—though Spinoza's movement is not, of course, a 'conversion to orthodoxy', nor does it respond to an external call or a superior authority. It is, instead, a 'natural' conversion.[23] Nevertheless, it is strikingly similar to Augustine's description of the philosopher's 'striving to be wise':

> What are we doing when we diligently strive to be wise? Do we not seek, with as much energy as we can command, to gather our whole soul somehow to that which we attain by the mind, to station ourselves and become wholly entrenched there, so that we no longer rejoice in our own private goods, which are bound up with ephemeral things, but

instead cast aside all attachment to times and places and apprehend that which is always one and the same? ... While we are striving thus—as long as we do so wholeheartedly—then we are on our way.[24]

Spinoza also echoes Augustine in showing that this existential change is radical, as well as is gradual. His conversion meant leaving behind not merely frivolity and shallowness, but the entire worldly way of being—encompassing much that seemed attractive and admirable—enshrined in the core collective values he discerned in his culture: 'wealth, honour, and sensual pleasure'.[25] These three notions occurred often in classical rhetoric, which Spinoza takes as a model for his own experience as a young man.[26] He describes himself wishing to become absolutely single-minded; he wanted the true good 'alone' to affect his mind, 'all other [goods] being rejected'. He suspected that seeking wealth, honour and sensual pleasure was incompatible with his pursuit of the 'true good'—not because these things necessarily conflicted, in themselves, with the true good, but because the human mind tends to become so 'distracted', consumed and lost in pursuing them that it is unable to gather its energies for the good that brings eternal happiness.[27]

Spinoza found himself most attached to honour: gaining the esteem of other people. He had learned quickly that 'after the enjoyment of sensual pleasure is past, the greatest sadness follows', yet he continued to find the desire for honour to be deeply distracting, 'for [honour] is always assumed to be good through itself and the ultimate end toward which everything is directed'.[28] He saw how the lure of honour is magnified by the social constitution of this good, grounded in the fact that we are highly conscious and acutely sensitive social beings. After early infancy, to be a human being in the world is to be aware of oneself as visible to other people, and as subject to their judgements. Our sophisticated, reflexive sociability makes honour a powerful human value, and Spinoza perceived it to be a dangerously inhibiting force: 'Honour has this great disadvantage: to pursue it, we must direct our lives according to other people's powers of understanding—fleeing what they commonly flee and seeking what they commonly seek.'[29] Spinoza hints at his own struggle to let go of the pursuit of honour: 'I saw, of course, the advantages that honour and wealth bring, and that I would be forced to abstain from seeking them, if I wished to devote myself seriously to something new and different.' For some time, he explains, he hoped to reach his new goal 'without changing the conduct and plan of life which I shared with other men. Often I tried this, but in vain.'[30] Eventually he saw that 'all these things'—wealth, honour, sensual pleasure—'stood in the way of my working toward this new goal, indeed were so opposed to it that one or the other must be given up'.[31]

The first seven paragraphs of the *Treatise on the Emendation of the Intellect* describe an inward revolution. 'At first glance' (*primo enim intuit*), Spinoza worried that he was 'losing something certain for something uncertain'; yet after an earnest exercise of attention (*postquam ... huic rei incubueram*) and 'persistent meditation' (*assidua autem meditatione*), he saw that, on the contrary, he 'would be giving up certain evils for a certain good'.[32] This exemplifies the 'conversion of looking' that Foucault identifies as a 'spiritual' element of philosophy.

However, even after grasping the certainty of the 'true good', Spinoza's conversion to his 'new goal' was slow, because his mind needed not merely to understand the nature of the true good, but to attend to it for an extended period of time.[33] A philosopher must do more than glance at the truth. Spinoza now found himself seeking a wisdom that *would* change his life, give him lasting joy; and this would not consist in the momentary acquisition of a piece of knowledge. Rather, the true good had to occupy his mind. It was, so to speak, a matter of changing the way his consciousness spent its time. His attention had to stop being absorbed by thoughts of wealth, pleasure and honour, and dwell in the company of 'the new goal' of eternal joy:

> By persistent meditation, I came to the conclusion that, if only I could resolve wholeheartedly [*modo possem penitus deliberare*] to change my plan of life, I would be giving up certain evils for a certain good. . . . But not without reason did I use these words *if only I could resolve in earnest*. For though I perceived these things so clearly in my mind, I still could not, on that account, put aside all greed, desire for sensual pleasure, and love of esteem. I saw this, however: that so long as the mind was turned toward these thoughts, it was turned away from those things, and was thinking seriously about the new goal. That was a great comfort to me. For I saw that those evils would not refuse to yield to remedies. And although in the beginning these intervals were rare, and lasted a very short time, nevertheless, after the true good became more and more known to me, the intervals became longer and more frequent.[34]

It was, in other words, a matter of time—of duration, a concept that would become a key element in Spinoza's mature philosophy. The Latin noun that Curley translates usually as 'goal', but also as 'plan of life', is *institutum*. This signifies not only 'intention', 'decree' and 'principle', but also 'custom' and 'habit', which involve a certain duration. (This semantic range is also suggested by Calvin's title for his monumental work, *Institutes of*

Christian Religion.) Spinoza is describing the process of adopting a new habit, or more precisely a new practice, if we understand practice to be a habit that is deliberately adopted and cultivated.[35] This practice became deeper and stronger through a combination of duration and repetition: at first, his intervals of attention to the good 'were rare, and lasted a very short time'; as he continued to devote himself to the practice, 'the intervals became longer and more frequent'.

As this passage shows, Spinoza's conversion was also a matter of desire. He found that clear perception was not enough to free him from his old desires. Gradually his mind spent less time wanting (and thus attending to) transient goods, and more time longing for (and thus attending to) the true good—though it did not yet fully know what this good consists in. Spinoza, like Descartes, found that while certainty, clarity and distinctness were the benchmarks of truth, these epistemic qualities did not constitute a resting-place for his philosophical enquiry—'For though I perceived these things so clearly in my mind, I still could not, on that account, put aside all greed, desire for sensual pleasure, and love of esteem.'[36] This was because his philosophical project was ethical in the deepest sense. It concerned *the way he spent his time*, or—in other words—how he lived: what he did with his mind and body, where he directed his consciousness, attention and desire. It required wholehearted resolution. The Latin adverb *penitus* is aptly translated as 'wholeheartedly', since it means 'thoroughly' and 'deeply' as well as 'inwardly'.

This allusion to the depth and inwardness of a human being may help us to make sense of the way Spinoza writes about the importance of his philosophical task. Remarkably, he suggests that pursuing the true good was a matter of life and death for him, making him feel subject to a certain necessity or imperative to pursue it:

> I saw that I was in the greatest danger, and that I was forced [*me cogi*] to seek a remedy with all my strength, however uncertain it might be— like a man suffering from a fatal illness, who, foreseeing certain death unless he employs a remedy, is forced to seek it, however uncertain, with all his strength. For all his hope lies there. But all those things people ordinarily strive for, not only provide no remedy to preserve our being, but in fact hinder that preservation, often cause the destruction of those who possess them, and always cause the destruction of those who are possessed by them.[37]

What kind of 'death' and 'destruction' is Spinoza envisaging here? Although he mentions that pursuing wealth, honour and pleasure can place people in physical danger, it seems unlikely that he is referring only to biological death.[38] He suggests that pursuing things that are not true goods—in other words, wasting his time—is akin to 'suffering from a fatal illness'. Spinoza seems to have in mind a kind of illness—and thus a kind of health and flourishing—that is not merely physical. This brings us back to the concept of spirituality that Foucault recovered from ancient philosophy. Spinoza felt the need, the necessity, to 'preserve' his bodily, affective and spiritual life with the wholeness and depth of his being, because it was precisely this existential wholeness and depth that was in danger of destruction if he neglected to pursue the true good.

Having thus emphasised the high stakes of his project, Spinoza explains that the threats to life that concerned him can be traced to 'the fact that all happiness or unhappiness is placed in the quality of the object to which we cling with love'.[39] It is a question of what we love, what we desire: of that to which we attach ourselves inwardly. 'For strife will never arise on account of what is not loved,' writes Spinoza, 'nor will there be sadness if it perishes, nor envy if it is possessed by another, nor fear, nor hatred—in a word, no disturbances of the mind [*commotiones animi*].'[40] Being seized by powerful affects which agitate the mind or soul constitutes a grave danger to our being.[41] All these disturbances happen, Spinoza continues, 'only in the love of those things that can perish, as [wealth, honour, sensual pleasure] can do. But love [*amor*] toward the eternal and infinite thing feeds the mind [*animum*] with a joy entirely exempt from sadness. This is greatly to be desired [*desiderandum*], and to be sought with all our strength.'[42]

Spinoza's gradual conversion from one way of life to another consisted in a reordering of his desire and love. Like Augustine, he found that his heart was turning from what is transient, perishable and destructive, to what is eternal, infinite and sustaining.

Having noted that the 'greatest danger' Spinoza sought to avert was the disturbance of his *animus*—his mind, soul or life-force—and perhaps its eventual destruction, it is worth pausing to note also how he characterises a soul that is at peace, free from such disturbances. In the course of describing the mind's immersion in sensual pleasure, Spinoza writes that 'the mind [*animus*] is so caught up in it, as if at peace in a [true] good [*ac si in aliquot bono quiesceret*], that it is quite prevented from thinking of anything else'.[43] Although the goodness of pleasure is illusory and futile, single-minded absorption in pleasure mimics the purity of mind that distinguishes devotion to the true good. Here, the state of being 'at peace' in a true good is expressed by the verb *quiescere*, meaning 'to rest'. The root *quies* denotes quietude and stillness, as well as repose. *Quiescere*, like the English verb 'to acquiesce', is generally used transitively with the preposition *in*, and this is how Spinoza uses it in this passage: *ac si in aliquot bono quiesceret*—'as if it [i.e., the mind] rests in something good'.

This gestures to an idea which we can follow to the last pages of the *Ethics*: a human being's proper relation to the good is to rest in it. Fundamental to the *Ethics* is the ontological distinction between duration and eternity, which corresponds to an existential (and experiential) distinction between fluctuation and stillness, restless desire and satisfaction. Repose in the good was, indeed, the new way of being which Spinoza was seeking to attain. His mind suffered from *commotiones* or *fluctuationes*, disturbance or unrest, and he wanted to find peace. His mind's unrest involved the affects named in the opening pages of this early *Treatise*: hatred, envy, sadness and, above all, fear. Spinoza wanted to replace these disturbing, unstable emotions with affects that would empower his being: love instead of hatred, generosity instead of envy, joy instead of sadness. And to fear is opposed not hope—which would be yet another agitating emotion—but peace.[44]

In the *Treatise on the Emendation of the Intellect* Spinoza does not discuss generosity, or any other antidote to envy. He does, however, reveal his ethical commitment to the flourishing of other people when he finally explains what he understands by 'the true good' and 'the highest good'. The concept of goodness is a complicated matter for Spinoza, who insists that 'good' and 'bad' are partial, relative terms: 'one and the same thing can be called both good and bad according to different respects. The same applies to perfect and imperfect. For nothing, considered in its own nature, will be called perfect or imperfect, especially after we have recognized that everything that happens, happens according to the eternal order . . . of Nature'.[45] Nevertheless, he continues, we naturally seek a model of perfection that emerges when we conceive 'a human nature much stronger and more enduring than [our] own'.[46] In this early text, Spinoza does not resolve the tension between his critique of the very notion of goodness, and his emphatic claim—grounded, he tells us, in his own experience—that pursuing the true good is the most important thing a human being can do.[47] However, he does clarify his views about the good in some important ways. Anything that helps an individual to attain the goal described at the beginning of the *Treatise on the Emendation of the Intellect* is, he affirms, 'a true good', but 'the highest good' is explicitly social: 'to arrive—together with other individuals if possible—at the enjoyment of [this goal]'. Spinoza clarifies that this 'enjoyment' involves 'the knowledge of the union that the mind [*mens*] has with the whole of nature'.[48]

So while Spinoza begins by presenting his pursuit of the true good as a personal and apparently rather solitary project, motivated by his own sense of being 'in the greatest danger', by the time he realises that the highest good is an empowered human nature, he wishes to enjoy this nature 'together with other individuals'. Indeed, he assumes a responsibility to cultivate this collective enjoyment. He wants to teach other people so that their minds and hearts will be brought into harmony with his own:

> This, then, is the end I aim at: to acquire such a nature, and to strive that many acquire it with me. That is, it is part of my happiness to take pains [*operam dare*] that many others may understand as I understand, so that their intellect and desire [*intellectus et cupiditas*] entirely agree with my intellect and desire. To do this it is necessary, *first* to understand as much of nature as suffices for acquiring such a nature; *next*, to form a society of the kind that is desirable, so that as many as possible may attain it as easily and surely as possible.[49]

Moreover, Spinoza advocates attentiveness to collective social endeavours such as the education of children, medical research, and 'mechanics', by which he means the development of new technologies to make material life easier.

Alongside this movement from an unsociable (or even anti-social) attitude to a deep interest in collective empowerment, is a similar movement in Spinoza's attitude towards worldly pursuits. He began by describing his need to 'abstain' from seeking wealth, honour and sensual pleasure, and to detach himself from his 'love of those things that can perish'. His suggestion that seeking these conventional human goods is incompatible with seeking the true good invokes an image of the philosopher swimming against the stream of ordinary norms and values, refusing to direct his own life 'according to other men's powers of understanding'.[50] However, Spinoza goes on to rehabilitate wealth, honour and sensual pleasure. Once he began to attend seriously to his 'new goal', he explains, he perceived more clearly the nature of these relative goods:

> I saw that the acquisition of money, sensual pleasure, and esteem are only obstacles so long as they are sought for their own sakes, and not as means to other things. But if they are sought as means, then they will have a limit, and will not be obstacles at all. On the contrary, they will be of great use in attaining the end on account of which they are sought.[51]

Spinoza reports that gaining this new insight actually helped him to focus on his new goal. He experienced 'longer and more frequent intervals' of attentiveness to the true good 'after' seeing that the acquisition of wealth, honour and sensual pleasure need not be obstacles, and that, on the contrary, they could aid his philosophical task. His progress towards the true good came not only by seeing through the emptiness and futility of ordinary goods, but also by resolving the conflict, within his own soul, between the conventional, collective values of his society and his own deepening love of a higher good.

With this resolution in view, the opening of the *Treatise on the Emendation of the Intellect* culminates in three 'rules of living':

1. To speak according to the power of understanding of ordinary people, and do whatever does not interfere with our attaining our purpose. For we can gain a considerable advantage, if we yield as much to their understanding as we can. In this way, they will give a favourable hearing to the truth.
2. To enjoy pleasures just so far as suffices for safeguarding our health.
3. Finally, to seek money, or anything else, just so far as suffices for sustaining life and health, and conforming to those customs of the community that do not conflict with our own.[52]

Spinoza introduces these rules by insisting that 'before anything else'—before reforming social organisation, education, medicine and so on—'we must devise a way of healing the intellect, and purifying it, as much as we can in the beginning, so that it understands things successfully ... all our activities and thoughts are to be directed to this end'.[53] The remainder of Spinoza's unfinished *Treatise* concentrates on this project of intellectual therapy. However, he points out that 'while we pursue this end, and devote ourselves to bringing the intellect back to the right path, it is necessary to live'.[54] He acknowledges a deep practical circularity here: we need to improve our minds in order to gain clear sight of the highest good, but we can make no progress in this so long as our minds are disturbed and disoriented by desires for what are not, in themselves, worthy goods. In other words, people live improperly because they are ignorant; but they cannot become less ignorant if they do not conduct themselves properly. Spinoza's proposed solution is to 'assume certain rules of living as good' while in the process of gaining true knowledge of the good.[55] Here he closely echoes Descartes, who in Part Three of his *Discourse on Method* lists three maxims forming a 'provisional moral code' to abide by while he is undergoing his intellectual training, and compares this 'code' to a temporary residence in which to 'live comfortably' while rebuilding his house.[56] Spinoza's three rules reflect his view that the human good should be pursued collectively, and his pragmatic commitment to social life and its conventions. They externalise the integration he achieved, within himself, of the established values of his community and his counter-cultural inclination towards a higher good, which had hitherto pulled him in contrary directions.

⁂

The first seventeen paragraphs of Spinoza's treatise thus describe an arc—of withdrawing from the ordinary social world and returning to it; of giving up this world and getting it back again. This is a movement of negation, followed by affirmation: his ascetic denial of worldly values and attachments is followed by a new sense of comfort in the world. This double movement fits with the early biographical accounts of Spinoza's habits of living in his later years: the long hours spent alone in his room in meditation, followed by mundane, easy conversations with his landlady and her family, in which he accepted and encouraged their conventional piety. It also fits with the way Spinoza avoided formal recognition by turning down a university professorship, yet was dedicated to communicating his philosophy in the most effective written form he could devise, arranging for the fruit of this intense labour, the *Ethics*, to be published shortly after his death.

Yet this arc is not simply biographical. It belongs to a philosophical tradition of thinking about how to live in the world while reaching for a truth that may transcend the readily available concepts and ideals of ordinary society. It thus echoes the parable, or visualisation, of the cave in Plato's *Republic*: the philosopher 'turns his soul' toward the light and climbs out of the dark cave of his social world, where everyone is ignorant and in chains—but then he returns to the cave to share his insight with his neighbours.[57] It also echoes the story of Jesus, who retreated to the wilderness of the desert, then returned to the towns and cities of Judea to teach the crowds. Of course, returning to the world did not turn out very well for Socrates or for Jesus, and Spinoza, whose watchword was '*Caute*', took a quieter, more prudent route into his seventeenth-century world. Nevertheless, the arc inscribed within the opening to the *Treatise on the Emendation of the Intellect* indicates what kind of rotation is required for the 'turning of the soul' described in the *Republic*. The soul turns not only away from the world and towards the true good, but then—having spent time with this true good, appropriated it, found rest in it—turns towards the world again. It is not a 180-degree turn, but comes full circle. This does not mean that it is any less of a transformation. On the contrary, it accomplishes a new way of being in the world, holds out the possibility of transforming other souls, and aspires to change a whole society.

As we have seen, Foucault suggests that spirituality, the labour of philosophy, may involve a 'conversion of looking'. In the *Treatise on the Emendation of the Intellect* Spinoza describes a conversion of looking at the world, as well as a conversion of his faith in and attention to the true good.[58] He also moves between uncompromising spiritual idealism and clear-eyed pragmatism about social realities. These features bring complexity to his account of the best kind of human life, and ambivalence to the role of conventional religion within it.[59] The *Theologico-Political Treatise* combines a rigorous critique of superstitious beliefs, underpinned by a critical analysis of both Jewish and Christian scriptures, with a defence of the attitude Spinoza expressed towards his landlady: *Your religion is a good one, you need not look for another, nor doubt that you may be saved in it, provided, whilst you apply yourself to Piety, you live at the same time a peaceable and quiet Life.* In that text he suggests that the truth of a person's beliefs is less important than their ethical conduct, a view that rehabilitates a broad range of religious ideals and practices, so long as they are adopted in the right moral spirit and contribute to justice and loving-kindness. The *Ethics*, however, traces a narrower and more demanding path, drawing normative distinctions between truth and falsehood, adequate and inadequate cognition, and describing the rare beatitude that rests on intuitive knowledge of God.

This difference between Spinoza's two great works—a difference concerning the status of truth—signals neither inconsistency nor a change of heart. Rather, it reflects his long effort to work through a tension already present in the opening pages of his *Treatise on the Emendation of the Intellect*. He could address this tension only by writing two quite different books. The *Theologico-Political Treatise* treats religious questions under their social and political aspect, while the *Ethics* is a work of philosophy giving form and expression to Spinoza's 'great desire of inquiring into truth', to borrow Pierre Bayle's words. The *Theologico-Political Treatise* is oriented primarily to a reordering of political and ecclesial power, the *Ethics* to a reordering of ethical and existential power.

At the very end of the *Ethics*, Spinoza names three features of the accomplishment of wisdom: it is excellent, it is difficult, it is rare.

> The wise person, insofar as he is considered as such, is hardly troubled in spirit, but being, by a certain eternal necessity, conscious of himself, and of God, and of things, he never ceases to be, but always possesses true peace of mind. If the way I have shown to lead to these things now seems very hard, still, it can be found. And of course, what is found so

rarely must be hard. For if salvation were at hand, and could be found without great effort [*sine magno labore*], how could nearly everyone neglect it? But all things excellent are as difficult as they are rare. (E5p42s)

Spinoza's extraordinary dedication to his philosophical work is evidence of his own devotion to this highest good. He also inspired devotion in others. Henry Oldenburg, for example, after visiting Spinoza at his lodgings in 1661, wrote to him from London that 'when I visited you recently in your retreat [*in secessu tuo*] at Rijnsburg, I found it so difficult to tear myself away from your side, that now I am back in England I hasten to reunite myself with you, so far as it is possible, even if it is only by correspondence.... What I, in my weakness, can provide, you may consider yours.' Oldenburg signed himself 'Yours in all love and devotion' (*Tuus omni affectu, et studio*).[60] In reply, Spinoza wrote that 'I think that friends must share all things, especially spiritual things' (*cogito amicorum omnia, pracipue spiritualia, debere esse communia*).[61] In a similarly affectionate letter, his friend Simon de Vries expressed his envy at a young student named Casearius who was lodging with Spinoza, and could 'talk to you about the most important matters at breakfast, at dinner, and on your walks', but consoled himself with the thought that he could commune with Spinoza from afar: 'though our bodies are separated from one another by such a distance, nevertheless you are very often present in my mind, especially when I meditate on your writings and hold them in my hands'.[62]

His circle of friends recognised something of deep, rare value in Spinoza—a connection to something which they also longed for—and they were eager to respond to this by offering something of themselves to him: attention, time, money. They tried to persuade him to let them support him financially—offers which Spinoza tended to decline—or help him publish his work. After his death, they worked for ten months preparing his *Ethics* for publication and producing a Dutch edition. These biographical details fit with his remarks in the *Ethics* about the importance of like-minded friends, and they also fit with the earliest literary portraits of Spinoza's devout life: pure-hearted, single-minded, religiously dedicated to inquiry into being and truth. Spinoza consistently called the object of this inquiry 'God', and he argued that 'blessedness' consists in a kind of union with God, a sharing in God's nature. Because this really *is* the highest human good, his closest readers—like his closest friends—find that the *Ethics* both elicits and gives shape to their own devotion to truth, however intermittent this may be.

CHAPTER TWO

What Is the *Ethics*?

SPINOZA MADE HIS LIVING as a lens-grinder, a profession that requires great skill and delicacy. His production of the *Ethics* also exhibits fine craftsmanship: Spinoza honed his text like glass, striving for clarity, attending minutely to the form and function of the finished object.[1] Many philosophers write extensively, composing treatise upon treatise, essaying new subjects, adding branch-lines to their intellectual network. Think of how Plato's dialogues stage an epic yet inconclusive conversation; how Kant extended his critical philosophy by writing a second and a third *Critique*; how Hegel's system towers like a high-rise building with panoramic views; how Kierkegaard's authorship flowed like surging water, driving the currents and torrents of his inner life through diverse literary channels. Though he wrote several works and experimented with literary genre, Spinoza laboured intensively, spending over eight years on the text that became the *Ethics*.[2] The form of this work is sculptural, architectural: it resembles an exquisitely carved crystal, cut as intricately on the inside as on the outside, hollowed into numerous interconnected chambers and corridors, its myriad colourless surfaces precisely formed and highly polished.

Once any text has been written, it has a double life. As a static or atemporal text it exists all at once, complete, while as a dynamic text it unfolds as a linear process through the act of reading. In the case of the *Ethics*, this doubleness is inscribed in the form of the work, producing two entities quite different in size, shape and significance. The static *Ethics* presents a theoretical system, set out according to the deductive order devised by Euclid to prove his geometrical theorems.[3] Its literary style is strikingly restrained, almost devoid of rhetoric; as Pierre Bayle noted in his *Dictionnaire philosophique et critique*, 'Spinoza has confined himself to a great precision in writing, without making use of figurative language, which so often prevents us from having just ideas of a body of doctrine.'[4] With the exception of summary sections, such as the 'Definitions of the Affects' at the end of Part Three and the Appendix to Part Four, there is little repetition in this text—for repetition has no theoretical value. Nothing is added to a philosophical system by reiterating one of its axioms or propositions.

By contrast, the dynamic *Ethics* which unfolds in the act of reading is replete with repetitions. Take, for example, the first proposition of Part One and its demonstration:

> P1. Substance is prior in nature to its affections.
> Dem. This is evident from def. 3 and 5.

Here the reader is directed to recall definitions 3 and 5, which she read a few moments earlier: she either brings them immediately to mind, or glances back at them to refresh her memory. And so she proceeds through the *Ethics*: each time Spinoza demonstrates a proposition by invoking an earlier element of the text as its logical foundation, she returns to that earlier element, whether by recollection or by flipping back through the pages of the book. Tracing the cross-references tunnelling through the text discloses a web of argumentative lines beneath its surface. When the *Ethics* is read sequentially, the act of reading follows a looping line, halting and circling back again and again to revisit elements of the text, as directed by Spinoza's demonstrations. Of course, like most philosophical texts, it can also be studied out of sequence. If a reader is focusing on a topic discussed in a cluster of propositions from the middle of the book, for example, she will need to trace their conceptual foundations back through to earlier parts in order to understand them fully.[5] Whether the text is read forwards or backwards, it generates repetitions. These repetitions are enacted by the motion of reading, and they exhibit, in time, a certain logical structure—what Spinoza calls 'the order and connection of ideas' (E2p7).

If the static, atemporal *Ethics* presents a theoretical system, the dynamic text constitutes a practical system. This means that the text is not only a representation of reality, but also a kind of training manual designed to lead the reader through a cognitive process that will shape her mind's habits of thinking.[6] We should remember that a circle of Spinoza's acquaintances studied his works together, and that at least some of his texts were written with this group of students in mind. A letter to Spinoza from Simon de Vries documents their study meetings: 'one of us (but each one takes his turn) reads through, explains according to his own conception, and then proves everything, following the sequence and order of your propositions'. When something proved difficult to understand, one of the group would write to the philosopher to ask for clarification, so that 'we may be able to defend the truth against those who are superstitiously religious and Christian, and to stand against the attacks of the whole world'.[7] Spinoza probably envisaged the finished version of the *Ethics* being studied in this way after his death.

A practical system is a discipline: an order or a rule that, when properly followed, forms (or re-forms) the practitioner in a certain way. Recalling Foucault's description of a philosophy that is also a 'spirituality', we can regard the dynamic *Ethics* as a spiritual exercise—a practice of reading— which guides the reader through 'conversions of looking' and 'modifications of existence'.[8] While repetitions are superfluous within a static theoretical system, they are indispensable to this kind of dynamic, temporal, practical system. Because most readers come to the *Ethics* with minds dimmed by entrenched customs and prejudices, they are at least partially resistant to the discipline it offers. Repetition, though not itself rational, can be put in the service of reason to overcome this resistance.

Philosophers in the early modern period were fascinated by the way repetition modifies the human mind. Descartes, Hobbes, Spinoza, Malebranche and Locke, followed by Hume and Reid, theorised about the role of repetition in processes of habituation and habit-formation, 'custom' and learning. In 1655, Hobbes defined habit as 'motion made more easy and ready by custom; that is to say, by perpetual endeavour, or by iterated endeavours', and Locke echoed this definition in his 1690 *Essay Concerning Human Understanding*, which states that habit is 'the power or ability in Man, of doing any thing, when it has been acquired by frequent doing the same thing'.[9] These general reflections on the effects of repetition were applied to the invisible activity of the human mind—in other words, to the process of thinking. In his *Search after Truth* (1674), Malebranche hypothesised that 'animal spirits' move along 'paths' formed by 'traces' in the brain: 'when the spirits have passed through these traces many times, they enter there more easily than other places', and thus habitual patterns of thinking, cognitive paths of least resistance, are formed in the mind.[10] Locke added a new chapter on the association of ideas to the fourth edition of the *Essay Concerning Human Understanding*, published in 1700.[11]

It is not surprising, then, that Spinoza's *Ethics* (considered as a theoretical system) contains an account of the psychological process whereby repetition produces a certain order of ideas in a person's mind. Here, however, this account explains how the *Ethics* itself (considered as a practical system) is meant to work upon the mind of the reader. Part Two of the text, which focuses on the nature of the human mind, identifies three kinds of cognition: 'opinion or imagination', 'reason' and 'intuition' (*scientia intuitiva*).[12] 'Imagination' signifies the activity of undisciplined, spontaneous, everyday, habitual thinking, which—in contrast to the other two types of cognition—produces 'inadequate' ideas. This imaginative process unfolds according to a basic principle of Spinoza's natural philosophy: bodies are affected by other bodies. When a body comes 'frequently' into contact with an external body, 'it changes its surface and, as it were, impresses on it certain traces [*vestigia*]' (E2post.V). In other words, bodies are characterised by plasticity: they are receptive to changes and may be modified by them, but they can also hold their form, so that 'traces' remain in bodies to mark the ways in which they have been affected. 'Images' are thoughts generated in this way, mental correlates of bodily traces. Imaginative thinking links together a series of images in the mind, according to a principle of 'association' that is engendered by repetition.

'For example,' explains Spinoza,

> from the thought of the word *pomum* a Roman will immediately pass to the thought of the fruit, which has no similarity to that articulate sound and nothing in common with it except that the body of the same man has often been affected by these two, that is, that the man often heard the word *pomum* while he saw the fruit. . . . And in this way each of us will pass from one thought to another, as each one's association [*consuetudo*] has ordered the images of things in the body. (E2p18s)

We fall into error when the order established by the habits of the imagination is confused with the nature of things.[13] In the Appendix to *Ethics* I, Spinoza identifies several 'prejudices' which persist because people 'judge things according to the disposition of their brain, and imagine, rather than understand them'; he argues that 'all the notions by which ordinary people are accustomed to explain Nature are only modes of imagining, and do not indicate the nature of anything, only the constitution of the imagination' (E1App). He illustrates this point by comparing the way two individuals will interpret the same sign:

> Each of us will pass from one thought to another, as each one's association has ordered the images of things in the body. For example, a soldier, having seen traces of a horse in the sand, will immediately pass from the thought of a horse to the thought of a horseman, and from that to the thought of war, and so on. But a farmer will pass from the thought of a horse to the thought of a plough, and then to that of a field, and so on. (E2p18s)

Towards the end of *Ethics* II, Spinoza extends his analysis of habitual thinking in considering general concepts, which he calls 'universal images'. Here, the image in question is not a mark in the sand, but the notion of humanity. This will vary according to our bodily dispositions:

For example, those who have more often regarded men's stature with wonder will understand by the word 'man' an animal of erect stature. But those who have been accustomed to consider something else, will form another common image of men—for example, that man is an animal capable of laughter, or a featherless biped, or a rational animal. And similarly concerning the others—each will form universal images of things according to the disposition of his body. (E2p40s1)

Again, Spinoza is suggesting that the way we interpret images reveals more about our past experience than about the nature of things. The chains of images in our minds reflect our particular habits, and no one will share exactly the same 'concatenations' of images with another person. As Hume would argue more forcefully in the eighteenth century, imaginary or habitual thinking is subjectively ordered, and there is nothing to guarantee its application to the objective 'order and connection of things'.[14] Spinoza claims that the mind has 'only a confused knowledge, of itself, of its own body, and of external bodies, so long as it is determined externally, from fortuitous encounters with things' (E2p29s). This knowledge by association is 'without order for the intellect', since it is drawn 'from random experience' (E2p40s2).

Spinoza's account of the inadequate cognition formed by 'opinion or imagination' shows the kind of minds—the patterns of thinking, the structures of attention—he expected people to bring to the task of reading the *Ethics*. When we attend to our own mental activity, his critique of imaginative thinking begins to appear even more radical than his critique of Descartes's metaphysics, or of Calvinist theology. A little introspection discloses a constant stream of thoughts passing through our minds: jumping from one train of associations to another, we realise that we are seldom the authors of our thoughts. It is difficult to disrupt the flow of images or ideas for longer than a few seconds, such is the force of habit. And it takes real effort to sustain a rational train of thought without distraction, even for a couple of minutes. In criticising imaginative thinking, Spinoza was not talking about an aberration, nor about something that is confined to a certain group of people (the uneducated, the stupid or the insane), but calling into question virtually all our ordinary mental activity.

Spinoza thought that genuine knowledge is gained by making the transition from imagination to reason, from the first to the second kind of knowledge. He emphasised that this transition is difficult. It involves a disruption of ordinary patterns of thinking, and a reordering of thought: a cognitive conversion from the order of habit—which is generated and consolidated by repetition—to the order of nature. Unlike Hume, Spinoza argued that the causal order of things is paralleled by a logical 'order and connection of ideas', which we can discern through reason. 'The order and connection of ideas is the same as the order and connection of things' (E2p7), and truly knowing something means understanding its causes: grasping how it fits into the whole of nature, to which it belongs and on which it depends. Our thinking needs to be trained to follow 'the connection of ideas which happens according to the order of the intellect, by which the mind perceives things through their first causes, and which is the same in all men' (E2p18s).

Spinoza's analysis of ordinary habitual thinking shows how repetition can produce lasting associations in the mind. When his demonstrations direct the reader to return to previous propositions, bringing them repeatedly to mind, he reinforces the logical 'order and connections of ideas' which the text has already traced. This process accomplishes not simply a demonstration of the validity of Spinoza's propositions, but a training in orderly, adequate cognition. Such a training will discipline the imagination to bring it into harmony with rational understanding.

Defining *imaginatio* as the 'first kind of cognition', Spinoza explains that it is a kind of thinking formed 'from signs, e.g., in hearing or reading certain words we remember things and form ideas of them similar to those which the things themselves first produced in us' (E2p40s2). We might apply this definition to the *Ethics* itself, considered as a practical system that involves 'hearing and reading certain words'—and we can also note that this account of *imaginatio* refers to remembering, or recollection, which is precisely what occurs when Spinoza cites previous propositions: the reader must call these elements to mind again. Furthermore, the mathematical example used to illustrate the difference between the first and second kinds of cognition refers to the 'demonstrations' within Euclid's *Elements*, the literary model for the *Ethics*. 'Merchants' find the fourth proportional number *either* 'because they have not forgotten what they heard from their tutor [*magistro*] without any demonstration, or because they have often tried the same process' *or* 'on the ground of the demonstration of Proposition 19, Book 7 of Euclid' (E2p40s2). The first case is *imaginatio*; the second is *ratio*. In the *Ethics*, Spinoza, as 'tutor', guides his readers through the demonstrations, leading them 'by the hand, as it were' (E2 Preface) through a training that involves 'often trying the same process' until their thinking proceeds from an understanding of his demonstrations. This process does not abandon *imaginatio*, but refashions it, so to speak, in the image of reason.

There is, of course, a 'third kind' of cognition: *scientia intuitiva*, intuitive knowing. Its significance becomes clearer in Part Five of the *Ethics*, and we will return to it in later chapters of this book: in particular, in Chapter 6, on Spinoza's concept of *acquiescentia*, we will see how *scientia intuitiva* grounds the mind's capacity for repose—for resting in itself, and at the same time resting in God. Spinoza's thinking on this point has deep sources. Medieval thinkers contrasted the mental exertion of *ratio* with a more restful, contemplative, intuitive kind of knowing, which participates in God's *intellectus*. Thomas Aquinas traced this philosophical ideal to the fourth of the ten commandments recorded in Exodus 20—'Remember the Sabbath day, and keep it holy'—which for Aquinas implied a 'moral precept' directing 'the mind to rest in God' (*quies mentis in Deo*).[15] As the Thomist philosopher Josef Pieper explained in his 1948 essay *Leisure the Basis of Culture*,

> The Middle Ages drew a distinction between *ratio* and *intellectus*. *Ratio* is the power of discursive, logical thought, of searching and examination, of abstraction, of definition and drawing conclusions. *Intellectus* [is] the capacity of *simplex intuitus*, of that simple vision to which truth offers itself like a landscape to the eye. Man's knowledge is both these things in one, according to antiquity and the Middle Ages, simultaneously *ratio* and *intellectus*; and the process of knowing is the action of the two together. The mode of discursive thought is accompanied and impregnated by an effortless awareness, the contemplative vision of the *intellectus*.[16]

While *ratio* requires 'real hard work', the simple, intuitive vision of *intellectus* 'is not work'.[17] Pieper argues that the possibility of intellectual rest was already in danger of being lost in the early modern era. Of course, any claim with such a sweeping historical scope is inevitably a generalisation, and another side to this story is the renewed interest in the Stoic ideal of tranquillity among sixteenth- and seventeenth-century thinkers. Nevertheless, Pieper's suggestion that during this period the pursuit of knowledge came to be construed solely as effortful work is borne out by Spinoza's own criticism of Francis Bacon, an early architect of modern science. In a 1661 letter to Henry Oldenburg, Spinoza criticised Bacon's view that 'the human intellect ... cannot stop or rest'.[18] This points to the broader context for Spinoza's insistence on a 'third kind' of knowing. The *Ethics* resists the tendency of modern thought to see *ratio* as the highest form of knowledge, and thus to deny the mind's repose. Spinoza's concept of *scientia intuitiva* places intellectual rest, alongside intellectual striving, at the heart of the human good.

The mind's awareness of its own cognitive activity is, I think, a paradigmatic instance of *scientia intuitiva*. Shortly after Spinoza introduces his distinction between three kinds of cognition at E2p40s2, he states that 'he who has a true idea at the same time knows [*simul scit*] that he has a true idea' (E2p43). This echoes his earlier remark that 'as soon as [*simulac*] someone knows something, he thereby knows that he knows it [*eo ipso scit*]' (E2p21s). By 'idea' Spinoza means an act of thinking, an act of understanding, not a static representation 'like a picture on a tablet' (E2p43s). Any act of thinking can be identified by its content, by what it is thinking *about*: for example, when I read the *Ethics*, I have a succession of ideas about substance, mode, attribute, desire, joy, sadness, virtue and all the other things discussed in the text. But an idea can also be considered in itself, without reference to its content, simply as an activity of thinking; Spinoza calls this 'the form of the idea insofar as this is considered as a mode of thinking, without relation to the object' (E2p21s). To pursue the same example, when I read and understand a proposition in the *Ethics*, I am aware of my own understanding. I have a true idea of the proposition, and at the same time I cognise my act of thinking: I know that I have a true idea.

This is an instance of *scientia intuitiva*, and we can see how it accompanies *ratio*, the second kind of knowing. Through *ratio* I grasp a proposition, and 'at the same time', through *scientia intuitiva*, I know that I am understanding it. One of the distinguishing features of *scientia intuitiva* is its immediacy or simultaneity: it arises 'as soon as' the act of thinking takes place. As soon as we have a true idea, we have an idea of this idea. Whereas in the case of *ratio* we can distinguish between what is known and the act of knowing it—on the one hand, say, a proposition in the *Ethics*, and on the other hand my act of understanding it—in the case of *scientia intuitiva* what is known and the act of knowing coincide. My mind knows itself; my act of understanding is both known and knowing. These are 'one of the same thing, which is conceived under one and the same attribute, viz. Thought' (E2p21s)—and this accounts for *scientia intuitiva*'s immediacy.[19]

Spinoza's own example of *scientia intuitiva* is not grasping a proposition in the *Ethics*, but the mathematical example that he uses to illustrate all three kinds of cognition. In the case of the simplest numbers, he remarks, neither the first nor the second kind of cognition is required to find the fourth proportional number: 'Given the numbers 1, 2 and 3, no one fails to see that the fourth proportional number is 6' (E2p40s2). Because we see 'in one glance' that 2 is twice as big as 1, we can immediately infer the number twice as big as 3, i.e., 6. This is precisely the kind of self-evident 'seeing' that is accompanied by a reflexive grasp of its truth: as soon as we have the true idea that the fourth proportional is 6, we know that we have the right answer. We cognise our own act of understanding.

Yet a very simple mathematical truth is so self-evident that we may pay little attention to the fact that we understand it. Perhaps a more palpable instance of *scientia intuitiva* is the sense of realisation and recognition that comes when we suddenly grasp something that was previously obscure: in this case, we really feel the transition in our mind, as we pass from not understanding something to understanding it. This transition is so evident—the contrast is so stark—that it is impossible not to notice it. To use Spinoza's own metaphor, it is like lighting a candle in a dark room (see E2p43s), and this is why, when we describe a sudden realisation, we sometimes say that it 'dawned on me'. The *Ethics* itself provides very ample opportunities to experience this dawning—the passage from darkness to light, from confusion to understanding—and to thereby feel our own intellectual activity, our own power of thinking. This is always an affective breakthrough, too, a passage from the frustrated, fumbling impotence of bewilderment to the happy power of clear vision. It can take time—minutes, days, years—to fully understand a single proposition, yet *as soon as* understanding comes, we recognise its truth and *at the same time* know that we have grasped this truth.

I should add, furthermore, that although knowing our own intellectual activity is the paradigmatic instance of *scientia intuitiva*, we may also know other things in this way. Again, the *Ethics* itself exemplifies this. The text is an articulation of Spinoza's intellectual activity: when we grasp one of its propositions, or a sequence of propositions, we are seeing not a mute image 'like a picture on a tablet', but an act of thinking. The immediacy that characterises our knowing of our own knowing applies here too. We might even say that our activity of thinking and Spinoza's activity of thinking become 'one and the same'. Thus *scientia intuitiva* permits its own kind of repetition, though one might argue that the different spatial-temporal conditions of these intellectual activities (Spinoza in the Netherlands in the seventeenth century, myself in London in the twenty-first century) are rendered so irrelevant by the immediacy of intuition that this is communion rather than repetition. And we form a community of readers, all of us, insofar as we understand the *Ethics*, sharing in the same reflexive intellectual activity. This too is intuitive repetition, and it is a great joy. Like Spinoza's very first readers, we do not encounter the *Ethics* alone: as we read and understand, maybe by very gradual degrees, we are participating together in understanding itself—participating, in other words, in the attribute of thought, in God's power of thinking. The metaphysics which grounds these cognitive possibilities will be explored in Chapters 3 and 5.

So the famous passage on the 'three kinds of cognition' offers a reflexive account of the work of the text itself, suggesting that the *Ethics* operates in all three modes of cognition, and seeks to bring them into agreement in its readers' minds. As Spinoza already perceived when he wrote his *Treatise on the Emendation of the Intellect*, this cognitive conversion has a deep ethical significance. In the *Ethics* he deploys the distinction between activity and passivity to argue that the conversion from habitual thinking to rational thinking will necessarily be empowering. As we develop adequate knowledge, we become more active, less subject to the vicissitudes of fortune which bring us into contact with this or that external influence, generating this or that sequence of associations. By exercising rational thought we come to understand the nature of things, to see how things affect one another, and this empowers us to order our own experience in a way that harmonises with reality and promotes our happiness. While imaginative, habitual thinking is based on 'random experience' and subject to its vicissitudes, rational thinking provides the basis for a wiser, more philosophical way of life.

The distinction between habit and experience on the one hand, and reason on the other, is a familiar trope of early modern and Enlightenment thought. This distinction was often correlated with a body–mind dualism in more or less normative ways, and of course Spinoza's metaphysics cuts through the dualism promoted by Descartes and his followers. His own distinction between thinking that is ordered by experience, and thinking that is ordered by reason—the distinction between the first and second kinds of cognition set out in E2p40s2—is unsettled by the fact that the *Ethics*, considered as a dynamic text constituted by an act of reading, is itself an experiential phenomenon. Like any other literary work, it is experienced by the reader as it unfolds in time. But the *Ethics* configures the experience of reading in a certain way: as we read, our minds follow its geometrical method, moving between ideas in a logical sequence. The dynamic text thus inculcates the discipline of rational thinking, as well as offering moments of *scientia intuitiva*. Although the habitual patterns of the imagination need to be undone and replaced by rationally ordered thinking, the force of habit can be weakened only by a corresponding counter-force: rationality needs to be entrenched by repetition.

―――

In Part Five of the *Ethics* Spinoza returns to the subject of repetition, and suggests that it has a vital role in reordering his readers' thinking 'according to the intellect'. Here the context is explicitly ethical: Spinoza is explaining how our emotions can be brought into harmony with a rational understanding of both ourselves and others.[20] 'So long as we are not torn by affects contrary to our nature,' he writes, 'we have the power of ordering and connecting the affections of the body according to the order of the intellect' (E5p10). Once we completely understand our emotions, he argues, we will cease to be passively subject to them. However, as he already saw when he composed his *Treatise on the Emendation of the Intellect*, 'while we . . . devote ourselves to bringing the intellect back to the right path, it is necessary to live'.[21] Complete self-knowledge is extraordinarily difficult to accomplish, and 'so long as we do not have perfect knowledge of our affects, the best thing we can do is to conceive a correct principle of living, or sure maxims of life, to commit them to memory, and to apply them constantly to the particular cases frequently encountered in life' (E5p10s).

Here the psychological mechanism whereby repetition generates and enforces habitual, imaginative thinking becomes the remedy for the condition which it had helped to produce. In the *Ethics* cognitive repetition thus exemplifies what Jacques Derrida called a 'pharmakon': a device that is both a poison and a cure.[22] Like the Stoics, Spinoza is advocating imaginative practices that will retrain the mind to follow a certain order of associations.[23] By way of an example, he suggests that the Christian exhortation to 'love your enemies' (see Matthew 5:44 and Luke 6:27)—or, as he rephrases it, the maxim 'that hate is to be conquered by love, by not repaying it with hate in return'—should be joined to the image of wrongdoing by 'frequently' meditating on 'the common wrongs of men, and how they might be warded off best by nobility'. Sufficient repetition will entrench the maxim as a habitual thought that 'will always be ready for us when a wrong is done to us'. Similarly, he suggests that the emotion of fear can be conquered if we 'recount and frequently imagine the common dangers of life, and how they can be best avoided and overcome by presence of mind and strength of character' (E5p10s). As he explains how these imaginative practices change the mind's patterns of thinking, Spinoza refers back to his analysis of habituation in *Ethics* II, particularly E2p18 (which is cited in E5p10s, E5p12 and E5p13). He states that 'as an image is related to more things, the more frequent it is, or the more often it flourishes, and the more it engages the mind' (E5p11), and that 'the more an image is joined with other images, the more often it flourishes' (E5p13).

This helps to explain what is happening when Spinoza's text directs the reader to recall or re-read an earlier proposition. For this is not mere repetition; rather, it is a repetition that involves variation. If a particular proposition is cited, say, six times over the course of the *Ethics*, each time the reader is sent back to it from a new place; the proposition is reiterated in association with six different propositions, with different conceptual contents. 'The more an image is joined with other images, the more often it flourishes'—and the revisited proposition functions just like an image that recurs in relation to many different images, and thus increasingly 'engages' the reader's mind.

It is possible, indeed, to analyse the dynamic structure of the *Ethics*— considered as a practical system, a philosophical discipline, a spiritual exercise—by measuring the frequency of each proposition. A small number of propositions are never cited; they are encountered just once in a single reading of the text. Others are repeated multiple times, demanding the reader's attention again and again. Each proposition thus gains a certain intensity, or intensive power. Within the text's architecture, this semantic power might be imagined as a weight or density which registers the proposition's significance in bearing a certain conceptual load. Propositions that are cited many times do a lot of work, both theoretically and practically: they support a large proportion of Spinoza's theoretical system, and through the practice of reading the *Ethics* they vigorously engage and form the mind of the reader who returns to them repeatedly. Just as Spinoza thought that individual entities (or modes), while inseparable from their relations to other modes, can be distinguished by their degree of power, so the interconnecting propositions of the *Ethics* have differing potencies.[24]

Reading the text in this way, we can identify a number of 'super-propositions', a term I reserve for those elements (there are definitions and scholia as well as propositions in this category) which are cited more than ten times. Often these super-propositions carry extensive scholia. Ten is an arbitrary number, but it yields a manageable selection of super-propositions: four from Part One, eleven from Part Two, nine from Part Three and two from Part Four.[25] These are listed at the end of this chapter.

Of course, simply counting the number of citations per proposition is simplistic: for example, a proposition might be cited just three times, but if these citations occur in demonstrations to three super-propositions, then the proposition supports elements which themselves bear a lot of the text's weight. No doubt someone could devise an algorithm to calculate the intensity of each element of the *Ethics*.[26] Nevertheless, our unsophisticated list of twenty-five super-propositions yields some rough yet interesting results. The two most powerful elements of the text are both in Part Three. The scholium to E3p11, cited twenty-seven times, explains that 'the [human] mind can undergo great changes, and pass at one time to a higher and at another to a lower degree of perfection', and defines the affects of joy and sadness in terms of these transitions to greater or lesser perfection. E3p7, cited twenty-five times, asserts that 'the striving by which each thing strives to persevere in its being is nothing but the actual essence of the thing'. Spinoza's definition of God, E1D6, is by far the most cited definition in the *Ethics*: 'By God I understand a being absolutely infinite, i.e., a substance consisting of an infinity of attributes, of which each one expresses an external and infinite essence.' From Part Two of the text, the distinction between three kinds of cognition at E2p40s2 and the discussion of imagination and error at E2p17s both make the list, as does the proposition that underpins Spinoza's metaphysical parallelism: 'The order and connection of ideas is the same as the order and connection of things' (E2p7).

Spinoza argues that we know a thing by knowing its cause, and no doubt he also held that his readers would understand any particular proposition of the *Ethics* once they understood all the elements—definitions, axioms, postulates, propositions—it rests upon.[27] Just as our understanding of a particular thing—for example, an organism, a meteorological event or a human emotion—expands as we trace the complex series of causes which conspire to produce it, so within Spinoza's philosophical system a complete grasp of any proposition depends on tracing the proliferating sequences of elements that constitute its conceptual foundations. To truly understand a proposition, the reader must first return to the elements cited in its demonstration, and then reach further back to all the elements cited in the demonstrations of these elements, and so on. This process yields an explication of each proposition *and* of its necessity; it also intensifies those propositions which constitute the foundation stones of Spinoza's system. Take, for example, a super-proposition from Part One: 'Whatever is, is in God, and nothing can be or be conceived without God (E1p15). This is cited seventeen times in the *Ethics*, and these seventeen elements are in turn cited sixty-five times, and these sixty-five elements are cited 146 times. In other words, if a reader were to trace Spinoza's argumentative lines by three conceptual steps—and she could, of course, follow his directions more diligently still, and trace every single proposition back to its first foundations—she would revisit E1p15 a total of 228 times, always from a different starting-point.

Most of the propositions in the *Ethics* are traversed by argumentative lines that reach back to Part One of the text, 'Of God'—and most frequently to the super-propositions of this Part: E1p11, which affirms God's necessary existence, and E1p16, which states that 'infinitely many things' follow 'in infinitely many modes' from God's nature, along with Spinoza's definition of God and E1p15: 'Whatever is, is in God, and nothing can be or be conceived without God.'

In Part Five of the *Ethics*, Spinoza refers to God—and to E1p15— immediately after discussing how the frequency and connectedness of images 'engages the mind':

> E5p11: As an image is related to more things, the more frequent it is, *or* the more often it flourishes, and the more it engages the Mind.
>
> E5p12: The images of things are more easily joined to images related to things we understand clearly and distinctly than to other images.
>
> E5p13: The more an image is joined with other images, the more often it flourishes.
>
> E5p14: The Mind can bring it about that all the Body's affections, *or* images of things, are related to the idea of God.
> Dem.: There is no affection of the Body of which the Mind cannot form some clear and distinct concept (by E5p4). And so it can bring it about (by E1p15) that they are related to the idea of God; q.e.d.

The 'spiritual exercise' of reading the *Ethics* is not, then, simply a formal training in logical thinking. It inculcates the practice of relating 'all images of things' to the idea of God—a practice mirrored in the structure of the text, which relates propositions about many different aspects of human activity and experience to propositions about God. To associate things with the idea of God is to connect them to the idea of their first cause, and for Spinoza this is precisely what it means to have genuine knowledge.

In offering readers a spiritual exercise that links things to the idea of God, and entrenching these associations by repetition, the *Ethics* resembles many religious practices, such as daily prayer, devotional reading and rituals of worship. It differs, of course, in offering a cognitive practice of enquiry. The *Ethics* is well suited to readers who, like Spinoza himself, are drawn to philosophy, and to the intellectual knowledge of God. Spinoza knew that people 'vary greatly in their mentality', and there is no reason to think that he wished to prevent anyone from following religious rituals which link things to God in ways that were chiefly devotional or contemplative, perhaps using figurative language and imaginative thinking—for example, by giving thanks to God for a shared meal, by regularly repeating the prayer Jesus taught his followers, or by laying out a prayer mat five times daily.[28] When such rituals were bound up with superstitious beliefs which gave rise to troublesome emotions, and when they were enforced by ecclesial authorities seeking to inhibit freedom of thought, then Spinoza was very critical of them. But the rituals themselves might be seen as complementary to the spiritual exercise of the *Ethics*, rather than contrary to it.

Though I have used architectural metaphors, drawn from the domain of extension, to convey the theoretical and practical power of the *Ethics*—and to identify the system's strongest foundations, its thickest load-bearing columns—we might also express its power by the metaphor of light, which has degrees of intensity. According to this metaphor, the text is a work of enlightenment. This has to be understood against the background of a particular configuration of darkness, or ignorance, which Spinoza discerned amongst his contemporaries. We might create a map of the *Ethics* that would resemble the constellations of the night sky, with some stars—the most intensive propositions—burning brighter than the others. As we have seen, the elements recurring most often in the dynamic text are those which Spinoza wants to impress most forcefully upon his readers' minds. It may turn out that these bright stars of Spinoza's philosophical constellation are points which correct his readers' deepest, darkest errors: belief in an anthropomorphic God; the idea that human beings are self-sufficient substances, which possess free will; fear of punishment and death; an individualistic and instrumental attitude to virtue and happiness; misguided conceptions of the nature of the human mind, and thus of elemental emotions such as desire, joy, sadness, love and hatred. Perhaps Spinoza's super-propositions signal where the most intensive work of enlightenment needs to be carried out.

Appendix: Super-propositions in the Ethics

Below I list the twenty-six 'super-propositions' in the *Ethics* (a couple of the longer ones have been abridged), with the number of direct citations of each given in brackets. Most of these elements will be explored in detail in the chapters to follow, but this list offers an overview, or a reminder, of the key points of Spinoza's philosophy.

DEFINITION OF GOD

1D6: By God I understand a being absolutely infinite, i.e., a substance consisting of an infinity of attributes, of which each one expresses an external and infinite essence. (13)

GOD EXISTS NECESSARILY

1p11: God, or a substance consisting of infinite attributes, each of which expresses eternal and infinite essence, necessarily exists. (10)

BEING-IN-GOD

1p15: Whatever, is in God, and nothing can be or be conceived without God. (17)

MODES FOLLOW NECESSARILY FROM GOD

1p16: From the necessity of the divine nature there must follow infinitely many things in infinitely many modes (i.e., everything which can fall under an infinite intellect). (17)

PARALLEL BETWEEN THE ATTRIBUTES OF THOUGHT AND EXTENSION

2p7: The order and connection of ideas is the same as the order and connection of things. (12)

THE HUMAN MIND

2p11: The first thing that constitutes the actual being of a human Mind is nothing but the idea of a singular thing which actually exists. (11)

THE HUMAN MIND IS PART OF GOD'S INTELLECT

2p11c: From this it follows that the human Mind is part of the infinite intellect of God. Therefore, when we say that the human Mind perceives this or that, we are saying nothing but that God, not insofar as he is infinite, but insofar as he is explained through the essence of the human Mind, *or* insofar as he constitutes the essence of the human Mind, has this or that idea; and when we say that God has this or that idea, not only insofar as he constitutes the nature of the human Mind, but insofar as he also has the idea of another thing together with the human Mind, then we say that the human Mind perceives the thing only partially, *or* inadequately. (11)

THE HUMAN MIND PERCEIVES ITS OBJECT (THE BODY) ENTIRELY

2p12: Whatever happens in the object of the idea constituting the human Mind must be perceived by the human Mind, *or* there will necessarily be an idea of that thing in the Mind; i.e., if the object of the idea constituting a human Mind is the body, nothing can happen in that body which is not perceived by the Mind. (10)

THE HUMAN MIND IS THE IDEA OF THE BODY

2p13: The object of the idea constituting the human Mind is the Body, *or* a certain mode of extension which actually exists, and nothing else. (19)

IDEAS OF EXTERNAL THINGS

2p16: The idea of any mode in which the human Body is affected by external bodies must involve the nature of the human Body and at the same time the nature of the external body. (11)

THE MIND AFFIRMS THE PRESENT EXISTENCE OF WHATEVER IT PERCEIVES

2p17: If the human Body is affected with a mode that involves the nature of an external body, the human Mind will regard the same external body as actually existing, or as present to it, until the Body is affected by an affect that excludes the existence or presence of that body. (15)

2p17c: Although the external bodies by which the human body has once been affected neither exist nor are present, the mind will still be able to regard them as if they were present. (10)

IMAGES AND IMAGINING

2p17s: We thus see why we frequently contemplate things that do not exist as if they were present. . . . [W]e clearly understand what is the difference between the idea of, say, Peter, which constitutes the essence of Peter's mind, and the idea of Peter which is in another person, say in Paul. For the former directly explains the essence of Peter's body, and involves existence only so long as Peter exists; but the latter indicates the condition of Paul's body more than the nature of Peter, and therefore while that condition of Paul's body of Paul lasts, Paul's mind will contemplate Peter as present to it, even though Peter does not exist. . . .

Next, to retain the customary words, the affections of the human Body whose ideas present external bodies as present to us, we shall call images of things, even if they do not produce the [external] figures of things. And when the Mind regards bodies in this way, we shall say that it imagines.

And here, in order to begin to indicate what error is, I should like you to note that the imaginations of the Mind, considered in themselves, contain no error, *or* that the Mind does not err from the fact that it imagines, but only insofar as it is considered to lack an idea that excludes the existence of those things that it imagines to be present to it. For if the Mind, while it imagined nonexistent things as present to it, at the same time knew that those things did not exist, it would, of course, attribute the power of imagining to a virtue of its nature, not a vice—especially if this faculty of imagining depended only on its nature, i.e. (by ID7), if the Mind's faculty of imagining were free. (12)

ASSOCIATION AND RECOLLECTION

2p18: If a human Body has once been affected by two or more bodies at the same time, then when the Mind subsequently imagines one of them, it will immediately recollect the others also. (10)

THREE KINDS OF COGNITION

2p40s2: From what has been said above, it is clear that we perceive many things and form universal notions:

I. From singular things which have been represented to us through the senses in a way that is mutilated, confused, and without order for the intellect; for that reason I have been accustomed to call such perceptions cognition from random experience.
II. From signs, e.g., from the fact that, having heard or read certain words, we recollect things, and form certain ideas of them, which are like them, and through which we imagine the things. These two ways of regarding things I shall henceforth call cognition of the first kind, opinion or imagination.
III. Finally, from the fact that we have common notions and adequate ideas of the properties of things. This I shall call reason and the second kind of cognition.
[IV.] In addition to these two kinds of cognition, there is (as I shall show in what follows) another, third kind, which we shall call intuitive knowledge. And this kind of knowing proceeds from an adequate idea of the formal essence of certain attributes of God to the adequate knowledge of the [formal] essence of things. (11)

DEFINITION OF ACTION

3D2: I say that we act when something happens, in us or outside us, of which we are the adequate cause, i.e., when something in us or outside us follows from our nature, which can be clearly and distinctly understood through it alone. On the other hand, I say that we are acted on when something happens in us, or something follows from our nature, of which we are only a partial cause. (12)

ACTIONS AND PASSIONS

3P3: The actions of the Mind arise from adequate ideas alone; the passions depend on inadequate ideas alone. (22)

STRIVING IS ESSENCE

3P7: The striving by which each thing strives to persevere in its being is nothing but the actual essence of the thing. (25)

WILL, APPETITE AND DESIRE

3p9s: When this striving is related only to the Mind, it is called Will; but when it is related to the Mind and the Body together it is called Appetite. This Appetite, therefore, is nothing but the very essence of man, from whose nature there necessarily follow those things that promote his preservation. And so man is determined to do those things.

Between appetite and desire there is no difference, except that desire is generally related to men insofar as they are conscious of their appetite. So *desire* can be defined as *appetite together with consciousness of the appetite*.

From all this, then, it is clear that we neither strive for, nor will, neither want, nor desire anything because we judge it to be good; on the contrary, we judge it to be good because we strive for it, will it, want it and desire it. (12)

THE MIND'S TRANSITIONS: JOY AND SADNESS

3p11s: We see, then, that the Mind can undergo great changes, and pass now to a greater, now to a lesser perfection. These passions, indeed, explain to us the affects of Joy and Sadness. By *Joy*, I shall understand in what follows that *passion by which the Mind passes to a greater perfection*. And by *Sadness*, that *passion by which it passes to a lesser perfection*.

I have explained in E3p9s what Desire is, and apart from these three I do not acknowledge any other primary affect. For I shall show in what follows that the rest arise from these three. (27)

LOVE AND HATE

3p13s: From this we understand clearly what Love and Hate are. *Love* is nothing but *Joy with the accompanying idea of an external cause*, and *Hate* is nothing but *Sadness with the accompanying idea of an external cause*. We see, then, that one who loves necessarily strives to have present and preserve the thing he loves; and on the other hand, one who hates strives to remove and destroy the thing he hates. (19)

EMPATHY

3p27: If we imagine a thing like us, towards which we have had no affect, to be affected with some affect, we are thereby affected by a like affect. (15)

DESIRE AND AVERSION

3p28: We strive to further the occurrence of whatever we imagine will lead to Joy, and to avert or destroy what we imagine is contrary to it, *or* will lead to Sadness. (14)

MALEVOLENCE AND BENEVOLENCE

3p39: He who hates someone will strive to do evil to him, unless he fears that a greater evil to himself will arise from this; and on the other hand, he who loves someone will strive to benefit him by the same law. (12)

WE STRIVE TO UNDERSTAND

4p26: What we strive for from reason is nothing but understanding; nor does the Mind, insofar as it uses reason, judge anything to be useful to itself except what leads to understanding. (10)

DESIRING THE GOOD OF OTHERS

4p37: The good which everyone who seeks virtue wants for himself, he also desires for other people; and this Desire is greater as his knowledge of God is greater. (10)

CHAPTER THREE

Being-in-God

'BEING-IN-GOD' is the fundamental tenet of Spinoza's thought. In the *Ethics* this is presented as an ontological principle and also, it seems, as an ethical task. In Part One, 'Of God', Spinoza states, 'Whatever is, is in God, and nothing can be or be conceived without God' (E1p15). In Part Four, which focuses on the human condition and its empowerment, or virtue, he writes that 'in proportion as we are affected with joy, we advance towards greater perfection, and consequently participate more fully in the divine nature [*eo magis de natura divina participamus*]'. Though this claim is, on the face it, purely descriptive, it is difficult to read the *Ethics* without regarding 'advancing towards greater perfection' and 'participating more fully in the divine nature' as a normative ideal. Chapters 4 and 5 in this book explore the idea that being-in-God is an ethical or spiritual task. Here, we will consider being-in-God as an ontological principle.

The first five words of E1p15—*Quidquam est in Deo est*—tell us something fundamental both about God, and about everything that exists. God contains 'whatever is', and 'whatever is' is in God. It is worth pausing for a moment to take in this radical ontological claim. *All* being is qualified as being-in-God. I have hyphenated this phrase to emphasise that there is, for Spinoza, no being apart from God, or prior to God—just as Heidegger's concept of *In-der-Welt-sein*, 'being-in-the-world', affirms that the human being is always already related to a world. According to Spinoza, the fundamental and immediate truth about anything that is—anything at all—is that it is in God.

The preceding chapter showed how the geometrical order of the *Ethics* generates repetitions in the act of reading the text: when Spinoza cites an earlier claim in the course of a demonstration, the reader should recall or re-read the cited proposition in order to discern the truth of the present proposition. Through the process of reading the *Ethics*, each proposition gains a degree of intensity, a degree of significance, according to how often it is cited by Spinoza, and thus repeated by the reader. Those propositions that are most often reinforced are the philosophical equivalent of load-bearing columns in a building, since they are holding up the greatest portion of Spinoza's philosophical system. According to these principles of literary engineering, E1p15 is the hardest-working proposition of *Ethics* I. It carries one of Spinoza's longest scholia, and is cited throughout the text, more frequently than any other element of Part One: eight times in Part One, seven times in Part Two, and twice each in Parts Four and Five. Through this repetition, the principle of being-in-God acquires over the course of the *Ethics* a semantic density, and correspondingly a psychological power in the mind of the reader.

Moreover, this principle is inscribed into the foundation stones of Spinoza's metaphysics: his concepts of substance and mode. The first axiom of the *Ethics* states, 'Whatever is, is either in itself or in another' (E1A1). Spinoza defines substance as 'that which is in itself [*in se est*]' (E1D3), while a mode is 'that which is in another [*in alio est*]' (E1D5). 'Nothing exists besides substances and modes', Spinoza writes in the Demonstration to E1p15, citing Axiom 1.[1] Since there is only one substance, namely God (see E1p14), everything that is, is in God. This includes God: God is substance, therefore God is *in se*.

But what does it mean to be 'in God'? In 1945, Étienne Souriau observed that 'the meaning of the little word *in* as it is found in [the first axiom of the *Ethics*] is the key to all of Spinozism', and more recently Don Garrett suggested that 'being in' is 'the most fundamental relation in Spinoza's metaphysics'.[2] It is safe to say that being-in-God does not mean spatial containment, nor does it mean being part of a whole. Rather, being-in-God is an ontological relation of dependency, which involves being 'caused by' God and being 'conceived through' God.

For Spinoza, our being-in-God participates in God's own being-in-God. God, as substance, is caused by and conceived through itself (see E1D3). God's own being-in-God is a being *in se*, while our being-in-God is a being *in alio*. This is an ontological difference, and it secures the relation of profound metaphysical intimacy between God and finite things—an intimacy indicated by some of Spinoza's key concepts: expression, participation, immanence.

So the little word 'in' plunges us into the deep end of Spinoza's metaphysics, since it is vital to the definitions of substance and mode, and to the relation between them—the relation of all things to God. Scholarly interpretations of the meaning and scope of the 'being in' relation not only differ, but lead to divergent interpretations of Spinoza's entire metaphysics.[3]

It is not surprising that even Spinoza's most accomplished readers struggle to make sense of being-in-God, or that his texts leave room for significant disagreement about what this means. One consequence of distinguishing between substance and mode, and insisting that substance is unique—that only God is substance—is that we cannot assume that our vocabulary, our grammar and our concepts which structure our understanding of entities within the world can yield an adequate account of God. Being-in-God does not mean the same thing as being in my house, being in a good mood, being in trouble, or being in a relationship; nor do even pure metaphysical concepts of relation, such as causation, apply to God in the same way as they apply to objects of experience. Our language applies to what Spinoza calls modes, and to the relations between modes. For this reason, Spinoza suggests that even to claim that there is only one substance—as he does in the *Ethics*—is, strictly speaking, to improperly apply to God the concept of oneness, which properly applies only to the kinds of things in the world that can be counted.[4]

In this respect, Spinoza's metaphysics departs from Descartes's metaphysics, which conceives human beings as finite substances and God as an infinite substance. Descartes recognised that our way of being a substance is very different from God's way of being a substance—so much so, he argued, that 'the term "substance" does not apply in the same sense to God and to other things, meaning that no clearly intelligible sense of the term is common to God and to created things'.[5] Yet treating these ways of being under a single category—substance—makes it possible to imagine the relations between God and the world to resemble relations between things in the world, since all these relations are relations between substances. This, in turn, paves the way for an anthropomorphic theology, which conceives God's nature and action on the model of human nature and action. Spinoza's distinction between substance and modes powerfully resists this anthropomorphism. As we shall see in the chapters to follow, it is true that Spinoza often suggests that modes—and especially human beings—can possess *to some degree* characteristics that substance possesses absolutely, perhaps even to the extent that singular things are capable of becoming 'quasi-substances', as Don Garrett puts it.[6] Nevertheless, the categorical distinction between substance and mode remains fundamental to Spinoza's metaphysics.[7]

For these reasons, we should allow the meaning of being-in-God to remain, to some extent, an open question: a question we attend to, and inhabit, whenever we read Spinoza. I think we should be prepared to understand 'being-in' to express both difference and identity. Of course, this will be a different difference, and a different identity, from the concepts of difference and identity we apply to things we encounter in the world. We need to be careful about the notion of otherness that Spinoza folds into his definition of a mode as that which is 'in another' (*in alio*). God is not other than ourselves in the same way that the house across the road is other than my house, nor in the same way that a house is other than a tree. While different things in the world compete, so to speak, for space and for agency, God does not get in the way of the space we occupy, nor does God's power detract from our agency. On the contrary, our agency *is*, in some sense, God's agency. Yet we are not identical to God in the way that two things in the world might be imagined to be identical to one another. Being-in-God does not mean being-God: the little word 'in' reminds us not to collapse the distinction between substance and mode. As Michael Della Rocca has explained, substance and modes stand in an 'asymmetrical relation': substance is not in (not conceived through, nor caused by) its modes, whereas modes are in (are conceived through and caused by) substance.[8] I am not God; I am a mode, while God is substance.

Part One of the *Ethics* constitutes a radical critique of anthropomorphism: the God under discussion here is not only unlike a human subject, but is not a subject at all.[9] Since Spinoza's God is neither a subject nor an object—of knowledge, of experience, of action—treating God as a grammatical subject or object is a linguistic contrivance that tends to obscure the unique nature of God's being. For this reason, the strands of negative theology running through all religious traditions have something to teach us about how to inhabit the Spinozist question of being-in-God. Perhaps negative concepts such as 'non-duality' and apparently paradoxical teachings—for example, Nicolas of Cusa's suggestion that God is 'not other' or, as one of my teachers used to say, 'not I, not other than I'—can gesture to the meaning of being-in-God.[10] And perhaps we get closer to the truth of being-in-God through silence than through speech, text, or linguistically ordered thinking. Like any theologian, Spinoza confronted these questions and constraints while writing the *Ethics*.

Nevertheless, Spinoza takes an important step to elucidate his principle of being-in-God by explaining that 'God is the immanent, not the transitive, cause of all things [*causa immanens, non vero transiens*]' (E1p18).

'Transitive' or 'transient' causation means the production of an effect outside its cause. In his *Short Treatise on God, Man and His Well-Being*, Spinoza states that '[God] is an immanent and not a transitive cause, since he does everything in himself, and not outside himself (because outside God there is nothing)'.[11] In a letter to Henry Oldenburg written in late 1675, towards the end of his life, Spinoza sought to clarify his views about the relationship between God and Nature: 'I favour an opinion concerning God and Nature far different from the one Modern Christians usually defend. For I maintain that God is the immanent, but not the transitive, cause of all things. That all things are in God and move in God, I affirm, I say, with Paul.'[12] As these sources show, Spinoza consistently used *immanens* to indicate that God causes all things to be in God, not outside God. This suggests that the way God causes all things to exist is qualitatively different from the causal relations between finite things, which can be understood as extrinsic or 'transitive' causes.[13]

As Spinoza's reference to 'Modern Christians' in his 1675 letter to Oldenburg suggests, his insistence that God is the 'immanent cause' of all things opposes a specific theological view. This 'modern' view involved the separation of God from Nature.[14] It can be discerned in both Calvinism and Cartesianism, the twin targets of the *Ethics*, which exemplify a decisive shift in early modern theology and philosophy. Calvinism and Cartesianism are in some important respects contrary bodies of thought—not least insofar as Calvin emphasised the authority of scripture, while Descartes emphasised the authority of human reason. Yet they both shaped worldviews that tend to separate God from nature, by producing voluntarist and anthropomorphic conceptions of God's activity. Though Dutch Cartesians and Calvinists engaged in hostile disputes over metaphysical and methodological questions, both factions emphasised God's supreme will.[15] Calvin himself described God as 'the supreme King and Judge',[16] while Descartes wrote that God 'lays down laws in nature just as a king lays down laws in his kingdom'.[17]

This early modern anthropomorphic governor-God subsequently ossified into the remote, skeletal God of eighteenth-century deism—which imagined that, having created the universe, God left it to function autonomously according to the mechanical laws he had designed—before crumbling into the vanishing God of nineteenth-century atheism.[18] If the seventeenth-century churches had been receptive to Spinoza, he could have been their Aquinas for the new modern era that stretched ahead of them: his profound refusal of anthropomorphism, voluntarism and the separation of God from nature might have insulated Christianity from the ravages of secularism to come. Instead, Protestants and Catholics alike denounced him as an atheist. Only after the intellectual influence of these churches had waned, thanks to the growing power of Enlightenment ideas, could Spinozism be taken seriously—but by then, of course, it was too late to save their God from empiricism and positivism, from Marx, Darwin, Nietzsche, Freud and their twentieth-century successors.

The *Ethics* criticises, with remarkable clarity, the theology that would prove so vulnerable to these modern ways of thinking: 'By God's power ordinary people [*vulgus*] understand God's free will and his right over all things which are, things which on that account are commonly considered to be contingent. . . . Further, they very often compare God's power with the power of Kings' (E2p3s). The twin targets of Calvinist theology and Cartesian philosophy can be discerned in the scholium to E1p15, which exhibits the critical force of Spinoza's principle of being-in-God. Spinoza begins the scholium by dismissing a popular theological view that imagines God to be 'like man, consisting of a body and a mind, and subject to passions'. He then argues, at greater length, with more sophisticated opponents—easily identifiable as Cartesians—who 'entirely remove corporeal or extended substance itself from the divine nature [and] maintain that it has been created by God'. This suggestion that God created an 'extended substance' that is outside, or 'removed from', God's nature, involves precisely the view of God as 'transitive cause' that Spinoza rejects in E1p18.

Whenever Spinoza employs the adjective 'immanent', it always designates a kind of causation, and is always opposed to 'transitive' causation.[19] Used in this way, the word emphasises that God is not a remote, external cause of 'whatever is', but an intimate, internal cause. Nowhere in Spinoza's works is immanence opposed to transcendence, and nowhere does Spinoza deny God's transcendence. He never uses the word 'transcendent', which was not commonly applied to God until late in the nineteenth century.[20] Nevertheless, his critique of the idea of God's 'transitive' creation is now often interpreted by readers as a wholesale rejection of a religious tradition involving belief in a transcendent God—a tradition usually labelled with overly generalising phrases such as 'classical theism' or 'traditional Christianity'. Spinoza was responding to something much more doctrinally and historically specific than this: a separation of God and nature that he recognised as distinctively modern. As any student of Aquinas knows, God can transcend creation without being separate from it.[21]

Spinoza's characterisation of God as an 'immanent cause' has led to some rather careless misreadings of his theological position. In 1970, Gilles Deleuze asserted that 'the entire *Ethics* is a voyage in immanence' and celebrated 'the Spinozan critique of all transcendence', and since then a chorus of researchers in philosophy and literary-cultural studies have heralded Spinoza as a thinker of 'pure immanence'.[22] Deleuze was an insightful reader of Spinoza: he rightly drew attention to the concept of power within the *Ethics*, and elaborated Souriau's insight into the significance of expression in Spinozism—but on the question of immanence his influence has been pernicious.[23] And this interpretation of Spinoza is not confined to commentators who follow Deleuze; it also dominates what we might call the common-sense secularist reading of Spinoza, eloquently articulated by Steven Nadler, who insists that for Spinoza 'there is no transcendent deity; there is no supernatural being.... There is only Nature, and what belongs to Nature.'[24] Commentators of either school who express this sort of view seem to associate transcendence with an image of God standing outside the universe, separate from nature—an image that Spinoza certainly did reject. When they deny the transcendence of Spinoza's God, they have in mind what Bruno Latour calls 'the wrong transcendence, the one that has immanence as its opposite rather than its synonym'.[25]

Transcendence and immanence are two sides of the same coin, and most contemporary theologians who follow the broadly Catholic trajectory shaped by Augustine and Aquinas recognise this when they describe God as transcendent. For them, affirming God's transcendence means affirming the ontological difference between creator and creation, between God and the universe. This difference secures the dependence of created beings on God. For Spinoza, being-in-God expresses his commitment to this dependence: 'Whatever is, is in God, and nothing can be or be conceived without God.'

The widespread tendency to frame Spinoza's philosophy as wholly immanent obscures the theological issues at stake in his work. While most philosophers assume that the *Ethics* rejects a conception of God that is central to Christian teaching, theologians accept the persistent rumour that Spinoza denies God's transcendence, assume that he has no theological insights to offer, and therefore pay little attention to the *Ethics*.[26]

We can begin to clear up this confusion by elucidating the distinction between pantheism and panentheism, and showing why Spinoza is not a pantheist. These terms, like the theological concept of transcendence, were not yet in use in Spinoza's time: 'pantheism' dates back to the early eighteenth century, and 'panentheism' to the nineteenth century. Spinoza has been described as both a pantheist and a panentheist (and also, of course, as an atheist), though pantheism is the most common label for his thought.[27]

Historically, pantheism is a rather slippery concept. In his 1720 work *Pantheisticon*, the Irish writer John Toland—often credited with coining the word 'pantheist' in 1704, and certainly one of the first to use it in published work—attributed to pantheists the view that 'All Things are from the Whole, and the Whole is from all Things', implying a mutual dependence between the one and the many. Toland described God as 'the Force and Energy of the Whole, the Creator and Ruler of All', insisting that, for pantheists, God is 'not separated from the Universe itself but by a Distinction of Reason alone'.[28] By the mid-nineteenth century, the denial that God is distinct from the world was seen as the distinguishing feature of pantheism: in 1836, S. T. Coleridge aligned pantheism with 'cosmotheism, or the worship of the world as God', and in 1848 Robert Wilberforce, a member of the Oxford Movement, wrote that the 'principle [of Pantheism] is to merge the personality of the moral Governor in the circle of His works'.[29] Pantheism is today commonly regarded as the belief that God is identical with the universe, 'the doctrine that God is everything and everything is God'.[30] This doctrine is considered a theological heresy by its critics precisely because it erases or understates the difference between God and creation.

Panentheism, by contrast, is the view that whatever is, is in God.[31] Both pantheism and panentheism are contrary to the theological dualism emerging from Calvinism and Cartesianism—and from later mechanical philosophies that posited a creator God—yet they are also squarely opposed to one another. While pantheism denies God's difference from the world, panentheism affirms this difference. Pantheism is often synonymous with the denial of divine transcendence; panentheism, on the other hand, offers one way to interpret divine transcendence. These 'ism' terms can be rather objectifying, as well as anachronistic, when applied to Spinoza, and they often close off questions rather than illuminating them. For these reasons, 'being-in-God' is a more appropriate expression: this is closer both to Spinoza's texts and to the existential, experiential dimensions of his metaphysics, and it articulates a question as much as it names a concept or a doctrine. Nevertheless, since Spinoza's philosophy has been so closely associated with pantheism, the distinction between pantheism and panentheism is an important one.

At first glance, the view that Spinoza is a pantheist seems much more credible than the charge of atheism. This interpretation has textual justification in the scholium to E1p29, where Spinoza distinguishes between *natura naturans* and *natura naturata*, and equates *natura naturans* with God:

> Before I proceed further, I will explain to the reader, or rather remind him, what I mean by *natura naturans* and what by *natura naturata*. For from the foregoing propositions it is, I believe, already evident that

> by *natura naturans* we are to understand that which is in itself and is conceived by itself, or such attributes of substance as express an eternal and infinite essence, *i.e.* (by E1p14c1 and E1p17c2), God considered as a free cause. By *natura naturata*, on the other hand, I understand everything that follows from the necessity of the nature of God or of any of his attributes, *i.e.*, all the *modes* of the attributes of God, considered as things which are in God and which cannot exist or be conceived without God. (E1p29s)

In this scholium, 'that which is in itself and is conceived by itself, or such attributes of substance as express an eternal and infinite essence' is offered as a metaphysical description that applies equally to God and to *natura naturans*. At the same time, Spinoza is emphasising that God cannot be equated with *natura naturata*. To put this point in more traditional theological language, he is accentuating the difference between the divine creator and created beings: *natura naturans* and *natura naturata* are not two distinct objects; nevertheless, they are not simply alternative labels for the same reality. The distinction between them signifies an ontological difference. Spinoza's description of *natura naturata* at the end of this scholium closely echoes E1p15: just as 'whatever is, is in God, and cannot be or be conceived without God', so *natura naturata* is 'in' *natura naturans*, and dependent on it. This relation of being-in expresses both difference and identity.

Most attempts to characterise Spinoza as a pantheist gloss over the highly distinctive conception of nature invoked in this discussion of *natura naturans*, and appeal instead to the striking phrase *Deus sive Natura*, frequently repeated as a kind of slogan for Spinozism. Commentators often assert that 'Spinoza identifies God with Nature', as if this claim were entirely uncontroversial, and as if no further explanation were required—and then they might implicitly project onto 'God or Nature' what Spinoza calls *natura naturata*, conceiving this in a specifically modern way as separate from God, and concluding that by *Deus sive Natura* Spinoza really means 'just Nature'.[32] Steven Nadler, for example, has argued that 'the phrase "God or Nature" is intended to assert a strict identity between God and nature (or some aspect of nature), not a containment relationship', and he admiringly sums up Spinoza's view as, 'God is nothing distinct from Nature itself. God is Nature, and Nature is all there is. This is why Spinoza prefers the phrase *Deus sive Natura*, "God or Nature".[33] In *A Secular Age*, the Catholic philosopher Charles Taylor offers a similar interpretation in a more disapproving tone, portraying Spinozism as a secularising force: 'following a path opened by Spinoza, we can see Nature as identical with God, and then as independent from God. . . . The immanent order can thus slough off the transcendent.'[34] Deleuze explicitly connects *Deus sive Natura* with pantheism when he declares that 'the *Ethics* demonstrates a substantial identity [between God and Nature] based on the oneness of substance (pantheism)'.[35]

The view that Spinoza is a pantheist rests on a persistent tendency not only to interpret *Deus sive Natura* too hastily, but also to give this phrase more weight than it deserves within Spinoza's philosophical system. *Deus sive Natura* occurs in just two passages in the *Ethics*. It does not appear in Part One, which is expressly focused on God; if Spinoza had wanted to make a robust metaphysical claim about the identity of God and Nature, surely this would have been the place to do it. Nor does Spinoza refer to *Deus sive Natura* in any of the text's definitions or propositions. The phrase occurs for the first time in the more loosely written Preface to Part Four:

> Nature does nothing on account of an end. That eternal and infinite being we call God, *or* Nature [*quod Deum, seu Naturam appellamus*], acts from the same necessity from which he exists. The reason, therefore, *or* cause, why God, *or* Nature, acts, and the reason why he exists [*cur Deus, seu Natura agit et cur existit*] are one and the same. (E4 Preface)

Here Spinoza conflates God and Nature in the course of ruling out final causes from both divine and natural agency. He is criticising a prevalent tendency to attribute purposes to nature, and since this tendency was closely allied to a misguided conception of God's providence and free will, it was natural for him to treat God and Nature together in this discussion. This passage, with its focus on activity, echoes E1p29s in showing that insofar as Spinoza is equating God and Nature, he has in mind *natura naturans*—Nature considered as an active power, expressed through infinite attributes—and not *natura naturata*. In applying the predicates 'eternal and infinite' to Nature, Spinoza is identifying Nature with a recognisable conception of God, rather than identifying God with (and thereby reducing God to) a familiar concept of Nature.

Normally, our broadest conception of 'Nature' comprises the whole universe, composed of—in Spinoza's terminology—thinking and extended substance, modified in so many ways as to produce a vast diversity of beings. When Spinoza identifies Nature with God, however, this conception of Nature must be expanded, beyond consciousness and extension, to comprise the infinity of attributes which, he declares, belong to God. Spinoza offers *Natura naturans* as, so to speak, an alternative name of God. This divine name works to free the concept of God from the cultural baggage—particularly the anthropomorphic and moralising connotations—it had acquired over many centuries.

After being thus introduced in Part Four's Preface, *Deus sive Natura* is then repeated twice in the demonstration of E4p4. Here again, Spinoza's primary concern is not to elucidate his conception of God. In this proposition he is asserting that human beings are necessarily 'part of nature' and subject to influences beyond their own power. Its demonstration emphasises that human beings are not autonomous or self-sufficient:

> P4. It is impossible that man should not be a part of Nature and should suffer no other changes than those which can be understood by means of his own nature alone, and of which he is the adequate cause.
>
> Dem.: The power [*potentia*] by which singular things (and consequently, [any] man) preserve their being, is the power of God, *or* Nature [*est ipsa Dei sive Naturae potentia*], not insofar as it is infinite, but insofar as it can be explained by man's actual essence. The man's power, therefore, insofar as it is explained through his actual essence, is a part of God or [*seu*] Nature's infinite power, *i.e.*, of its essence. (E4p4 and E1p4d)

In the first part of this demonstration, Spinoza makes clear that he is talking about God in a highly qualified sense: 'not insofar as [God's power] is infinite'. The issue at stake here is the relationship between an individual person's power and the power of 'God or Nature'; Spinoza is explaining that these powers are distinct but not separate, identical but not the same. In the second part of the passage, the words *seu Naturae* might themselves be read as signalling the very qualified sense of *Deus* at work here. While Spinoza suggests that human power is 'part of' the 'infinite power ... of God or Nature', this claim cannot be true of God considered absolutely, since in Part One of the *Ethics* he has argued that God is neither composed of parts nor divisible into parts.[36] Indeed, his suggestion in E4p4d that 'the power of man ... is a part of the infinite power ... of God or Nature' is further qualified by his claim that an individual's power '*is* the power of God or Nature ... insofar as [God] can be explained by the actual essence of human nature' (emphasis added). Metaphysically, being *identical with* divine power (appropriately qualified) is quite different from being *part of* divine power. Spinoza's treatment of the metaphysical issue of parts and wholes, or 'mereology', counts against giving undue weight to the phrase 'God or Nature' and treating this as a robust pantheist claim. Though in the demonstration to E4p4 Spinoza conflates God and Nature, in the course of insisting that human beings are 'part of nature', it is precisely this mereological issue that demands a clear distinction (though not, of course, a separation) between God and Nature. Substance is simple, indivisible; modes are not parts of substance (see E1p13). Spinoza never claims that a human being—or any other finite being or thing—is 'part of God', while he frequently asserts that we are 'part of Nature'.[37] He is unusually imprecise when he writes that 'the power of man ... is a part of the infinite power ... of God or Nature', precisely because within his philosophical system it does not make sense to treat God and Nature as the same thing. 'God' and 'Nature' refer to distinct (though not separate) realities: Nature has parts, while God is simple, neither composed of parts nor divisible into parts.[38] The point Spinoza really wants to emphasise in this passage is that our power is inseparable from the wider reality in which we participate. He is arguing that we are mistaken when we take ourselves to be autonomous beings, or—to put it in more technical and more obviously Cartesian terms—when we take ourselves to be substances.

Read in context, then, Spinoza does not appear to be making a decisive metaphysical declaration about the identity of 'God' and 'Nature' when he uses the phrase *Deus sive Natura* early in Part Four of the *Ethics*. In contrast to the shaky support for pantheism offered in these passing references to 'God or Nature', we find in Part One of the *Ethics* clear and prominent textual evidence for being-in-God (or, if you like, panentheism). The phrase *Deus sive Natura* is not even a straightforward metaphysical claim, let alone a load-bearing tenet of Spinoza's philosophical system, whereas the assertion of being-in-God at E1p15 is, as noted, one of the most significant propositions of the *Ethics*.

Spinoza's principle of being-in-God establishes an asymmetry between God and the universe, which is confirmed by his distinctive use of the concepts of substance and mode. Spinoza employs these concepts to assert the dependence of all things on God: to be a mode is to be constitutionally dependent, 'in another' and conceived through another, whereas substance is self-sufficient, 'in itself' and conceived through itself. This insistence on one-way ontological dependence distinguishes Spinoza's theology as sharply from pantheism as from the doctrine of a separate, anthropomorphic God which the *Ethics* explicitly refutes. We might call this latter doctrine the deist tendency, and Spinoza rejects it forcefully: 'God is not only the cause of things' beginning to exist, but also of their persevering in existing, *or* (to use a Scholastic term) God is the cause of the being of things [*causam essendi rerum*]' (E1p24c).

Although deism and pantheism appear to be theological opposites, they are alike in denying the asymmetry between God and the world, and in thus compromising our deep ontological dependence as beings-in-God. Pantheism privileges God's immanence at the cost of transcendence, while deism offers a false, hollow transcendence. Affirming the Spinozist alternative to these two positions is not a matter of finding a balance or a 'mean' between immanence and transcendence, as if we must avoid an excess of either quality. Rather, Spinoza recognises immanence and transcendence as inseparable features of one theological reality, securing true immanence *and* true transcendence.[39]

On Spinoza's own terms, the stakes of this issue are high. If we overemphasise immanence, then it makes little difference whether we think of ourselves as beings-in-God, or parts of *natura naturata*: either way, we come to know ourselves as constitutionally dependent beings. Yet there are different kinds of dependence. As parts of nature, we are dependent on a network of ever-shifting finite things, while as beings-in-God we are *also* grounded in eternal, indivisible, immutable, necessary being. Unlike pantheism, the principle of being-in-God affirms the ontological difference that offers us this grounding: God is not identical with nature, but the ground of nature. This grounding secures Spinoza's fundamental commitment to the intelligibility of being, which involves the claim that everything must have a reason or cause for its existence.[40] Without the concept of God (or *Natura naturans*) as ontological ground, finite things could be explained by other finite things, but nature as a whole would have no explanation. It would be radically contingent. Spinoza's metaphysics needs the concept of something that causes itself, and exists necessarily—that is, the concept of substance—to secure the intelligibility of nature as a whole. Part One of the *Ethics* proposes God as precisely this ground of being, and guarantor of intelligibility.

By means of his concept of substance, Spinoza accentuates the uniqueness of God, which is part of what divine transcendence signifies for modern theologians. Only God is substance, while everything else is a mode of substance, and God is thus ontologically different from all things, without being separate from anything. Furthermore, as we have seen, the causal relationship between God and finite things is qualitatively different from the causal relations among finite things: God as substance is the immanent cause of the modes, in contrast to the 'transitive causation' that operates between the modes. These are two kinds of causal relation, and also of dependence relation.

God's transcendence in a more relative and epistemic sense—our recognition that God's being exceeds and surpasses everything we can know, conceive or imagine—is secured by Spinoza's claim that God has an infinite number of attributes:

> E1d6: By God I understand a being absolutely infinite, i.e., a substance consisting of an infinity of attributes, of which each one expresses an eternal and infinite essence. [*Per Deum intelligo ens absolute infinitum, hoc est, substantiam constantem infinitis attributis, quorum unumquodque aeternam, et infinitam essentiam exprimit.*]
>
> Exp.: I say absolutely infinite, not infinite in its own kind; for if something is only infinite in its own kind, we can deny infinite attributes of it.[41]

Spinoza defines an attribute as 'what the intellect perceives of substance, as constituting the essence of substance' (E1D4). However, when he defines God as a substance with an infinity of attributes, he describes an attribute not just as that which *is perceived*, but also, more actively, as that which *expresses*. An attribute is a way of being, a way in which something expresses its essence. Each attribute is infinite in its own kind, but God is absolutely infinite, since God has an infinity of infinite attributes. This robust doctrine of divine infinity underscores the qualitative difference between God and finite beings. In 1674 Spinoza wrote to his friend Hugo Boxel, 'Truly, I confess I still don't know in what respect spirits are more like God than other creatures are. I know this: that there is no proportion [*nullam esse proportionem*] between the finite and the infinite; so the difference between the greatest, most excellent creature and God is the same as that between the least creature and God.'[42]

Spinoza's insistence on God's infinite attributes signals the epistemological as well as the ontological import of God's transcendence.[43] Human beings are constituted by their participation in two of God's attributes: thought and extension. Spinoza defines the human mind as the idea of the body, or, in other words, consciousness of the body.[44] A human mind perceives only two attributes: its own way of being, which is thought or consciousness; and extension, the way of being of the body which is its object. This means that the fullness of God's being eludes us. The metaphysical conjunction of immanence and transcendence running through Spinoza's philosophy thus finds an epistemological correlate in the conjunction of divine revelation and divine hiddenness. God's essence insofar as it is expressed through the attributes of thought and extension can be known by human beings, yet the infinity of attributes expressing God's being remain inaccessible to us.

Postscript: Knowing-in-God

Spinoza's affirmation that being-in-God is the fundamental principle of all existence has immediate consequences for the task of philosophy—for this task must itself be undertaken in God. Philosophy thus becomes theological through and through. And its labour of thinking is shaped, stretched and tested by the following question: how is it possible to thematise, comprehend and articulate a reality 'in which we live and move and have our being'?

Spinoza shares this question with all philosopher-theologians who are committed to the principle of being-in-God. Although panentheism is now often regarded as a distinct (and rather idiosyncratic) metaphysical position, it is more productively understood as a tendency within all the great theistic traditions: Hinduism, Judaism, Christianity and Islam.[45] Moreover, affirmations of being-in-God are not confined to the margins of these traditions. Saint Augustine, for example, the intellectual father of the western Christian churches, taught that 'all things are in God' (*omnia igitur in ipso sunt*), though in a special sense, since God is 'not a place'.[46] In the seventh century, John of Damascus wrote in his treatise *The Orthodox Faith* that 'toward God all things tend, and in God they have their existence'.[47]

As I explained in the Introduction to this book, situating Spinoza within any religious or theological tradition risks denying him the freethinking perspective which he maintained after he left his Jewish community in 1656, and which is fundamental to his thought. Yet I also suggested that situating Spinoza within modern secularism would likewise be a forced assimilation, carrying the different risk of suppressing the deeply theological orientation of the *Ethics*. In order to bring into view the distinctive philosophical task that follows from the principle of being-in-God, we may place Spinoza in dialogue with Christian theology, which constituted the immediate context for his philosophical work. This opens up a conceptual space that lets the theological issues at stake in the *Ethics* show themselves more clearly—provided we follow the example Spinoza set in his own life by situating his work within a theological discourse without seeking to convert that work to Christianity.

In the Latin Christian tradition, being-in-God gained a decisive philosophical expression in Anselm's *Proslogion*. This short work, composed in a monastery in the eleventh century, deserves to be regarded as the founding text of western philosophical theology (or theological philosophy), precisely because it opens a conceptual space configured by being-in-God. As a matter of fact—though not for this reason—Anselm's brief, accessible and enormously rich work is a core text of the undergraduate curriculum in a subject named, rather misleadingly, 'philosophy of religion'.[48] Today the *Proslogion* is most famous for setting out what Kant called the 'ontological argument' for the existence of God, and for Anselm's description of his own philosophical endeavour as 'faith seeking understanding'.[49]

Though it remains a reference-point for scholarly debates about God's existence, the *Proslogion* is quite different from the kinds of text written by contemporary philosophers. It abounds with biblical references, and its arguments are embedded in a prayer—of praise, petition and confession—that is addressed directly to God. It is also an account of philosophical labour. When we attend to its dramatic form, we discern contemplative and devotional features of Anselm's project which resonate with the early biographical descriptions of Spinoza by Colerus and Bayle discussed in my first chapter. Anselm was actually a monk when he composed his works, while Spinoza in his later years created the quasi-monastic conditions of reclusive quietude demanded by his 'great desire of inquiring into truth without any interruption', as Bayle put it. Monasteries could be busy places, so even within the cloister there were varying degrees of retreat from the world. In the opening chapter of the *Proslogion*, entitled 'A rousing of the mind to the contemplation of God', Anselm gathers his dispersed attention in order to seek God with his 'whole heart':

> Come now, insignificant man, fly for a moment from your affairs, escape for a little while from the tumult of your thoughts. Put aside now your weighty cares and leave your wearisome toils. Abandon yourself for a little to God and rest for a little while in Him. Enter into the inner chamber of your soul, shut out everything else save God and what can be of help in your quest for Him and having locked the door seek Him out.[50]

Here Anselm is undertaking an exercise in being-in-God: 'rest for a little while in Him' (*requiesce aliquantulum in eo*). This expresses an aspiration rather than an accomplished state. Though being-in-God is, as he will assert in Chapter 19 of the *Proslogion*, an ontological fact, Anselm does not *feel* that he is resting in God. On the contrary, he finds himself 'separated from God', desperately seeking God, and he implores God to 'teach my heart where and how to seek You'. Language of unfulfilled desire, often echoing the Psalms, abounds in this opening chapter:

> What shall Your servant do, tormented by love of You [*anxius amore tui*] yet 'cast off far from Your face' (Ps. 31:22)? He yearns to see You [*Anhelat videre te*] and Your countenance is too far away from him. He desires to come close to You [*Accedere ad te desiderat*] and Your dwelling place is inaccessible; he longs to find you [*Invenire te cupit*] and does not know where You are; he is eager to seek you out [*Quaerere te affectat*] and does not know your face.... How wretched man's lot is when he has lost that for which he was made![51]

The *Proslogion* thus characterises being-in-God as both an ontological truth and a spiritual task. Anselm situates his philosophical labour in the mysterious gap between the source of his being and a longed-for encounter with this source; between his desire for God and the knowledge, love and joy 'in God' for which he hopes.

Indeed, Anselm finds that being-in-God makes it peculiarly difficult to know God. Because God encompasses him, surrounds him, he can never step back and *see* God. He cannot grasp God as a concept, imagine God as a figurative form, or posit God as an object. God is too close, too ubiquitous, as well as too immense, for him to gain any purchase. Anselm tells God that his soul is 'overwhelmed by Your immensity'.[52] When he finally arrives at a definition of God, this very definition asserts the impossibility of defining God: 'Not only are you that than which a greater cannot be thought, but You are also something greater than can be thought.'[53] Anselm confesses that God's 'inaccessible light' is 'too much' for him:

> It shines too much and [my understanding] does not grasp it nor does the eye of my soul allow itself to be turned towards it for too long. It is dazzled by its splendour, overcome by its fullness, overwhelmed by its immensity, confused by its extent. O supreme and inaccessible light; O whole and blessed truth, how far You are from me who am so close to You! How distant You are from myself while I am so present to Your sight! You are wholly present everywhere and I do not see You. In You I move and in You I have my being and I cannot come near to You.[54]

At apophatic moments like these, Anselm seems to be lost in God—and his bewilderment is an epistemic consequence of being-in-God. He goes on to suggest that the difficulty of encountering God is compounded by his own human limitations. Though his soul participates in God, 'the senses of my soul, because of the ancient weakness of sin, have become hardened and dulled and obstructed'.[55]

In the course of his philosophical prayer Anselm makes several claims that will be familiar to readers of Spinoza's *Ethics*: God's existence is necessary; God's existence is entirely self-sufficient; God is 'unlimited and eternal ... in a unique way'; God is simple, being neither composed of parts nor divisible into parts.[56] And throughout the text Anselm returns repeatedly to his contemplative affirmation of being-in-God. 'In You I move and in You I have my being,' he writes in Chapter 16 of the *Proslogion*, transposing Acts 17:28 into the second person. In Chapter 19 he explains that '[God] is not in place or time but all things are in Him', and confesses to God that 'You, though nothing can be without You, are nevertheless not in place or time but all things are in You. For nothing contains You, but You contain all things.' Anselm concludes in Chapter 20 that 'You therefore permeate and embrace all things' (*Tu ergo imples et complecteris omnia*), gesturing to God's simultaneously immanent and transcendent activity: the verb *implere* means 'fill up', 'infuse', while *complecti* means 'encircle', 'include'.

Chapter 19 of the *Proslogion* indicates that Anselm's principle of being-in-God ('all things are in You') is closely connected to his affirmation that all things depend on God ('nothing can be without You'). As we have seen, whereas pantheism equates God with everything that exists, so that God might be identified with Nature, panentheism entails the absolute asymmetry between God and 'all things'. Anselm emphasises that while all things depend on God, God does not depend on anything: 'You ... are completely sufficient unto Yourself, needing nothing, but rather He whom all things need in order that they may have being and well-being.'[57] This ontological asymmetry is, in turn, closely connected to God's transcendence. Anselm explains that God is not only 'before' all things, but also 'beyond' all things. An eternal God is 'before' all things which come into existence, *and* 'beyond' even eternal things, 'because these things can in no way exist without You, though You do not exist any the less even if they return to nothingness'.[58]

Like the *Ethics*, the *Proslogion* folds human experience—most immediately, that of author and reader—into its panentheist metaphysics. Anselm's reflections on joy suggest that his ontological principle of being-in-God has powerful affective and ethical consequences. Citing Matthew 25:21, Anselm conceives human beatitude as 'enter[ing] into the joy of the

Lord'.[59] God is 'the good', 'which contains [*continet*] the joyfulness of all [particular] goods'—just as God himself 'contains all things'.[60] In the final chapter of the *Proslogion*, Anselm quotes John 16:24: 'Ask and you will receive, that your joy may be complete.' He suggests that the 'complete' joy given to a human being is exceeded by an 'infinite' joy, so that 'those who rejoice will enter into that [infinite joy]'. Anselm confesses that in God he has discovered

> a joy that is complete and more than complete. Indeed, when the heart is filled with that joy, the mind is filled with it, the soul is filled with it, the whole person is filled with it, yet joy beyond measure will remain. The whole of that joy, then, will not enter into those who rejoice, but those who rejoice will enter wholly into that joy.[61]

This is a description of the affective, experiential manifestations of being-in-God. All things are in God, while God pervades all things; when people are truly joyful, they are in a joy that exceeds yet pervades their being. Although Anselm says he has 'discovered' this joy, by the end of the *Proslogion* he is still hoping and searching for beatitude: 'I pray, O God, that I may know You and love You, so that I may rejoice in You.'[62]

The *Proslogion* articulates the philosopher's task as knowing a God in whom we live, move and have our being. Anselm finds that this involves thinking God's transcendence and immanence together, as one and the same thing. The effort to know God will be frustrated by any attempt to determine God by a concept, to posit God as an object or to represent God in an image. Anselm's own approach to this philosophical project is aporetic and open-ended. The *Proslogion* concludes with its author's hope, desire and resolution to continue pursuing his 'God of truth'.[63] Later philosophers who were faithful to this task—Thomas Aquinas being pre-eminent among them—retained Anselm's apophatic appeal to faith while thinking (in) God more systematically. Others deviated from Anselm's path by inclining either towards pantheism, thereby privileging immanence over transcendence, or towards deism, thereby privileging transcendence over immanence.

We can read Spinoza's *Ethics* as accomplishing, in a purely philosophical medium, the task set out in Anselm's *Proslogion*. Spinoza remains committed to the principle of being-in-God throughout the *Ethics*, compromising neither immanence nor transcendence. While Anselm's biblical and poetic language articulates an experience of being lost in God, crying out to God for rescue within a boundless sea of divine magnitude, Spinoza achieves a rigorous philosophical knowing *in* God. This can equally be described as a theological knowing, a knowing of the order of God—though since it makes no appeal to faith, it is not theological in the sense in which Spinoza himself uses this term.

The character of this theological knowing is illuminated by the distinction drawn, in *Ethics* II, between three kinds of cognition: imagination, reason and intuitive knowledge. Reason and intuition both yield 'adequate' or true knowledge. Yet while reason cannot avoid conceptualising God—positing God as an object, albeit in panentheist terms—intuition is inseparably a knowing-of-God and a knowing-in-God. Even this knowledge cannot, however, deliver the fullness of God's being. It apprehends God through, and indeed within, just two of God's infinite attributes. Unlike apophatic theologians such as Anselm or Aquinas, Spinoza does not refer transcendent truths about God's inaccessible nature to eschatological hope or to the mystery of faith. The *Ethics* is simply silent on whatever lies beyond the attributes of thought and extension.[64]

Spinoza, like Anselm, acknowledged how difficult it is for a human mind to become fully conscious of the fact that it 'participates in God'. He distrusted the language of sin that is so fundamental to Christian discourse, believing that his culture's collective self-image of sinfulness, with its emphasis on weakness and deviance, fostered a punitive moralism which inhibited the truly ethical task of human enlightenment and empowerment. Nevertheless, Spinoza's metaphysics and epistemology, grounded on the principle of being-in-God, frame his diagnosis of a natural propensity to error. The *Ethics* characterises error as a 'privation of knowledge', often involving a tendency to mistake a part for the whole, to form confused ideas, and to attribute free will and autonomy to conditioned, dependent beings (see E2p35).

In a 1665 letter to Henry Oldenburg, Spinoza resorted, uncharacteristically, to a metaphor in order to convey human ignorance. 'Let us imagine', he wrote, 'that there is a little worm living in the blood ... as we do in this part of the universe.' This worm can distinguish 'the particles of blood, lymph, etc.' and it will naturally, though mistakenly, 'consider each particle of blood as a whole, not as a part'.[65] It is no coincidence that this is an image of a creature's immersion in its native element. We are beings-in-God who cannot see the whole of God, and our perspective is limited to the elements (or the attributes) in which we live and move and have our being.

When we reflect on Spinoza's metaphor of the worm in the blood, and its analogical structure, some interesting epistemological questions emerge. The worm is, Spinoza suggests, analogous to a human being, and the blood in which it lives is analogous to 'this part of the universe'. Not only is each distinct particle of blood 'a part' (mistaken for the whole) of the blood, but blood itself is a part of an organism's body—just as the 'part of the universe' in which we dwell is a part (mistaken for the whole) of the entire universe. We can discern here a twofold relation of being-in: the worm is in the blood, and the blood is in the body. Analogously, we are in 'this part of the universe', which in turn is in the entire universe. Perhaps this is what Spinoza would call the whole of nature, that is, *natura naturata*. At every level of complexity 'whatever is, is in God':

(a) worm	human being	→	is in God
(b) blood	this part of the universe	→	is in God
(c) body	the entire universe	→	is in God

On this model, our epistemic range is limited to (a) and (b). Of course, when we look back to Spinoza's century we see that there was much that remained to be discovered about 'this part of the universe'—and while modern science has made great leaps, we still have an incomplete grasp of 'this part of the universe', the object of our scientific enquiries, knowable in principle though by no means thoroughly known in practice. We can only suppose that the relation between our part of the universe and the whole of nature is analogous to the relation between the blood and the body. This analogy accentuates the dazzling complexity of the unseen whole, and suggests that *natura naturata* is as elusive as *natura naturans*.[66]

Spinoza's letter to Oldenburg does not venture into these speculations. Indeed, the analogical force of his metaphor of the worm in the blood breaks down towards the end of his letter, where he suggests that the blood stands for 'natural bodies' rather than for 'this part of the universe'. Spinoza emphasises that he is 'in ignorance' as to how 'each part of nature agrees with its whole'. To answer such a question, he explains, 'we should have to know the whole of nature and its several parts'—and he says that he does not have this knowledge.

What Spinoza does claim to know in the *Ethics*, however, is that everything is in God, regardless of the enormously complex interconnections of wholes and parts throughout *natura naturata*. There is a striking contrast between the complex knowledge of the networks and sequences of finite causes that shape each thing, and the simple, singular knowledge of each thing's being-in-God. This is illustrated by the mathematical example Spinoza provides to explain his three kinds of cognition:

> Suppose there are three numbers, and the problem is to find a fourth which is to the third as the second is the first. Merchants do not hesitate

to multiply the second by the third, and divide the product by the first, because they have not yet forgotten what they heard from their teacher without any demonstration, or because they have often found this in the simplest numbers, or from the force of the Demonstration of P7 in Book VII of Euclid, viz. from the common property of proportional. But in the simplest numbers none of this is necessary. Given the numbers 1, 2 and 3, no one fails to see that the fourth proportional number is 6—and we see this much more clearly because we infer the fourth number from the ratio which, in one glance, we see the first number to have to the second. (E2p40s2)

Although the second and third kinds of cognition—*ratio* and *scientia intuitiva*—both yield adequate knowledge, they are very different in character. People who possess *ratio*, a certain form of cultivated reason, can find the fourth proportional number on the basis of Euclid's demonstration. By contrast—and this case illustrates the simplicity, immediacy and clarity of *scientia intuitiva*—'in the simplest numbers there is no need of this demonstration'. We can simply see that one is to two as three is to six.

Analogously, perceiving that God's essence—which is simply existence itself—is expressed in any existing thing, we may see in one glance that the thing is in God. 'What do we understand more clearly than . . . what existence is?' wrote Spinoza in 1663.[67] The givenness of things, their bare being, discloses to us 'the very nature of existence', that is to say, 'God's eternal and infinite essence' (E2p45s, E2p47). This means that 'God's infinite essence and eternity are known to all' (E2p47s), given immediately to our minds in our awareness of any existing thing, and perhaps most obviously in our self-awareness. 'And since all things are in God and are conceived through God, it follows that we can deduce from this knowledge [of God's essence-and-existence] a great many things which we know adequately, and so can form that third kind of knowledge of which we spoke in E2p40s2'—that is, *scientia intuitiva* (E2p47s).

However, our intuitive knowledge of God's essence-and-existence often gets covered over or drowned out by the clamour of imaginative thinking. People tend to 'join the name *God* to the images of things they are used to seeing' (E2p47s). Equally, our knowledge of singular things' being-in-God, which is given in every simple intuition of their existence, usually eludes us, because our ideas of other things are confused with our own reactions to them: 'the ideas we have of external bodies indicate the condition of our own body more than the nature of the external body' (E2p16c2). This is the predicament of imaginative thinking, and although rational thinking overcomes its confusions, it knows things by their common properties rather than in their singularity. Only in *scientia intuitiva* do we receive things in their singularity, their givenness, their simple presence. Intuition does not add anything new; it is always already there, like the sun behind clouds, and it shines forth, becomes knowledge, whenever the busy clamour of imaginative thinking settles down.

When our minds and bodies become quieter, less agitated and crowded by images conjured by 'memory or imagination', we naturally become open to the simple truth of things: 'very much conscious of ourselves, and of God, and of things' (E5p39s), as Spinoza puts it in Part Five the *Ethics*. Anyone can see in one glance how an extended being—a tree, for example—is in God. I cannot perceive the tree without perceiving that it participates in extension, one of the attributes that expresses God's nature, and thus perceiving its relation to God as clearly as I perceive the relations between the numbers one and two, and three and six. Likewise, simply through my awareness of my own embodied, conscious being, I perceive myself through the attributes of extension and thought—and thus I feel myself to be in God. Our thinking is not set apart from nature; it participates in the natural-divine activity of consciousness—and things are intelligible, and real, only insofar as they are in God. For Spinoza, as for Anselm and other apophatic theologians, we cannot know God as an object. What can be known, however, is our own being-in-God, and the being-in-God of other bodies and minds.

In the thought of the deepest medieval theologians, such as Anselm and Aquinas, it makes little sense to distinguish ontology from theology. I think this is also true of the *Ethics*—as long as we understand theology simply as a thinking of God, which is not the way Spinoza himself used the term when he criticised theology and theologians in his *Theologico-Political Treatise* and his letters. We separate theology and ontology only by regarding theology as what Heidegger called an 'ontic science': an enquiry into a determinate entity, conceived as a subject or an object, about which the question of whether it exists can meaningfully be asked.[68] In contrast, those who argue that God exists necessarily, that God cannot be conceived not to exist—as Saint Anselm argues in his *Proslogion*, and as Spinoza argues in the *Ethics*—do not simply give an emphatically affirmative answer to the question of whether God exists.[69] Rather, elucidating God's necessary existence shows why, properly understood, the existence of God is not a question at all.[70]

CHAPTER FOUR

Whatever We Desire and Do

'OUR HEART IS RESTLESS [*inquietum*] until it rests in you [*requiescat in te*],' Augustine wrote—addressing God—at the beginning of his *Confessions*. This eloquent suggestion that our inner life is marked by an experience of unrest or anxiety, revealing a deep desire for being-in-God, is not in itself distinctively Christian. It captures rather well Spinoza's view of the human condition, which likewise involves a diagnosis of the soul's unrest (*animi commotiones* and *animi fluctuationes*) and proposes a resting-place (*animi acquiescentia*) constituted by being-in-God.[1]

In the Appendix to Part Four of the *Ethics*, Spinoza offers one of his clearest summaries of the ethical task he sets before his readers:

> It is therefore of the first importance in life to perfect our intellect, *or* reason, as far as possible. In this one thing consists man's highest happiness, *or* blessedness [*felicitas seu beatitudo*]. For blessedness is nothing else than the peace of mind [*animi acquiescentia*] which springs from the intuitive knowledge of God; and to perfect the intellect is nothing else than to understand God and the attributes and actions of God which follow from the necessity of God's nature. So the ultimate aim [*finis ultimus*] of the man who is led by reason, *i.e.*, his highest desire [*summa cupiditas*], by which he endeavours [*studet*] to govern all other desires, is that which leads to the adequate knowledge of himself and of all objects which can be embraced by his understanding [*intelligentiam*]. (E4App4)[2]

Readers may be surprised to find Spinoza writing in this way of our 'aims', 'desires' and 'endeavours'. By this point in the text, he has criticised teleological thinking and denied human beings any free will. Don't we need some conception of freedom, and of teleology, in order to believe that there is a good way to live, and that human beings desire and strive for this good?

Human desire is both ontologically and ethically crucial for Spinoza. In this chapter we shall see that our desires are, so to speak, the feeling of being: the feeling of being human, the feeling of being alive, the feeling of being-in-God. Desire is also a motor for action or agency, and the foundation of our emotional life. It is not surprising, then, that desire forms the basis of Spinoza's religion. The final super-proposition in the *Ethics* affirms that 'the good which everyone who seeks virtue wants for himself, he also desires for other people; and this desire is greater as his knowledge of God is greater' (E4p37). In the scholium to this proposition, 'religion' is defined as 'whatever we desire and do [*quicquid cupimus, et agimus*], insofar as we have the idea of God as cause, or insofar as we know God' (E4p37s). And when, in Part Five, Spinoza asserts that 'the mind's highest striving [*summus mentis conatus*], and its highest virtue' (E5p25) is to know intuitively both God and singular things, he follows this with two propositions which associate this knowledge first with desire, and then with rest:

> The more capable the mind is of knowing things by the third kind of cognition, the more it desires [*cupit*] thus to know things. (E5p26)

> From this kind of cognition there arises the highest possible repose of mind [*mentis acquiescentia oritur*]. (E5p27)

So, if we want to understand Spinoza's account of our highest good—and thus of our ethical or religious task—we must attend to the way he understands desire and action.

In the background to Spinoza's distinctive conception of human striving is the formalised teleological thinking of medieval and early modern theology. This was shaped by Jewish, Christian and Islamic scholars' appropriations of Aristotle's fourfold analysis of causation, which distinguished between efficient, material, formal and final causes.[3] While Aristotle developed this account to explain how things come to be by natural processes and by human craft, theologians such as Moses Maimonides and Thomas Aquinas adapted his concepts to divine agency. God was said to be the efficient, formal and final cause of creation—but emphatically not the material cause, since God was not a material being who created the universe out of himself. (Against the opposite heresy, that God created out of pre-existing matter—as dualists like the Manicheans had argued—arose the doctrine that God made matter *ex nihilo*, 'out of nothing'.[4])

Within the Christian tradition which directly shaped Spinoza's philosophical milieu, Aquinas emphasised a desire for God animating creation as a whole, and human lives in particular. Giving a cognitive gloss to Augustine's insight that human hearts are restless until they find rest in God, Aquinas wrote, 'Our natural desire to know cannot be at rest in us until we know the first cause by its essence.... But the first cause is God, therefore the final end of an intellectual creature is to see God essentially.'[5] Denying that God has extrinsic purposes, Aquinas ascribed to God what we might call an intrinsic or immanent teleology: 'nothing apart from God is the end of God [*finis Dei*], yet God himself is the end with respect to all things made by him ... the object of the divine will is its own goodness, which is its essence'.[6]

By the early seventeenth century, the medieval habitus of teleological thinking was being called into question, notably by the Jesuit philosopher Francisco Suárez, who influenced Descartes.[7] Both thinkers prioritised efficient causation, which became the core explanatory category of the new natural philosophy, the basis of modern science; in 1620, Francis Bacon argued that 'the final cause rather corrupts than advances the sciences'.[8] Hobbes extended the denial of final causation to the moral realm, declaring that 'there is no such *finis ultimus* (utmost end) nor *summum bonum* (greatest good), as is spoken of in the books of the old moral philosophers'.[9]

Most seventeenth-century thinkers did not go so far as Hobbes, however, and this distinctively modern shift away from teleological explanation was usually restrained by the demands of Christian orthodoxy. Descartes emphasised efficient causation while equivocating on the question of God's teleological agency; he certainly did not deny outright that God has purposes. In the *Meditations* he writes, rather craftily, that God 'is capable of countless things whose causes are beyond my knowledge. And for this reason alone I consider the customary search for final causes to be totally useless in physics; there is considerable rashness in thinking myself capable of investigating the purposes of God.'[10]

In the domain of ethics, meanwhile, Descartes was happy to attribute teleological agency to human beings. Writing to Princess Elisabeth of Bohemia in 1645, he explained that 'virtue' and 'happiness' (*la béatitude*) are our 'supreme good' and 'final end'.[11] And in a 1647 letter to Queen Christina of Sweden, he declared that the will's 'firm and constant resolution to carry out to the letter all the things one judges to be best ... by itself constitutes all the virtues; this alone produces the greatest and most solid contentment in life'. Here Descartes describes free will as 'the noblest thing we can have, since it makes us in a way equal to God and seems to exempt us from being [God's] subjects'. He insists that the right exercise of our free will is 'the greatest of all the goods we can possess ... nothing but free will can produce our greatest happiness'. There is a slight hint here of the intrinsic or immanent teleology that Aquinas attributed to God: Descartes is suggesting that our highest good lies within ourselves, in the quality of our own willing, rather than in anything external to us. 'The peace of mind and inner satisfaction felt by those who know they always do their best to discover what is good and to acquire it is, we see, a pleasure incomparably sweeter, more lasting and more solid than all those which come from elsewhere,' he advised Queen Christina.[12]

The question of God's purposes is a different issue, of course, from our own teleological orientation—whether towards God, or towards our own happiness. Nevertheless, these issues easily become confused when God is conceived anthropomorphically, so that human purposes are ascribed to divine activity. In the Appendix to Part One of the *Ethics*, Spinoza continues the early modern critique of teleological thinking about natural processes, stating—more decisively than Descartes—that 'Nature has no pre-established end, and all final causes are nothing more than human fictions'. Like Descartes, though, he seems to allow for teleological human action, and warns his readers against projecting their own motivations onto the natural world:

> all the prejudices which I here undertake to show, depend on this, namely, that people commonly suppose all natural things to act, as they themselves do, for the sake of an end, and even regard it as certain that God himself directs everything to a particular end, for they may say that God made everything for the sake of man, and man that he might worship God. (E1App)

Attributing final causes to both God and nature gives rise, Spinoza argues, to prejudices 'concerning *good* and *evil*, *merit* and *sin*, *praise* and *blame*, *order* and *confusion*, *beauty* and *deformity*'—in other words, to the whole assemblage of concepts that governed conventional moral thinking in the seventeenth century, and still shape moral life today.[13]

Perhaps surprisingly, Spinoza's attitude towards divine purposes seems closer to Aquinas than to Descartes. Instead of espousing Descartes's sceptical claim that we cannot know the purposes of God, he echoes Aquinas in asserting that God simply cannot have extrinsic purposes—as Aquinas put it, 'nothing apart from God is the end of God [*finis Dei*]'. In Part One of the *Ethics*, Spinoza criticises the opinion that 'God produces all things according to the rule of the Good', on the grounds that this 'seems to posit something outside God, which does not depend on God, to which God attends as a model in what he does, and at which he aims, as at a certain goal. This is simply to subject God to fate' (E1p33s2). In the Preface to Part Four, he seems to go further, suggesting that the very notion of divine purpose is incoherent: 'As God exists for the sake of no end, he acts for the sake of no end: his action, as well as his existence, has no ground of commencement and no end which is related to it as a motive' (E4 Preface).

Spinoza departs more conspicuously from Descartes in denying that we possess a faculty of will—which was, so to speak, the organ of human teleology for Christian thinkers, both medieval and modern.[14] In rejecting free will, Spinoza clarifies that he is referring to 'the power of affirming and denying [what is true and what is false], and not *desire* [*cupiditatem*]', and argues that 'these faculties are universal notions, with no existence distinct from the particulars whence we derive them' (E2p48s). Enquiring 'whether volitions are anything else than the ideas of things', he offers the following conclusion:

> In the mind (by E2p48) there is no absolute faculty of willing and not willing, but single volitions only, namely, this or that affirmation, this or that negation. Let us therefore conceive any single volition, for example, the mode of thought by which the mind affirms that the three angles of a triangle are equal to two right angles. This affirmation ... can neither be nor be conceived without the idea of a triangle. Further, the idea of a triangle must involve this same affirmation, namely, that three of its angles are equal to two right angles. Hence *vice versa* also, the idea of a triangle can neither be nor be conceived without this affirmation; and thus this affirmation belongs to the essence of the idea of a triangle, and can be nothing else than that essence. But what we have said of this volition (since we have taken it indifferently) is also to be said of any volition whatever, namely, that it is nothing else than the idea itself; q.e.d. (E2p49d)

> Will and intellect are one and the same. (E2p49c)

Part Two of the *Ethics* concludes with this proposition's lengthy scholium, which refers not only to the denial of human free will in E2p49, but also to 'preceding propositions' concerning the nature of will and intellect, and our knowledge of God. Here Spinoza looks ahead to lessons to be learned through the remainder of the *Ethics*:

> It remains to indicate how much the knowledge of this doctrine is to our advantage in life, which we may easily gather from the following considerations. First, it teaches us that we act solely from God's command, that we share in the divine nature [*divinaeque naturae esse participes*], and that we do this the more, the more perfect our actions are, and the more we understand God. So this doctrine, as well as rendering the mind thoroughly calm [*animum omnimode quietum reddit*], also teaches us wherein consists our greatest happiness, *or* blessedness: namely, in the knowledge of God alone, by which we are led to do only those things which are in harmony with piety and love. From this we clearly understand how far they stray from the true valuation of virtue, who expect to be honoured by God with the highest rewards for their virtue and best actions, as for the greatest service, as if virtue itself, and the service of God, were not happiness itself, and the greatest freedom. (E2p49s)[15]

This is a pivotal passage in the text, marking the transition from Part Two to Part Three, and also anticipating key points of Parts Four and Five. The passage sketches an ethical-religious telos, giving the reader plenty to strive for: a mind at rest in knowledge of God; participation in divine nature; blessedness, happiness and the greatest freedom. These are, in fact, alternative descriptions of one and the same ideal.

Though Spinoza denies that we possess any distinct faculty of will, he certainly incorporates what we might call the *energy* of willing in his account of human nature. This is present in his conception of 'ideas' as acts of thinking which involve affirmation; in his claim that the mind 'strives [*conatur*] to persevere in its existence for an indefinite period, and is conscious of this effort [*conatus*]' (E3p9); and in his closely related view that desire is not only one of the fundamental human affects (E3p9s), but the very essence of each human being. The significance of these concepts of striving and desire is attested by the fact that the key passages asserting them, E3p7 and E3p9s, are among the nine 'super-propositions' found in Part Three of the *Ethics* (see the Appendix to Chapter 2).

Many philosophers, from Stoics to medievals to early moderns, have argued that organic beings have an appetite for self-preservation. Drawing on these sources—in particular, the fourteenth-century Talmud scholar and rationalist Gersonides, as well as Descartes—Spinoza extends this insight beyond the organic realm and makes it universal, claiming that 'each thing [*unaquaeque res*], insofar as it is in itself [*quantum in se est*], strives [*conatur*] to persevere in its being [*in suo esse*]' (E3p6).[16] Spinoza's concept of *conatus*, or striving, is ontological in a double sense: it is a striving to persevere *in being*; and this striving is 'the actual essence of the thing' (E3p7). When this striving 'is related to the Mind and Body together, it is called Appetite. This Appetite, therefore, is nothing but the very essence of man [*hominis essentia*]' (E3p9s).

On the basis of this concept of appetite, Spinoza defines desire (*cupiditas*) as 'appetite together with consciousness [*conscientia*] of the appetite'. He explains that 'between appetite and desire there is no difference, except that desire is generally related to men insofar as they are conscious of their appetite' (E3p9s).[17] Towards the end of Part Three he claims that desire, like appetite, is the essence of the human being, clarifying the relation between appetite and desire as follows:

> Desire is the very essence, *or* nature, of each [man] insofar as it is conceived to be determined, by whatever constitution he has, to do something. (E3p56s)

> Desire is the very nature, *or* essence, of each [individual] (see the definition of Desire in E3p9s). . . . Joy and Sadness are passions by which each one's power, *or* striving to persevere in his being, is increased or diminished, aided or restrained. But by the striving to persevere in one's being, insofar as it is related to the Mind and Body together, we understand Appetite and Desire (see E3p9s). So Joy and Sadness are the Desire, *or* Appetite, itself insofar as it is increased or diminished, aided or restrained, by external causes. (E3p57d)

> Desire is man's very essence, insofar as it is conceived to be determined, from any given affection of it, to do something [*ad aliquid agendum*].
>
> Exp.: We said above, in E3p9s, that Desire is appetite together with the consciousness of it. And appetite is the very essence of man, insofar as it is determined to do [*determinata est ad ea agendum*] what promotes his preservation. But in the same scholium I also warned that I really recognise no difference between human appetite and Desire. For whether a man is conscious of his appetite or not, the appetite still remains one and the same. And so—not to seem to commit a tautology—I did not wish to explain Desire by appetite, but was anxious so to define it that I would comprehend together all the strivings of human nature that we signify by the name of appetite, will, desire, or impulse. (E3Def.Aff.1)

From this rather complex sequence of passages, we can draw two slightly contrary insights. On the one hand, Spinoza recognises that there is a difference between an appetite of which we are conscious, and an appetite of which we are not conscious—and of course, modern psychology and psychoanalysis have taught us that this difference may be very significant with respect to our experience and our actions. On the other hand, Spinoza also wants to claim that ontologically this difference is not so significant: both appetite and desire can properly be regarded as the essence of the human being—an essence which, regardless of the extent to which we are conscious of it, determines us to activity, to a 'doing' (*agendum*) that promotes our preservation. Furthermore, as he argues in his demonstration of E3p57, 'Appetite and Desire' is the medium, the base element, the very stuff of our emotional life: *Joy and Sadness are the Desire, or Appetite, itself insofar as it is increased or diminished*. Desire is the conscious feeling of our *conatus*. It is the experiential meeting-point of activity and consciousness, the sensation of being-in-God.

In concluding Part Two of the *Ethics* with a critique of those people 'who expect to be honoured by God with the greatest rewards for their virtue and best actions', Spinoza challenges the distinction between means and ends that tends to structure our thinking about human action. Here he identifies 'happiness itself, and the greatest freedom', which might naturally be identified as the goal of ethical life, with what readers are accustomed to regard as the means to this goal: 'virtue and the service of God' (E2p49s). Spinoza returns to this criticism of instrumental moral thinking in Part Four, where he writes—echoing the argument of Plato's *Republic*— that 'virtue is to be desired for its own sake, and not for the sake of something else, there being nothing better, or more useful to us, on account of which virtue should be sought' (E4p18s). And the very last proposition of the *Ethics* repeats that 'blessedness is not the reward of virtue, but is virtue itself' (E5p42). This is a more robust statement of the intrinsic relation of virtue and happiness which Descartes invoked in his correspondence with Princess Elisabeth and Queen Christina; in this respect, at least, Spinoza agreed with the Cartesian position, though he developed it more philosophically and asserted it more rigorously. This presented a direct challenge to the psychological basis of superstitious Christianity: while Catholic ideas of spiritual merit were one of the main targets of Protestant theology, Calvin's teaching continued to separate earthly virtue and piety from its heavenly reward.[18]

Spinoza's conflation of means and ends in his remarks on virtue suggests a more immanent, more intrinsic teleology than we usually find in accounts of volition and practical reason, whether theological or secular. Virtue as conceived in the *Ethics* has no extrinsic goal, no reward beyond itself. Spinoza asserts that 'no one strives to preserve his being for the sake of any end outside himself' (E4p52s). Here he seems to transfer to human beings the Thomist argument that God cannot have extrinsic purposes. This accomplishes a kind of inversion of anthropomorphic thinking: Spinoza is suggesting that instead of projecting an extrinsic notion of human teleology onto God, we should model our own activity and desire on a traditional conception of God's intrinsic, immanent teleology.

Indeed, Spinoza inverts ordinary teleological reasoning as soon as he defines 'appetite' and 'desire' in Part Three of the *Ethics*. As we have seen, 'appetite' is the effort of both mind and body to persevere in existence, while 'desire' is what we feel when we are conscious of this appetite. 'It results from all this', Spinoza continues, 'that a thing is not the object of our effort, will, appetite and desire because we have judged it to be good; but that, on the contrary, we judge a thing to be good because it is the object of our effort, volition, appetite and desire' (E3p9s). Again, the good is here drawn into our activity as striving, desiring beings, rather than posited outside the will as an extrinsic final cause of its preferences and inclinations.

One way of describing Spinoza's position regarding teleology within human life—including, of course, our ethical and religious life—is to say that he replaces final causation with efficient causation in the domain of human activity, just as for natural processes. This certainly makes sense of his remarks about final causes in his Preface to Part Four:

> What is called a final cause is nothing else than a human desire considered as the originating principle or primary cause of anything. For example, when we say that habitation was the final cause of this or that house, we mean nothing else than that a man, because he imagined to himself the conveniences of domestic life, had a desire to build a house. Hence habitation, considered as a final cause, is nothing more than this particular appetite or desire, which in fact is the efficient cause; and this men consider as the primary cause, being commonly in ignorance of the causes of their appetites. (E4 Preface)

At the same time, we can see Spinoza's way of thinking about human desire and action as reshaping teleology, rather than simply abandoning it. One consequence of this reshaping is a softening of the distinction between efficient and final causes. For desire's momentum is shaped by our grasp of the highest good, just as the very notion of goodness is constituted by our desire. Spinoza explicitly insists on the 'immanence' of God's efficient causal agency in his metaphysics (see E1p18), and he implicitly endorses a kind of immanent final causation in his ethical philosophy. This allows him to use teleological language—to write enticingly of our 'highest good' and 'ultimate end', thereby forming or re-forming the reader's desire in a certain direction—while criticising conventional means–end teleological thinking in theology, natural philosophy and ethics.

For Spinoza, then, our telos does not lie outside our activity, our life, our being, but within it. While Suárez categorised both efficient and final causes as 'extrinsic causes'—in contrast to formal and material causes, which inhere in their effects—Spinoza reconfigures both efficient and final causation as immanent, though in different ways.[19] If being-in-God is at once our source and our telos, then our ethical task is, in some sense, to become what we are. We find a strong hint about this immanent teleology in Spinoza's claim in the scholium to E2p49 that his account of freedom, volition and our knowledge of God teaches us that we 'share in the divine nature'. This remark has a clear affinity with Spinoza's core ontological principle that 'whatever is, is in God' (E1p15). Here, however, it has an ethical as well as an ontological resonance, being closely connected with his claim that 'the more perfect our actions are, the more we understand God'. Human actions, he is suggesting, can be more or less perfect, and although 'perfection' is not to be understood moralistically—for Spinoza, it means both 'reality' and activity—this 'more or less' takes us onto ethical territory.[20] This becomes more explicit in Part Four of the *Ethics*, where he argues that the more we progress towards perfection, the more joyful we become, and 'the more we necessarily participate in the divine nature' (E4p45c2s).

Just as Anselm's *Proslogion* characterises being-in-God as both an ontological truth and a spiritual task, and suggests that accomplishing this task necessarily involves an experience of joy, so in Spinoza's *Ethics* being-in-God has this twofold significance. Having been proposed in Part One as an unconditional ontological principle, it is then, in Part Four, considered in a specifically human context as an ethical task that admits variable degrees. This means that Spinoza's theology is both radically inclusive and unequivocally hierarchical. On the one hand, being-in-God is the fundamental feature of everything that exists, without exception, and this fact grounds the qualitative difference between God *qua* substance and things *qua* modes of substance. On the other hand, all beings do not share in God's nature to the same degree. Indeed, Spinoza also seems to suggest that all beings are not in God to the same degree. Of course, the alternative to being-in-God is not being outside God: nothing is outside God. Since Spinoza conceives all being as being-in-God, *being in God* to a greater or lesser extent means *being* to a greater or lesser extent: having more or less reality, more or less perfection, more or less power.

This differentiation applies to diverse types of thing (a human being might be more in God than an insect), or to things of the same type (one human being might be more in God than another human being). It also applies to a single being, whose being-in-God fluctuates over the course of its life. This existential fluctuation is fundamental to Spinoza's account of finite things in general, and human beings in particular: the most repeated super-proposition in the entire *Ethics* begins with the assertion that 'the mind can undergo great changes [*mutationes*], and pass at one time to a higher and at another to a lower degree of perfection' (E3p11s).

This reveals the error of those readers—Schelling, for example—who have accused Spinozism of being static, lifeless, inert, allowing no becoming.[21] On the contrary, in arguing that there are degrees of being and in drawing attention to the fluctuations between them, Spinoza's metaphysics opens up a way, a path (*via*) for human beings to follow (see E5p42s). We can draw from the *Ethics* an image of the cosmos as an infinite number of interconnected beings, with varying degrees of being-in-God, like a starry sky full of lights burning, each for a certain duration and with varying degrees of intensity. The light of each individual being waxes and wanes—especially the lights of human beings, whose existence fluctuates dramatically between non-being and reality or perfection. This image of the cosmos reflects the image of the *Ethics* itself, invoked in my second chapter, as a philosophical constellation, with some textual elements (definitions, propositions, scholia, etc.) shining brighter than others. In the case of the text, a bright light indicates semantic intensity, while in the case of the cosmos a bright light indicates a high degree of activity and power.

Spinoza's view that things can have more or less reality, more or less power, echoes a Platonic idea of degrees of being that can be discerned in many theological thinkers—including in Plotinus, where it informs a doctrine of emanation; in Augustine, where it facilitates a response to the 'problem of evil' that characterises evil as non-being; and, through the medieval period, in Anselm, in Kabbalistic authors and in Aquinas.[22]

Descartes, in his *Meditations*, puts the point negatively when he writes that 'I am, as it were, something intermediate between God and nothingness ... insofar as I participate in nothingness or non-being, that is, insofar as I am not myself the supreme being and am lacking in countless respects.'[23] Spinoza's reception of this ontology could have been mediated, indirectly or otherwise, through any of these sources; he certainly notes Descartes's view that 'there are different degrees of reality, *or* being' in his exposition of the *Principles of Philosophy*.[24] But in the *Ethics* it grounds a conception of affect, or emotion, as the *feeling*, within the mind and body, of an existence which fluctuates in its degree of being, its power, its intensity. Through this distinctive theory of affect, Spinoza brings the Platonic and Neoplatonic doctrine of degrees of being directly into human experience.

The *Ethics* identifies desire, joy and sadness as the three elemental affects from which all others are derived. Desire, the first of the affects introduced in the text, relates to both the mind and the body at once. Indeed, it is related to the mind in a double sense: it involves the mind and body together striving to persevere in being (i.e., appetite), *and* the mind's consciousness of this striving (i.e., desire). The conceptual structure is different in the case of joy (*laetitia*) and sadness, which are defined primarily in relation to the mind alone, and have other variants—cheerfulness (*hilaritas*) and melancholy—which involve both mind and body. Joy is the mind's feeling of transition to a greater degree of reality, while sadness is the opposite feeling:

> the mind can undergo great changes, and pass at one time to a higher and at another to a lower degree of perfection; and these passions explain to us the emotions of joy and sadness [*laetitiae et tristitiae*]. By joy I shall understand in the following pages a passion whereby the mind passes to a higher degree of perfection; by sadness a passion whereby the mind passes to a lower degree of perfection. (E3p11s)[25]

If human life did not admit of degrees of being, we would know neither joy nor sadness—nor, indeed, any other affects.[26] Spinoza's definition of joy as the feeling of transition to a higher perfection explains why our ethical progress toward 'perfection'—being more fully in God—will always be a joyful experience.

Spinoza's principle that 'whatever is, is in God' provides the anchor for his accounts of knowledge, of affect and of virtue, as well as for his metaphysics. It underlies the distinction between rational and intuitive knowledge—the second and third kinds of knowing—which becomes crucial in *Ethics* V, where Spinoza asserts that human freedom, or blessedness, consists in living according to the truth of being-in-God. And as we have seen in this chapter, it is integral to his ontological theory of desire, action and affectivity. The more we share in God's perfection, or reality, the more joyful we feel. This joy is not a reward for virtue; it is simply the experience of being virtuous. Our immanent ethical task is to become who we are: to express our being-in-God by knowing it, and desiring it.

CHAPTER FIVE

Participating in Divine Nature

IN PART FOUR of the *Ethics*, Spinoza suggests that the more joyful we feel, the more we participate in divine nature. He distinguishes this empowering, joyful religious attitude from the moralising, self-diminishing ethic promoted by contemporary Christian teachers. In a scholium to Proposition 45 ('Hatred can never be good'), Spinoza criticises 'a harsh and dismal superstition [which] prohibits enjoyment.' He clearly has in mind ascetic practices and puritanical teachings that valorise the affects accompanying diminished power: humility, abjection, pity, melancholy and so on, all species of sadness. 'My opinion at least is the following, and I have regulated my mind [*animum*] accordingly,' he writes:

> No deity [*numen*], nor anyone else, unless he is envious, takes pleasure in my lack of power and misfortune; nor does he ascribe to virtue our tears, sighs, fear, and other things of that kind, which are signs of a weak mind [*animi*]. On the contrary, the greater the joy with which we are affected, the greater perfection to which we pass, *i.e.*, the more we must participate in the divine nature [*eo nos magis de natura divina participare necesse est*]. (E4p45c2s)

Spinoza repeats this point in Part Four's Appendix: 'in proportion as we are affected with joy, we advance towards greater perfection, and consequently participate more fully in the divine nature [*eo magis de natura divina participamus*]' (E4App§31). Note that these references to joyful participation concern not God *per se*, but God's nature. While we are all 'in God', we may share to a greater or lesser degree in God's nature, which Spinoza specifies as 'perfection'.

The English translations of these sentences introduce the preposition 'in' to express the relation of participation. In medieval and later Latin, the verb *participare* does not usually go with the preposition *in*: often it takes no preposition, and may refer to a noun in the accusative, genitive, dative or ablative case; or it is used with *de*, signifying a relation of 'from' or 'of'. Spinoza, quite conventionally, always uses *participare* with *de*. (Alternative translations of *de natura divina participare* might be 'partake of the divine nature' or 'share the divine nature'.) This grammatical point could have significant metaphysical implications, since the phrase *de natura divina participare* need not express a relation of being-in-God at all. However, in the context of the *Ethics*, Spinoza's ontological principle that 'whatever is, is in God [*in Deo est*]'—coupled with his claim that we are modes of substance, and thus constituted by a relation of being 'in another' (*in alio*)—provides a metaphysical anchor that makes the English grammar of participation rather felicitous. For Spinoza, 'participate in the divine nature' does indeed signify participation in God's nature, since it is a way of being-in-God.

Let's speculate a little about what this means. Early in *Ethics* III, when he introduces his concept of *conatus*, Spinoza writes that 'each thing, so far as it is in itself [*quantum in se est*], strives to persevere in its being' (E3p6). The little phrase *quantum in se est* is ambiguous: as Edwin Curley explains, it is a classical Latin idiom that means 'insofar as it can' or 'insofar as it has the power to', and this is how he chooses to translate *quantum in se est* in this proposition.[1] It could, however, be taken in a more literal and thus more metaphysical sense, echoing Spinoza's definition of substance: 'By substance I understand that which exists in itself [*in se est*] and is conceived through itself' (E1D3). Spinoza seems to bring together the idiomatic and metaphysical meanings of *quantum in se est* in the demonstration of E3p6, where he repeats that each thing perseveres in its being, 'insofar as it can and [insofar as it] is in itself' (*quantum potest et in se est*) (E3p6d)—so perhaps we do not need to choose between these two interpretations. After all, the *Ethics* brings the concepts of power and being so close together as to render them almost equivalent.[2]

Don Garrett interprets *quantum in se est* in its metaphysical sense, arguing that while only God can be 'absolutely' *in se*, 'a straightforward reading of E3p6 implies that singular things can be *in* themselves to limited but varying degrees'.[3] On this reading, although modes are constitutively dependent beings, by definition 'in another', they can possess, to some degree, the qualities that substance possesses absolutely. To say that substance is *in se* is to say that it causes itself and is conceived through itself. Garrett suggests that insofar as they are in themselves, modes are 'quasi-substances'. It is important to add that the phrase *quantum in se est* signals both a similarity and a difference between substance and modes: this phrase applies only to modes, and not to substance or God, which is *in se* not to some degree, but absolutely, as Garrett points out. We know that modes can never be entirely in themselves—caused by and conceived through themselves—not only because this would betray the very definition of a mode, but also because Spinoza emphasises that 'we can never bring it about that we require nothing outside ourselves [*extra nos*] to preserve our being' (E4p18s).

This metaphysical reading of *quantum in se est* is supported by several key elements of Spinoza's ethical philosophy. The affect of *acquiescentia in se ipso*, 'resting in oneself'—which, as the next chapter will show, is at the heart of the account of the highest human good put forward in the *Ethics*—suggests that being *in se* is something we humans can strive for. And Spinoza's definition of action indicates that we can be, to some degree, in ourselves: 'I say that we act when something happens, in us or outside us, of which we are the adequate cause, i.e., when something in us or outside us follows from our nature, which can be clearly and distinctly understood through it alone' (E3D2, one of the super-propositions of *Ethics* III). In other words, we can be to some degree immanent causes of effects within ourselves, as God is always an immanent cause; we can be to some degree intelligible through, and to, ourselves. We can be more or less powerful, real or perfect, and thus more or less joyful, as Spinoza affirms when he writes, in *Ethics* IV, that 'the greater the joy with which we are affected, the greater perfection to which we pass, i.e., the more we must participate in the divine nature'. And we find further support for this interpretation of *quantum in se est* in Spinoza's enigmatic suggestion that we, as finite modes, can be to some degree eternal.

It is God's nature, as substance, to be *in se*, so the more we are in ourselves, the more we share in God's nature. As this way of putting it suggests, being more 'in ourselves' does not mean we are any less 'in God'. On the contrary: the more we are in ourselves, the more we are in God—because the more we simply *are*, and, as Spinoza insists in E1p15, all being is being-in-God. Our being, or power, does not compete with God's being, or power. This is one reason why the distinction between substance and mode remains so important, even when modes seem to approach the nature of substance by becoming more 'in themselves': two substances would, Spinoza suggests, always limit one another (see E1p8d), while substance does not limit modes, but empowers them. Our being-in-God is not a competitive relation, but a relation of sharing, or participation.

All this is, admittedly, quite a lot to hang on the ambiguous little phrase *quantum in se est*, tucked away at the beginning of *Ethics* III. Yet this interpretation coheres with other elements of Spinoza's view of the human good, which will be explored in the chapters to follow. For the remainder of this chapter, I want to excavate the philosophical and theological significance of the verb *participare*, which Spinoza uses to articulate our relation to God's nature, and to claim that this relation is a matter of degree.

Spinoza's use of *participare* in the *Ethics* echoes similar uses of this verb in some of his earlier texts, particularly the *Theologico-Political Treatise*, and these earlier uses illuminate its significance in the *Ethics*.

In 1665 Spinoza used *participare* in a letter to Willem van Blyenbergh, a Calvinist merchant who had drawn him into a lengthy correspondence about theological issues. One of Blyenbergh's most pressing questions concerned the source of human evil, which is indeed a challenging issue for any theology which refuses to separate God from nature (including human nature). Spinoza's response to Blyenbergh emphasises that 'perfection' and participation in 'godliness' are, in effect, the same thing, and a matter of degree: 'It is indeed true that the godless [*impios*] express God's will in their fashion. But that doesn't make them comparable with the pious, because the more perfection a thing has, the more it shares in godliness [*magis de Deitate participat*] and the more it expresses God's perfection [*Deique perfectionem exprimit magis*].' In this letter Spinoza explains that people who are 'impious', or unethical, 'lack the love of God that comes from knowledge of God and through which alone we are said—putting this in terms that we can understand—to be "servants of God"'. He suggests that a person who does not know God is powerless, perhaps even annihilated by his own ignorance: 'nothing but a tool . . . that serves unknowingly and is consumed in serving'. By contrast, pious people 'serve knowingly, and become more perfect by serving' (*conscii servient, & serviendo perfectiores evadunt*).[4]

The references to participation in the *Theologico-Political Treatise*, which Spinoza began in late 1665, circle around these themes of knowledge and love of God. And as in his letter to Blyenbergh, the uses of *participare* in this text indicate that participating in God's nature happens to a greater or lesser degree. In Chapter 1 of the *Theologico-Political Treatise*, Spinoza asserts that prophetic knowledge—that is, direct knowledge of

God—should include 'natural knowledge', which is 'common to all men'. This knowledge, he insists, 'can be called divine with as much right as anything else, since God's nature, in so far as we participate in it [*Dei natura, quatenus de ea participamus*], and [God's] decrees, as it were, dictate it to us',[5] Because the human mind 'contains God's nature objectively in itself, and participates in it' (*Dei naturam objective in se continet, et de eadem participat*), our minds can be considered 'the first cause of Divine revelation'.[6] We know God by knowing ourselves—our own thinking, our own being-in-God—and venerating supposed sources of 'revealed' knowledge such as miracles, prophesy, and the biblical texts themselves amounts to idolatry.[7] Here Spinoza uses the concept of participation to propose what others thinkers called a 'natural theology', taking the human mind as the principal object of investigation into God. Yet this Spinozist natural theology is quite different from the English versions of natural theology that would be so influential in eighteenth century, leading Anglican thought in a decidedly deist direction.

In Chapter 4 of the *Theologico-Political Treatise*, Spinoza uses *participare* in a more ethical context. Here he discusses 'the highest good', asserting that 'the intellect is the better part of us', and that 'our supreme good and perfection depend only on the knowledge of God'. As in the Appendix to *Ethics* IV, he urges his readers to 'perfect [the intellect] as much as we can'.[8] He invokes the dependence of all things on God—'without God nothing can exist or be conceived'—in support of his claim that when we expand our knowledge of nature, we gain 'greater and more perfect knowledge of God'. In this passage, Spinoza uses the word *participat* to describe someone who shares in the highest blessedness:

> Since nothing can be or be conceived without God, it is certain that all things in nature involve and express the concept of God, in proportion to their essence and perfection. Hence the more we know natural things, the greater and more perfect is the knowledge of God we acquire—or, since knowledge of an effect through its cause is nothing but knowing some property of the cause, the more we know natural things, the more perfectly we know God's essence, which is the cause of all things. So all our knowledge, i.e., our supreme good, not only depends on the knowledge of God, but consists entirely in it. That knowledge of God is our supreme good also follows from the fact that man is more perfect in proportion to the nature and perfection of the thing which he loves before all others, and conversely. Therefore, the man who is necessarily the most perfect and who participates more in

supreme blessedness [*adeoque ille necessario perfectissimus est, et de summa beatitudine maxime participat*] is the one who loves above all else the intellectual knowledge of God, the most perfect being, and takes the greatest pleasure [*maxime delectatur*] in that knowledge.[9]

Although Spinoza refers here to participation in blessedness, rather than participation in God's nature, he connects this sharing of beatitude to love and knowledge of God. Throughout the passage he evidently conceives participation not only as a matter of degree, but also as something that we can (and should) strive for and cultivate.

When he returns to these themes of love and knowledge of God in Chapter 14 of the *Theologico-Political Treatise*, Spinoza situates his discussion in a Christian context. Emphasising the close connections between 'faith', knowledge of God, and ethical conduct, he refers his reader to Chapter 2 of the biblical Letter of James, and highlights in particular James 2:17: 'Faith without works is dead'—a verse beloved by Catholics and inconvenient to Lutheran Protestants, as it seems to undermine Luther's insistence on justification *sola fide* (by faith alone).[10] Spinoza invokes this New Testament text to support his key claim that 'works', which he initially equates with 'obedience' or good conduct, are the inevitable consequence and sure sign of 'faith'.

Here Spinoza defends a 'true religion' that consists not in believing the right dogmas, but in behaving in the right way. This religion is defined primarily in ethical terms: good conduct is the criterion for possessing 'knowledge of God'. Spinoza expresses this complicated thought by moving from the Letter of James to the First Letter of John, then back to James 2:17:

> And John says (in 1 John, 4:7–8): whoever loves (i.e., loves his neighbour) is born of God, and knows God; whoever does not love does not know God, for God is loving-kindness [*Deus est Charitas*]. From these things it follows next that we can judge no one faithful or unfaithful except from their works. If the works are good, they are still faithful, however much they may disagree with other faithful people in their doctrines. Conversely, if the works are bad, they are unfaithful, however much they may agree in words with other faithful people. For where there is obedience, there is also faith, and faith without works is dead.[11]

Spinoza then cites 1 John 4:13, the verse he chose as the epigraph for the *Theologico-Political Treatise*. Having repeated James 2:17, this time without quotation marks—implying, perhaps, that it reflects his own view— he suggests that 'John teaches the same thing explicitly in verse 13 of the same chapter: *by this*, he says, *we know that we remain in God and that he remains in us, because he has given us of his spirit*, viz. Loving-kindness [*Charitatem*].'12

In glossing the 'works' of the Letter of James as the 'love' of the First Letter of John, Spinoza suggests that his triangulation of faith, knowledge of God, and ethical conduct is robustly ontological. God *is* love (1 John 4:7), and God-as-love is a reality on which we depend, and in which we exist. In Paul's words, 'in [this reality] we live and move and have our being'.

These pages of the *Theologico-Political Treatise* are certainly ambiguous. Spinoza could be claiming that God is nothing more than the love, or kindness, which people show to one another, thereby dissolving religion—the human relation to God—into ethical life. Or he might be arguing that whenever we show this human love, we do so only by participating in God's love. Without suppressing this ambiguity—which may well be essential to the text—we can see how the metaphysics of *Ethics* I inclines us to the latter reading. Far from emphasising human autonomy—the principle underlying Kant's argument that true religion is nothing more than ethical life—Part One of the *Ethics* accentuates our absolute dependence, our constitutive being-in-God. Within the *Theologico-Political Treatise* Spinoza articulates this view in another short, dense passage elucidating 1 John 4:13:

> [The author of 1 John] had said previously that God is Loving-kindness [*Deum esse Charitatem*], from which (according to his principles, accepted at that time) he infers that he who has Loving-kindness really has the Spirit of God. Indeed, because no one has seen God, he infers from that that no one is aware of God, or acknowledges God [*neminem Deum sentire, vel animadvertere*], except by Loving-kindness toward his neighbour, and that in fact no one can come to know any other attribute of God beyond this Loving-kindness, in so far as we participate in it [*praeter hanc Charitatem, quatenus de eadem participamus*].[13]

Here again we find a reference to participation qualified by a *quatenus*, suggesting that human beings may participate in God's loving-kindness to varying degrees. Spinoza's interpretation of 1 John 13 highlights how the author of this letter conflates knowledge and love of God, and also love of God and love of neighbour: no one knows God except by loving his neighbour, and no one knows God's nature except by knowing God's love. Both knowledge and love are gained, or possessed, through participation in the love that constitutes God's being.[14]

Spinoza draws from these theological and scriptural reflections a polemical conclusion, targeted at the brutal dogmatism of the seventeenth-century Christian churches. It is both hypocritical and perverse, he suggests, for Christians to persecute people in the name of their 'faith', since true faith is demonstrated by loving one's neighbours, not by oppressing them. 'The real enemies of Christ', he declares, 'are those who persecute honest men who love justice, because they disagree with them, and do not defend the same doctrines of faith they do. For we know that loving justice and loving-kindness are enough to make a man faithful; and whoever persecutes the faithful, is an enemy to Christ.'[15] Here Spinoza follows both the letter and the spirit of the First Letter of John, which was itself addressed to a nascent Christian community riven by conflicts over points of doctrine. This contextual parallel between the *Theologico-Political Treatise* and John's letter helps to explain why Spinoza took a verse from this New Testament text—not without a certain irony—as the motto for his book.

As we have seen, Spinoza insists that 'our supreme good and perfection ... depend only on the knowledge of God', and he urges his readers to 'perfect' their intellects as far as possible. Yet his reflections on the First Letter of John—and his confrontation, through the lens of this biblical text, with real-life religious communities whose members manifest varying degrees of ignorance, intolerance and egotism—seem to draw him to a more pragmatic view of knowledge. 'It follows', he writes, 'that faith requires, not so much true doctrines, as pious doctrines which move the heart to obedience, even if many of them do not have even a shadow of truth.'[16] Here again Spinoza affirms the principle of being-in-God, and traces this to a biblical text which his Christian opponents regarded as authoritative. Faith, he repeats, requires 'doctrines necessary for obedience, which strengthen our hearts in love towards our neighbours [*quae scilicet animum in amore erga proximum confirment*]. It is only because of this love that each of us (to speak with John) is in God and that God is in each of us.'[17]

When Spinoza writes about participation in God's nature in the *Theologico-Political Treatise*, he connects this with love—sometimes *charitas*, sometimes *amor*; when he explores the same theological idea in Part Four of the *Ethics*, he connects it with joy.[18] His analysis of the affects in the *Ethics* shows that love and joy are closely linked: love (*amor*) is a species of joy, being defined as 'joy, coupled with the idea of the cause of this joy'. Love and joy are both affects of empowerment, feelings of an increase in our desire, our essence, our power. Love is distinguished from joy by being inherently cognitive, always involving an idea—that is to say, an act of thinking—of whatever is perceived to cause joy. These affects are at the heart of an experience of being-in-God which Spinoza describes, at the end of the *Ethics*, as 'beatitude'.

Spinoza's multiple references to participation in texts written during the 1660s form the background to his use of the verb *participare* in the *Ethics*. When in Part Four he invokes the possibility of 'advanc[ing] towards greater perfection, and consequently participat[ing] more fully in the divine nature', this description of our ethical task can be understood in light of the biblical context that is made explicit in the *Theologico-Political Treatise*. At the same time, it should be read as continuing Spinoza's polemic against the powerful churches of his day—a polemic that put New Testament texts in the service of a critique of Christian teachers who held those texts to be the authoritative word of God.

{~~~}

Spinoza's remarks about participation in divine nature in *Ethics* IV may be situated in a longer history of Christian thought, in which New Testament sources are blended with Greek metaphysics. In addition to those verses from Acts and 1 John which Spinoza quoted in various letters as well as in the *Theologico-Political Treatise*, a key passage from the Second Letter of Peter offers a more specifically Christian gloss on participation. The author of this Letter tells his readers that through Christ's 'great promises' they may 'become participants of the divine nature [*genesthe theias koinonoi phuseos*]' (2 Peter 1:4). In the Latin Vulgate edition of the New Testament, this Greek phrase is rendered as *efficiamini divinae consortes naturae*: the Greek word *koinonoi*, translated into English as 'participants', 'sharers' or 'partakers', becomes *consortes* in the Latin, rather than a word deriving from the verb *participare*. In 1 Corinthians 10, Paul twice uses *koinonia* to describe the Eucharistic ritual: 'Is not the cup of thanksgiving for which we give thanks a *koinonia* in the blood of Christ? And is not the bread that we break a *koinonia* in the body of Christ? Because there is one loaf, we, who are many, are one body, for we all share [*metachomen*] the one loaf' (1 Corinthians 10:16–17). The Latin Vulgate renders these verses in a way that rather obscures the Greek text, translating the first *koinonia* as *communicatio* and the second as *participatio*, and translating *metachomen* as *participamus*: 'Calix benedictionis, cui benedicimus, nonne communicatio sanguinis Christi est? et panis quem frangimus, nonne participatio corporis Domini est? Quoniam unus panis, unum corpus multi sumus, omnes qui de uno pane participamus.'

From these intertextual biblical roots we can trace the development of a Latinised metaphysics of participation, which found its most sophisticated and influential exponent in Thomas Aquinas. In his *Summa Theologiae* Aquinas explains that 'God is essential being, whereas other things are beings by participation [*per participationem*]'; 'all beings apart from God are not their own being, but are beings by participation'.[19] Drawing this distinction anticipates Spinoza's claim in *Ethics* I that God, as substance, 'is in itself' whereas anything else, as a mode of substance, 'is in another'.

This is certainly not to deny that Aquinas's metaphysics—and not least his doctrine of creation—is fundamentally different from Spinoza's in several important respects. Nevertheless, Aquinas's concept of participation does similar metaphysical work to Spinoza's concepts of substance and mode, in distinguishing between what exists by virtue of its own being (i.e., God) and what exists 'by participation' (i.e., created things). Aquinas expands on this distinction when he sets out the causal relation between God and creatures:

> God is the first and most perfect Being. Therefore God must be the cause of being in all things that have being.... [W]hatever has some perfection by participation, is traced back, as to its principle and cause, to what possesses that perfection essentially. Thus molten iron has its incandescence from that which is fire by its essence.... God is existence itself; hence existence belongs to God in virtue of God's essence, but pertains to all other things by participation.[20]

Here Aquinas emphasises the ontological asymmetry between God and creation, and creation's ontological dependence on God. Rather like Spinoza's ontological principle of being-in-God, Aquinas's concept of participation secures the simultaneous transcendence and the immanence of God's relation to the created universe.[21] God is 'in everything', and thus inseparable from creation:

> God is said to be in everything [*dicitur Deus in omnibus esse*] by essence, power, and presence. God is in everything by God's essence inasmuch as the existence of each thing is a certain participation in the divine essence [*est quaedam participatio divini esse*]; the divine essence is present to every existing thing, to the extent that it has existence, as a cause is present to its proper effect. God is in all things by God's power, inasmuch as all things operate in virtue of God. And God is in all things by God's presence, inasmuch as God directly regulates and disposes all things.[22]

Of course, the cautionary note about using the preposition 'in' when translating the verb *participare* applies here, as it does to Spinoza's texts—and Aquinas's metaphysics does not offer quite such robust grounds for affirming the English construction 'participation in'.

Scholars disagree about whether Aquinas's theology of participation elucidates the theological principle of being-in-God that is expressed more directly in earlier Christian writers such as Augustine, John of Damascus and Anselm.[23] When he considers the question of God's omnipresence—'Whether God is in all things?'—Aquinas quotes Augustine's teaching that 'all things are in [God], and argues that this is compatible with the claim that God is in all things. He takes care to gloss Augustine's insistence that being in God is meant 'in a special sense', since the preposition 'in' customarily applies to physical things:

> Although corporeal things are said to be in another as in that which contains them, nevertheless, spiritual things contain those things in which they are; as the soul contains the body. Hence also God is in things containing them; nevertheless, by a certain similitude to corporeal things, it is said that all things are in God; inasmuch as they are contained by God.[24]

Aquinas's language—if not his doctrine—is closest to Spinoza's when he discusses grace, for here he writes of 'participation in the divine nature', quoting 2 Peter. He argues that the 'infused virtues' of faith, hope and love, which are given by God, 'dispose the human being . . . in relation to a participation in the divine nature [*in ordine ad naturam divinam participatam*], according to 2 Peter 1:4: "He has given us most great and precious promises, that by these you may be made partakers of the divine nature [*divinae consortes naturae*]." And it is in respect of receiving this nature that we are said to be born again sons of God.' Grace, explains Aquinas, is prior to virtue, and lies 'in the essence of the soul' rather than in the soul's powers, which are its virtues: 'As the human being by intellectual powers participates in divine knowledge through the virtue of faith, and by the power of will participates in divine love through the virtue of charity, so also by the nature of the soul he participates in the divine nature, through a certain likeness, through a certain regeneration or re-creation.'[25]

Aquinas's doctrine of the 'beatific vision' enjoyed by human beings in the afterlife also turns on the concept of participation. Beatitude, or blessedness, is the 'ultimate end of man', and this 'consists in the vision whereby [a human being] sees God in His essence'. Just as human beings already participate in being and goodness, so they will finally participate in God's beatitude: 'Of course, man is far below God in the perfection of his beatitude. For God has this beatitude by His very nature, whereas man attains beatitude by being admitted to a share in the divine light [*per divini luminis participationem*].'[26] Aquinas accentuates this point when he writes that 'all who share in blessedness can be happy only by participation in the blessedness of God, who is essential goodness itself, even though one human being helps another to tend toward, and arrive at, blessedness'.[27]

In setting out this theology of participation, Aquinas drew on a Platonic philosophical tradition as well as on biblical sources. The way he moves easily between the ideas of divine participation and 'likeness with God' reflects an equivocation between the concepts of *methexis* (participation) and *mimesis* (imitation) in Plato's works. Plato developed these concepts to propose a solution to the ancient metaphysical problem of the relation between the One and the Many, between universals and particulars.[28] In his *Metaphysics*, Aristotle criticised Plato for conflating *methexis* and *mimesis*. Tracing the history of the concept of *methexis* back to Pythagoras, Aristotle argued that neither the Pythagoreans nor the Platonists gave a satisfactory account of how the multiplicity of singular things share in the One, whether by imitation (*mimesis*) or participation (*methexis*).[29] For Aristotle, Platonic participation relied on an overly transcendent conception of form—conceived as the higher, unchanging reality in which lower, ephemeral beings participate—and he proposed a more immanent account of the relation between particular things and their idea or form.[30] Though Neoplatonic thinkers developed concepts of participation which attempted to mediate between Plato and Aristotle, Aquinas has been credited with achieving the fullest synthesis of Platonic transcendence and Aristotelian immanence.[31]

Participation is a concept with a long history—a history that is 'Christian' in a broad sense that encompasses the Latinisation of diverse biblical texts and ancient Greek metaphysics, mediated by medieval Arabic and Jewish sources. Equally, Aquinas's doctrine of participation is a large subject which poses deep interpretative questions, and within a few pages it is possible only to cite a few indicative texts and point to some of the linguistic, historical and conceptual issues they raise. Nevertheless, this glimpse into the genealogy of participation helps to show what is at stake, theologically, when Spinoza uses the verb *participare* to elucidate the relation of being-in-God. We can see that he combines the ideas of *methexis*, sharing, and *mimesis*, imitation, which have structured the concept since it emerged in Plato's works. Being-in-God, which expresses our causal and conceptual dependence on God, means that we exist, and are intelligible, only insofar as we share in God's being, while a mode's striving to be more *in se*—and thereby participate more fully in God's nature—might be interpreted as an imitation of God, who is absolutely *in se*.

Since the concept of participation combines difference and identity—accentuating the ontological difference between creator and creation, while also affirming God's omnipresence—this concept helped Spinoza to resist the specifically modern tendency to separate God and nature that he discerned in both Cartesian philosophy and Calvinist theology. However, Spinoza also resisted the distinction between nature and grace which structures Aquinas's account of participation.[32] For Spinoza, our sharing in God's nature is not a special gift of grace, but a natural state—though it is nevertheless variable, a matter of degree that depends on (or corresponds to) an individual's intellectual and ethical condition. Indeed, Spinoza implies that all natural agency is also divine agency. His phrase 'God or Nature' provides a useful corrective to the view that natural and divine agency are in competition, and even pulling in opposite directions—although, as I argued in Chapter 3, we should not take 'God or Nature' to imply that divine agency is reduced to what we know as natural processes, since God's power is expressed through infinite attributes, not simply through the spatio-temporal conditions of extension and duration.

Drawing on Aquinas to help clarify the theological significance of participation need not lead us to claim that his works were a direct or indirect source for Spinoza's use of the concept.[33] And we can note parallels between the way the concept of participation functions philosophically in Aquinas's works and in the *Ethics*, while recognising that Spinoza's view of God, and of God's relation to human beings, differs from Aquinas's theological vision in several significant respects. Perhaps most importantly, Aquinas (like Aristotle and Descartes) regarded individual beings as substances, which Spinoza, of course, denied. Aquinas saw God as uncaused, while Spinoza conceived God as *causa sui*.[34] Spinoza rejected creation *ex nihilo*, a core Thomist doctrine, though he did so for reasons that accord with the spirit, if not the letter, of Aquinas's theology.[35] As we saw in the previous chapter, he also criticised the Aristotelian notion of a 'final cause' that formed the deep structure of Aquinas's thinking and characterised scholastic thought more broadly. And while Aquinas locates the beatific vision of God in the afterlife, Spinoza suggests that *beatitude* is attainable—though very rarely attained—in this life; we can point again here to Spinoza's unwillingness to distinguish nature from grace. Furthermore, Aquinas's elaborate hierarchical cosmology includes strata of angelic beings, which have no place in Spinoza's more economical metaphysics—though his view that God has an infinity of attributes points to an ontological variety that remains unexplored in his philosophical system.[36]

It is not necessary to understate the theological and cultural differences between Thomism and Spinozism in order to recognise that the philosophical elements of Aquinas's doctrine of God are similarly elemental in the *Ethics*.[37] For both thinkers, God is eternal, infinite, simple and immutable, and God's essence and existence are inseparable.[38] Aquinas's preferred name for God is '*Ego sum qui sum*', from the Latin translation of Exodus 3:14—'I am who I am'—since this name, Aquinas suggests, denotes 'simply existence itself' or 'the infinite ocean of substance'.[39] 'I am who I am' translates, with a certain theological word-play, the four Hebrew letters known as the tetragrammaton: יהוה, or YHWH. This unpronounceable name of God can be vocalised as 'Yahweh', which was Latinised as *Jehova*, and this in turn was Anglicised as 'Jehovah'. In Latin, then, *Ego sum qui sum* and *Jehova* are virtually equivalent, since they are both ways of transcribing the most ontological name of God. Aquinas's preference for this divine name reflects his philosophical definition of God as the pure act of being (*actus essendi*), which he explicates through an Aristotelian conception of being (*esse*) as activity, 'as ontological affirmation and positivity'.[40]

In the *Theologico-Political Treatise* Spinoza echoes Aquinas (along with other Jewish and Christian thinkers) in emphasising that the tetragrammaton is 'the unique name of God':

> there is no name in the Bible except *Jehova* which makes known the absolute essence of God, without relation to created things. And therefore the Hebrews contend that this is, strictly speaking, the only name of God, the other names being merely common nouns. And really, the other names of God, whether they are substantives or adjectives, are attributes which belong to God in so far as God is conceived in relation to created things, or is manifested through them.[41]

This account of God's 'absolute essence' resonates with the explication of God in Part One of the *Ethics*. Though Spinoza makes few explicit biblical references in the *Ethics*, Exodus 3:14 certainly remains in the background to his theological metaphysics of substance.

Aquinas distinguished those 'truths' about God's essence and existence which can be known by human reason—and which can therefore be accepted by non-Christian 'philosophers'—from 'other things about God at which [these philosophers] could not arrive, things communicated to us in the teaching of Christian religion, about which Christian faith instructs us beyond human understanding'.[42] These articles of faith include the doctrine of the Trinity, which affirms Christ's unique ontological status and unique relation to God. Spinoza agreed with Aquinas not only on the core philosophical doctrine of God, but also in distinguishing this rational knowledge from other doctrines, scriptural or ecclesial, which belong to what Aquinas called 'faith' and Spinoza called 'theology'. As a teacher of his monastic order and his Church, Aquinas expounded both the philosophical and the non-philosophical elements of Christian teaching. Spinoza, by contrast, insisted on his philosophical doctrine of God while treating matters of faith or theology in an agnostic and anti-dogmatic spirit.

The divergence between Spinozism and the specifically modern, post-Reformation Christian theology that he addressed was indeed wide, and within this context the charges of heresy and even of atheism against him are unsurprising. Yet when we read the *Ethics* in light of the theology proposed by Aquinas—who though controversial in his own time has long been regarded as an exemplar of theological orthodoxy—Spinoza's views about God and our relations to God seem rather less heretical than many commentators suppose.[43] The *Ethics* might be read as pushing certain Thomist insights further, rather than as moving in an entirely different theological direction. For Aquinas, the concept of participation names an ontological distinction between creation and creator, while affirming the intimacy emphasised by Paul when he wrote that 'God is not far from each one of us, for in him we live and move and have our being'. This shows why we cannot attribute to Aquinas a one-sided insistence on divine transcendence at the expense of divine immanence. It also calls into question the prevailing interpretation of the *Ethics* as advancing a radical secular philosophy of 'pure immanence' that contrasts with the unequivocal transcendence espoused by theologies vaguely defined as 'traditional' or 'orthodox'.[44] In fact, Spinoza, like Aquinas, affirms both ontological difference and being-in-God, and thus rejects both pantheism and deism.[45] Of course, Spinoza articulates this ontological difference in a new way: by arguing that God alone is substance, which exists through itself, while finite things are not substances but modes, which *by definition* exist not through themselves, but through God. Yet one result of this innovation is that, for Spinoza as for Aquinas, participating in God's nature signifies both essential difference and intimate relationship, for these are two aspects of the same principle of absolute dependence on God.

So, without overlooking or understating the differences between Spinozism and Thomism, tracing the concept of participation from its early Greek roots to its apotheosis in Aquinas's thought helps to situate Spinoza's ethics within a rich philosophical and theological context. This context does not prescribe the religious valence of Spinoza's references to participation, but it does provide some orientation in thinking through what this might be. It is only by grasping the full ontological *and* ethical force of our being-in-God that we can begin to understand Spinoza's claim that 'self-contentment' (*acquiescentia in se ipso*) and an 'intellectual love of God' (*amor Dei intellectualis*) belong to 'the greatest human perfection'.

Postscript: Spinoza and Christ

Reading Spinoza alongside Aquinas suggests that it is Spinoza's view of Christ, and not his doctrine of God, which most clearly distances him from Christianity. The question of Christ's distinctiveness from other human beings, and the extent to which faith in Christ's special status is a requirement for salvation, are, of course, decisive tests of Christian orthodoxy. For centuries after the death of Jesus, theologians sought to articulate a cogent doctrine of Christ's unique ontological status, often making creative advances in metaphysics and logic in order to systematise the New Testament's claims that Jesus was the 'son of God', even the *logos* which 'was God and was with God', 'from the beginning'.[46]

When Aquinas sought to demonstrate Christ's uniqueness, he began by setting the question of Christ's relation to God within the framework of his hierarchical doctrine of participation in God's goodness. He then located Christ beyond this participatory range. Commenting on 'the fullness of Christ's grace', Aquinas explains that divine grace was given to Christ 'not by participation, but by nature':

> The closer any creature draws to God, the more it shares in God's goodness [*bonitate eius magis participat*], and the more abundantly it is filled with gifts infused by God. Thus someone who comes closer to a fire, shares to a greater extent in its heat. But there can be no way, nor can any be imagined, by which a creature more closely adheres to God, than by being united to God in unity of person. Therefore, in consequence of the very union of Christ's human nature with God in unity of person, Christ's soul was filled with habitual gifts of graces beyond all other souls. . . .

The possession of infinite grace is restricted to Christ. To other saints is given the grace of being gods or sons of God by participation, through the infusion of some gift. Such a gift, being created, must itself be finite, just as all other creatures are. To Christ, on the contrary, is given, in his human nature, the grace to be the Son of God not by participation, but by nature.[47]

In this way, Aquinas suggests that when a human life participates as fully as it can in divine goodness—a participation that occurs through an intellectual activity motivated by love for God—it draws closer to the life of Christ, without ever attaining the 'personal' union with God that is 'restricted to Christ'.

Where does Spinoza stand on this question? His divergence from Aquinas's position is evident, though not unambiguous. In the first chapter of the *Theologico-Political Treatise*, he argues that Christ had an exceptionally direct connection to God, which surpassed ordinary human knowledge:

> I do not believe that anyone else has reached such perfection [in knowledge], except Christ, to whom the decisions of God, which lead men to salvation, were revealed immediately—without words or visions. So God revealed himself to the Apostles through Christ's mind, as previously God had revealed himself to Moses by means of a heavenly voice. And therefore Christ's voice, like the one Moses heard, can be called the voice of God. And in this sense we can also say that God's Wisdom, that is, a Wisdom surpassing human wisdom, assumed a human nature in Christ, and that Christ was a way to salvation [*et Christum viam salutis fuisse*].
>
> But I must warn here that I'm not speaking in any way about the things some of the Churches maintain about Christ. Not that I deny them. For I readily confess I don't grasp them [*ea non capere*]. What I have just affirmed I conclude from Scripture itself. . . . If Moses spoke with God face to face, as a man usually does with a companion (i.e., by means of their two bodies), Christ, indeed, communicated with God mind to mind.[48]

There is deep ambiguity in this passage: since Spinoza did not think that Moses literally conversed with God as with an embodied companion, where does this leave his suggestion that Christ, by contrast, 'communicated with God mind to mind'? In Chapter 4 of the *Theologico-Political Treatise* Spinoza draws a similar contrast between Christ and the prophets, asserting that

All the prophets who wrote laws in the name of God [did] not perceive God's decrees adequately, as eternal truths. . . . I say this only about the prophets . . . and not about Christ. For however much Christ too may seem to have written laws in the name of God, nevertheless we think that he perceived things truly and adequately. Christ was not so much a prophet as the mouth of God. . . . From the fact that God revealed himself immediately to Christ, *or* to Christ's mind—and not, as he did to the prophets, through words and images, the only thing we can understand is that Christ perceived truly, *or* understood, the things revealed.[49]

Here, Spinoza attributes to Saint Paul the view that 'everyone, by the natural light, clearly understands God's power and eternal divinity', while suggesting diplomatically that people may certainly plead ignorance when it is a question 'of the supernatural light, and of the fleshly passion of Christ [*de carnali Christi passione*] and his resurrection etc'.[50] In other words, Spinoza was happy to see Christ as an exemplar—even the highest exemplar—of the human mind's capacity to know (and thereby reveal) God. Interpreted in this naturalistic way, he could accept the Christian doctrine of the incarnation.

In 1675 Spinoza echoed that cautious, qualified endorsement of the incarnation in a letter to Henry Oldenburg, written in response to Oldenburg's request to clarify his position on Christian doctrine. Here Spinoza denies that 'knowing Christ according to the flesh' is necessary for salvation: 'We must think quite differently about the eternal son of God, i.e., God's eternal wisdom, which has manifested itself in all things and chiefly in the human mind, and most of all in Jesus Christ [*et omnium maxime in Christo Jesu manifestavit*].' Without this eternal, divine wisdom, he explains, 'no one can attain to a state of blessedness, since this alone teaches what is true and false, good and evil'. However: 'as for what certain Churches add to this—that God assumed a human nature—I warned expressly that I don't know what they mean. Indeed, to confess the truth, they seem to me to speak no less absurdly than if someone were to say to me that a circle assumed the nature of a square.'[51] In a subsequent letter to Oldenburg, continuing the same conversation, Spinoza connects his interpretation of Christ's divinity with the opening of John's Gospel: 'as I said in my [previous] letter, God manifested himself most in Christ. To express this more powerfully, John said that the word became flesh.'[52]

Though the *Ethics* makes no pronouncement about Christ, its philosophical categories may illuminate the views Spinoza expressed in these earlier texts. We might interpret his remark about the absurdity of God taking on human nature in terms of the concepts of substance and mode. To say that God assumed a human nature amounts to claiming that eternal, infinite substance became a finite mode, and for Spinoza, this simply does not make sense. His willingness to write that 'God's eternal wisdom, which has manifested itself in all things, but most in the human mind, and most of all in Christ Jesus', suggests that in the attribute of thought God's essence might be expressed, or manifested, more or less fully—and this allowed Spinoza to claim that in Jesus's human mind God's 'eternal wisdom' was manifested 'most of all'. Perhaps this accords with the logic of degrees of perfection suggested in the *Ethics*, where 'the greater the perfection to which we pass' equates to 'the more we participate in the divine nature' (E4p45s). And Spinoza's remarks about the immediacy and truth of Christ's knowledge of God resonate with his account of *scientia intuitiva*.

In his letters, as in the *Theologico-Political Treatise*, Spinoza was prepared to recognise a difference between Christ and other human beings, while insisting that this is a matter of degree rather than an essential difference. Whereas Aquinas, a Trinitarian theologian, regarded Christ's uniqueness as both ontological and moral, since it consists in a non-participatory union with God's being and goodness, Spinoza suggests that Christ's being-in-God *was* participatory, and thus no different in kind from that of other human beings. This allows Spinoza to treat Christ as a human exemplar: a model for how far a human mind might be—or become—an expression, a manifestation or a participator in 'God's eternal wisdom'.

Spinoza's way of thinking about both the similarity and the difference between Christ's mind and other human minds might be interpreted as a critique of more figurative claims about the incarnation expressed in the official confessions and liturgies of the Christian churches. Alternatively, his remarks might provide philosophical grounding for the view that these figurative claims express some truth. The texts are, I think, open to both interpretations. Perhaps this is because Spinoza thought that people should be free to accept or to ignore these Christian teachings; they do not belong in his list of universal religious tenets in the *Theologico-Political Treatise*. He expressed approval for the universal reach of Christianity: 'Christ was sent to teach, not only the Jews, but the whole human race. So it was not enough for him to have a mind accommodated only to the opinions of the Jews; he needed a mind accommodated to the opinions and teachings universal to the human race, i.e., to common and true notions.'[53] However, the claims of Christian churches that human salvation is possible *only* through Christ jarred with this universalism, and turned it into dogmatism. While the gospel of incarnation and resurrection was offered to all, anyone who did *not* embrace it was deemed to be excluded from truth and blessedness, and in practice this exclusion often hardened into persecution and oppression. By contrast, there is a certain flexibility in Spinoza's remarks about Christ that accommodates orthodox Christian belief—and perhaps even illuminates it—while refusing to require it.

This open-mindedness appealed to the early German Romantics who embraced Spinozism at the end of the eighteenth century. 'It is very one-sided and presumptuous to assert that there is only one Mediator,' declared Friedrich Schlegel in his pioneering journal *Athenäum*: 'To the ideal Christian—and in this respect the unique Spinoza comes nearest to being one—everything ought to be a Meditator.'[54]

CHAPTER SIX

Acquiescentia

IN PART FOUR of the *Ethics* Spinoza writes that '*acquiescentia in se ipso* is really the highest thing we can hope for' (E4p52s). Traditionally, theologians had described a deep human desire to rest in God—an ideal powerfully expressed by Augustine, Anselm and Aquinas, among others. When seventeenth-century philosophers dismantled the teleological worldview of their medieval forebears, they called into question the possibility of ever finding rest. Hobbes, for example, argued in *Leviathan* (1651) that 'the felicity of this life consisteth not in the repose of a mind satisfied', and discerned in 'all mankind a perpetual and restless desire of power after power, that ceaseth only in death'.[1]

In 1661 Spinoza criticised Bacon for assuming that 'the human intellect is unquiet, it cannot stop or rest [*neque consistere, aut acquiescere possit*]', and, like Bacon, he uses the verb *acquiescere* to signify the mind's capacity for repose.[2] His claim in the *Ethics* that '*acquiescentia in se ipso* is really the highest thing we can hope for' seems to revive the ancient ideal of rest. But *acquiescentia in se ipso* means resting in oneself, not resting in God. Was Spinoza replacing traditional theological teaching with the humanist ideal of autonomy that would become a defining feature of the modern, enlightened age? Yes and no.

Acquiescentia in se ipso appears in the enumeration of the affects in Part Three of the *Ethics*, and remains an important concept right through to the end of Part Five. It is also a complex concept, since its meaning is comprised of three elements. First, there is Spinoza's definition of *acquiescentia in se ipso* as a joy arising from contemplating ourselves, or, in other words, self-love (see E3p55s). All love, according to Spinoza's definition, is joy accompanied by the idea of its cause (see E3p13s), so self-love is joy accompanied by the idea of oneself as the cause of one's joy. The second and third elements of *acquiescentia*—more implicit, but certainly no less significant—are drawn from the word itself. The verb *acquiescere* carries the sense of acceptance, submission or obedience conveyed by the English 'acquiesce', while the Latin root *quies* signifies stillness, quiet, repose. *Acquiescentia in se ipso* has, then, a threefold meaning, combining self-love, or joy in one's own causal activity; obedience and acceptance; peace and rest.

This threefold meaning indicates the affective, experiential character of the freedom, virtue and blessedness which Spinoza opposes to an unfree, illusory kind of existence—and particularly to an unfree, illusory kind of religion. *Acquiescentia in se ipso* conveys the feeling-quality of the highest human good. It thus takes its place among the distinctive cluster of concepts that define Spinozist *beatitudo*: intuitive knowledge, intellectual love of God, the mind's eternity, and *acquiescentia in se ipso*.

Not surprisingly, given its philosophical richness and semantic complexity, Spinoza's translators have struggled to find an adequate English translation of *acquiescentia in se ipso*. Translating it literally, as 'acquiescence in oneself', leaves out the element of joy that is integral to Spinoza's definition of this affect.[3] Furthermore, 'acquiescence in oneself' suggests passivity, whereas *in se ipso* echoes the definition of substance as what is 'in itself', *in se* (E1D3)—and the more we share in the nature of substance, the more active we become. 'Self-acceptance' sounds a little more active than 'acquiescence in oneself', yet misses the crucial sense of repose, and leaves out the important little word 'in'. Marian Evans—who took the pseudonym George Eliot soon after completing the first English translation of the *Ethics* in 1856—chose 'self-contentment', which remains perhaps the best rendering of *acquiescentia in se ipso*, and has been revived by Spinoza's most recent translators.[4] Late nineteenth-century translators preferred 'self-approval' or 'self-satisfaction', while in the 1980s Edwin Curley opted for 'self-esteem', noting that 'self-satisfaction' sounds a little smug.[5]

Our modern notion of 'self-esteem' captures very well Spinoza's definition of *acquiescentia in se ipso* as a self-love that involves an idea of oneself, or an attitude towards oneself. We human beings live in relation to ourselves, with a certain self-understanding or self-awareness, and this reflexivity always has an affective dimension. Yet translating *acquiescentia in se ipso* as 'self-esteem' neglects the element of *quies*, stillness and rest. It also conceals the continuity between Spinoza's discussion of *acquiescentia in se ipso* in Parts Three and Four of the *Ethics*, and the 'true peace of mind' (*vera animi acquiescentia*) he attributes to the wise person in Part

Five (see E5p27, E5p42). Curley uses different English words for *acquiescentia* over the course of the *Ethics*—and with good reason, since the meaning of *acquiescentia* varies according to the epistemic, psychological and ethical condition of the person who experiences it. Nevertheless, the concept has an integrity throughout the text, which is obscured for Anglophone readers by these shifting translations of *acquiescentia*. In this chapter I will leave *acquiescentia in se ipso* untranslated, in order to retain its integrity while exhibiting its rich and multiple significance.

Because *acquiescentia in se ipso* always involves an idea of oneself, it is an inherently cognitive affect. Ideas, for Spinoza, are not static images, like 'mute pictures', but acts of thinking that affirm their object (see E2p49s). So any idea of oneself is an act of thinking that affirms one's own existence in a certain way. Spinoza distinguishes between three kinds of thinking—imagining, reasoning and intuiting—and one's idea of oneself can take any of these cognitive forms. When our self-understanding is based on imagination, our *acquiescentia* is a hollow, volatile, egotistical satisfaction. When it is rooted in the second, rational kind of knowledge, it becomes a stable joy that can be shared with others. Within *scientia intuitiva*, the third kind of knowledge, *acquiescentia* signifies the feeling-quality of participation in God's eternity, giving experiential content to the apparently abstract idea of intellectual love of God. Just as there is a hierarchy among Spinoza's three kinds of cognition, so there is a hierarchy among their corresponding forms of *acquiescentia*. In the *Theologico-Politico Treatise* Spinoza uses a concept of '*acquiescentia*', distinguished by the clearest knowledge, to define human blessedness: 'true salvation and blessedness [*vera salus & beatitudo*] consists in true peace of mind [*vera animi acquiescentia*], and we truly find peace [*vera acquiescimus*] only in those things we understand very clearly'.[6] The *Ethics* makes the same argument, while providing a much fuller discussion of the *acquiescentia* that belongs to the inadequate ideas of ourselves produced by imagination.

The relationship between *acquiescentia in se ipso* and Spinoza's three kinds of cognition bears witness to the continuity and coherence of his discussion of *acquiescentia*, on the one hand, and to the 'polyvalence' of the concept, on the other. *Acquiescentia in se ipso* is a single affect, always conforming to its definition as self-love, that is, joy arising from contemplating ourselves. However, it is characterised by varying forms of stillness and obedience, according to the kind of cognition that produces it.[7] Indeed, these variations are ethical and experiential qualities by which the different kinds of cognition can be recognised and distinguished—for it is through the various forms of *acquiescentia* that we *feel* the effects of our self-knowledge (or lack thereof) within our own being.

{⸻}

Spinoza's discussion of *acquiescentia in se ipso* has a deep philosophical significance. This affect links his critiques of free will, of Cartesian philosophy, and of superstitious religion, and it also links these critiques to his own account of true freedom and blessedness.

Spinoza took the concept of *acquiescentia in se ipso* from Henri Desmarets's Latin translation of Descartes's *Les Passions de l'âme* (*The Passions of the Soul*), completed in 1650, just a year after the French original was published.[8] Desmarets used *acquiescentia* to translate the French *satisfaction*. In the second part of *Les Passions de l'âme*, Descartes defines and discusses a series of particular passions, among them *la satisfaction de soy-mesme*, 'self-satisfaction', which he opposes to 'repentance'. Desmarets chose *acquiescentia in se ipso* to translate *la Satisfaction de soy-mesme*, and *dat nobis acquiescentiam interiorem* for *nous donne une Satisfaction intérieure*. Descartes returns to *la satisfaction de soy-mesme* in Part Three of *Les Passions de l'âme*, and here Desmarets translated this as *Satisfactio sive Acquiescentia in se ipso*.[9]

Descartes emphasises that the *satisfaction de soy-mesme* of a consistently virtuous person has a quality of stillness or rest: 'la Satisfaction, qu'ont tous-jours ceux qui constamment la vertu, est une habitude en leur âme, qui se nomme tranquillité & repos de conscience'.[10] Desmarets translated the latter part of this sentence as *Tranquillitas & Quies Conscientiae*, and he amplified Descartes's point by identifying the passion of *la satisfaction* as *acquiescentia* as well as *satisfactio*. Although the idea of stillness or rest may be implicit in *satisfactio*, it is much more explicit in *acquiescentia*. So while Descartes explicates *la satisfaction* in terms of 'tranquillity and repose', Desmarets makes *quies* integral to this passion, and thus inseparable from it—a subtle yet significant difference.

Spinoza's incorporation of *acquiescentia in se ipso* into his own discussion of the affects in *Ethics* III and IV engages closely with Descartes's *Passions of the Soul*.[11] Though Spinoza is clearly indebted to the Cartesian account of *la satisfaction de soi-même*, he responds to it critically.[12] His discussion of *acquiescentia in se ipso* echoes seven features of Descartes's discussion of *la satisfaction de soi-même*:

(1) *La satisfaction de soi-même* is a joy relating to one's own action: 'We may consider the cause of a good or evil, present as well as past. A good done by ourselves gives us an internal satisfaction.' This joy, Descartes emphasises, 'depends completely on ourselves'.[13] Similarly, Spinoza states that 'I shall call Joy accompanied by the idea of an internal cause, *Acquiescentia in se ipso*' (E3p30s), and that '*Acquiescentia in se ipso* is a Joy born of the fact that a man considers himself and his own power of acting' (E3Def.Aff.25). Descartes's idea of a joy that 'depends completely on ourselves' resonates with the self-sufficiency of Spinoza's substance, captured by the words *in se* that link his definition of substance to *acquiescentia in se ipso*.

(2) *La satisfaction de soi-même* is coupled with, and opposed to, repentance (*le repentir*). Descartes defines repentance as 'a kind of sadness' that 'results from believing we have done an evil deed'.[14] Likewise, Spinoza identifies 'the sadness contrary to *acquiescentia in se ipso*' as 'repentance' (E3p30s). However, in his 'Definitions of the Affects' he distinguishes between two senses of *acquiescentia in se ipso*: one is the opposite of repentance, and the other is the opposite of humility.

(3) Descartes elevates *la satisfaction de soi-même* above the other passions, describing it as 'the sweetest of all the passions'—whereas repentance is 'the most bitter . . . because its causes lie in ourselves alone'.[15] As we have seen, Spinoza suggests that '*acquiescentia in se ipso* is really the highest thing we can hope for'.

(4) *La satisfaction de soi-même* can be either 'a habit of the soul' or 'a passion', depending on whether it accompanies the steadfast pursuit of virtue, or arises as a 'fresh satisfaction' following the performance of 'an action we think good'.[16] Spinoza echoes this distinction in his account of *acquiescentia in se ipso*. Like all the affects, *acquiescentia* can be predominantly passive, 'a confused idea', and fleeting, contributing to 'vacillations of mind' (E3Gen. Def.Aff; E3p59s). A wise person enjoys lasting *acquiescentia*: he 'always possesses true peace of mind [*vera animi acquiescentia*]' (E5p42s).

(5) Having distinguished between the 'habit' and the 'passion' of *la satisfaction de soi-même*, Descartes suggests that the passion may be either true or false, genuine or 'vain'. When the cause of our self-satisfaction 'is not just, i.e., when the actions from which we derive great satisfaction are not very important or are even vicious,

[then our] satisfaction is absurd.[17] Similarly, Spinoza states that some instances of *acquiescentia* are *vana*: empty, futile or false (E3p58s), while others are *vera*: true, genuine, properly named, well-founded. However, this is not simply a binary distinction, since within true *acquiescentia* we can make the further distinction between that which arises from reason, and that which arises from *scientia intuitiva*.

(6) Descartes associates 'vain' self-satisfaction with 'impertinent arrogance'.[18] Spinoza identifies the vain, deluded form of *acquiescentia in se ipso* as pride (*superbia*), defined as 'thinking more highly of oneself than is just, out of love for oneself' (E3p26s; Def.Aff.28). Pride is a species of *acquiescentia in se ipso*: 'it can also be defined as love of oneself, or *acquiescentia in se ipso*, insofar as it so affects a man that he thinks more highly of himself than is just' (E3Def.Aff.28).

(7) Descartes illustrates his description of vain self-satisfaction by the example of religious bigotry, hypocrisy and violence, which he describes with great vividness. The 'vanity' and 'impertinent arrogance' of deluded self-satisfaction, writes Descartes,

> is noticeable especially in those who believe themselves devout, but are merely bigoted and superstitious. These are people who—under the pretext of frequently going to church, reciting many prayers, wearing their hair short, fasting, and giving alms—think that they are absolutely perfect and imagine that they are such close friends of God that they could not do anything to displease him. They suppose that anything their passion dictates is a commendable zeal, even though it sometimes dictates the greatest crimes that men can commit, such as the betrayal of cities, the killing of sovereigns, and the extermination of whole peoples for the sole reason that they do not accept their opinions.[19]

The detail and vigour of this passage suggests that Descartes's observations of violent religiosity—vividly displayed in the sectarian wars that divided Europe during his lifetime—not only furnish an example of vain self-satisfaction, but motivate his account of this passion. Likewise, Spinoza's critique of superstition certainly provides an important context for his analysis of the affects and of 'human servitude'. He analyses superstition in both epistemic and affective terms: superstition is based on inadequate cognition and is manifest in the passion of fear, and it is contrasted with the freedom and blessedness arising from adequate understanding and manifest in an active affect of love.[20] This account of superstition is paralleled by his description of the 'empty' *acquiescentia in se ipso* 'that is encouraged only by the opinion of the multitude', not only because it is irrational but because it makes people both fearful and violent: 'he who exults at being esteemed by the multitude is made anxious daily . . . [and] this gives rise to a monstrous lust of each to crush the other in any way possible' (E5p58s).[21]

Spinoza's discussion of *acquiescentia in se ipso* appropriates these seven characteristics of *la satisfaction de soi-même* in a manner that critiques and subverts the Cartesian passion. This appropriation targets a central tenet of Descartes's philosophy: the freedom of the human will. For Descartes, virtue consists in the rational exercise of free will—and this is particularly pertinent to the twin passions of self-satisfaction and repentance, since we deserve to be praised or blamed only when we are free to act well or badly. Self-satisfaction and repentance accompany deeds 'done by ourselves', caused by 'ourselves alone', through our own volition. 'There is only one thing in us which could give us good reason to esteem ourselves, namely, the exercise of our free will and the control we have over our volitions,' writes Descartes.[22] *La satisfaction de soi-même* is closely connected to the virtue of *générosité*, which is 'the key to all the other virtues and a general remedy for every disorder of the passions'.[23] *La générosité* involves both an affirmation of human freedom and the 'constant resolution' to use this freedom well.[24]

As we have seen, Descartes distinguishes between true and illusory *satisfaction de soi-même*, and associates the latter with superstitious religion. Spinoza, however, assigns the whole Cartesian concept of *satisfaction de soi-même*—along with its mirror image, repentance—to the category of illusion. A 'decision of the mind which is believed to be free is not distinguished from imagination itself', writes Spinoza, concluding that those who 'believe that they do anything from a free decision of the mind, dream with open eyes' (E3p2s); the idea of free decision is a 'fiction' (E3Def. Aff.6exp). Throughout the *Ethics* he treats belief in free will as a symptom of ignorance: 'men think themselves free, because they are conscious of their volitions and their appetite, and do not think . . . of the causes by which they are disposed to wanting and willing, because they are ignorant of those causes' (E1App).[25] In fact, Spinoza states plainly, 'the will cannot be a free cause, but only a necessary one' (E1p32).[26]

When Spinoza defines *acquiescentia in se ipso* alongside repentance in his 'Definitions of the Affects', he links both affects to an erroneous belief in free will.[27] He distinguishes this inadequate *acquiescentia in se ipso* from a more neutral version of the affect, paired with humility, which does not involve the idea of free will:

> *Acquiescentia in se ipso* is opposed to Humility, insofar as we understand by it a Joy born of the fact that we consider our power of acting. But insofar as we also understand by it a Joy, accompanied by the idea of some deed which we believe we have done from a free decision of the Mind, it is opposed to Repentance, which we define as follows[:] ... Repentance is a Sadness accompanied by the idea of some deed we believe ourselves to have done from a free decision of the Mind. (E3Def. Aff.26exp; E3Def.Aff.27)

In his Explanation of the latter definition, Spinoza refers the reader back to Part Two: 'On the free decision of the Mind, see E2p35s.' This scholium takes free will as an example to elucidate the proposition that 'falsity consists in the privation of knowledge which inadequate, *or* mutilated and confused, ideas involve'—'men are deceived in thinking themselves free.... [T]hey say that human actions depend on the will, but these are only words for which they have no idea. For all are ignorant of what the will is' (E2p35 and schol.). In this way, Spinoza declares the Cartesian affects of *acquiescentia in se ipso* and repentance to be intrinsically inadequate, bound up with a host of negative connotations: falsity, 'mutilated and confused' ideas, self-deception, ignorance.

Descartes suggested that when *la satisfaction de soi-même* is vain, it can lead to violence and persecution: 'it sometimes dictates the greatest crimes that men can commit, such as ... the extermination of whole peoples'. For Spinoza, however, it is the misguided commitment to free will which produces, or at least stimulates, this kind of violence. The fiction of free will, he argues, exacerbates the affects of both love and hatred: 'because men consider themselves to be free, they have a greater love or hate toward one another than toward other things' (E3p49s). Spinoza returns to this point in Part Five, where he emphasises the link between the idea of free will and ignorance: 'imagining a thing as free can be nothing but simply imagining it while we are ignorant of the causes by which it has been determined to act' (E5p5s). Believing in human free will, for Spinoza, is just like believing in divine miracles: both beliefs are equally superstitious, equally rooted in ignorance.[28] When he describes the emotional consequences of belief in free will at the end of his account of the affects, he refers specifically to *acquiescentia in se ipso* and repentance. Having repeated his definition of these affects as joy or sadness 'accompanied by the idea of oneself as cause', he adds that 'because men believe themselves to be free, these affects are very violent' (E3p51s).

This rejection of free will rids *acquiescentia* and repentance of the moral force of their corresponding Cartesian passions.[29] While Descartes defines *la satisfaction de soi-même* and repentance with reference to 'good' or 'evil' deeds, Spinoza omits these terms from his definitions. He suggests that repentance and its corresponding *acquiescentia* have acquired a moral valence by 'education' and 'custom', which conditions people to have certain emotional responses to their own actions:

> it is no wonder Sadness follows absolutely from all those acts which from custom are called *wrong*, and Joy, from those which are called *right*. For from what has been said above we easily understand that this depends chiefly on education. Parents—by blaming the former acts, and often scolding their children on account of them, and on the other hand, by recommending and praising the latter acts—have brought it about that the emotions of Sadness were joined to the one kind of act, and those of Joy to the other.
>
> Experience itself also confirms this. For not everyone has the same custom and Religion . . . [and] according as each one has been educated, so he either repents of a deed or exults at being esteemed for it (E3Def.Aff.27exp).

When Spinoza presents his neutral definition of *acquiescentia in se ipso*, which is paired with humility, he characterises both affects simply in terms of power: '*Acquiescentia in se ipso* is a Joy born of the fact that a man considers himself and his own power of acting. . . . Humility is a Sadness born of the fact that a man considers his own lack of power, or weakness' (E3Def.Aff.25 and 26).

Spinoza associated both moralism and immorality—especially the kind that accompanies superstitious religion—with the illusory belief in free will. This was not merely a critique of Descartes, who expressed an outlook that had come to dominate his Christian culture. Spinoza does, however, suggest that Descartes, being a philosopher, should have known better.[30]

{⁂}

The concept of *acquiescentia*, with its connotations of acceptance and obedience, helped Spinoza to counter the moral outlook grounded on belief in free will with an alternative ethics grounded on understanding and accepting necessity. Indeed, in the *Ethics*, *acquiescentia* implies a distinctive ideal of obedience. We tend to associate obedience with heteronomy, submission to an external authority; relatedly, 'acquiescence' usually refers to a rather passive acceptance of another's will that is reluctant, helpless, or perhaps indifferent. This was equally true in the seventeenth century. Hobbes, for example, used the verb *acquiescere* to describe heteronomous submission to an external authority when discussing the interpretation of scripture in *De Cive* (1642).[31] Yet Spinoza's use of *acquiescentia* suggests a different kind of obedience, which encompasses both following the laws of one's own nature and wisely accepting the necessity of divine law.

According to this Spinozist conception of obedience, being in oneself, *in se ipso*, and being-in-God become indistinguishable—for neither relation is heteronomous. This is an immanent obedience. Though he does not use this language, Spinoza does explicitly state that there is a kind of service to God that is synonymous with human freedom: 'virtue itself, and the service [*servitus*] of God, [are] happiness itself, and the greatest freedom' (E2p49s).[32] As Nancy Levene has observed, 'when Spinoza uses the term *servitus*, he means to set the question of freedom on an entirely different basis'.[33]

We must distinguish this notion of immanent obedience, drawn from Spinoza's account of *acquiescentia in se ipso*, from the practical obedience that Spinoza makes central to his definition of true religion in the *Theologico-Political Treatise*:

> the intellectual *or* exact knowledge of God is not a gift common to all the faithful, as obedience is. . . . Men, women, children, everyone in fact, is equally able to obey on command. But not everyone is equally able to be wise. . . . God asks of man no other knowledge than knowledge of God's divine justice and loving-kindness [*Charitatis*]. This knowledge is not necessary for intellectual understanding [*ad scientias*], but only for obedience.[34]

This obedience need not involve knowledge of God's nature. Even here, however, Spinoza's discussion coheres with the more philosophical concept of immanent obedience suggested by his analysis of *acquiescentia* in the *Ethics*. The *Theologico-Political Treatise* goes on to argue that 'it does not matter, as far as faith is concerned' whether people believe that God 'directs things from freedom or by a necessity of nature, or [whether] God prescribes laws as a prince or teaches them as eternal truths, or whether man obeys God from free will or from the necessity of the divine decree'.[35] We know from the *Ethics* that the wise person embraces the second of each of these alternatives. The philosopher's obedience is grounded in his insight into 'the necessity of the divine decree', this 'decree' being synonymous with 'eternal truth' and the 'necessity of nature'.

Earlier I suggested that *acquiescentia* is correlated to the three kinds of knowledge, since it is an inherently cognitive affect, always involving a certain idea of oneself. Just as there are three kinds of knowledge, so there are three kinds of *acquiescentia*. This threefold structure produces three different modes of obedience. False *acquiescentia*, arising from the first kind of cognition, involves heteronomous obedience, and is characterised by a failure of immanent obedience. We fail to follow the laws of our own nature when our idea of ourselves is determined by external causes. Because this idea is an inadequate self-image, mediated by the inconstant opinions of the multitude, the self we take satisfaction in is not really *our* self at all. At the same time, we disobey—that is to say, we refuse to accept—natural or divine necessity, insofar as we hold on to belief in free will. Our *acquiescentia in se ipso* does not live up to its name: it is not 'in itself', but subject to external influences.

Adequate or true *acquiescentia*, arising from the second and third kinds of knowledge, involves an obedience to oneself, which means actively following the laws of one's own nature. At the beginning of Part Three, Spinoza opposes action to passivity, and defines it in these terms: 'we act when something happens, in us or outside us, of which we are the adequate cause, i.e., when something in us or outside us follows from our nature' (E3D2). In Part Four, he links this definition of action with *ratio*, the second kind of knowledge: 'acting from reason is nothing but doing those things which follow from the necessity of our nature, considered in itself alone (by E3p2 and E3D2)' (E4p59d). So when Spinoza considers the *acquiescentia in se ipso* arising from reason, he reminds readers that 'man's true power of acting, or virtue, is reason itself, which man considers clearly and distinctly', explaining that 'while a man considers himself, he perceives nothing clearly and distinctly, *or* adequately, except those things which follow from his [own] power of understanding' (E4p52d and schol.) True *acquiescentia in se ipso* is how it feels to obey, or express, our nature 'considered in itself alone'.

Spinoza picks up this thread of argument in Part Five, referring back to E4p52 in stating that 'the highest satisfaction of mind [*summa animi acquiescentia*] stems from the right principle of living' (E5p10s). We should 'keep this in mind', he advises, together with the fact that 'men, like other things, act from the necessity of nature'. Whereas the 'fiction' of free will exacerbates the affects of love and hate, when our reason recognises how all beings follow 'the necessity of nature', this produces the peace of *acquiescentia in se ipso*. In the Appendix to Part Four, Spinoza recommends the calming effects of accepting necessity, even when we are subject to the vicissitudes of fortune:

> We do not have absolute power to adapt things outside us to our use. Nevertheless, we shall bear calmly [*æquo animo feremus*] those things which happen to us contrary to what the principle of our advantage demands, if we are conscious that... we are a part of the whole of nature, whose order we follow. If we understand this clearly and distinctly, that part of us which is defined by understanding, i.e., the better part of us, will be entirely satisfied [*plane acquiescet*] with this, and will strive to persevere in that satisfaction [*acquiescentia*]. For insofar as we understand, we can want nothing except what is necessary, nor absolutely be satisfied [*in veris acquiescere*] with anything except what is true. (E4App32)

This passage echoes remarks about calm acceptance of 'matters of fortune' at the end of Part Two, where Spinoza emphasises 'how much knowledge of [the will's necessity] is to our advantage in life'. There he explains that understanding necessity 'teaches us how we must bear ourselves concerning matters of fortune, or things which are not in our power, that is, concerning things which do not follow from our nature—that we must expect and bear calmly [*æquo animo exspectare, et ferre*] both good fortune and bad', adding that 'all things follow from God's eternal decree with the same eternal necessity as from the essence of a triangle it follows that its three angles are equal to two right angles' (E2p49s). On the one hand, *acquiescentia* of the second kind involves a familiar modern idea of autonomy— acting according to one's own nature and understanding—yet on the other hand it also involves recognising and accepting how much lies beyond our power.

In the passage from the Appendix to Part Four, the two semantic elements of *acquiescentia*—obedience and stillness—come together. Someone who obeys necessity is able to 'bear [it] calmly', and Spinoza connects this to an *acquiescentia* that 'wants nothing except what is necessary'; that is to say, nothing except what *is*. This suggests a kind of desire that rests in itself, rather than seeking something it feels is lacking. Spinoza has already outlined such a desire, in discussing love at the end of Part Three: there he explained that the 'will' (*voluntatem*) to join oneself to a beloved object consists in 'an *acquiescentia* in the lover on account of the presence of the thing loved, by which the lover's Joy is strengthened or at least encouraged' (E3Def.Aff.6). This 'will' rests content with what it has; because it does not want anything else, it can rest (or acquiesce) in the present moment.

While *acquiescentia* of the second kind involves an immanent obedience to the laws of one's own nature, the third and highest kind of *acquiescentia* sees these laws as divine laws, so that obedience to oneself becomes indistinguishable from obedience to God—and also, as we shall soon see, from resting in God. Obedience to the God of superstitious religion, mediated by a confused amalgamation of imagination and received opinion, must be a heteronomous submission: superstitious people surrender their own power of acting to a God imagined as external, and to an ecclesial authority which competes with their power, and diminishes it. *Acquiescentia* of the second kind reverses this weakening effect by making obedience immanent and autonomous. But it is in *acquiescentia* of the third kind, whereby one's dependence on God is the core truth grasped in intuitive knowledge, that the highest human freedom is found.[36] This is quite different from the usual Enlightenment concept of autonomy. It combines fidelity to one's own finite power with the understanding that this power both depends on, and expresses, an infinite power.[37]

Though Spinoza inherited the concept of *acquiescentia* from Descartes (or rather, from Desmarets's translation of Descartes), he made it his own by imbuing it with an undefined yet powerful notion of immanent obedience, thereby both criticising and replacing the Cartesian free will that he rejected as a 'fiction'. *Acquiescentia* indicates a freedom that is identical to necessity. Insofar as this is a 'human freedom'—as the title of Part Five of the *Ethics* indicates—it participates in divine freedom. 'God acts from the laws of his nature alone, and is compelled by no one', and 'God alone is a free cause, for God alone exists only from the necessity of his nature' (E1p17 and cor.2). Through our *acquiescentia* we can approximate, share in or imitate this freedom-in-necessity, 'being, by a certain eternal necessity, conscious of [ourselves], and of God, and of things'.

Immanent obedience concerns our implicit (or possibly explicit) metaphysical self-understanding: our sense of how our agency relates to the world. The other semantic elements of *acquiescentia*—stillness, peace, repose, joy, self-love—are more experiential, more affective. This is a question, to put it simply, of how a person feels about being herself. But it is also a question of how one's whole experience of being in the world is coloured: whether by anxiety and unease, or contentment and peace of mind.

So what do the three kinds of *acquiescentia in se ipso* feel like? We have already glimpsed the unsettled quality of *acquiescentia* based on imaginative thinking, in considering Spinoza's critique of the equivalent Cartesian passion, *la satisfaction de soi-même*. Indeed, when Spinoza introduces *acquiescentia in se ipso* and defines it for the first time, he connects it to imagination: 'If someone has done something which he imagines affects others with Joy, he will be affected by Joy accompanied by the idea of himself as cause, or he will regard himself with Joy' (E3p30). And when he defines it a second time, this time in conjunction with repentance, he emphasises that 'the things which [a person] believes will make for Joy or Sadness, and which he therefore strives to promote or prevent, are often only imaginary', and links this with the 'inconstancy' of human nature and judgement (E3p51s). It is here that he adds, 'Because men believe themselves free, these affects [of *acquiescentia in se ipso* and repentance] are very violent.'

Spinoza's discussion of the affects in Part Three of the *Ethics* emphasises their general instability. Summing up, he links the affects with 'vacillations of mind'—*affectus, animique fluctuationes*—and writes that 'from what has been said it is clear that we are driven about in many ways by external causes, and that, like waves on the sea, driven by contrary winds, we toss about, not knowing our outcome or our fate' (E3p59s). Early in Part Five, the affects are again associated with fluctuation or agitation: here Spinoza refers to *animi commotionem, seu affectum* and suggests that love and hate cause *animi fluctuationes* (see E5p2). With regard to *acquiescentia* (of the first kind) in particular, he identifies two related consequences of this instability: it makes people anxious within themselves, and troublesome to others.

The first kind of cognition encompasses 'opinion' as well as 'imagination' (see E2p40s), and Spinoza's discussion of *acquiescentia* makes it clear that 'opinion' means the opinions of other people. 'When the mind considers itself and its power of acting, it rejoices, and does so the more, the more distinctly it imagines itself and its power of acting,' writes Spinoza (E3p53), adding that 'this Joy is more and more encouraged the more a man imagines himself to be praised by others. For the more he imagines himself to be praised by others, the greater the Joy with which he imagines himself to affect others' (E3p53c). This *acquiescentia* is conditioned by the attitudes and opinions of society in general, and of our own circle of acquaintances in particular, which are often (though not necessarily) prejudices and superstitions. Because the affects of *acquiescentia* and *gloria*—translated by Curley as 'love of esteem'—are closely connected, our relationship to ourselves is intimately bound up with our relationships to others (see E4p52s). For this reason, the problems associated with imaginative *acquiescentia* are often compounded by social influences.

Spinoza hints at the anxiety-provoking character of *acquiescentia* in the scholium to E3p55, where we find his third definition of the affect—this time named 'self-love [*Philautia*] or *Acquiescentia in se ipso*'—as 'Joy arising from considering ourselves'. Because this joy 'is renewed as often as a man considers his virtues, or his power of acting, it also happens that everyone is anxious [*gestiat*] to tell his own deeds, and to show off his powers, both of body and of mind'. Spinoza adds here that human beings, 'for this reason, are very troublesome to one another' (*homines hac de causa sibi invicem molesti sint*) (E3p55s).

He amplifies this point when he returns to the subject of vain, empty *acquiescentia*, based on the first kind of cognition, in Part Four. Here opinion, rather than imagination, emerges as the distinctive feature of the self-understanding that gives rise to vain *acquiescentia*:

> The love of esteem [*Gloria*] which is called empty [*vana*] is *acquiescentia in se ipso* that is encouraged only by the opinion of the multitude. When that ceases, the *acquiescentia in se ipso* ceases, i.e. (by p52s), the highest good that each one loves. That is why he who exults at being esteemed by the multitude is made anxious daily, strives, sacrifices and schemes [*quotidiana cura anxius nitatur, faciat, experiatur*], in order to preserve his reputation. For the multitude is fickle and inconstant; unless one's reputation is guarded, it is quickly destroyed. (E4p58s)[38]

As well as making us anxious and envious, pursuing this 'vain' *acquiescentia* makes us aggressively competitive with other people. Indeed, those who succeed in gaining it may be the worst of all. In this struggle for *acquiescentia*, 'the one who at last emerges as victor exults more in having harmed the other than in having benefited himself'. Of course, this competitive spirit is deeply embedded in our culture, so often entrenched by educational, professional and political systems, even the most civilised. Too many examples present themselves; I often think of Spinoza's analysis of *acquiescentia* when an American university asks me to rank a tenure candidate in comparison with her peers—and I remember that Spinoza refused the offer of a professorship. There is a tragic irony here: it is because we long for contentment, yet fundamentally misunderstand it, that we are driven to behave in ways that produce the opposite effects. Spinoza emphasises that it is precisely because *acquiescentia* is the 'highest thing we can hope for', 'the highest good that each one loves', that the false *acquiescentia* arising from inadequate understanding has such destructive consequences: 'since this struggle is over a good thought to be the highest, this gives rise to a monstrous lust of each to crush the other in any way possible'. Here, then, Spinoza argues that the first kind of *acquiescentia* is as volatile as the opinions it rests upon, generating agitation within both individuals and communities. In other words, it not only fails to produce the *quies* that belongs to genuine *acquiescentia*, but actually encourages unrest. Not surprisingly, then, Spinoza concludes that 'this love of esteem, or *acquiescentia*, then, is really empty, because it is nothing [*Est igitur haec gloria, seu acquiescentia revera vana, quia nulla est*]' (E4p58s).

Right at the end of the *Ethics*, where he contrasts the 'wise person' with the 'ignorant person', Spinoza returns to this idea that someone who lacks adequate knowledge is restless, anxious, agitated, 'troubled in many ways [*multis modis agitatur*] by external causes, and unable ever to possess true peace of mind [*vera animi acquiescentia*]' (E5p42s). Our power of acting is limited, and we are all influenced by external things; Spinoza thinks it is impossible not to be (see E4p3 and E4p4). But being subject to forces beyond our control—so that we feel their effects within us—does not necessarily mean that we are 'driven about' and destabilised by them. The ignorant man described at the end of the *Ethics* is dominated by external causes: he is so entirely determined by them that they constitute his very existence, so that 'as soon as he ceases to be acted on, he ceases to be' (E5p42s).

This emphasis on the power of external causes might appear at odds with Spinoza's definition of *acquiescentia in se ipso*, which refers to the idea of an internal cause, or the idea of oneself as a cause. Yet even the 'empty' *acquiescentia* that depends on external factors, such as the approval of other people, involves an idea of oneself, of one's own agency— an idea which is itself subject to external causes. This is a 'mutilated' and 'confused' idea, in which our own power and activity, our assumptions— formed by customs and education—about the moral status of certain actions, the opinions and reactions of others, and our (perhaps mistaken) perception of those opinions and reactions are all mixed up together. This is certainly an inadequate self-image, produced by a combination of imagination and opinion, but it is still an idea of oneself, and thus of an internal cause.

In contrast to the emotional volatility that accompanies the first kind of knowledge, the feeling-quality of adequate understanding is much more even (*æquo*) and peaceful. The stillness experienced in *acquiescentia* of the second kind is a quality of stability and equanimity. When the mind thinks about 'those things which it perceives clearly and distinctly, and with which it is fully satisfied [*plane acquiescit*]', then not only are the affects of 'love, hate, etc.' destroyed (here Spinoza refers us back to his discussion of *animi commotiones* and *animi fluctuationes*), but also 'the appetites, *or* desires, which usually arise from such an affect, cannot be excessive' (E5p4s).[39] Spinoza is not here espousing the Stoic view that desire should be restrained or reduced by reason. After all, desire is our very essence, and whenever it is diminished this brings sadness. Rather, he is arguing that when desire is accompanied by understanding, there cannot be too much of it. 'A desire which arises from reason . . . is the very essence, *or* nature, of man', and it makes no sense to say that human nature 'could exceed itself, *or* could do more than it can' (E4p61 and dem.).

The essence of each being is its desire or striving, and adequate *acquiescentia* does not lessen or halt this striving, but stabilises it, making it more immanent and less restless. The quietude of adequate *acquiescentia* is active and self-expressive, not self-limiting, and certainly not repressive. Given our inherent sociability and interdependence, the internal stability of individuals whose *acquiescentia* comes from the second kind of knowledge will be conducive to political stability—and vice versa.[40] During a discussion of religious conflict in the *Theologico-Political Treatise*, Spinoza uses the verb *acquiescere* to signify agreement or concord between people: 'the common mentality of human beings is extremely variable, and not everyone is equally accepting of all things [*nec omnes in omnibus aeque acquiescere*]. Opinions govern people in different ways.'[41]

The mental stability of the second kind of *acquiescentia* has a bodily correlate in *hilaritas*, usually translated as 'cheerfulness': 'the affect of joy which is related to the mind and body at once' (E3p11s). Spinoza states that 'the idea of any thing that increases or diminishes, aids or restrains, our body's power of acting, increases or diminishes, aids or restrains, our mind's power of thinking' (E3p11). In contrast to pleasure (*titillatio*)—which is also a joy relating to both mind and body—cheerfulness affects all parts of the body equally. It is a condition of overall stability, equilibrium and well-being, just as genuine, rational *acquiescentia* involves intellectual stability, equanimity and contentedness. When the body is affected by cheerfulness, 'all its parts maintain the same proportion of motion and rest to one another'; cheerfulness 'is always good, and cannot be excessive'—since stability cannot be excessive (E4p42d). Spinoza reflects that this stable joy is, unfortunately, very rare, 'more easily conceived than observed' (E4p44s).⁴²

Scientia intuitiva, Spinoza's 'third kind of cognition', is a direct, immediate comprehension of God and of the way all things follow necessarily from God's nature. While reason grasps, by 'common notions', ideas and properties which a certain group of entities share, intuitive knowledge sees singular things.⁴³ Spinoza writes that 'the greatest satisfaction of mind [*mentis acquiescentia*] there can be arises from this third kind of knowledge' (E5p27). This *acquiescentia* is constituted by the consciousness of being-in-God, and is closely related to the intellectual love of God. In this affect, divine and human consciousness (and joy) come together. Spinoza gives this idea a biblical expression in the *Theologico-Political Treatise*, citing Paul's Letter to the Galatians on the 'fruits of the Holy Spirit' and suggesting that 'the Holy Spirit . . . is in truth simply the mental peace [*animi acquiescentiam*] that arises in the mind from good actions'.⁴⁴

The *acquiescentia* accompanying *scientia intuitiva* shares the qualities of stability, equanimity and obedience to one's own nature that distinguish *acquiescentia* of the second kind from its false counterpart. But—as we might expect, given the nature of the third kind of cognition—it differs from *acquiescentia* of the second kind in its connection to God. Having argued that 'the greatest virtue of the mind, that is, the mind's power, *or* nature, *or* its greatest striving, is to understand things by the third kind of knowledge', Spinoza explains that 'he who knows things by this kind of knowledge passes to the greatest human perfection, and consequently is affected with the greatest joy, accompanied by the idea of himself and his virtue. Therefore the greatest satisfaction [*acquiescentia*] there can be arises from this kind of knowledge' (E5p27d). In *scientia intuitiva*, the idea of oneself includes the idea of being-in-God: the mind 'knows that it is in God and is conceived through God' (E5p30). This means that *acquiescentia* of the third kind is a joy accompanied by the idea of God, as well as by the idea of oneself:

> Whatever we understand by the third kind of knowledge we take pleasure in [*eo delectamur*], and our pleasure is accompanied by the idea of God as cause.
>
> From this kind of knowledge there arises the greatest satisfaction of Mind [*summa . . . Mentis acquiescentia*] there can be (by p27), i.e.

(by Def.Aff.25), Joy; this Joy is accompanied by the idea of oneself, and consequently (by p30) it is also accompanied by the idea of God, as its cause, q.e.d. (E5p32 and dem.)

Spinoza introduces the intellectual love of God in the corollary to this proposition: 'from this kind of knowledge there arises Joy, accompanied by the idea of God as its cause, i.e., love of God, not insofar as we imagine him as present, but insofar as we understand God to be eternal. And this is what I call intellectual love of God' (E5p32c).

In Part Three of the *Ethics*, the affects of *acquiescentia* and love are distinguished insofar as the former is a joy accompanied by the idea of an internal cause (i.e., the idea of oneself), while the latter is a joy accompanied by the idea of an external cause (i.e., the idea of something or someone else). But the demonstration of E5p32 suggests that in the third kind of cognition this distinction between internal and external causes is unsettled. In place of two distinct ideas—an idea of oneself, and an idea of God—intuitive knowledge offers a single idea of oneself as 'in' God, or (to put it another way) of God's nature as containing and expressing *this* singular existing being. This idea is an immediate awareness of being-in-God. Thus Spinoza explains that

> the mind's intellectual love of God is the very love of God by which God loves himself. . . . It is an action by which the mind contemplates itself, with the accompanying idea of God as its cause (by P32 and P32C), that is, an action by which God, insofar as he can be explained through the human mind, contemplates himself. . . . Whether this love is related to God or to the mind, it can rightly be called satisfaction of mind [*animi acquiescentia*], which is not really distinguished from Glory. For insofar as it is related to God, it is joy (if I may still be permitted to use this term), accompanied by the idea of himself [as its cause]. And similarly insofar as it is related to the mind. (E5p36d and schol.)[45]

Although the intellectual love of God can be distinguished conceptually from *acquiescentia* of the third kind, phenomenologically they are inseparable. Both are a joy arising from the idea of one's being-in-God—in other words, a joyful awareness of being-in-God.

We have seen that the stillness belonging to *acquiescentia* of the second kind is not stasis, but stability, which contrasts with the instability accompanying the first kind of knowledge; it is an equanimity of mind, mirrored by equilibrium in the body (*hilaritas*). This stability is a prerequisite for gaining the third kind of knowledge, and enjoying all that arises from it. While *acquiescentia* of the second kind involves stability over time, or duration, *acquiescentia* of the third kind involves the stillness of eternity. As Spinoza writes at the very end of the *Ethics*, the wise person 'is hardly troubled in spirit [*vix animo movetur*], but being, by a certain eternal necessity, conscious [*conscius*] of himself, and of God, and of things, he never ceases to be, but always possesses true peace of mind [*sed semper vera animi acquiescentia*]' (E5p42s). 'Never ceasing to be' and 'always possessing true peace of mind' are presented here as two aspects or two descriptions of the same condition. Spinoza's closing remarks reinforce his suggestion that *acquiescentia* of the third kind is linked to what 'remains' of the mind after the body perishes: 'because the highest *acquiescentia* there can be arises from the third kind of knowledge, it follows from this that the mind can be of such a nature that the part of the mind which we have shown perishes with the body is of no moment in relation to what remains' (E5p38s). The peace and stillness that characterise *acquiescentia* of the third kind is the feeling of eternity.[46]

The three kinds of *acquiescentia* thus express three different qualities of thinking: the unsettled, confused, anxious thinking of imagination and opinion; the stable, ordered thinking of reason; and the intuitive thinking that understands things immediately, as they are in God, *sub specie aeternitatis*. While the second kind of cognition consists in a process of reasoning that traces, step by step, the logical connections between ideas and the causal connections between things, intuitive thinking is not a process at all: it grasps the truth immediately.[47] Yet *acquiescentia* of the third kind is not merely an absence of emotional disturbance. While it brings deep rest and peace, it also expresses the highest degree of activity and striving. Spinoza states that 'the greatest virtue of the mind, that is, the mind's power, *or* nature, *or* its greatest striving, is to understand things by the third kind of knowledge' (E5p25d); and just two propositions later he asserts that 'the greatest *acquiescentia* there can be arises from this kind of knowledge' (E5p27). He seems to acknowledge that the very notion of affect, involving movement and transition, becomes problematic in the third kind of cognition: there is inevitably an element of 'feigning' in speaking of an eternal joy, and of the 'passage' to the third kind of *acquiescentia*.[48]

As a joy accompanied by the idea of oneself, *acquiescentia* signifies the feeling-quality of our relation to ourselves, our sense of our own power and agency. We have seen that this affect can be true or false, authentic or inauthentic, depending on whether it arises from adequate or inadequate self-understanding. In moving from the first to the third kind of *acquiescentia* we see an increase in stillness or repose, *quies*, that is also, crucially, an increase in activity or power, involving a distinctively Spinozist conception of immanent obedience. Inadequate *acquiescentia* falls short of all these criteria, while adequate *acquiescentia* fulfils them.

Tracing the correlation between *acquiescentia* and the three kinds of cognition brings into view the threefold structure of Spinoza's account of *acquiescentia*. Corresponding to the three kinds of cognition—

(1) imagination   **(2) reason**   **(3) intuition**

—are three kinds of relation, according to the criterion of obedience:

(1) heteronomy   **(2) autonomy**   **(3) being-in-God**

—and three kinds of experience, according to the criterion of stillness:

(1) agitation   **(2) stability**   **(3) rest**

—and three psychological states:

(1) anxiety   **(2) equanimity**   **(3) peace**

One of Spinoza's seventeenth-century critics, Pierre Poiret—a disciple of the visionary mystic Antoinette Bourignon—described *acquiescentia in se ipso* as 'the head and root of all vices, and true atheism'.[49] His critique assumed that, in proposing *acquiescentia in se ipso* as our highest good, Spinoza was replacing the Christian virtues of humility and repentance with the sin of pride. Our threefold analysis of this affect exposes the error of Poiret's view. The *acquiescentia in se ipso* that is distinguished from humility and repentance is *acquiescentia* of the first kind. This *acquiescentia* belongs, together with these two affects, within the domain of the imagination—the basis of superstitious religion—and Spinoza argues that all three affects are equally volatile, confused and debilitated.

Rather than simply inverting the traditional Christian schema of virtue and vice, which opposed humble obedience to prideful self-assertion, Spinoza showed why this whole moral schema rests on misunderstanding. Poiret's critique was itself rooted in cognition of the first kind: it was a symptom of the superstition that Spinoza was challenging. The account of adequate *acquiescentia* developed through Parts Four and Five of the *Ethics* lies at the heart of this challenge. In fact, the highest kind of *acquiescentia* is very far from hubristic, and is absolutely opposed to atheism.[50] It involves an obedience based on consciousness of being-in-God, and yields a certain kind of humility—although Spinoza does not give it this name—since it is a consciousness of ontological dependence on God.[51] And far from being a sign of weakness or smallness, this humility is a feeling of the highest degree of power or activity that a human being can express, by virtue of 'participation in the divine nature' (E4p45s).

According to the popular religious imagination, joy, peace and rest were a heavenly reward for obedience to the extrinsic will of God—meditated in Catholicism by obedience to the teachings of the Church, and in Protestantism by obedience to the commands written in the Bible. For Spinoza, blessedness is not the reward of virtue: it is virtue itself. Immanent obedience and self-contentment are one and the same thing: *acquiescentia in se ipso*, a single affect in which cognition—ideas about oneself and one's relation to God—is thoroughly blended with feeling. Of course we may distinguish them conceptually—as I am doing here—as two elements or aspects of *acquiescentia in se ipso*, but this is only to explain why they are inseparable.

Acquiescentia in se ipso is a polyvalent concept, and in the *Ethics* Spinoza defines it more than once. So our analysis of this affect is, inevitably, complex. Yet the thing itself is very simple. Do we feel anxious or contented? Are we agitated or at peace? Spinoza offers this feeling of being ourselves as a guide to the depth of our self-understanding, the adequacy of our metaphysics and our theology, the truth of our religion.

CHAPTER SEVEN

How to Love God

IN CHAPTER 4 of the *Theologico-Political Treatise*, entitled 'On Divine Law', Spinoza asserts that the highest human good is 'to know God and to love him'. Attaining this good is, he explains, our 'true liberty':

> A man is more perfect in proportion to the nature and perfection of the thing which he loves before all others. Therefore, the man who is necessarily the most perfect and who participates more in supreme blessedness is the one who loves above all else the intellectual knowledge of God, the most perfect being, and takes the greatest pleasure in this knowledge. Our supreme good, then, and our blessedness come back to this: the knowledge and love of God....
>
> Since, then, the love of God is man's highest happiness and blessedness, and the ultimate end [*finis ultimus*] and object of all human actions, the only one who follows the divine law is the one who devotes himself to loving God [*qui Deum amare curat*], not from fear of punishment, nor from love of another thing, such as pleasures or reputation, etc., but only because he knows [that] the knowledge and love of God is the highest good.... This good consists only in contemplation and in a pure mind [*in sola speculatione et pura mente consistit*].[1]

In the *Ethics* Spinoza offers a fuller and more philosophical account of this religious ideal, bringing to full maturity a view he had expressed in his earliest works. The short passages on *amor Dei intellectualis*—the intellectual love of God—late in Part Five mark the culmination of Spinoza's many years of labour in pursuit and contemplation of this 'highest good'.

Spinoza's doctrine of divine love is summarised in the claim that 'our salvation, or blessedness, or freedom, consists ... in a constant and eternal love of God, or [*sive*] in God's love for human beings' (E5p36s). His phrasing here indicates that *amor Dei intellectualis* involves both our love for God, and God's love for us. This suggestion of reciprocity could be misleading, had he not already taken pains to correct an anthropomorphic image of divine love. 'Strictly speaking God loves no one and hates no one,' he insisted a few propositions earlier. Love and hate are species of joy and sadness respectively, defined as transitions to greater or lesser perfection—and God, being immutable, is 'without passions, and is not affected by any affect of Joy or Sadness' (E5p17 and cor.; E1p20c2). Therefore, 'he who loves God cannot strive that God should love him in return' (E5p19).

Spinoza offers these remarks just before the turning-point of Part Five, where he declares that 'we have now concluded everything that concerns this present life'. This transition signals a shift in perspective, and his account of *amor Dei intellectualis* begins on the far side of it. The scholium to E5p36 suggests that it is appropriate to speak of a mutual love relationship between ourselves and God only if this is conceived not in terms of reciprocity, but in terms of identity. Of course, this must be a kind of identity that does not compromise the ontological difference marked by Spinoza's distinction between substance and its modes: a difference that consists, at the very least, in an asymmetrical relation of dependence. In linking our love for God to God's love for us with the word *sive*, the inclusive Latin 'or', Spinoza indicates that this is one love, conceived in two different ways: 'a constant and eternal love of God, or [*sive*] . . . God's love for men'.

Spinoza was developing his distinctive view of divine love at least since the early 1660s, when he wrote his *Short Treatise on God, Man and His Well-Being*. There he argues that if God loved us in return for our devotion, this would 'produce a great mutability in God. Where previously God had neither loved nor hated, he would now begin to love and to hate, and would be caused to do this by something that would be outside him.'[2] Ordinary human love is responsive, preferential, and mutable: it arises and passes away, waxes and wanes, and depends at least to some extent on the activity or condition of its object. In the *Cogitata Metaphysica* appended to his 1663 guide to Descartes's *Principles of Philosophy*, Spinoza contended that 'God is improperly said to hate things, and love others . . . God does not love things in the way in which ordinary people persuade themselves he does.'[3] As Warren Zev Harvey has shown, Spinoza knew how these theological questions had been addressed by the medieval Jewish philosophers Maimonides (who refused to attribute passionate love, ḥesheq, to God) and Gersonides (who argued that God 'passionately loves' the world).[4]

Spinoza's remarks in these early texts suggest that while God's love is not like human love, there may be a way or a sense in which God *does* 'love things'. And while he thought it incoherent to imagine God to be mutable, subject to external causes and susceptible to desires and preferences, he did not understand God to be remote or abstract.[5] On the contrary, the *Short Treatise* invokes the ontological principle of being-in-God to explain that the intimacy between God and human beings is too close to admit a conventional notion of love:

> When we say, however, that God does not love man, that must not be understood as if he left man, as it were, to proceed on his own; rather, that because man, together with all there is, is so in God, and God so consists of all of these, there cannot be in him any real love toward something else, since everything consists in one unique thing which is God himself.[6]

In this first, unfinished attempt to elaborate his philosophy, Spinoza conceived both love and knowledge as a kind of union or unity, and this led him to formulate a religious ideal of 'union with God.' Love, he explains in the *Short Treatise*, means 'enjoying a thing and being united with it', and 'the most perfect man is the one who unites with the most perfect being', who is God.[7]

This union is achieved through the highest kind of knowledge, which is

> an immediate manifestation of the object itself to the intellect. And if the object is magnificent and good, the soul necessarily becomes united with it . . . this knowledge is what produces love; so if we come to know God in this way, then we must necessarily unite with God . . . our blessedness consists only in this union with God.[8]

In the *Ethics*, this highest knowledge is defined as *scientia intuitiva*. Here Spinoza no longer speaks of a union with God, though of course he retains (and consolidates) his grounding principle of being-in-God. Perhaps he came to regard the idea of union with God as, ironically, too dualistic, since suggesting that there are two separate things which come into union or unity actually betrays the principle of being-in-God. In the *Ethics* he no longer defines love as 'enjoying a thing and being united with it', but as 'joy'—that is, a person's feeling of an increase in her desire and power—'accompanied by the idea of an external cause' of this joy (E3p13s, E3Def. Aff.6). However, this definition of love poses further problems when it is applied to God. It introduces mutability or fluctuation into the very concept of love, and specifies the beloved object as an 'external cause', which—more directly and more obviously than the notion of union with God—threatens the principle of being-in-God.

In the *Ethics*, then, Spinoza must confront these challenges, for he not only repeats his earlier critiques of anthropomorphic ideas of divine love, but also seeks a positive account of *amor Dei intellectualis* that encompasses, in a single affect, both our love for God and God's love for us. This love, he argues, belongs to 'the greatest human perfection'; it is 'the greatest joy' and 'the greatest satisfaction [*acquiescentia*] there can be' (see E5p27, E5p32).

By the time Spinoza introduces *amor Dei intellectualis* in *Ethics* V, he has already explicated its three components: God, knowledge (for *intellectualis* signifies a certain kind of knowing or understanding) and love. These three components are condensed within his concept of *amor Dei intellectualis*, and we must consider each of them in order to understand the nature of divine love, and how human beings may come to share in it.

Spinoza's theology has been explored in the third and fifth chapters in this book, so we need only review it briefly here. Part One of the *Ethics* argues that God is neither an anthropomorphic, personal deity, nor a remote abstraction. God is the eternal, self-causing, unique substance; God is absolutely infinite, expressing infinite power in infinitely many ways (i.e., through infinite attributes); God is reducible to nothing else, not even the whole universe. This is the God in which all things exist, the source of all beings—'not only the cause of things' beginning to exist, but also of their persevering in existing. . . . the cause of the being of things' (E1p24c). From Part Two onwards, Spinoza's focus narrows to human beings, and to the two divine attributes—thinking and extension—through which we exist and know everything we conceive and encounter, including ourselves. Although our being-in-God is an ontological fact which we share with all things, 'participation in the divine nature' becomes a normative ethical principle within human life: 'the greater the joy with which we are affected, the greater the perfection to which we pass, that is, the more we participate in the divine nature' (E4p45s). In Part Five, Spinoza asserts that human freedom, or blessedness, consists in living according to the principle of being-in-God. This means expressing the truth of our ontological constitution, as individual beings-in-God, by actively knowing it and resting at peace in it.

We may clarify the nature of this knowing—the second component of *amor Dei intellectualis*—by returning to Spinoza's distinction, in Part Two of the *Ethics*, between three kinds of cognition, or kinds of thinking. The first is 'opinion or imagination'; the second is reason (*ratio*); and the third is intuitive knowing (*scientia intuitiva*). To recall: these are different qualities of thinking, or states of mind: the first is characterised by fluctuation and, often, agitation; the second is a stable, orderly process; the third shares in the stillness of eternity. The first kind of cognition is inadequate, or false, and the second and third kinds are adequate, or true. Reason, the second kind of cognition, grasps the common properties of things, tracing logical connections between ideas and causal connections between bodies. Intuition, the third kind of cognition, involves insight into being-in-God: it conceives things truly 'under a species of eternity', for it is a simple, direct, immediate comprehension of the way singular things 'are contained in God and follow from the necessity of the divine nature' (E5p29s). Through *scientia intuitiva*, we know singular things—including ourselves, and other human beings—in their being-in-God. 'Insofar as our mind knows itself and the body under a species of eternity,' explains Spinoza, 'it necessarily has knowledge of God and knows that it is in God' (E5p30).[9] His epistemological distinction between rational and intuitive knowing is closely linked to his metaphysical distinction between duration and eternity, and to his phenomenological distinction between fluctuation and *quies*: stillness, contentment, rest.

Love, the third component of *amor Dei intellectualis*, is defined in Part Three of the *Ethics* as joy, accompanied by the idea of the cause of that joy. Joy is pure affect, since it is simply the feeling of an increase in power, but love always has a cognitive element, since it involves the idea of a cause. Conversely, we may equally say that love always follows from true knowledge, because knowing is an activity that increases our power. Love, for Spinoza, 'proceeds from true knowledge as necessarily as light does from the sun'.[10]

Because Spinoza understands love to be an inherently cognitive affect, his threefold account of cognition generates a threefold taxonomy of love. An emotion of joy may be incorrectly attributed to a cause that is merely imagined (either because the object itself is imaginary, or because its causal link to the affect is imaginary); it may be correctly attributed to a cause that is rationally understood; or it may be correctly attributed to a cause that is intuitively known. Joy shares in the quality of the cognition it is based upon: it may be vacillating, and thus fragile and fickle; it may be stable and well-grounded; it may be deeply peaceful, manifesting the immutability of eternity. *Amor Dei intellectualis* belongs to this third category: it arises from *scientia intuitiva*, consists in 'Joy, accompanied by the idea of God as its cause' (E5p32c), and is 'eternal' (E5p33).

Spinoza's definition of love also admits a distinction between external and internal objects of love. We love things, or animals, or other people, when we know (or imagine) them to cause our joy, and we love ourselves when we know (or imagine) our own power and actions to be the cause of our joy. *Amor Dei intellectualis* is a love of God considered less as an external cause than as an internal or immanent cause. Like the *Theologico-Political Treatise*, the *Ethics* advances a robust critique of the doctrine of divine love that imagines God as a heteronomous cause outside the world, external to and indeed far beyond each individual. According to this anthropomorphic theology, the relational dynamic between ourselves and God is often imagined to be like that between an uncomprehending child, who is anxious for approval and fearful of punishment, and her remote, forbidding, inscrutable father. In place of this superstitious doctrine, which he consigns to the imagination—the 'first kind' of cognition that yields error and confusion—Spinoza outlines a non-dualist account of true blessedness in which love for God entails the recognition that we are in God, and that God's power is inseparable from our own power of acting and existing. Just as Spinoza's God does not intervene in nature, so God does not compete with or disrupt human agency. On the contrary, God facilitates all our activity: when we express ourselves, we express something divine—and when we understand this and do not try to resist it, our power is enhanced. This means recognising our ontological dependence, which involves overcoming misguided views of ourselves as substances, and as possessing free will.

As a form of love related to an internal cause, Spinoza's conception of *amor Dei intellectualis* emerges from his account of self-love, defined as 'joy arising from considering ourselves' (E3p55s), or 'joy accompanied by the idea of an internal cause' (E3p30s).[11] Self-love is a species of *amor*, yet named as a distinct affect, '*philautia* or *acquiescentia in se ipso*' (E3p55s). As we saw in the last chapter, *acquiescentia in se ipso* always rests on a certain kind of self-understanding. This might be a deluded, inadequate self-image formed by imagination or opinion (or some combination of these two); or a self-understanding based on reason; or a self-understanding arising from intuitive knowledge.

Spinoza introduces his concept of *amor Dei intellectualis* in the corollary to a demonstration concerning this 'third kind' of *acquiescentia*:

> E5p32: Whatever we understand by the third kind of knowledge we take pleasure in [*eo delectamur*], and our pleasure is accompanied by the idea of God as cause.
>
> Dem.: From this kind of knowledge there arises the greatest satisfaction of Mind [*Mentis acquiescentia*] there can be (by P27), that is

(by Def. Aff. 15 [i.e., Spinoza's definition of *acquiescentia in se ipso*]), Joy; this Joy is accompanied by the idea of oneself, and consequently (by P30) it is also accompanied by the idea of God, as its cause, q.e.d.

Cor.: From the third kind of knowledge there necessarily arises an intellectual love of God. For from this kind of knowledge there arises (by P32) joy, accompanied by the idea of God as its cause, that is (by Def. Aff. 6 [i.e. Spinoza's definition of love]), love of God, not insofar as we imagine him as present (by P29), but insofar as we understand God to be eternal. And this is what I call intellectual love of God.

As Spinoza's demonstration indicates, the crucial link in his reasoning from *scientia intuitiva* to *amor Dei intellectualis* is E5p30, which states that 'insofar as our mind knows itself and the body under a species of eternity, it necessarily has knowledge of God, and knows that it is in God'. This form of knowing not only understands, in a rational way, the principle of being-in-God—the general fact that 'whatever is, is in God'—but also has an immediate insight into singular things *as* 'contained in God' (E5p29s). More precisely, in *scientia intuitiva* a person knows *herself* to be in God: she has an intuitive grasp of her own being-in-God. The highest kind of self-knowledge includes an intimate knowledge of God, and the highest kind of self-love includes love of God.

Spinoza thus introduces his concept of *amor Dei intellectualis* by suggesting that, in the third kind of knowing, *acquiescentia in se ipso* becomes indistinguishable from love of God. In Part Three, where the affects are considered primarily as they arise from the first kind of cognition, as confused and mutable passions, *acquiescentia* and *amor* are distinct insofar as *acquiescentia in se ipso* is a joy accompanied by the idea of an internal cause (that is, the idea of oneself), while *amor* is a joy accompanied by the idea of an external cause (that is, the idea of something or someone else). However, the demonstration of E5p32 suggests that in *scientia intuitiva* this distinction between internal and external causes is dissolved. In place of two distinct ideas—an idea of oneself, and an idea of God—intuitive knowing offers a single insight into oneself as 'in' God. To put it another way, one knows God's nature as containing and expressing *this* singular existing being. This insight is an immediate awareness of being-in-God.

In an important paper on *amor Dei intellectualis*, Yitzhak Melamed asks how Spinoza's concept of love, which involves the idea of an external cause, can be applied to God, who neither has an external cause, nor is an external cause of anything else. Recognising that the love of God seems closer to the affect of *acquiescentia in se ipso*, Melamed suggests that in

Part Five of the *Ethics*, Spinoza 'attaches the additional title of "intellectual love"' to this affect, and wonders why he does so. We can respond to this question by showing how the affects of *acquiescentia* and love that are clearly distinct in Part Three converge to a single point in Part Five, when they are related to the third kind of cognition. Here, the idea of external causation is absorbed or dissolved into the singular truth of being-in-God, so that *acquiescentia* of the third kind and *amor Dei intellectualis* are two aspects of the same affect.[12] Although the intellectual love of God can be distinguished conceptually from *acquiescentia* of the third kind, phenomenologically they are inseparable. Both are a joy arising from the idea of one's being-in-God, or, in other words, a joyful awareness of being-in-God.

As he continues his discussion of *amor Dei*, Spinoza pushes this point further, first by attributing the affect of self-love to God, and then by assimilating this divine self-love to human self-love. He asserts that 'God loves himself with an infinite intellectual love' (E5p35), before arguing that 'the mind's intellectual love of God is the very love of God by which God loves himself' (E5p36). God does not love 'things'—including ourselves— as distinct objects: 'From this it follows that insofar as God loves himself, he loves men, and consequently that God's love of men and the mind's intellectual love of God are one and the same' (E5p36c). Reaching for a way to express this identity, Spinoza describes *amor Dei intellectualis* as 'an action by which the mind contemplates itself, with the accompanying idea of God as its cause, that is, an action by which God, insofar as he can be explained through the human mind, contemplates himself' (E5p36d). He concludes that 'Whether this love is related to God or to the mind, it can rightly be called satisfaction of mind [*animi acquiescentia*]' (E5p36s). This meeting-point, or coincidence, of divine and human love can also, Spinoza adds, be called 'Glory', which signifies our joyful consciousness of God's love for us, and God's joyful consciousness of our love for God. Again, this deep mutuality is really an identity: the joy of *gloria* is, like the human and divine love that grounds it, 'one and the same'. Unusually in the *Ethics*, Spinoza appeals explicitly to 'the sacred scriptures' here, leaving scholars to trace possible source texts for his remarks about *gloria*—or *kavod*, in Hebrew.[13]

Though he has defined love in terms of joy, Spinoza now signals that it is questionable to use the concept of joy when writing of divine love. Insofar as love 'is related to God', he writes, 'it is Joy (if I may still be permitted to use this term), accompanied by the idea of himself' (E5p36s). If joy is the idea, or the consciousness, of an increase in power, then the corresponding divine affect would be consciousness of God's plenitude of power. This affect (though again, we might ask whether it is appropriate to apply this concept to God) is both like and unlike joy, which is why Spinoza uses the word while calling it into question. The translation of *animi acquiescentia* as 'satisfaction of mind' is quite felicitous here, for satisfaction denotes fullness. On the one hand, this contrasts with a process of increase, yet on the other hand, it is the *telos*, the resting-place, of such a process.

In this proposition, which marks the culmination of his discussion of *amor Dei intellectualis*, Spinoza achieves a realisation of the non-duality which has, in fact, constituted his philosophy from the beginning—as expressed in E1p15, 'Whatever is, is in God.' While affirming this non-duality, he is careful to preserve the asymmetry between God and finite individuals, which follows from the fact that God is at once transcendent and immanent, ontologically different from all finite things as well as intimately present to them. God's self-love is identical to the individual's intellectual love of God 'not insofar as [God] is infinite, but insofar as God can be explained by the human mind's essence, considered under a species of eternity; that is, the mind's intellectual love of God is part of the infinite love by which God loves himself' (E5p36).[14] In his scholium Spinoza moves from asserting the identity of our love for God and God's love for us to emphasising the dependence of human beings on God. Again, this dependence indicates the ontological asymmetry at the heart of Spinoza's theology. 'Because the essence of our mind consists only in knowledge, of which God is the beginning and foundation,'—and here Spinoza makes his eighteenth and final reference to E1p15—'it is clear to us how our mind, with respect both to essence and existence, follows from the divine nature, and continually depends on God' (E5p36s).

In the *Ethics* Spinoza defines religion as 'whatever we desire and do of which we are the cause insofar as . . . we know God' (E4p37s1). He could have added affectivity to this definition—'whatever we desire and do *and feel* insofar as we know God'—since the affects are central to his discussion of religion. Spinoza thought that both the Dutch Reformed Church and the Roman Catholic Church promoted a superstitious popular religion characterised by passive affects, many of them species of sadness (the feeling of diminishing desire and power), bound up with confused ideas about God and human beings. To these superstitious affects he opposes the active affects of joy and peace arising from a true understanding of our participation in God's nature; he shows how our affects vary depending on the kind of cognition, and particularly the kind of self-understanding, in which they are grounded. His account of *acquiescentia in se ipso*, for example, identifies a single affect of self-love that encompasses the worst vices and the highest virtues—from grotesque, destructive pride to beatific divine love. This is why knowledge of God—which is excluded from the first kind of cognition, and belongs only to *ratio* and *scientia intuitiva*—provides one criterion for distinguishing true religion from superstition.

Yet Spinoza criticised superstitious religion not simply because it was grounded on ignorance, but also for its pernicious consequences: it diminished the power of those who believed and practised it, disrupted order and prevented peace. He witnessed directly how the seventeenth-century churches fuelled anxiety, conflict and violence. Affects based on a confused understanding perpetuate instability; the opinions of 'the multitude' are always 'fickle and inconstant' (E4p58s). In a specifically religious context, the passions of hope and fear—which were encouraged by Christian doctrines of an afterlife, comprising either eternal happiness or eternal damnation—are inherently 'inconstant' and destabilising.[15] These fluctuating affects, including the self-love that is based on a confused self-image, make people aggressively competitive and 'very troublesome to one another' (E3p55s).[16] Spinoza perceived that self-aggrandisement and self-diminishment were two manifestations of the same underlying condition.

The enlightened love in which, through the third kind of knowledge, human self-love becomes inseparable from divine self-love, is nothing like the vacillating, egotistical passion that Spinoza criticises so forcefully. Someone who attains *scientia intuitiva* knows that her own power is not in competition with the power of others, nor with the power of God: she understands herself and others as beings-in-God, and thus as channels for the expression of divine power. Indeed, this understanding gives rise to a certain kind of humility. Spinoza urges his readers to a recognition of finitude and dependence which is very different from the species of sadness that he identifies as *humilitas*. This recognition is, in fact, empowering: 'if we suppose that [a] man conceives his lack of power because he understands something more powerful than himself, by the knowledge of which he determines his own power of acting, then we conceive nothing but that the man understands himself distinctly or [*sive*] that his power of acting is aided' (E4p53d).

Spinoza's discussion of *amor Dei intellectualis* accentuates the empowering character of true religion. Having argued that this divine love constitutes our 'salvation, *or* blessedness, *or* freedom', and having emphasised that the mind, like all things, depends on God, he explains that 'I thought this worth the trouble of noting here, in order to show how much the knowledge of singular things I have called intuitive, *or* knowledge of the third kind, can accomplish, and how much more powerful it is than the universal knowledge I have called knowledge of the second kind' (E5p36s). This reflection on the difference between *ratio* and *scientia intuitiva* throws light on Spinozistic religion, not least because it indicates that it really is religious—a way of life involving ethical conduct, inward virtue and the cultivation of transformative affects.

Though true understanding and active, joyful affects may arise from *ratio*, the joy and peace belonging to *scientia intuitiva* are deeper and longer lasting, even eternal. The 'wise person' (*sapiens*), who grasps the being-in-God of all things, is still subject to the fluctuations of embodied existence, under the attribute of extension, but his consciousness, while registering these bodily changes, does not itself fluctuate; he 'is hardly troubled in spirit; but being, by a certain eternal necessity, conscious of himself, and of God, and of things, he never ceases to be, but always possesses true peace of mind [*vera animi acquiescentia*]' (E5p42s). It is clear, writes Spinoza, 'how much [this] wise person is capable of, and how much more powerful he is than one who is ignorant'. He also indicates that this *sapiens* is more empowered than a merely rational person. Though in Part One of the *Ethics* he demonstrated 'legitimately and beyond all chance of doubt' that 'all things (and consequently the human mind also) depend on God both for their essence and their existence', he admits that this rational demonstration 'still does not affect the mind as much as when this is inferred from the very essence of any singular thing [i.e., known by intuition] which we say depends on God' (E5p36s). The 'power' of the third kind of knowledge consists in the way it produces affects—and these particular affects are themselves especially empowering.

Love has a particularly important place within Spinoza's account of the affects, and also, therefore, within his religion. Augustine taught that misdirected love—which pursues finite things instead of God—is the deepest human error, and likewise Spinoza argued that loving the wrong things, or loving things in the wrong way, is a particularly damaging affective state.[17] Conversely, a love that is constant and grounded in truth secures eternal happiness, peace, liberation. Before he turns to consider eternal life in the final twenty-two propositions of the *Ethics*, Spinoza concludes his analysis of 'everything that concerns this present life' by noting that

> sickness of the mind and misfortunes take their origin especially from too much love toward a thing that is liable to many variations and which we can never fully possess. For no one is disturbed or anxious concerning anything unless he loves it, nor do wrongs, suspicions, and enmities arise except from love for a thing which no one can really fully possess. (E5p20s)

By contrast, 'clear and distinct knowledge—and especially that third kind of knowledge, whose foundation is the knowledge of God itself' transforms the mind by producing 'love toward a thing immutable and eternal' (E5p20s). Here Spinoza references recent propositions indicating that this love is a fusion of love of God and *acquiescentia in se ipso*, and he then goes on to define this fusion as *amor Dei intellectualis*.

Scientia intuitiva 'begets a love toward a thing immutable and eternal, which we really fully possess, and which therefore cannot be tainted by any of the vices which are in ordinary love, but can always be greater and greater, and occupy the greatest part of the mind, and affect it extensively' (E5p20s).[18] At this point Spinoza refers the reader all the way back to E2p45 for an explanation of how we 'really fully possess' the eternal and immutable 'thing' that becomes the object of our love. This proposition concerns the being-in-God of singular things:

> E2p45: Every idea of a body, or of an individual thing actually existing, necessarily involves the eternal and infinite essence of God.
>
> Schol.: By existence I do not here understand duration, i.e., existence conceived abstractly and as a certain form of quantity. I speak of the very nature of existence, which belongs to individual things because there follows from the eternal necessity of the nature of God an infinity of modes themselves infinitely modified. I speak, I say, of the existence of individual things so far as they are in God.

The idea of any singular thing 'must involve an eternal and infinite essence of God' (E2p45d). Its being-in-God is not a fluctuating, durational existence, but a participation in divine nature.

Since *amor Dei intellectualis* is a species of self-love—the merging of human and divine self-love—it might seem to be a solitary experience of mystical union that excludes other people. On the contrary: we love others most purely, actively and productively when we understand and respect them in their eternal aspect, 'insofar as they are in God'. Here again, Spinoza's philosophy, while it refutes some of the dichotomies of post-Reformation theology, has affinities with an older Christian tradition. His account of religious love has a deeply communal dimension, and he reiterates Thomas Aquinas's view that self-love is the basis of love for other people, just as it can provide a starting-point for loving God.[19] The *acquiescentia in se ipso* arising from true knowledge of the self's being-in-God not only overcomes the agonistic, competitive, anti-social tendencies of affects based on the first kind of cognition, but also, more positively, opens up a new way of relating to others in *their* being-in-God. As Spinoza asserts in E1p15, being-in-God is something we share with all beings; and, as he suggests in the scholium to E4p35, we share it most fully with human beings whose understanding and ethical conduct align with and express (or, in other words, obey) their ontological constitution. The more truly we understand ourselves and others, the less competitive and the more cooperative we become. 'The greatest good of those who seek virtue is common to all, and can be enjoyed by all equally,' explains Spinoza. Moreover 'the good which everyone who seeks virtue wants for himself, he also desires for other men; and this desire is greater as his knowledge of God is greater' (E4p36, E4p37).

Amplifying this moral generosity further—and echoing Jesus's exhortation to 'love your enemies, do good to those who hate you' (Luke 6:27; Matt. 5:44)—Spinoza argues that 'he who lives according to the guidance of reason strives as far as he can to compensate the hatred, anger, contempt, etc. of others towards him with love or generosity' (E4p46). These ethical teachings culminate in the last proposition of Part Four, and its scholium:

> E4p73: A man who is guided by reason is more free in a society, where he lives according to a common decree, than in solitude, where he complies only with himself. . . .
>
> Schol.: These and similar things which we have shown concerning the true freedom of man are related to strength of character [*ad fortitudinem*], i.e. (by E3p59s), to tenacity and generosity [*ad animositatem, et generositatem*]. I do not consider it worthwhile to demonstrate separately here all the properties of strength of character, much less to show that a man strong in character [*vir fortis*] hates no one, is angry with no one, envies no one, is indignant with no one, scorns no one, and is not at all proud. For these and all things which relate to true life and

religion, are easily proven from E4p37 and p46, viz. that hatred is to be conquered by returning love, and that everyone who is led by reason desires for others also the good which he wants for himself.

When this communitarian ethic is understood in light of Spinoza's principle of being-in-God, it suggests a religious ethic of loving both oneself and others as 'in God'. On this point, Spinoza shares Augustine's view that joyful communion with others is our highest happiness: 'that we may thoroughly enjoy God and that all of us who enjoy God may enjoy one another in God'.[20]

CHAPTER EIGHT

Eternal Life

HALFWAY THROUGH PART FIVE of the *Ethics*, Spinoza pauses. He will now, he declares, turn from what 'relates to this present life'—the various 'principles of self-government' and 'remedies of the emotions' he has enumerated thus far—and consider the eternity of our minds (E5p20s).[1] Having asserted that 'the human mind cannot be absolutely destroyed with the body, but something remains of it, which is eternal' (E5p23), he repeats the verb *sentire* three times in quick succession to emphasise that we know this truth with the intimacy and immediacy of 'feeling':

> It is impossible that we should remember ourselves to have existed before the body, since there are no traces in the body of this preexistence, and eternity is not defined by time, nor can it have any relation to time. Nevertheless we feel, we experience [*sentimus, experimurque*], that we are eternal. For the mind no less feels [*sentit*] those things which it conceives by the understanding, than those which it has in the memory. For the eyes of the mind, by which it sees and observes things, are themselves demonstrations. Although, therefore, we do not remember that we have existed before the body, we feel our mind [*sentimus mentem nostram*], so far as it involves the essence of the body under the form of eternity, to be eternal, and in this sense its existence cannot be defined by time or explained by duration. (E5p23s)

Spinoza's rather surprising juxtaposition of 'experience' and eternity here recalls the very first line of his *Treatise on the Emendation of the Intellect*, discussed in Chapter 1: 'After experience [*experientia*] had taught me that all the things which regularly occur in ordinary life are empty and futile . . . I resolved at last to try to find out whether there was something which, once found and acquired, would continuously give me the greatest joy, to eternity.'[2]

Many years later, in the *Ethics*, Spinoza claims that even ordinary people are 'conscious [*conscios*] of the eternity of their minds' (E5p34s). Forms of the word *conscientia* recur several times in the text's final propositions: the more we achieve *scientia intuitiva*, the third kind of knowledge, argues Spinoza, the more we know ourselves 'under a species of eternity', and the more we are 'conscious' of ourselves and of God—and the more 'perfect and blessed' we become (E5p30, E5p31s).

For Pierre-François Moreau, whose 1994 book *Spinoza: L'expérience et l'éternité* follows the arc from the beginning of the *Treatise on the Emendation of the Intellect* to Part Five of the *Ethics*, Spinoza's appeal to our feeling of eternity 'proves nothing', demonstrates nothing, yet plays a different role: 'it incites'. Experiencing that we are eternal, 'in other words, that the necessity which we discover is a matter for us, makes us aspire to live this from the inside [*à la vivre de l'intérieur*]'. This human experience invites us 'to search [*à nous mettre en quête*] for an eternity that is at once promised and given, to take the path which will lead us to knowledge and blessedness [*vers la connaissance et la béatitude*]'.[3]

Spinoza's references to *sentire* and *conscientia* in *Ethics* V suggest an intimate form of knowing in which the knower is not separate from what is known. More specifically, the human mind knows itself (see E5p30), not by positing itself as an object, but by sensing itself immediately, intuitively: 'the mind ... feels those things which it conceives ... we feel our mind ... to be eternal'. In this intellectual feeling, or consciousness, one has an immediate grasp of oneself and of other things; of the connections between oneself and others; and of the intelligibility of the causal chain considered as a whole. This is a knowing of God, on whom all beings, their activities and their mutual relationships, depend for their intelligibility and causal power. Spinoza wants us, his readers, to become 'more ... conscious of [ourselves] and of God' (E5p31s), 'highly conscious of [our minds], of God, and of things' (E5p39s). This intensification of consciousness is figured as a growth or expansion of being-in-God, so that love (and thus knowledge) of God 'must occupy or constitute the greater proportion of [the] mind', producing 'a mind the greater proportion of which is eternal' (E5p39d).[4]

This recalls Spinoza's brief discussion of the third kind of cognition in Part Two of the *Ethics*, which we considered in Chapter 2. As Kristin Primus has pointed out, there is a link (which Spinoza does not make explicit) between his remark that 'the idea of the mind, i.e., the idea of the idea, is nothing but the form of the idea insofar as this is considered as a mode of thinking without relation to the object' (E2p21s) and his announcement in the middle of Part Five that 'it is time now to pass to those things which pertain to the mind's duration without relation to the body' (E5p20s).[5] Spinoza has explained that *scientia intuitiva* comprehends the truth immediately, 'in one glance' (E2p40s2), and this oracular metaphor recurs in his remark that 'the eyes of the mind, by which it sees and observes things, are themselves demonstrations', which he appears to offer as a kind of explanation, or confirmation, of his insistent claim that 'we feel, we experience, that we are eternal'.[6] In Chapter 2, I suggested that in *scientia intuitiva* there is no distinction between what is known and the act of knowing it; Spinoza gestures to this when he writes that 'the idea of the mind and the mind itself are one and the same thing, which is conceived under one and the same attribute, viz. Thought' (E2p21s), and this kind of epistemic non-duality seems to be echoed much more intensely in the latter part of Part Five. Although the account of eternal life presented in the *Ethics* is complex—and for some readers simply baffling—the mind's intuition of its own eternity, so immediate that we simply see it, feel it, can be a touchstone as we navigate this difficult terrain. Spinoza suggests that this intuition underlies even erroneous doctrines of immortality: the core insight into our eternity is true, but it tends to be theorised and represented in misleading ways.

Nevertheless, Spinoza also treats human eternity as an accomplishment, indeed as a transformation. *Scientia intuitiva* can seem mysterious in this respect: do we all possess this knowledge, or is it something very rare?[7] The answer, I think, is 'both'—because we have a consciousness of eternity that is distorted by fluctuating thoughts and clouded by imaginative thinking, and particularly by doctrines of immortality inculcated by superstitious religion. Even the rational thinking developed through the practice of reading the *Ethics* struggles to grasp our eternity, both because it divides the knower from what is known, and because it is durational: it takes time to think through a logical sequence of propositions.[8]

Scholars disagree about whether intuitive knowledge should be attributed to Spinoza. Beth Lord argues that 'Spinoza did not *have* the third kind of knowledge. His writing, in these ten final propositions of the *Ethics*, is therefore strange and incoherent: it reflects the paradox of an enduring rational mind trying to imagine what eternal intuitive knowing might be like,' while Gilles Deleuze suggests that the final section of the *Ethics*, from E5p21 onwards, is written from the perspective of the third kind of knowledge.⁹ The idea that *Ethics* V documents an attempt to imagine intuitive knowledge (or relies on the testimony of others who claim to have possessed it) undermines the basic epistemological position that Spinoza maintains throughout his work, since his remarks about this form of knowing and all that it can achieve would be merely an instance of the inadequate 'first kind' of knowledge. Furthermore, if intuitive knowledge were merely a hypothesis, it is not clear what could motivate such speculation for a thinker as scrupulous as Spinoza. We would do well to follow H. F. Hallett's advice, offered to the readers of *Mind* in 1928: 'it is to *Scientia Intuitiva* that we must look for our main clue to the Spinozistic conception of eternity, but it is not necessary, indeed it would be pernicious, to separate the second section of Part V of the *Ethica* from the rest of the work. Spinoza means to tell a single story.'[10]

In interpreting the end of the *Ethics*, we have to take a middle path between rationalism and mysticism. To suggest that ordinary rational understanding—already a significant achievement, in Spinoza's view—fails to do justice to *Ethics* V need not entail a mystical claim that access to this part of the text is denied to all but those few readers who have attained a special state of union with God. It is, however, to remain open-minded about the distinctive features of the third kind of knowledge that are emphasised there: the possibility of transformation, and the possibility of an immediate, non-dualist awareness of being-in-God, which perhaps resembles the kind of awareness that can arise during meditation or contemplation. This open-mindedness certainly does not involve relinquishing our critical faculties—on the contrary, discernment between truth and falsity, between intuition and imagination, is extremely important—but it is nevertheless a refusal to refuse what cannot be captured by rational thinking and logical analysis. This is, I think, the only way to accommodate the *possibility* that Spinoza is right about intuitive knowledge.

It is not surprising, then, that when Spinoza discusses the eternity of the mind there is a disparity between the content of his account—which foregrounds *scientia intuitiva*—and its literary form, which like the rest of the *Ethics* consists in a series of propositions to be followed by rational thinking, unfolding in time:

> Our mind, so far as it knows itself and its body under the form of eternity, has necessarily the knowledge of God, and knows itself to be in God and to be conceived by and through God. (E5p30)

> The third kind of cognition depends on the mind as its formal cause, so far as the mind itself is eternal. (E5p31)

> From the third kind of cognition necessarily arises the intellectual love of God. For from this kind of cognition arises joy in connection with the idea of God as a cause, i.e., the love of God, not imagined as present but understood as eternal; and this is what I mean by the intellectual love of God. (E5p32c)
>
> The intellectual love of God, which arises from the third kind of cognition, is eternal. (E5p33)

Both intuitive knowledge and the mind's eternity are closely connected to our dependence on God. And just as being-in-God is an unconditional ontological principle while 'participating in the divine nature' is a matter of degree, something to strive for, so our mind's eternity has this twofold structure. On the one hand, the mind *is* eternal; on the other hand, it has the ethical (or religious) task of becoming eternal.[11]

Although Spinoza suggests that the mind's eternity is a truth known in our inward experience, our intellectual feeling, our consciousness, the way this truth is elucidated in Part Five of the *Ethics* is deeply cultural. Spinoza's account of human eternity took shape within a milieu saturated by Christian teachings about the afterlife, in which, it was believed, people would either enjoy eternal bliss or suffer eternal damnation.[12] In order to uncover the intuition of eternity, to restore it to the 'natural light' of a human mind which knows itself to be in God, Spinoza had to dismantle these powerful, emotive images. He was in no doubt that the doctrine of personal immortality taught by the Christian churches—both Catholic and Reformed—was a pernicious superstition, and the *Ethics* offers several different arguments against it.[13]

One line of argument challenges its theoretical basis. Belief in immortality rests on a confused image of eternity, combined with mistaken ideas about personal identity. 'If we attend to the common opinion of men,' Spinoza observes, 'we shall see that they are conscious of the eternity of their minds, but that they confound it with duration, and attribute it to the imagination or memory, which they believe to remain after death' (E5p34s). Note that Spinoza here suggests that ordinary beliefs about immortality evince a mixture of truth and falsity: people *are conscious of the eternity of their minds, but they confound it with duration*. He reminds readers of his ontological definition of eternity in Part One of the *Ethics*, where he distinguishes sharply between eternity and duration, and rules out conceiving eternity in temporal terms, as if it meant existing for an infinite period of time:

> By eternity I understand existence itself, conceived as following solely and necessarily from the definition of the thing which is eternal.
>
> Exp.: For existence so conceived is an eternal truth, inasmuch as it is the essence of the eternal thing; consequently, it cannot be explained by duration or time, even though the duration be conceived without beginning or end (E1D8).

'Eternity cannot be explained by duration (by E1D8 and its explanation)', asserts Spinoza, before clarifying that there are two ways of conceiving things as actual: 'either as existing with relation to a certain time and place, or as contained in God and following from the necessity of the divine nature. But the things which are conceived in the second way as true or real, we conceive under the form of eternity, and the ideas of them involve the eternal and infinite essence of God' (E5p29d and schol.).[14]

Spinoza's account of the human mind shows how our identity as persons is grounded in our imagination, our memory, and our emotions. It is impossible for any of this to continue after we die: 'The mind can imagine nothing, nor can it remember past things, except during the existence of the body,' (E5p21), and 'a passion is an act of imagination insofar as it indicates the present constitution of the body; and thus the mind is liable to [passions] only during the existence of the body' (E5p34d).

As well as challenging these theoretical foundations of Christian belief in personal immortality, Spinoza criticised the affective and ethical consequences of this belief. Popular doctrines about the Last Judgement— whether these reflected Calvinist ideas of predestination, or the Catholics' more meritocratic view of salvation—caused believers to fluctuate between hope for reward in heaven and dread of punishment in hell. The experience of anxiety which motivated and shaped Luther's theological breakthrough bears witness to the emotional instability generated by the Christian doctrine of salvation. Protestant reformers did not solve this problem, but merely reconfigured it: Calvin, for example, argued that knowledge of God ought to 'awaken and arouse us to the hope of a future life ... to which is reserved the vengeance due to iniquity, and the reward of righteousness'.[15] This 'arousal to hope', inseparable from dread of divine vengeance, was for Spinoza the antithesis of the deep rest, *acquiescentia in se ipso*, which the *Ethics* recommends as the highest human good. As Daniel Garber has shown, Spinoza's discussion of the eternity of the mind is oriented to the practical project of overcoming the fear of death. If Spinoza's discussion is 'disappointing' insofar as 'the person who has attained eternity in the sense Spinoza promises it has not conquered the death of the body', writes Garber, *Ethics* V nevertheless achieves something 'perhaps just as important': conquering the fear of death. 'In place of the false hope Christianity offers, Spinoza offers us a *real* hope, the hope for a kind of happiness and peace of mind beyond anything the Christian can offer.'[16]

More than this, however, Spinoza thought that the very idea of extrinsic rewards and punishments, whether worldly or eschatological, was a corruption of true piety and virtue. He articulated this view in his letter to Ostens in 1671, written in response to Velthuysen's accusation of atheism:

> Is someone who holds that our greatest happiness and freedom consist only in [the love of God] irreligious? Or that the reward of virtue is virtue itself, whereas the punishment of folly and weakness is folly itself? . . . But I think I see what mud this man is stuck in. He finds nothing in virtue itself, or in understanding, which delights him, and he would prefer to live according to the impulse of his affects, if one thing did not stand in his way: he fears punishment.[17]

Hoping for eternal life as a reward for virtue, or fearing it as a punishment for vice, not only reveals an ignorant superstition, but also undermines genuine virtue. Part Two of the *Ethics* concludes by confirming that 'we clearly understand how far they stray from the true valuation of virtue, who expect to be honoured by God with the greatest rewards for their virtue and best actions, as for the greatest service [*servitude*]—as if virtue itself, and the service [*servitus*] of God, were not happiness itself, and the greatest freedom' (E2p49s). Spinoza believed that Church teachings about heaven and hell, election and damnation, actually undermined the intrinsic value of virtue, and thus threatened moral life itself.

Spinoza reiterates this point near the end of Part Five, where he connects it explicitly with the question of human eternity. 'Even if we did not know our mind to be eternal,' he argues, 'still piety and religion, and everything we have shown in the Fourth Part to belong to courage and generosity, would be the primary objects of life' (E5p41). Yet, he notes, those who hope for heavenly rewards do not value these virtues—piety, religion, courage, generosity—for their own sake. On the contrary, they regard them as a burden, and long to be free of them:

> For most people apparently believe that they are free to the extent that they are permitted to yield to their lust, and that they give up their right to the extent that they are bound to live according to the rule of

the divine law. Morality [*pietatem*], then, and religion, and absolutely everything related to strength of character [*animi fortitudinem*], they believe to be burdens, which they hope to put down after death, when they also hope to receive a reward for their servitude [*servitutis*], that is, for their morality and religion [*pietatis et religionis*]. (E5p41s)

Here, however, Spinoza takes a rather surprising turn. Although eschatological hope and fear are destabilising affects, he suggests that insofar as they provide moral incentives for 'the vulgar', they are the lesser of two evils:

They are induced to live according to the rule of the divine law (as far as their weakness and lack of character [*impotens animus*] allows) not only by this hope, but also, and especially, by the fear that they may be punished horribly after death. If people did not have this hope and fear, but believed instead that minds die with the body, and that the wretched, exhausted with the burden of morality [*pietatis*], cannot look forward to a life to come, they would return to their natural disposition, and would prefer to govern all their actions according to lust, and to obey fortune rather than themselves. (E5p41s)

In this passage we see Spinoza's caution and pragmatism mitigating his critique of superstitious religion. As an ethical idealist, he argued that fear and the idea of extrinsic punishment are opposed to virtue and to freedom. Insofar as he was also a pragmatist, he regarded fear of hell—together with other elements of Christian morality that he criticised on philosophical grounds—as an effective means for preventing social disorder: 'Because men rarely live from the dictates of reason, these two affects, Humility and Repentance, and in addition, Hope and Fear, bring more advantage than disadvantage. . . . The mob is terrifying, if unafraid' (E4p54s). This ambivalence towards fear reflects Spinoza's recognition that the failure to live rationally and virtuously was so pervasive, so entrenched in customs and beliefs, that basic social conditions of peace and stability had to be prioritised, in order to facilitate the pursuit of freedom and blessedness. Yet this pragmatism does not alter, or even qualify, his principled claim that the Christian doctrine of eternal life both rests on and perpetuates ignorance about the intrinsic goodness of virtue.[18]

Spinoza's insistence that belief in personal immortality was motivated, for good or ill, by fear of death offered a bold challenge to Church teachings.

At the same time, his argument drew deeply on the biblical texts that these same churches claimed as their own. Here, once again, he engaged in sophisticated ways, constructively as well as critically, with layers of scriptural tradition. This biblical engagement is explicit in the *Theologico-Political Treatise*, and it is also discernible, though less conspicuous, in the *Ethics*.

The New Testament's teaching on eternal life is bound up with a narrative concerning human sinfulness.[19] In Paul's letters, sin is linked to the body, to the flesh and to death, and all of these are presented as a condition of bondage; Paul declares that Christ's resurrection accomplishes liberation from sin, and thus from death. As he wrote to the first Christians in Rome,

> When you were slaves to sin, you were free from the control of righteousness. What benefit did you reap at that time from the things you are now ashamed of? Those things result in death! But now you have been set free from sin and become slaves of God, the benefit you reap leads to holiness, and the result is eternal life. For the wages of sin is death, but the gift of God is eternal life in Christ Jesus (Romans 6:20–23).

Through Christ, Paul explains, we are given new life—a life of the spirit rather than of the flesh—and released from the bonds of sin: 'to set the mind on the flesh is death, but to set the mind on the spirit is life and peace' (Romans 8:6).[20]

In Chapter 15 of the First Letter to the Corinthians, which discusses resurrection, Paul presents Christ as a counterpart to Adam. While Adam's sin brought death to the human race, Jesus is a second Adam who restores us to life: 'For as in Adam all die, so in Christ all will be made alive. . . . So it is written: "The first man Adam became a living being" [Genesis 2:7]; the last Adam, a life-giving spirit' (1 Corinthians 15:22, 45).[21] In this way, Paul at once invokes and subverts Jewish teaching, emphasising both fulfilment of the tradition and a new beginning.

Spinoza rejected the concept of sin for philosophical reasons, and he distrusted the morbid or moralising concern for human sinfulness voiced frequently by Christian leaders in his day. Nevertheless, his analysis of bondage and freedom, death and life, mirrors Paul's in interesting ways. Parts Four and Five of the *Ethics* deal with 'human servitude' and 'human freedom' respectively. Part Four takes up the Stoic critique of bondage to the passions, emphasising the link between existential servitude and fear—but Spinoza places this idea in a theological context, presenting his own gloss on the story of Adam's fall into sin narrated in Genesis 2: 'God prohibited a free man from eating of the tree of knowledge of good and evil, and that as soon as he should eat of it, he would immediately fear death, rather than desiring to live' (E4p68s).[22] This gives a mythical resonance to Spinoza's assertion, in the preceding proposition, that 'a free man [*homo liber*] thinks of nothing less than of death, and his wisdom is a meditation on life, not on death. A free man, i.e., one who lives according to the dictate of reason alone, is not led by Fear, but desires the good directly' (E4p67). These passages echo the exegesis of Genesis 2:17 in the *Theologico-Political Treatise*, where Spinoza suggests that God wanted Adam to recognise the intrinsic value of virtue, and to be motivated by love of the good, rather than by fear of evil:

> Let us . . . survey Holy Scripture to see what it teaches concerning the natural light and [the] divine law. The first thing that strikes us is the story [*historia*] of the first man, where it is related that God told Adam not to eat the fruit of the tree of knowledge of good and evil. This seems to mean that God told Adam to do and seek the good for the sake of the good [*bonum agree, et quaerere sub rationi boni*], and not insofar as it is contrary to evil, i.e., that he should seek the good from love of the good [*ut bonum ex amore boni quaereret*], and not from fear of evil. For . . . he who does good from a true knowledge and love of the good acts freely and with a constant heart [*libere et constanti animo agit*], whereas he who acts from fear of evil is compelled by evil, acts like a slave [*serviliter agit*], and lives under the command of another.[23]

On Spinoza's interpretation, the Fall dramatised in Genesis 2, and repeated through all generations descended from Adam, is not from immortality to mortality, but from *desire for life* to *fear of death*. Its consequence is servitude, slavery—as in Paul's analysis of the fall into sin. This Fall is a corruption of life itself: it is the mark of a life that has degenerated into fear of death, squandering its vitality in the weakest of passions. While desire for life is an active affect, expressing our own essence or nature, fear of death is a passive affect, since death—according to Spinoza—always comes from an external source (see E3p3).

In the Appendix to Part Four of the *Ethics*, this critique of fear is explicitly linked to superstitious religion: 'Superstition . . . seems to maintain that the good is what brings sadness, and the evil, what brings joy. . . . [H]e who is led by fear, and does the good only to avoid evil, is not governed by reason' (E4App31). Similarly, in the Preface to the *Theologico-Political Treatise*, Spinoza suggests that the essence of superstitious passion is fear, and especially fear of punishments to be administered in the afterlife.[24]

He warns there that this degenerate religiosity is not only founded on ignorance, but also leads to the conflict, oppression and social unrest that threatened the stability of the Dutch Republic in his own lifetime.[25] Spinoza's reinterpretation of the Genesis narrative thus implies a provocative critique of established religion. He presents 'superstition' as a corrupted form of religiosity that people mistake for true faith, and he reads the Fall as a descent into this superstitious religion.

Part Four of the *Ethics* is concerned, then, with our bondage not simply to the passions in general, but to the particular passions associated with beliefs instilled by the established churches. Spinoza's philosophical anthropology shows that if we live in fear of death, then—as finite modes who are constitutionally vulnerable to external influences—we experience our very being as a state of bondage. The freedom that constitutes our salvation involves a turn from death to life that echoes the message of Paul's theology, yet at the same time exposes the error of those contemporary religious authorities which claimed Paul's teachings as their own. As we have seen, Spinoza nevertheless affirms the value of superstitious teachings for purely pragmatic reasons—but only for so long as people remain ignorant of their true good.

For Spinoza, the fear that sustains superstition is not simply debilitating, but perverse. All fear is a passion, and therefore a weakness, since a fearful person suffers on account of the external things that frighten her. But someone who fears death, because she fears punishment in an afterlife, has been determined by an external power—specifically, by the teachings of the Church—to fear the consequences of her own actions. Such a person is made afraid of *her own power*, and this means that she is afraid of her own existence. It is difficult to imagine a state in which a human being lives less in accordance with his nature—to conceive, in Spinozist terms, a life less virtuous. Spinoza's critique of superstition echoes Paul's inversions of Jewish tradition, in a manner specifically accommodated to seventeenth-century religious life. While Paul's Christ is a new Adam who conquers death by life, through release from the bondage of sin, Spinoza proposes a new exemplar: a 'wise person' (*sapiens*) or a 'free person' (*homo liber*) who models freedom from the bondage of Christian superstition, overcoming the fear of death with desire for life.

When Spinoza discusses eternal life in Part Five of the *Ethics*, he refers back to his reading of the Fall in Part Four. Among the cluster of propositions that deal with the third kind of knowledge and the love of God, he presents his account of blessedness as a remedy for the fear of death: 'The more the Mind understands things by the second and third kind of knowledge, the less it is acted on by affects which are evil, and the less it fears death[;] . . . death is less harmful to us, the greater the Mind's clear and distinct knowledge, and hence, the more the Mind loves God' (E5p38 and schol.). Readers are reminded here that 'evil' affects are those 'which are contrary to our nature' and 'the cause of sadness' (E5p38, referencing E4p30). Spinoza then explains that 'because human bodies are capable of a great many things . . . they can be of such a nature that they are related to minds which have a great knowledge of themselves and of God, and of which the greatest, *or* chief, part is eternal. So they hardly fear death' (E5p39s). As he approaches his conclusion to the *Ethics*, Spinoza contrasts his own account of human freedom with conventional Christian beliefs, which persuade people to persist in their servitude 'especially by the fear that they may be punished horribly after death' (E5p41s). Here, 'servitude' is explicitly identified with superstitious beliefs and practices. As we have seen, Spinoza suggests that most people regard virtue as a 'burden' which 'they hope to put down after death, when they also hope to receive a reward for their servitude, that is, for their Morality and Religion'.

When this passage is read in context, it is clear that 'Morality and Religion' here refers not to *any* morality or religion, but specifically to the superstitious doctrines taught by the Reformed and Roman Catholic churches, which formed the minds of the multitude. Overlooking Spinoza's distinction between religion and superstition leads very quickly to the view that his critique of 'morality and religion' is a sign of atheism. But, of course, superstition can be criticised as vehemently for the sake of 'true religion' as from an atheistic perspective, and Spinoza seems to be doing just this when he expresses his wish to see 'religion again free of all superstition'.[26]

Replacing fear of death by desire for life involves not simply a transition from ignorance to knowledge (although it is also that), nor from superstitious passion to rational understanding (although it is this as well), but a conversion of a passive affect to an active one (see E4D3; also E4App1-4). The fear of death that characterises superstition is passive— that is to say, due to external causes—in several ways: this fear is shaped by heteronomous authorities (inculcated, that is, by priests, theologians and the superstitious beliefs of others); death always comes from an external cause; and the judgement and punishment envisaged after death are attributed to the heteronomous decree of an anthropomorphic God. Desire for life, on the other hand, both arises from one's own essence, as striving for preservation, and takes this essence as its object. It is an intrinsic or immanent fulfilment, rather than a striving for extrinsic reward.

Another New Testament epistle, the First Letter of John, helps to illuminate what Spinoza's religion teaches about human life, death and eternity. This epistle was traditionally believed to be written by the author of John's Gospel, since it has the distinctive characteristics of Johannine theology, influenced by Greek philosophy—Stoicism and Platonism—as well as by the teachings of Jesus and their Jewish background.[27] The First Letter of John was one of Spinoza's favourite biblical texts: in Chapter 14 of the *Theologico-Political Treatise* he makes several references to it (including to 1 John 4:7, 'God is love'), and he placed one of its verses on the title page of this work—'By this we know that we abide in [God] and he in us' (1 John 4:13). This epigraph, of course, invokes the surrounding text: 'If we love one another, God lives in us and his love is perfected in us. By this we know that we abide in him and he in us, for he has given us his spirit' (1 John 4:12–13).

The author of 1 John concludes his letter by reminding its readers that 'I write these things to you . . . so that you may know that you have eternal life' (1 John 5:13). This epistle is particularly germane to Part Five of the *Ethics*, since it explores the interconnected themes of love of God, love of other people, and 'eternal life'.[28] As in other Johannine texts, eternal life is here understood as the life of God that human beings can share in. This divine life is qualitatively different from natural life (*psyche*), which is characterised by duration; eternal life 'is not a *human* life that never ends, but the very life of God that by its nature is unending'.[29] The author of 1 John suggests that this eternal life can be possessed in the present, rather than only at some future point at the end of time—a doctrine described by modern biblical scholars as 'realised eschatology'.[30] Particularly distinctive to 1 John, moreover, is the idea that gaining eternal life is immediately dependent on ethical action: 'We know that we have passed from death to life because we love one another. Whoever does not love abides in death. All who hate a brother or sister are murderers, and you know that murderers do not have eternal life abiding in them' (1 John 2:14–15). Here, both 'life' and 'eternal life' are gained by loving others. In describing a 'passage' from death to life, these verses indicate that eternal life involves radical existential transformation—a deep conversion, a 'new birth'.[31]

Although the author of 1 John regards life and death in spiritual or ethical terms—that is, as ways of being in this present life—he also presents the transition to eternal life as an ontological change. This 'passage' is not simply a metaphor for ethical improvement.[32] The essentially religious thought here is that love has, and indeed is, a transforming power: *we have passed from life to death because we love one another.*

Furthermore, the First Letter of John emphasises that fear is opposed to love. Its author suggests that fear is connected to death just as love is connected to (eternal) life. 'There is no fear in love, but perfect love casts out fear, for fear has to do with punishment, and whoever fears has not reached perfection in love' (1 John 4:18). Such a statement would not be out of place in the *Ethics*, and this is no coincidence. Like the author of 1 John, Spinoza addressed readers who lived in a diverse society unsettled and fractured by religious tensions. Indeed, the *Ethics* might plausibly be read as a philosophical exposition of the theology of 1 John, situating the biblical text in the seventeenth-century European context by accentuating (and explaining with rational arguments) the harmful psychological and social effects of fear, and by insisting that hatred fuelling sectarian conflict must be overcome by love.[33] Spinoza's critique of superstition—and of the violence and repression it generates—can thus be interpreted as a call to return to a 'true religion' articulated in New Testament sources. Read in this way, Spinoza is criticising the morbidly fearful religion of superstition for the sake of a positively religious conception of life and love.

Immortality may seem to be a metaphysical or eschatological issue, and sin primarily an ethical category. However, the close connections between sin and death, faith and eternal life within Christian theology suggest that both doctrines combine ethical and eschatological aspects. Indeed, in the First Letter of John we encounter an equivocation between ethical and eschatological, or natural and supernatural, interpretations of eternal life. This is mirrored in Part Five of the *Ethics*, where ethics and eschatology become inseparable from Spinoza's ontology. Here the *Ethics* is describing a way of being in which human life participates more fully in the eternal life of God.

Spinoza repeatedly links love with life, and hatred and fear with death. Towards the end of Part Four, he tells us that all those things 'which relate to true life [*vita*] and religion' follow from the principles 'that hate is to be conquered by returning love, and that everyone who is led by reason desires for others also the good he wants for himself' (E4p73s). He also invokes life, *vita*, when he elucidates the interconnectedness of human desire, virtue and being: 'No one can desire to be blessed, to act well and to live [*vivere*] well, unless at the same time he desires to be, to act, and to live, that is, to actually exist. . . . For [this desire] is the very essence of man, that is, the striving by which each one strives to preserve his being'

(E4p21). And he states that 'a free man['s] wisdom consists in the contemplation not of death, but of life. . . . [He] is not led by fear, but desires the good directly, that is, acts, lives and preserves his being from the foundation of seeking his own advantage' (E4p67).[34] Here again, we find echoes of the opening of the *Treatise on the Emendation of the Intellect*, discussed in my first chapter. I asked there what conception of life—and death—Spinoza had in mind when he compared himself to 'a man suffering from a fatal illness, who, foreseeing certain death unless he employs a remedy, is forced to seek it, however uncertain, with all his strength', and realised that those things people ordinarily strive for 'not only provide no remedy to preserve our being, but in fact hinder that preservation . . . and always cause the destruction of those who are possessed by them'.[35] His coupling of 'true life and religion' in the scholium to E4p73 suggests that—like Paul, who wrote that 'to set the mind on the spirit is life and peace', and like the author of 1 John, who wrote that 'we have passed from life to death because we love one another'—Spinoza proposes a conception of human life that combines moral, spiritual and biological vitality.

If, as Spinoza claims, death can be caused only by an external force, then there are two alternative ways to resist death, to desire life. We might either close ourselves off from outside influences, or open and expand ourselves to embrace external things. The contracting response is fear; the expansive, inclusive response is love. Spinoza believed that the fearful response is not in fact viable for us—it is contrary to our nature—since we cannot prevent ourselves from being affected and influenced by external beings and events.[36] The alternative possibility, on the other hand, may help to explain his insistence on the human capacity for eternity. While the ignorant person is determined heteronomously, constituted by affects brought about 'by external causes', so that 'as soon as he ceases to be acted upon, he ceases to be', the wise person's existence is not circumscribed in this way. Rather, his mind embraces many things, perhaps even infinitely many: 'being, by a certain eternal necessity, conscious of himself, and of God, and of things, he never ceases to be, but always possesses true peace of mind' (E5p42s).

Spinoza thought that how we live conditions who we are in the strongest sense. Though he maintains that an 'eternal essence' of each person is eternally in God, he also conceives our ethical task as *becoming* eternal.[37] This is where ethics meets ontology: at the heart of the *Ethics* is the idea that how we think, act and relate to others constitutes our identity (see E4p39s; E5p39s). It would not make sense to say that overcoming fear of death is 'merely' an ethical or a psychological task, for it involves a change in our being. And this, I think, is how Spinoza's account of the eternity of the mind should be understood: certainly not as the continuance of personal duration in an afterlife, nor as a mere technicality lacking in practical significance—but rather as a transformation, at once ethical and ontological, that softens the distinction, perhaps even to a vanishing point, between a human being's finite life and the eternal life of God.

The ethical orientation of Spinoza's account of human eternity is reflected in the structure of his text. The sequence of propositions concerning eternity are preceded and followed by passages explaining that virtue involves the transformation of the lived body.[38] In the first half of Part Five, readers are advised to forge stronger and stronger links between their own experience and the idea of God through an imaginative practice: 'The mind can bring to pass that all the affections of the body or images of things shall be connected with the idea of God' (E5p14).[39] Propositions 11 to 13 discuss how 'frequent' connections between images of things lead to the 'flourishing' of these images in a way that 'engages the mind'—and here Spinoza reminds us of his analysis of habituation in Part Two.[40] Once the eternity of the mind has been demonstrated, Spinoza summarises its practical implications: 'In this life, then, we strive especially that the child's body may change (as much as its nature allows and assists) into another, capable of a great many things and related to a mind very much conscious of itself, of God, and of things' (E5p39s). He seems to be arguing that the path of spiritual transformation leads through the imagination, through the body, yet finally leaves this embodiment behind to arrive at intuitive knowledge: the mind's direct 'seeing' or 'feeling' of its own eternity. Our 'striving' for eternal life requires us to develop bodily capacities to act and to feel in many different ways, in order to seek a condition in which 'whatever is related to [the body's] memory or imagination is of hardly any moment in relation to the intellect' (E5p39s).[41]

Although Spinoza refuses to console or to frighten us with a doctrine of personal immortality, his understanding of human eternity is not simply formal or abstract. It has everything to do with how we live and act, think and feel. The *Ethics* conceives human eternity as a way of existing in God, and thereby participating in God's eternity while still living.[42] In this respect, eternal life is primarily an ethical principle rather than a theological belief. For Spinoza, however, questions about how to act and to live, what to desire and do, are inseparable from the religious question of how to be in God.[43]

CHAPTER NINE

Spinoza's Religion

WHAT IS RELIGION? Addressing this question in his *Summa Theologiae*, Thomas Aquinas turned to earlier authors for insight into the origins and meanings of the word *religio*. According to Cicero, a person is said to be religious 'because he often ponders over, and, as it were, reads again [*relegit*], the things which pertain to the worship of God'. *Legere* can also mean to choose, and to gather, as well as to read. Augustine—who thought that 'true religion' existed throughout history and across different cultures— offered two different etymologies: in *The City of God* he suggested that we must cultivate *religio* because 'we ought to seek God again [*Deum religere debemus*], whom we had lost by our neglect', while his treatise *On True Religion* connected *religio* with *religare*, meaning to bind together. 'Whether religion take its name from frequent reading, or from a repeated choice of what has been lost through negligence, or from being a bond,' concluded Aquinas, 'it denotes properly a relation to God'.[1]

Aquinas classified *religio* among the virtues, and discussed it within the part of the *Summa Theologiae* known as the 'Treatise on Justice and Prudence'. Following Aristotle's formal definition of virtue as the mean between deficiency and excess, he identified both 'irreligion' and 'superstition' as vices contrary to true religion.[2] *Religio* is the virtue of paying due honour to God, and is thus closely connected with justice, which means giving to each person his or her due.[3] Aquinas declared that 'religion excels among the moral virtues', since its actions 'are directly and immediately ordered to the honour of God'.[4] While *religio*, like other virtues, has both an inward and an outward aspect, it is constituted chiefly by internal acts of devotion and prayer.[5] For Aquinas, as for his predecessors, *religio* had very little to do with beliefs or metaphysical doctrines.

In the seventeenth century, during Spinoza's lifetime, the concept of religion was undergoing a deep shift, from the medieval view crystallised by Aquinas to the modern category of religion that is still with us today. Spinoza, however, resisted the emerging conception of religion as a particular set of teachings, beliefs and practices, circumscribed and regulated by ideals of orthodoxy and orthopraxy. He discusses *religio* in eight passages in the *Ethics*, and like Aquinas he consistently situates it amongst the virtues. At the end of Part Four he states that 'all the painful emotions which people feel towards each other are directly opposed to justice, equity, honour, piety and religion' (E4App§24). The penultimate proposition of Part Five asserts that 'even if we did not know our mind to be eternal, still piety and religion, and everything we have shown in the Fourth Part to belong to courage and generosity, would be the primary objects of life' (E5p41). Here Spinoza associates 'piety and religion' with 'everything which belongs to strength of mind [*animi fortitudinem*]' (E5p41s).

In the *Ethics*, 'strength of mind' or 'fortitude' is a broad virtue associated with the core affect of desire, based on true understanding and conducive to our 'true freedom'. Fortitude encompasses various forms of courage, defined as 'the desire by which everyone strives to persevere in his existence according to the dictate of reason', and of generosity, 'the desire by which everyone strives to aid other people and unite with them in friendship' (E3p59s). Summing up the 'characteristics' of this virtue in the final proposition of Part Four, Spinoza concludes that

> I do not think it worthwhile to demonstrate separately all the properties of fortitude [*fortitudinis*], and much less to show that a man strong in character [*vir fortis*] hates no one, is angry with no one, envies no one, is indignant with no one, scorns no one, and is not at all proud. For these and all things which relate to true life and religion [*ad veram vitam, et religionem*] are easily proven from E4p37 and E4p46; namely, that hatred is to be conquered by returning love [*Amore*] and that everyone who is led by reason desires that the good which he seeks for himself may be possessed by others. (E4p73s)

Fortitude, love and generosity, then, 'relate to true life and religion'. The two prior propositions that Spinoza cites in this passage confirm, respectively, the form and the content of *religio*. Proposition 37 states that 'the good which everyone who desires virtue follows for himself, he desires for all human beings, and the more, in proportion as he has greater knowledge of God'. It is in the scholium to this proposition that Spinoza comes closest to defining religion: 'whatever we desire or do, or cause to be done, in virtue of our having the idea of God, or of knowing God, I relate to religion' (E4p37s1).

For Spinoza, *religio* encompasses both inwardness and expression. Just as Aquinas recognised in the virtue of *religio* both an internal and an external aspect, so Spinoza's definition includes both desire—that is, conscious appetite—and action.[6] Proposition 46 states, in philosophical terms, the familiar Christian exhortation to 'love your enemies, and do good to those who hate you' (Luke 6:27): 'He who lives according to the guidance of reason strives as far as he can to compensate the hatred, anger, contempt, etc. of others towards him with love or generosity.' Spinoza refers again to these passages in the Appendix to Part Four, where he places *religio* alongside other virtues: 'The things that produce concord are those things belonging to justice, equity, and being honourable.... Especially necessary to bring people together in love, are those things which concern religion and piety [*Amori autem conciliando illa apprime necessaria sunt, quae ad Religionem, et Pietatem spectant*]. On this, see E4p37s1 and s2, E4p46s, and E4p73s' (E4App§15). This sense of *religio* is echoed in letters exchanged with Henry Oldenburg at the end of 1675, which discuss Oldenburg's fears that Spinoza's *Ethics*, if published, would 'destroy the practice of religious virtue [*religiosæ virtutis praxin*]'.[7]

Just as Spinoza treats religion as a virtue, so, conversely, he associates the lack of virtue with false religion. He argues that people who are 'more ready to denounce vice than to teach virtue, and not knowing how to strengthen minds but only how to crush them, are burdensome both to themselves and others. That is why many, from too great an impatience of mind and a false zeal for religion, have preferred living among the lower animals than among men' (E4App§13). He also states that 'self-depreciation has a false appearance of piety and religion' (E4App§22). In just one passage in the *Ethics* he considers religion apart from virtue, associating it instead with customary morality: 'Not everyone has the same custom and religion [*consuetudo et religio*]. On the contrary, what is holy [*sacra*] to some is unholy [*profana*] to others; and what is honourable for some is dishonourable for others. Hence, according as each person has been educated, he either repents of an action or glories in it' (E3Def. Aff.27exp.). Here 'religion' is seen to be socially constructed, and this is closer to a recognisably modern concept of religion. Again, though, this sense of *religio* has both an inward and an outward aspect. It involves a recognition of sacredness, which is a special kind of value, and this attitude will guide thoughts, emotions and moral conduct as well as acts of devotion, reverence and worship.

For Spinoza, *religio* is a relation to oneself, as well as—echoing Aquinas's definition—a relation to God. In considering Spinoza's remarks about religion alongside Aquinas's discussion of this virtue, I am not seeking to trace a line of influence from the *Summa Theologiae* to the *Ethics*. Rather, I want to draw attention to the fact that Spinoza and Aquinas share a similar category of *religio*. They treat it as a virtue, having both inward and outward aspects, rather than as a system of beliefs or as membership of a faith community. Of course, in Spinoza's philosophy, virtue itself gains a distinctive meaning: it is no longer an Aristotelian concept, theorised as a habit (*hexis*, *habitus*), as it was for Aquinas, nor is it a moral concept, as it was for Descartes. 'By virtue and power I understand the same thing,' declares Spinoza at the beginning of Part Four of the *Ethics*: 'virtue, insofar as it is related to man, is the very essence, or nature, of man, insofar as he has the power of bringing about certain things, which can be understood through his nature alone' (E4D8). He understands *religio* according to this definition of virtue, just as Aquinas understood it according to his own account of virtue. Recognising this formal similarity—along with the formal difference it brings into view—helps us to approach Spinoza's writing about religion in light of the conceptual shift from the medieval to the modern era, and to appreciate his distinctive response to a new way of thinking about religion that rose to precedence in his own century. It also shows how inappropriate and misleading it would be to impose onto Spinoza's works our twenty-first-century assumptions about what religion is, and what it means to be religious.

In his 2011 Gifford Lectures, published in 2015 under the title *The Territories of Science and Religion*, the historian Peter Harrison analysed a 'remarkable change in the understanding of religion . . . that can be traced back to the early modern period'.[8] During the sixteenth and seventeenth centuries, *religio* became objectified in a double sense: first, as a system of propositional beliefs, inculcated by printed creeds and pedagogic practices of catechism; and second, as an empirical social reality, so that one might speak of 'the Christian religion' or 'the Jewish religion'. It was this objectified form of religion, characterised by belief and belonging, which would eventually be 'privatised', as a matter of personal choice, within secular societies espousing values of 'religious liberty' and 'religious toleration'.[9] When J. S. Mill articulated these values in *On Liberty*, he recognised that they had their roots in an intensification of religious difference during the upheavals, conflicts and persecutions of the sixteenth-century Protestant reformations.[10]

The 1555 Peace of Augsburg identified two 'religions': Roman Catholicism ('the old religion') and Lutheranism, which was defined in terms of the Augsburg Confession's twenty-eight articles. 'For the first time,' writes Harrison, '"religion" could be understood as a political and legal construct.'[11] While many preachers and theologians continued to emphasise the interior aspects of their own religion, they identified 'other' religions by more observable features such as doctrines and rituals.[12]

Summarising this shift to the new idea of religion, Harrison suggests that

> the philosophical exercises and bodies of knowledge employed in the inculcation of the interior virtue [of] *religio* came to stand in for the thing itself in its entirety. The content of catechisms that had once been understood as techniques for instilling an interior piety now came to be thought of as encapsulating the essence of some objective thing—religion. Religion was vested in creeds rather than in the hearts of the faithful.[13]

This modern conception of religion allows us to identify plural 'religions', distinguished chiefly by their scriptures, creeds and practices. While the virtue of religion, in the medieval sense, can only be properly understood from the inside, modern religion can become an object of study for historians, sociologists, anthropologists and philosophers.[14] An early work of comparative religion was Edward Herbert of Cherbury's *De religione gentilium*, published posthumously in 1663, which surveyed ancient religions for evidence of five 'common notions' of a rationalist 'true religion', which Herbert had set out in his major work *De veritate* (1624).[15] At the end of the seventeenth century, William Turner, a Sussex vicar, published *The History of all Religions in the World: From the Creation down to this Present Time*. The title page of this weighty tome indicated that it was divided into two parts, 'the First containing their THEORY, and the other relating to their PRACTICES; Each divided into Chapters, by the several Heads, or Common Places of Divinity, viz. The Object of Religious Worship, the Place, the Time, the Persons Officiating, the Manner, and the Parts of Worship, & c.' Turner's book included a 'Table of Heresies' and a 'Geographical Map, Showing in what Country Each Religion is Practised'. Turner proudly declared his work to be 'Written in a different Method from anything yet published on this Subject'—and thus summed up, on a single page, the modern conception of religion.[16]

Harrison argues that one indicator of this new way of understanding religion is 'the changing grammar of "religion" in the early modern period'. Since the Latin language has no articles, translators of Latin works must choose whether to render *religio* as 'religion', 'a religion' or 'the religion'. These translation choices changed dramatically during the middle decades of the seventeenth century. In 1632—when Spinoza was born—the phrase 'Christian religion' (without an article) occurred in English books roughly twice as often as 'the Christian religion', while by 1660, when Spinoza began to compose his philosophical works, this proportion had been inverted, 'the Christian religion' now occurring twice as often as 'Christian religion'. The deeper significance of this grammatical shift is illustrated by different translations of the title of Calvin's *Institutio Christianae religionis*: this was first rendered into English, in 1561, as *The Institution of Christian Religion*, whereas a 1762 edition was entitled *The Institution of the Christian Religion*.[17] In the earlier title, 'Christian Religion' might be replaced with 'Christian Virtue', with little change in meaning, while the addition of 'the' suggests a more objectified notion of 'religion' as a doctrine or a social group.

Several reasons might be given for this emergence of modern 'religion' during Spinoza's century. Successive reformations and counter-reformations—involving a series of disputes over the means of salvation, the laity's access to scriptures and sacraments, and the question of clerical marriage—generated a sharpened sense of religious difference, as each Christian faction asserted its claim to 'true religion' and denounced alternative views. This politicised sectarianism tended to objectify 'religion' in terms of theological belief and institutional belonging.

These social changes were accompanied by a slow philosophical revolution in which the concept of virtue was replaced, in both natural and moral philosophy, by a concept of law. Medieval philosophers had understood individual things to be animated by inner principles, powers and potencies, which had a teleological orientation to God. *Virtus*, the Latinised concept of Greek *arête*, meaning excellence or virtue, had connotations of strength, power and manliness as well as moral goodness. Early modern philosophy is characterised by a movement away from the Aristotelian physics and metaphysics that had shaped this worldview. Suárez, Descartes, Bacon and Hobbes all questioned teleological accounts of nature, and sought to expel scholastic notions of *telos, virtus, habitus* and *dispositio* from their accounts of natural processes. Refusing to invoke final causes, these natural philosophers argued that bodies are moved not by intrinsic powers and principles, but by forces—and according to laws—external to themselves.

This new vision of nature extended to human beings, and was paralleled by a new vision of intellectual and moral life.[18] As the Dutch Calvinist theologian Gisbert Voetius argued, the Cartesians' refusal to recognise inherent powers throughout nature undermined appeals to an inner *habitus* as the cause or explanation for moral action.[19] And sure enough, as the modern image of a mechanistic, law-governed universe took shape, concepts of moral law and divine command replaced Aristotelian virtue as the organising principle of a broadly Christian moral philosophy. As questions about the good life were reconfigured around the concept of law (and the associated concepts of duty and obligation), autonomy emerged as the core moral ideal, grounded on the distinction between laws imposed on individuals from the outside—whether by religious authorities, rulers of states or unspoken customs and traditions—and laws we impose freely, rationally, on ourselves. This ideal of autonomy became the hallmark of Enlightenment thinking, exemplified above all by Kant's moral philosophy.

While this is partly a narrative about the intertwined rise of modern philosophy and science, scholastic accounts of human virtue came under attack for distinctively theological reasons too. Luther denounced the view of pagan thinkers, such as Aristotle and Cicero, that a virtuous *habitus* could be cultivated by human effort, arguing that our all-pervading sinfulness means we could only be justified by divine grace. Calvin, similarly, condemned the 'very false opinion, that man has in himself sufficient ability to ensure his own virtue and happiness'.[20] More fundamentally, these reformers rejected the idea that righteousness is a condition of a person's inner being. Luther, in particular, did not think that grace changed a person's nature: the individual remained sinful, and his righteousness or justification meant that he now stood in the right relation to God, even as a sinner. Salvation was certainly not a reward for good works facilitated by a divinely infused virtue or *habitus*. In other words, Luther ceased to think about faith and righteousness in terms of the concepts of virtue and habit.[21] His polemic against scholastic and humanist accounts of virtue suppressed the very notion of human power, whether individual or collective. And perhaps—despite an Enlightenment 'ideal of mastery' being one of the clichés of modern scholarship—this suppression continued in the new natural philosophies of the seventeenth century, in which nature was understood mechanistically, and human freedom was set apart from nature, no longer conceived as a channelling, cultivation and refinement of natural powers.

During the seventeenth century, then, as Harrison argues, 'the fate of the inherent virtues of natural things was intimately related to the fate of the moral and intellectual virtues.... As a consequence of challenges to Aristotelian understandings of virtues both natural and human, *religio* took on a new meaning, and was increasingly associated with systems of thought, belief, and social organisation in the familiar modern sense.'[22]

Of course, the older concept of *religio*, closely associated with virtue, piety, devotion and attention to the inner life, continued to be asserted— often by those who recognised the intellectual and social reification of religion, and sought to resist it. In the Catholic tradition, Francis de Sales and Pascal wrote influential works exploring the inward relation to God. Quakers and Christian 'enthusiasts' emphasised personal experience. And Lutheran 'pietists' revived pre-Reformation devotional and mystical works. Medieval writers like Thomas à Kempis and Johannes Tauler inspired Johann Arndt's *True Christianity*, a popular pietist guide to the holy life, which was published in over a hundred editions between 1605 and 1740. Arndt, like Pascal, located religion in the heart, while emphasising charitable works. German Romanticism, which challenged both doctrinal and institutional religion, was a marriage of pietism and Spinozism, mixed with new elements: an expansive sexual morality, and devotion to art. The Romantic theologian Friedrich Schleiermacher, who was educated at a Moravian pietist school, famously described religion as 'a feeling of absolute dependence'. Søren Kierkegaard, the most significant religious thinker of the nineteenth century, channelled both pietism and Romanticism into his searing critiques of objectified religion: he argued that academic theology rationalised faith; that the Danish State Church taught a worldly, bourgeois, civic religion; that Hegelian philosophy externalised religious life as *Sittlichkeit*, given form by customs and institutions. Kierkegaard's emphasis on inwardness, subjectivity and spiritual 'upbuilding' directly addressed the modern idea that religion is a set of doctrines that can be understood through propositional knowledge, or a social phenomenon known by empirical methods.

Spinoza did not, of course, belong to the Christian tradition which produced these successive efforts to draw religion back into the human heart. Nevertheless, situating his treatment of *religio* within this broader milieu helps us to appreciate how he too offered philosophical resistance to the modern concept of religion that took shape following the Reformation. Harrison traces its development through the seventeenth century without mentioning Spinoza—perhaps because the discussion of *religio* in the *Ethics* bears little trace of the objectifying, intellectualising view of religion that Harrison's book seeks to explain—or perhaps because Spinoza has so often been read as an opponent of religion of any kind.

Why would Spinoza, in many respects such a radical thinker, be exempt from this new way of thinking about religion? Why does the *Ethics* employ a concept of *religio* that is structurally similar to Aquinas's use of this term? In some ways, this is not surprising: Spinoza did not share the motivations that led other philosophers and theologians to reject the scholastic view that *religio* is a virtue, a habitual disposition. Since he dismissed Christian teachings about sin, he was untroubled by the idea that the highest good could be attained by human effort. Indeed, his concept of *conatus*, or striving, placed this effort centre-stage. More profoundly, Spinoza's critique of human free will and his insistence on being-in-God amount to a refusal to draw the distinction between divine and human agency, between grace and nature, which underpinned and structured Christian debates about this issue. And while Spinoza joined Descartes, Bacon and Hobbes in rejecting a teleological metaphysics of nature, expelling final causes from scientific enquiry, his assertion that everything strives to persevere in its being echoes the medieval conception of *virtus* as both inward power and outward expression. Spinoza's streamlined approach to virtue, or power, is quite different from the elaborate psychology of the scholastics, who attributed all sorts of powers, faculties, virtues and tendencies to natural things. Yet it is also fundamentally different from the philosophies of nature advanced by those seventeenth-century thinkers who argued that bodies are moved not by intrinsic powers and principles, but by forces external to themselves, in accordance with mechanistic laws.[23]

Although the passages on *religio* in the *Ethics* show that Spinoza did not espouse the modern view of religion, we have to look beyond the *Ethics* to appreciate his intense interest in the category of religion itself. Spinoza was keenly aware of the changing discourse among his contemporaries, and—as we might expect—he did not simply cling to an unreconstructed medieval conception of *religio*. Rather, he actively resisted the tendency to equate religion with beliefs and doctrines, and to objectify 'other' religious creeds and practices—because he saw this as a cause as well as a symptom of sectarian conflict. Before he completed the *Ethics*, he was working out these ideas in his letters and, of course, in the *Theologico-Political Treatise*.

Two of Spinoza's later letters, quoted in my Introduction, directly confront the modern concept of religion. Written during the years following the publication of the *Theologico-Political Treatise*, these letters show how vigorously Spinoza defended his non-sectarian understanding of *religio* as an ethical virtue, rather than a confession of faith in ecclesial doctrines. In 1671, he responded to Lambert van Velthuysen's charge that 'to avoid being faulted for superstition, he [had] cast off all religion' by challenging Velthuysen's concept of religion:

> What he understands by Religion, and what by Superstition, I don't know. Has someone who maintains that God must be recognized as the highest good, and that he should be freely loved as such, cast off all religion? Is someone who holds that our greatest happiness and freedom consist only in this [love of God] irreligious? Or that the reward of virtue is virtue itself, whereas the punishment of folly and weakness is folly itself? And finally, that each person ought to love his neighbour and obey the commands of the supreme power?[24]

This passage implies that Spinoza considered his philosophy to be religious precisely insofar as it states that God must be loved as the highest good, that virtue is intrinsically good, and that neighbour-love and a law-abiding pacifism should be the guiding principles of social life.

Spinoza's letter to Albert Burgh, written in the winter of 1675–76 following news of Burgh's conversion to Roman Catholicism, shows awareness of different religious traditions as well as different Christian sects. Here Spinoza uses the word 'religion' in the modern sense, yet he immediately corrects himself, as if calling this sense of 'religion' into question: 'you ... presume you have at last discovered the best Religion, or rather the best men, to whom you have abandoned your credulity'. How did Burgh know, asked Spinoza, that his new-found Catholic teachers 'are the best among all those who have ever taught other Religions, still teach them, or will teach them in the future? have you examined all those religions, both ancient and modern, which are taught here, and in India, and everywhere throughout the globe? And even if you had examined them properly, how would you know you have chosen the best?'[25] Spinoza was not actually advising Burgh to undertake studies in comparative religion. Rather, he challenged not only Burgh's claim to have found *the* true religion, but also—more importantly—the sectarianism underpinning this claim, by treating *religio* as a virtue: a matter of honour, justice, loving-kindness and 'holiness of life', which can be 'common to all'.

'In every Church', writes Spinoza,

> there are many very honourable men, who worship God with justice and loving-kindness. We know many men of this kind among the

Lutherans, the Reformed, the Mennonites, and the Enthusiasts. And, not to mention others, you know your own ancestors, who in the time of the Duke of Alva, with equal constancy and freedom of mind, suffered all kinds of torture for the sake of Religion. So you ought to concede that holiness of life [*vitae sanctitatem*] is not peculiar to the Roman Church, but is common to all. And because we know by this—to speak with the Apostle John—that we remain in God, and God remains in us, it follows that whatever distinguishes the Roman Church from the others is completely superfluous, and so has been established only by superstition. For as I have said, with John, justice and loving-kindness are the unique and most certain sign of true Catholic faith [*verae fidei Catholicae*].[26]

Here Spinoza reminds Burgh of the destructive consequences of sectarianism: the Duke of Alva had brutally repressed the Reformation in the Netherlands, on behalf of the Spanish king, Philip II, son of the Holy Roman emperor Charles V. Spinoza cleverly challenges Burgh's own sectarianism by using the word 'Catholic' in its original sense—in distinction from 'the Roman Church'—to denote a universal, inclusive faith. In the *Ethics*, of course, he asserts this universality and inclusivity through his principle of being-in-God. *Everything* is in God, and this includes all people, and all their religious ideas and practices.

This letter, like his response to Velthuysen, echoes the argument set out in the concluding chapters of the *Theologico-Political Treatise*. Here Spinoza offers a robust critique of an objectified, excessively doctrinal conception of religion. Chapter 19 of the *Treatise* explicitly distinguishes between external and internal *religio*—between 'the exercise of piety [and] the external practice of religion [*externo religionis cultu*]' and 'piety itself and the internal worship of God [*Dei interno cultu*]'.[27] This distinction between what is 'external' and what is 'internal' echoes Spinoza's remarks, earlier in the *Treatise*, about God's 'internal aid' and the human being's 'internal virtue'. There he appealed to the Proverbs of Solomon to argue that

> natural knowledge [*Scientia naturali*] . . . teaches Ethics and true virtue [*Ethicam docet, et veram virtutem*]. . . . Solomon agrees that the happiness and peace [*felicitas et tranquillitas*] of one who cultivates the natural understanding [*naturalem intellectum*] does not depend on the rule of fortune (i.e., on God's external aid), but chiefly on his internal virtue (i.e., on God's internal aid) [*a sua interna virtute (sive Dei auxilio interno)*].[28]

This significant passage implies a preference for internal virtue, which is aligned with 'true virtue' and also with 'natural knowledge'. Returning to Chapter 19, we may detect an analogous preference for 'internal religion', which, Spinoza argues, cannot be commanded by human authorities. External religion 'receives the force of law only from the decree of those who have the right to rule', that is, from the sovereign ruler of a republic, and not from separate ecclesial authorities. Moreover, sovereigns have a right of command over external religion 'provided only that they do not allow the doctrines of Religion to be increased to a great number or to be confused with knowledge [*cum scientiis*]'.[29]

Spinoza offers these suggestions in a pragmatic spirit, observing that 'men are likely to make great mistakes in matters of religion, and to compete vigorously in inventing many things, according to the differences in their mentality'. Given these human tendencies, 'if no one were bound by law to obey the supreme power in the things he thought pertained to religion', society would be thrown into chaos. 'The right of the state would depend on the varying judgement and affect of each person', according to 'his faith and superstition', and people would be deprived of the security and peace that is 'the supreme exercise of loving-kindness'.[30] Since Spinoza thinks 'true religion' consists in loving-kindness, these remarks suggest that his political strictures on 'external' religious life seek to protect and facilitate this true religion.

The claims about the nature and scope of *religio* set out in Chapters 13 and 14 of the *Theologico-Political Treatise* constitute the core argument of the book. These clarifications of the concept of religion are, Spinoza writes, 'the main points I have been aiming at in this treatise'.[31] He concludes Chapter 14 by entreating the reader 'most earnestly to take the time to read these two Chapters quite carefully, to weigh them again and again, and to be persuaded that we did not write them with the intention of introducing any novelties, but only to correct distortions [*ut depravata corrigeremus*], which we hope one day, finally, to see corrected'.[32] Following Spinoza's advice to review carefully these chapters of the *Theologico-Political Treatise*, we find that the 'distortions' he sought to correct involve an objectifying, overly theoretical conception of religion.

The title of Chapter 13 of the *Treatise* announces the ethical orientation of Spinoza's own concept of religion: 'that Scripture teaches . . . nothing about the divine Nature, except what men can imitate by a certain manner of living'. Spinoza quickly professes himself confounded by the 'mentality' of people who have 'introduced into religion so many matters of philosophic speculation that the Church seems to be an Academy, and Religion, a science [*scientia*], or rather, a disputation'.[33] He argues briskly that scriptural or 'revealed' religion requires obedience, not knowledge, before emphasising the importance of this point: 'because the judgement of the whole of Religion depends on this [*quia hinc totius Religionis decisio pendet*], I want to show the whole matter more carefully and to explain it more clearly'.[34]

The more detailed argument that follows is twofold. First, Spinoza explains that we do not all have equal access to intellectual knowledge of God. Anticipating the objection that mere belief, rather than knowledge, is required of the faithful, he argues that

> anyone who says this is talking nonsense. Invisible things, and those which are the objects only of the mind, can't be seen by any other eyes than by demonstrations. Someone who doesn't have demonstrations doesn't see anything at all in these things. If they repeat something they have heard about them, it no more touches or reveals their mind than do the words of a parrot or an automaton, which speaks without a mind or without meaning.[35]

Second, Spinoza states that *religio* consists in neither theoretical knowledge nor propositional beliefs, but in the virtues of justice, loving-kindness and mercy. He turns to the Bible to support this claim:

> God through the Prophets asks from us no other knowledge than knowledge of his divine Justice and Loving-kindness [*quam cognitionem divinae suae Justitiae, et Charitatis*], i.e., such attributes of God as people can imitate in a certain way of life. Jeremiah teaches this most explicitly: *Your father, indeed, ate, and drank, and passed judgement, and did justice, and then it was well with him; he judged the right of the poor and the needy, and then it was well with him; for this is to know me, said Yahweh* (22:15–16). No less clear is the passage in 9:23: *let each one glory in this, that he understands me and knows me, that I, Yahweh, practice loving-kindness, judgement and justice on the earth, for I delight in these things, says Yahweh.*
>
> We infer this also from Exodus 34:6–7. There, when Moses wants to see and to come to know him, God reveals only those attributes which display divine Justice and Loving-kindess.
>
> Finally, we should note especially the passage in John, where, because no one has seen God, he explains God only through

loving-kindness, and concludes that whoever has loving-kindness really has and knows God.

We see, then, that Jeremiah, Moses and John sum up the knowledge of God each person is bound to have by locating it only in this: that God is supremely just and merciful, *or*, that he is the model of the true life.[36]

Spinoza concludes Chapter 13 by rejecting an objectifying view of *pietas*, a virtue that was traditionally associated closely with *religio*, and in this instance is virtually synonymous with it. Piety, suggests Spinoza, is a matter of 'how' rather than 'what': a matter of how one thinks and behaves, not a matter of what one knows or believes—'So we should not for a moment believe that opinions [*opiniones*], considered in themselves and without regard to works, have any piety or impiety in them. Instead, we should say that a person believes something piously only insofar as his opinions move him to obedience, and impiously only insofar as he takes from them a license to sin or rebel.' Indeed, Spinoza claims that piety has nothing to do with propositional beliefs, even if those beliefs happen to be true: 'So, if anyone becomes insolent [*contumax*] by believing truths [*vera credendo*], he is really impious; on the other hand, if he becomes obedient by believing falsehoods [*falsa credendo*], he has a pious faith [*piam habet fidem*].'[37]

He repeats this point in a slightly different way in Chapter 14, where he condemns 'sectarians' for 'persecuting, as God's enemies, everyone who does not think as they do, even though they are very honest and obedient to true virtue. On the other hand they still love, as God's elect, those who give lip service to these opinions, even though they are most weak-minded.' He adds here that 'nothing more wicked or harmful to the republic can be imagined'.[38] The subject of this chapter is faith (*fides*), which has more cognitive connotations than *religio*; Spinoza's chief task here is to 'separate faith from Philosophy'—which is, he declares, 'the main purpose of this whole work'. Commentators often interpret this as a call for freedom to philosophise, by limiting the reach of religious authority, and it is certainly this—but it is also an attempt to circumscribe the scope of faith itself, in order to defend Spinoza's ethical conception of religion.[39]

Ironically, this chapter offers two lists which bear a passing resemblance to the creedal statements, summarising theological doctrines in propositional form, which crystallised sectarianism during the sixteenth century. Spinoza's lists are notably short in comparison with the Augsburg Confession of the Lutheran Church, or the Belgic Confession of the Reformed Church. Doctrinal minimalism was a strategy pursued by others who wished to settle sectarian conflicts.[40] More than this, however, the content of Spinoza's lists subverts the epistemic, confessional concept of *fides* that is intimately connected to the modern objectification of *religio*.

The first list comprises a definition of faith, followed by five propositions which follow from this definition. In each case Spinoza pushes the concept of faith away from theoretical knowledge or belief, and towards virtue. Faith, he states, 'certainly [*nempe*] can be nothing other than knowing [*sentire*] such things about God that, were you unaware [*ignoratis*] of them, obedience to God would be destroyed, and that the mere fact of obedience implies'.[41] It is striking that, in this carefully worded definition, Spinoza chooses the verb *sentire*, 'to feel', in order to articulate the kind of awareness of God involved in faith. It would have been more natural to use *scire* (to know), or *noscere* (to be acquainted with; to recognise)—both of which occur in the passage from 1 John that Spinoza cites in this chapter: 'we know [*scimus*] that we know [*novimus*] God if we keep God's commandments' (1 John 2:3–4). *Sentire* suggests an immediate, affective cognition, rather than propositional understanding. This is emphasised further by Spinoza's claim that faith is *certainly nothing other than* this feeling-knowing of certain features of God.[42]

And what are these features of God? As Spinoza has already suggested in the preceding chapter, they are moral qualities—loving-kindness (*charitas*), justice and mercy—and we 'know' God insofar as we embody these qualities. The five propositions which follow from his definition of faith are all connected with inward or outward virtue:

I. Faith is not saving by itself, but only in relation to obedience.
II. If someone is truly obedient, he must have a true and saving faith.
III. We can judge no one faithful or unfaith except from their works.
(Here Spinoza cites James 2:18: 'I shall show you my faith from my works,' and 1 John 4:7–8: 'whoever loves [*diligit*] is born of God and knows God . . . for God is loving-kindness [*charitas*]'.)
IV. The real Antichrists are those who persecute honest men who love Justice, because they disagree with them, and do not defend the same doctrines of faith they do.
V. Faith requires, not so much true doctrines, as pious doctrines, i.e., doctrines which move the heart to obedience, even if many of them do not have even a shadow of truth.[43]

Having thus elaborated his concept of faith, Spinoza proceeds to 'enumerate the tenets of the universal faith [*fidei universalis dogmata*]'. This second list comprises seven *dogmata*, each with a practical orientation to virtue. As Susan James explains, 'whereas tenets of faith were usually presented [by religious authorities] as accredited truths to which the faithful must consent, Spinoza's are designed not to communicate the truth but to guide our actions'. Equally, 'evidence of one's commitment to the tenets is not supplied by one's ideas but by one's actions'.[44] Mogens Lærke has developed this insight by tracing in the *Theologico-Political Treatise* a 'systematic distinction' between faith as a theoretical foundation (*fundamentum*) and 'true religion' as a practical standard (*norma*): 'no doctrine will qualify as being of universal faith unless it measures up to the practical standard of true religion [i.e., justice and loving-kindness]. Conversely, doctrines of universal faith form the speculative or theoretical foundation of true religion.'[45] As Spinoza puts it, 'the person who displays the best arguments is not necessarily the one who displays the best faith; instead it's the one who displays the best works of justice and loving-kindness'.[46] Here Spinoza singles out one of the most divisive theological questions of post-Reformation Christendom—the relative significance of faith and works—and appeals to a particularly contentious New Testament text, James 2:17 ('faith without works is dead'), to underscore his point.[47] Yet he is not merely criticising the Protestants' elevation of faith above works, and thus siding with the Catholic Church. Rather, he is advancing a philosophical argument that rejects the sectarianism underlying the whole debate.

When Spinoza sets out his seven *dogmata* of universal faith, he links each tenet to a negative claim, in the form of a theoretical question which, he insists, 'does not matter, as far as faith is concerned'. So his list of *dogmata* is not determined simply by a practical religious 'standard', as James and Lærke point out; it also explicitly excludes certain theoretical issues. If we consider this Spinozist creed as a clarification of the very concept of faith, it becomes a repudiation of theory itself:

I. *God exists, i.e., there is a supreme being, supremely just and merciful*, or *a model of true life*. Anyone who does not know, or does not believe [*nescit, vel non credit*] that God exists cannot obey God or know God as a Judge.
    i. [It does not matter for faith] what God (or that model of true life) is, whether fire, spirit, light, thought, etc.
II. *God is unique.* No one can doubt that this too is absolutely required for supreme devotion, admiration and love towards

God. For devotion, admiration and love arise only because the excellence of one surpasses that of the rest.

    ii. [It does not matter for faith] how God is a model of true life, whether because God has a just and merciful heart, or because all things exist and act through God (and hence we too understand and see through God what is truly right and good).

III. *God is present everywhere, or everything is open to God [omnia ipsi patere].* If people believed some things were hidden from God, or did not know that God sees all, they would have doubts about the equity of the justice by which God directs all things— or at least they would not be aware of it.

    iii. [It does not matter for faith] whether God is everywhere according to God's essence, or God's power.

IV. *God has a supreme right and dominion over all things, and does nothing because he is compelled by law, but acts only according to his absolute good pleasure and special grace.* For everyone is absolutely bound to obey God, whereas God is not bound to obey anyone.

    iv. [It does not matter for faith] whether God directs things from freedom or by a necessity of nature.

V. *The worship of God and obedience to God consist only in justice and loving-kindness, or in love towards one's neighbour.*

    v. [It does not matter for faith] whether God prescribes laws as a prince or teaches them as eternal truths.

VI. *Everyone who obeys by living in this way is saved; the rest, who live under the control of pleasures, are lost.* If people do not firmly believe this, there would be no reason why they should prefer to obey God rather than pleasures.

    vi. [It does not matter for faith] whether we obey God from freedom of the will or from the necessity of the divine decree.

VII. *God pardons the sins of those who repent.* No one is without sin. So if we do not maintain this, everyone would despair of his salvation, and there would be no reason why anyone would believe God to be merciful. Moreover, whoever firmly believes that God, out of mercy and the grace by which he directs everything, pardons our sins, and who for this reason is more inspired by the love of God [*et hac de causa in Dei amore magis incenditur*], that person really knows Christ according to the Spirit, and Christ is in him.

vii. [It does not matter for faith] whether the reward of the good and punishment of the evil are natural or supernatural.[48]

When we lay out Spinoza's *dogmata* like this, with each tenet accompanied by a statement of what is irrelevant to faith, it appears more like an anti-creed than a creed. This is fundamentally at odds with Calvin's approach to doctrine: the preface to the *Institutes of Christian Religion* complains that Catholic priests are too willing to accept ignorance of the 'true religion' taught in Scripture, since 'they think it unimportant what anyone holds or denies concerning God and Christ'.[49]

While creeds aim to unify a community, they are also inherently sectarian. The creeds of the early Christian church settled disputes and established boundaries between orthodoxy and heresy, while the plural creeds and confessions that emerged following the Reformation articulated the differences between churches. Spinoza's *dogmata*, by contrast, propose a 'universal faith'.[50] They are offered to the predominantly Christian readership of the *Theologico-Political Treatise* as tenets that all Christians—whether Catholic or Calvinist, Cartesian or non-conformist—may accept.[51] Spinoza's *dogmata* are, in fact, quite loosely Christian. Only the final tenet mentions Christ, and not as a requirement for salvation, but as a way of understanding what it means to acknowledge God's mercy and grace, and to participate more fully in divine love.

Spinoza's doctrinal minimalism does not, however, indicate that he thought people should have thinned-down, minimal religious lives. On the contrary, while his seven *dogmata* define what can be universally shared, he urges his readers to 'interpret' and 'embrace' these foundations in ways particular to their own minds and hearts. Spinoza does not merely permit this personal appropriation, but insists on it:

> each person is bound [*tenetur*] to accommodate these tenets of faith [*fidei dogmata*] to his own power of understanding, and to interpret them for himself, as it seems to him easier for him to embrace them without any hesitation, with complete agreement of the heart [*integro animi consensus amplecti*], so that he may obey God wholeheartedly [*Deo pleno animi consensus obediat*].[52]

This existential requirement opens the door to a much richer religious life than is implied by the *dogmata* themselves.[53] Wholeheartedly embracing the 'universal faith' might involve engaging with a wide and diverse range of ideas, images, stories and practices. Participating in rituals of worship and undertaking rigorous philosophical work could be equally conducive to appropriating Spinoza's *dogmata* and practising 'true religion'. As Michael Rosenthal has argued, the *dogmata* 'provide a bridge between the inner and outer forms of religion', disclosing 'the indissoluble links between the imaginative practices of outer religion and the rational ones of inner religion'.[54]

Having read the *Ethics*, we know that Spinoza pursued answers to the questions which the *Theologico-Political Treatise* puts beyond the scope of faith. His philosophical enquiries yield knowledge that applies directly to the *dogmata* enumerated in the *Treatise*: (i) God is infinite and eternal substance, expressed through infinite attributes; (ii) all things exist and act through God, and hence we understand through God what is truly right and good; (iii) God is everywhere according to his essence and his power, since God's essence and power are one and the same; (iv) God directs things by a necessity of nature—which coincides with divine freedom; (v) divine laws are eternal truths; (vi) we obey God from the necessity of divine decree; and (vii) goodness is rewarded and evil is punished naturally, not supernaturally.

For Spinoza, faith and philosophy are separable precisely because they are analogous to one another: they both offer a kind of knowledge of God, or at least an idea of God. The virtue of *religio* does require some knowledge—for all virtues require knowledge. Courage, for example, involves knowledge of the good, since it is virtuous to fight bravely for a good cause, but not for an unjust cause; justice involves knowing what is due to each person. Since *religio* is a kind of justice towards God, it requires some understanding of God, and of how it might be appropriate to honour God. *Religio* can discern God either through faith, or through philosophy. Either way, Spinoza argues, the virtue of *religio* will involve desires and actions that embody justice and loving-kindness.

The *Theologico-Political Treatise* considers *religio* in relation to faith, while the *Ethics* shows how this virtue can be cultivated on the basis of a philosophical understanding of God, and particularly by knowing our own being-in-God, which we share with all other people and things.

Spinoza's inclusive definition of *religio* in the *Ethics* accommodates these alternatives of faith and philosophy: 'whatever we desire and do, insofar as we have the idea of God, or insofar as we know God [*quatenus Dei habemus ideam, sive quatenus Deum cognoscimus*], I relate to religion' (E4p37s1). The ideas we have of God may be adequate or inadequate, and—as Spinoza emphasises in the *Theologico-Political Treatise*—they will, either way, provide a foundation for true religion as long as they inspire justice and loving-kindness. In other words, *religio* may be based on imaginative thinking about God, or on reason, or on intuition. Whether *religio* is grounded in faith or in philosophy, it need not require propositional knowledge. Of course, it might involve this kind of knowledge (or belief), but *religio* certainly would not *consist* in this. Spinoza's *religio* is neither a doctrine nor a belief, neither a sect nor a church. It is a virtue, and it consists in desire and action—'whatever we desire and do'—that is oriented not only to God, but also to singular things in their being-in-God.

In Chapter 3, I suggested that the seventeenth-century Christian churches might have been better fortified against the challenges of modernity if they had embraced Spinozism. I think this is also true of ourselves, and our culture. Spinoza's philosophy of religion accommodates the religious diversity that now shapes modern cities, schools and universities. It also offers resistance and critique to many of the tropes now diagnosed—by humanities scholars, at least—as diseases of modernity: dualism, nihilism, voluntarism, reductive materialism, subjectivism. When we dwell in the world of the *Ethics*, these philosophical pathologies simply don't arise. While contemporary theologians often seek refuge in a more enchanted medieval cosmology, built by thinkers who knew only one true faith, Spinozism can confront modernity without nostalgia, yet with *religio*.[55]

AFTERWORD

'The path to these things'

IN THE *ETHICS* Spinoza proposes both a speculative theology and a philosophy of religious life. The first concerns our being, while the second concerns our becoming. These two aspects of the *Ethics*—the ontological or metaphysical, on the one hand, and the ethical or existential, on the other—are intimately connected. In Part One, Spinoza argues that God, a substance consisting of an infinity of attributes, necessarily exists, and that whatever is, is in God. For each individual mode this entails causal and conceptual dependence, which can give the impression that we are trapped in a rigid determinist system. As we move through the *Ethics*, however, Spinoza's metaphysics of human being-in-God unfolds: we see that we can be more or less, that we are continually passing between various degrees of being—and that our fluctuating existence, with its striving to persist and increase, opens up a path to follow in pursuit of the highest good. This ethical journey, way or path (*via*) expresses our nature, yet it involves effort, emendation, learning, growth in virtue and self-understanding.

Religious life consists in keeping to this demanding path, or, perhaps more realistically, in returning to it again and again. Its task is to appropriate, live out and remain faithful to the truth of our being-in-God—the truth that constitutes the core of Spinoza's theology. This is the meaning of 'human freedom', as the title of *Ethics* V suggests.

Spinoza ends Part Five with a word of encouragement to follow his difficult path of freedom: 'If the path [*via*] I have shown to lead to these things now seems very hard [*perardua videatur*], still, it can be found' (E5p42s). In fact, he suggests, the path only *seems* arduous. When it is found and followed, even if only for a short time, it turns out to be a place of rest.

Religio joins a number of concepts in the *Ethics*—being-in-God, *scientia intuitiva*, participation, *acquiescentia*, *amor Dei intellectualis* and eternity—which are gathered in this book under the title *Spinoza's Religion*. These concepts touch one another, illuminate one another, and each might be placed at the heart of the gathering. Whichever concept takes centre-stage, the *Ethics* discloses ways of being, knowing, desiring, feeling and acting that are entirely natural to human beings, yet also high ideals which inspire strivings of devotion and cultivation. We considered, in Chapter 2, how the text itself exemplifies and guides these strivings. The *Ethics* addresses readers with mixed minds, and seeks to train their imaginations as well as model the clear, orderly thinking of *ratio* and the immediate, penetrating insight of *scientia intuitiva*.

Spinoza is often described as a rationalist—and he is certainly committed to the intelligibility of being. Yet his conception of knowledge seems much broader than the epistemologies that dominate contemporary philosophy. He understands human cognition to be intimately tied to our embodiment, our affective experience, our duration. His use of the verb *cognoscere* throughout the passages in the *Ethics* dealing with our knowledge of God suggests a process of getting to know God, which requires sustained attention. Similarly, he chooses the verb *noscere*—meaning to recognise, to become acquainted—to describe a process of getting to know ourselves: 'it is necessary to know [*noscere*] both the power and the weakness of our nature' (E4p17s). This suggests that we should seek to know, by intimate acquaintance, both our sadness and our joy: though Spinoza celebrates joy, and criticises the idea that forms of sadness should be cultivated as spiritual virtues, this does not mean we should resist or refuse sadness when it arises—for how else can we come to know 'the power and the weakness of our nature', except by feeling its fluctuations? *Sentire* denotes the mind's feeling of its own eternity, while *scientia intuitiva* likewise conveys the immediacy and simplicity of sensation: a capacity to see, in one glance, the being-in-God of singular things. Spinoza suggests that our minds can connect to God in all these ways, and he shows why this connection naturally, necessarily, brings us joy and peace—our highest activity, and our deepest repose.

We are not autonomous beings, and we do not strive for these goods alone. We seek like-minded companions, and the more we taste the immanent rewards of consciously being-in-God, the more we wish to share them with others. This is precisely what Spinoza himself desired—and what he did. The very fact that he spent many years writing the *Ethics*, without extrinsic reward, is, I think, an extraordinary demonstration of his own virtue of *religio*.

In my Introduction, I suggested that the *Ethics* may be ambiguous on the question of religion. This is partly because Spinoza approaches this question neither in terms of orthodoxy, nor in terms of orthopraxy; both these alternatives belong to the modern objectification of religion, which he sought to resist. More fundamentally, the religious ambiguity of the *Ethics* contributes to this resistance. It is possible to interpret the text so that the concept of God becomes a theoretical vanishing-point, evacuated of recognisably religious significance—and many people have read it this way. I find it remarkable that Spinoza's philosophy accommodates twenty-first-century atheism along with the simple piety of his landlady. This profound inclusivity is a great strength at a time when there are deep sectarian divisions not only between different 'religions', but between what we have become accustomed to call 'religious' and 'secular' perspectives. Unlike many other religious philosophies, Spinoza does not alienate non-religious readers.[1]

Nevertheless, if we exclude the insights I have considered under the heading 'Spinoza's Religion', we miss much of the richness and depth of the *Ethics*. We also miss the opportunity to allow Spinoza to challenge the dogmatism of the secular view that now dominates our culture, just as he challenged Christian and Jewish dogmatisms in his own time. If we insist on Spinoza's atheism, we cannot appreciate his core principle of being-in-God, and have little choice but to dismiss much of Part Five of the *Ethics*. If we assume that *Deus sive Natura* simply reduces God to a familiar modern notion of nature, stripped of any theological meaning, then we lose the conception of God (or *Natura naturans*) as ontological ground which is so integral to Spinoza's metaphysics, with its deep commitment to the intelligibility of being.[2]

Spinoza offers us the freedom to name this ontological ground 'God' or 'Nature', 'YHWH' or 'substance', or perhaps something else. Any name can only gesture to a plenitude of being that eludes us—although we cannot exist, or conceive ourselves, apart from it. Yet *how* we gesture to the ground of our being matters a great deal, since this gesture is a fundamental way of making, or disclosing, meaning in our world. Since 'God' names this excessive, elusive, omnipresent fullness of being in a manner that draws human beings into communities of devotion and enquiry, equipped with long histories and rich philosophical, contemplative and poetic traditions to draw upon, this is both a good name and a risky one. In the seventeenth century it had a very broad appeal, and offered a promising basis for universality as well as enormous potential for theological discord. Perhaps this is why Spinoza retained it in the *Ethics* as well as in the *Theologico-Political Treatise*, while addressing, in both texts, the misunderstandings and conflicts generated by dogmatic 'belief in God'.

To speak personally for a moment, I feel ambivalent towards the word 'God', but one of the things I like about it is that it places us in what Étienne Souriau called 'a questioning situation'.[3] I find that this word opens up, rather than circumscribes, the Kierkegaardian 'question of existence'— What does it mean to be a human being?—that guides my philosophical work and what I hesitatingly call my spiritual life.[4] The Catholic theologian Karl Rahner wrote that the word 'God' (or equivalent words in other languages) 'is so very much without contour', and for this reason is 'obviously quite appropriate for what it refers to'. Using the word 'mystery' in a sense similar to Souriau's 'questioning situation', Rahner suggests that 'the concept "God" is not a grasp of God by which a person masters the mystery, but it is letting oneself be grasped by the mystery which is present and yet ever distant'.[5]

The name of God, spoken with due care, has a remarkable power to hold open the question of religion. Since Spinoza retains the classical conception of *religio* as the virtue of giving honour to God, his decision to name God as the ground of being in Part One of the *Ethics* raises the question: what does it mean to give honour to God? This prompts theoretical, theological questions—What is God? Where is God? How am I connected to God?—and while the *Ethics* does offer compelling answers to these questions, it also suggests that pursuing them will cultivate a sense of our own epistemic limitations. Such questions flow from, and are intimately connected to, the practical religious question of *how* we might give honour to God. Spinoza refuses to answer this question in terms of religious belief or religious practice. In place of orthodoxy or orthopraxy, he holds open the ethical, existential or spiritual *question* of religion: 'How . . . ?' This is a working question, a guiding question, a question that is genuinely asked only insofar as it is lived.[6]

One clear answer that emerges from Spinoza's works is the kind of devotion I discussed in Chapter 1: a willingness to spend time, to pay attention, to offer these resources of one's life—as Foucault put it, 'the price that must be paid for access to the truth'. Paying this 'spiritual' price is what it means to honour God, and perhaps, as Latour suggests, 'learning to redirect attention is religion itself'.[7] Yet precisely how we spend our time, precisely where we direct our attention, may remain open—for devotion can be expressed through philosophical and theological enquiry;

through contemplation and meditation; through rituals and liturgies; or simply through ethical life. *Religio* might take the form of seeking God, or giving praise and thanks to a God already given through a cultural tradition. It might be cultivated and communicated in hymns and mantras, in speech and writing, in works of love or in silence.

Spinoza's conception of God as ontological ground not only secures the intelligibility of being, but also provides a resting-place for desire. In other words, this grounding is affective and experiential, as well as metaphysical. If we were not consciously grounded in God, we could not feel, or 'know by experience', that we are eternal—not even for a moment. The *Ethics* suggests that we do have this knowledge, and that we can rest in it, regardless of religious belief or belonging. Without God, our hearts would remain restless; our desire and love would be drawn only to mutable, perishable things. Spinoza's writings give philosophical expression to an eternal desire and love, which has been articulated in many ways, in many traditions, throughout human history. We can trace the stakes of this issue to the beginning of the *Treatise on the Emendation of the Intellect*, where Spinoza describes how our minds, or souls, are disturbed and diminished by 'the love of those things that can perish'—whereas 'love [*amor*] toward the eternal and infinite thing feeds the mind [*animum*] with a joy entirely exempt from sadness. This is greatly to be desired [*desiderandum*], and to be sought with all our strength.'[8]

This affirmation of eternity does not make Spinozism a dualistic, life-denying, other-worldly philosophy. On the contrary: all the things of this world have some share in God's eternity, and deserve to be seen and loved as beings-in-God. When things express themselves most truly, they participate most fully in God's nature. For a Spinozist, it would be poetic, but not untrue, to call their being-in-God 'glory', and to say that every creature on the earth sings its own peculiarly glorious song in praise of its creator.

ACKNOWLEDGEMENTS

SEVEN FRIENDS AND FELLOW PHILOSOPHERS read a draft of this book, and offered their comments: Yitzhak Melamed, who kindly welcomed me in when I turned up on the doorstep of the seventeenth century, and whose work on Spinoza has been an inspiration; Mogens Lærke, whose detailed critiques and generous encouragement were enormously helpful; Michael Della Rocca, whose reflections on the metaphysical questions at stake in the book were so enriching and clarifying; Chris Insole, whose philosophical-theological work on Kant makes him a kind of fellow-traveller in the terrain explored here; John Milbank, who set out a helpful critique of Spinoza from the perspective of Trinitarian Christianity; King Ho Leung, whose expertise in both Deleuze and theology helped sharpen my argument; and John Tresch, my most brilliant friend, who encouraged me to write this book six years ago and then, when it was nearly finished, helped me to see it from a reader's point of view.

This book has also been shaped by countless conversations with a wonderful community of Spinoza scholars—not least the three mentioned above—and by their work. I'm particularly indebted to Edwin Curley's fine translations of Spinoza's texts.

A special thank-you to Susan James, who introduced me to Spinoza in 1997, when I was an undergraduate at Cambridge. Without her inspiring lectures and attentive supervision, I might never have understood the *Ethics* well enough to fall in love with it. (I happened to meet my future husband at those lectures, too.) I'm also grateful to Susan for her friendship and collegiality in more recent years: being part of the London Spinoza Circle, which she founded, invariably brings me joy.

I am grateful, as ever, to King's College London for supporting my research, and to my great colleagues there, particularly my collaborators in the King's History of Philosophy Seminar and the King's Theology Seminar, and Daniel Hadas, Latinist extraordinaire.

And thanks to everyone at Princeton University Press, especially my editor Ben Tate, who has been cheerfully committed to this book from proposal to publication.

Clare Carlisle
Autumn 2020

NOTES

Introduction: The Question of Religion

1. See Nadler, *Spinoza: A Life*, pp. 153–54. Pierre Bayle describes Spinoza's departure from the Jewish community as follows: 'It is said that the Jews offered to tolerate him, provided he would comply outwardly with their ceremonies, and even that they promised him an annual pension; but he could not resolve upon such a hypocrisy. However, it was only by degrees that he left their synagogue; and perhaps he would not have broken with them so soon, had he not been treacherously attacked coming from a play, by a Jew who gave him a thrust with a knife. The wound was slight but he believed the assassin designed to kill him. From that time he left them altogether, which was the cause of his excommunication.'—Bayle, *Dictionnaire historique*, p. 416.

2. According to Johannes Colerus, a Lutheran pastor and Spinoza's early biographer, 'the Jewish Doctors . . . did not doubt that he would soon leave them, and make himself a Christian. Yet, to speak the truth, he never embraced Christianity, nor received the Holy Baptism: And tho' he had frequent Conversation with some learn'd Mennonites, as well as with the most eminent Divines of other Christian Sects, yet he never declared for, nor profest himself to be a Member of any of them.'—Colerus, *The Life of Benedict de Spinoza*, p. 8.

3. Curley vol. 2, p. 475 / IV 320a / Letter 76 (Spinoza to Albert Burgh, late 1675 or early 1676). Spinoza also claims that truth is self-evident in the *Ethics*: 'He who has a true idea at the same time knows himself to have a true idea, and cannot doubt of its truth. . . . As light makes both itself and darkness plain, so truth is the criterion of itself and of falsehood' (E2p43 and schol.). See Parkinson, '"Truth Is Its Own Standard"'.

4. Curley vol. 2, pp. 475–76 / IV 320a / Letter 76 (Spinoza to Albert Burgh, late 1675 or early 1676). Spinoza is here quoting Burgh's words back to him, substituting 'religion' for 'philosophy'. Writing with news of his conversion to Catholicism, Burgh had suggested to Spinoza that his philosophy was 'sheer illusion and a Fantasy', and asked, 'How do you know that your Philosophy is the best of all those which have ever been taught in the world, are still taught, or will ever be taught in the future? Not to get into the discoveries of future ages, have you examined all the Philosophies, both ancient and modern, taught here, and in India, and everywhere else on the planet? And even if you have examined them all properly, how do you know that you have chosen the best?'—Curley vol. 2, p. 441 / IV 281 / Letter 67 (Albert Burgh to Spinoza, September 1675). See Curley, 'Spinoza's Exchange'.

5. Curley vol. 2, p. 474 / IV 318a; p. 477 / IV 323a / Letter 76 (Spinoza to Albert Burgh, late 1675 or early 1676).

6. Curley vol. 2, p. 118 / III 50 / TTP ch. 3; p. 125 / III 56 / TTP ch. 3. See Harvey, 'Spinoza's Counterfactual Zionism'; Smith, *Spinoza, Liberalism*; Yovel, *Spinoza and Other Heretics*, vol. 1, pp. 190–92.

7. See Israel, *Radical Enlightenment*, especially pp. 159–74. Two landmark philosophical studies of secularism written from a Christian perspective—the first criticising the concept of the secular, the second criticising secularisation as a cultural phenomenon—likewise treat Spinoza as a secularising figure: see Milbank, *Theology and Social Theory*, pp. 19–21, and Taylor, *A Secular Age*, pp. 363, 543. John Milbank, however, has proposed that 'an important project for postmodern theology might be to "Spinozize" Augustine . . . and at the same time to "Augustinize" Spinoza'—*The Word Made Strange*, p. 166; see also p. 155.

8. Charles Taylor distinguishes between the "porous selves" of pre-modernity and the bounded, "buffered selves" of modernity (see *A Secular Age*, pp. 37–43). In Part Two of the *Ethics* Spinoza sets out an account of human minds and bodies that suggests that 'the boundary between mind and world is porous', as Taylor puts it (p. 39). However, many of Taylor's examples of porosity involve what Spinoza would call 'superstition'. It is typical of Spinoza's ambivalent relation to modernity that he proposes a porous self within a worldview purged of superstitious thinking.

9. Charles Webster has argued that Bacon's systematisation of modern scientific method enacts in the sphere of knowledge the shift that Max Weber discovered in the sphere of economics: a new ideal of labour and industriousness, influenced by Lutheran and Calvinist theologies. See Webster, *The Great Instauration*.

10. See Weber, *The Protestant Ethic*.

11. See Bacon, 'Of Superstition', p. 374; Calvin, *Institutes*, vol. 1, ch. 4 §§1, 3; ch. 5 §12; ch. 6 §3; ch. 11 §§1, 2; vol. 2, ch. 5 §§8, 10; ch. 7 §3; Cameron, *Enchanted Europe*; James, *Spinoza on Philosophy*, pp. 14, 24–26; MacPhail, 'Montaigne, Hobbes and Bayle'. See also Curley vol. 2, pp. 66–68 / III 5–7 / TTP Preface. In Chapter 12 of the TTP, Spinoza writes that 'both reason itself and the statements of the Prophets and Apostles clearly proclaim that God's eternal word and covenant, and true religion, are inscribed by divine agency in men's hearts, i.e., in the human mind, and that this is the true original text of God, which he himself has stamped with his seal, i.e., with the idea of him, as an image of his divinity'—Curley vol. 2, p. 248 / III 158 / TTP ch. 12.

12. Curley vol. 2, p. 477 / III 323a / Letter 76 (Spinoza to Albert Burgh, late 1675 or early 1676).

13. See Curley vol. 2, pp. 65–68 / III 5–6 / TTP Preface. On fluctuations, see James, 'The Interdependence'.

14. See Curley vol. 2, pp. 413–15 / IV 250–53 / Letter 54 (Spinoza to Hugo Boxel, October 1674). See also E1p17s.

15. On the concept of 'true religion' in relation to Spinoza's work and its broader intellectual context, see Topolski, 'Spinoza's True Religion'.

16. Curley vol. 2, p. 374 / VI 207 / Letter 42 (Lambert van Velthuysen to Jacob Ostens, January 1671). On Velthuysen's critique and Spinoza's response, see Rosenthal, 'Why Spinoza is Intolerant'.

17. Curley vol. 2, pp. 386–87 / IV 220b–21b / Letter 43 (Spinoza to Jacob Ostens, February 1671).

18. In 2010 this manuscript—the only surviving manuscript of the *Ethics*—was discovered by Leen Spruit and Pina Totaro in the archives of the Library of the Congregation for the Doctrine of the Faith in the Vatican City: see Totaro, 'On the Recently Discovered Vatican Manuscript'.

19. See Carlisle and Melamed, 'God-Intoxicated Man'; Kneller, 'Early German Romanticism', pp. 305-6.

20. Froude, 'Spinoza', pp. 342-43. For further discussion of Froude's interpretation of Spinoza, see Carlisle (ed.), *Spinoza's Ethics*, pp. 27-33.

21. See Latour, *An Inquiry*, pp. 295-325.

22. See Lærke, *Spinoza and the Freedom*, pp. 167-92.

23. Curley vol. 2, p. 616.

24. James, *Spinoza on Philosophy*, p. 229. See also Fraenkel, *Philosophical Religions*, especially pp. 213-80.

25. Curley vol. 2, p. 75 / III 12 / TTP Preface.

26. See Curley vol. 2, p. 281 / III 188 / TTP ch. 15; James, *Spinoza on Philosophy*, pp. 7-14; 215-30. James shows how Spinoza followed Dutch Cartesians (Abraham Heidanus, Christopher Wittich, Lambert van Velthuysen, Johannes de Raey) in separating philosophy and theology, institutionally as well as in principle; she also shows how in the *Theologico-Political Treatise* Spinoza went further than these thinkers, 'drawing the line between philosophy and theology in a different place [and] substantially enlarging the scope of philosophical enquiry so that it can yield not only truths about nature but truths about God and morality as well.... Still more importantly, [Spinoza] does not accept that theology and philosophy are entirely independent enterprises. While theology as he interprets it retains a degree of autonomy, it remains in some ways subservient to the greater intellectual power of philosophical thought' (pp. 217-18). For more historical detail on these issues, see Douglas, *Spinoza and Dutch Cartesianism*. See Kant, *The Conflict of the Faculties*, for a development of Spinoza's argument that philosophy should be autonomous, rather than serving theology.

27. Calvin, *Institutes*, vol. 1, ch. 6 §2; ch. 7 §1.

28. See Carlisle and Melamed, 'God-Intoxicated Man'.

29. See, for example, Nadler, '"Whatever Is, Is in God"': 'It is absolutely clear... that Spinoza is an atheist. Novalis got it wrong when he called Spinoza a 'God-intoxicated man'. Spinoza did not elevate nature into the divine. On the contrary, he reduced the divine to nature—he naturalised God—in the hope of diminishing the power of the passions and superstitious beliefs to which the traditional conceptions of God gave rise. If there is a theism in Spinoza, it is only a nominal one' (p. 70).

30. Yirmiyahu Yovel ascribes to Spinoza 'a skill for equivocation and dual language' and argues that this was a distinctively Marrano characteristic: see Yovel, *Spinoza and Other Heretics*, vol. 1, pp. 28ff. See also Strauss, *Persecution*, pp. 142-201; Israel, 'Meyer, Koerbagh'. In Letter 43 Spinoza considers—and rejects—the accusation that he 'teaches atheism by disguised and counterfeit arguments': see Curley vol. 2, p. 389 / IV 226 / Letter 43 (Spinoza to Jacob Ostens, February 1671).

31. While the phrase 'hermeneutics of credulity' is my own somewhat tongue-in-cheek invention, 'hermeneutics of suspicion' comes from Ricoeur's discussion of Marx, Nietzsche and Freud, the 'masters of suspicion': see Ricoeur, *Freud and Philosophy*, pp 32-36. 'Hermeneutics of suspicion' has since taken on a broader application: for an overview that pushes back against a broadly suspicious (or 'unmasking') method of critique, see Felski, 'Critique and the Hermeneutics of Suspicion', and for further discussion see the works cited at the end of her article. Felski calls for a 'postcritical'

literary hermeneutic, and my own reading of Spinoza fits well with the alternative interpretative strategies explored in her bold study *The Limits of Critique*.

32. See Rosenthal, 'Why Spinoza is Intolerant', pp. 820–21, and 'Persuasive Passions'.

33. For influential modern expressions of apophatic theology, see, for example, Rahner, *Foundations*; McCabe, *God Matters*.

34. See Kierkegaard, *Fear and Trembling*, Preface; *Concluding Unscientific Postscript*, passim.

35. See Hatfield, 'Descartes's *Meditations*'; Jones, 'Descartes's Geometry' and *The Good Life*, pp. 13–86.

36. Harvey, 'The Judeo-Christian Tradition's Five Others', pp. 213–14. Edward Feld argues that 'Spinoza was educated in an extraordinarily unique and sophisticated Jewish community, quite aware of the secular learning and Christian theology of its day. In addition to his traditional education within the Jewish community, probably at the noted Amsterdam school [Yeshivat] Etz Hayim where the major Rabbinic figures taught, Spinoza associated with several Jewish heretics who had been educated in Spain and Portugal and who had brought their skepticism with them to the Amsterdam ghetto' (p. 105); 'Spinoza studied with the Chief Rabbi, Saul Levi Morteira, who taught the advanced classes at the school. . . . Morteira was born in Venice of Marrano origin [and] his parents had been forced to convert and practice Christianity. . . . The bulk of his works . . . are apologetic attacks on Christianity including a report of his conversations with Calvinist Dutch clergymen. These works demonstrate that Morteira was quite aware of contemporary Christian theologies and was in contact with the non-Jewish world of the Netherlands'—Feld, 'Spinoza the Jew,' pp. 107–8.

37. Curley vol. 2, p. 121 / III 54 / TTP ch. 3.

38. See Roth, *Spinoza, Descartes, and Maimonides*; Wolfson, *The Philosophy of Spinoza*; Brykman, *La Judéité de Spinoza*; Harvey, 'A Portrait of Spinoza' and 'Du mysticisme'; Popkin, 'Spinoza, Neoplatonist Kabbalist?'; Ravven, 'Some Thoughts'; Ravven and Goodman, *Jewish Themes*; Fraenkel, 'Maimonides's God'; Chalier, *Spinoza lecteur de Maimonide*; Seeskin, 'From Maimonides to Spinoza'. Wiep van Bunge sets out a critique of Jewish readings of Spinoza in 'Spinoza's Jewish Identity' and *From Stevin to Spinoza*. For an excellent overview of this literature, including Van Bunge's critique, see Nadler, 'The Jewish Spinoza'.

39. See Verbeek, *Spinoza's Theologico-Political Treatise*; James, *Spinoza on Philosophy*; Douglas, *Spinoza and Dutch Cartesianism*. An exception is Graeme Hunter's *Radical Protestantism in Spinoza's Thought*, which includes two chapters on the *Ethics*; in my view, Hunter goes too far in assimilating Spinoza to Protestantism (and thus to Christianity). Also notable are Charlie Huenemann's suggestive *Spinoza's Radical Theology*, which positions Spinoza as 'a religious reformer rather than as one presenting a complete rejection of religion' and claims that 'reading his philosophy as an overall attempt at constructing a theology is the best way of reading him' (pp. xv–xvi); and Nancy Levene's wide-ranging *Spinoza's Revelation*, which convincingly argues that 'the standard theological pieties concerning God's unmoving pre-eminence are certainly turned on their heads in Spinoza. But it is not, as some of his opponents would like to think, in order to abandon religion for naturalism or science or atheism' (p. 63).

40. Nadler, 'The Jewish Spinoza', p. 505. Edward Feld emphasises that Amsterdam's Jewish community was itself ecumenical, or at least extremely diverse: 'The community the Amsterdam Rabbis presided over should be seen as one composed of extraordinary diversity: some Converso families returning to Judaism were anxious to throw themselves fully into the religious life of their ancestral faith while others had developed patterns of life and thought which they found hard to change even though they now found themselves within a community in which they could be fully Jewish'— 'Spinoza the Jew', pp. 106–7.

41. See Van Bunge et al. (eds), *The Continuum Companion to Spinoza*, pp. 60–62, 70–74; Verbeek, *Descartes and the Dutch*.

42. See Nadler, *Spinoza: A Life*, pp. 155–81. Nadler writes that most of Spinoza's intellectual circle 'were committed primarily to religious reform and toleration, to the freedom of the individual to worship God in his own manner[;] . . . their motivations were deeply religious; and the truth to which reason led them was usually a devout Christian one' (pp. 169–70). Nadler considers circumstantial evidence that Spinoza associated with Quakers in Amsterdam in the late 1650s, following his excommunication, and possibly translated a Quaker pamphlet (pp. 158–63). Among Spinoza's close friends were Jarig Jellesz, Mennonite author of *Confession of the Universal and Christian Faith*, which recommended 'a purely rational communion with the divine understanding' (p. 168); Pieter Balling, Mennonite author of *The Light Upon the Candlestick*, which claimed that 'a natural, intuitive, "inner" experience of the divine is possible for everyone' (p. 169); Adriaan Koerbagh, a 'radical political and religious thinker' who 'denied the trinity and the divine nature of Jesus' and was imprisoned for blasphemy in 1669 (pp. 170–71); and Lodewijk Meyer, a Lutheran who wrote a rationalistic treatise titled *Philosophy, Interpreter of Holy Scripture* (p. 172). On the religion of Jelles and Balling, see Kołakowski, *Chrétiens sans église*, pp. 206–25.

43. See Servaas van Rooijen, *La Bibliothèque*, pp. 131, 135–37, 147–48, 180, 183, 191, 195. Spinoza's edition of Calvin's *Institutes* was a 1597 Spanish translation of the Latin original.

44. See Carlisle, 'Spinoza's Philosophy of Religious Life'.

45. Haight (ed.), *The George Eliot Letters*, vol. 5, p. 290. On George Eliot's translation of Spinoza and its influence on her fiction, see my Introduction to *Spinoza's Ethics*, pp. 1–59.

46. On repetition and religion see, for example, Pickstock, *Repetition and Identity*; Latour, *An Inquiry*, pp. 306, 309–13; Carlisle, 'The Self and the Good Life' and *Philosopher of the Heart*, pp. 147–64.

1. *Philosophy and Devotion*

1. Bayle, *Dictionnaire historique*, p. 417.
2. Bayle, *Dictionnaire historique*, p. 417.
3. Bayle, *Dictionnaire historique*, p. 416.
4. Bayle, *Dictionnaire historique*, pp. 424–25.
5. Colerus, *The Life of Benedict de Spinoza*, pp. 39–42.
6. Colerus, *The Life of Benedict de Spinoza*, p. 39. Here Colerus also provides a physical description of Spinoza: 'He was of middle size, he had good features in his

Face, the Skin somewhat black, black curl'd Hair, long Eyebrows, and of the same Colour, so that one might easily know by his Looks that he was descended from Portuguese Jews.'

7. See Nadler, *Spinoza: A Life*, pp. 107-10; 193-95. Spinoza's teacher Franciscus van den Enden was fond of classical drama, and staged two of Terence's comedies at Amsterdam's municipal theatre: *Andrea* in 1657, and *Eunuchus* in 1658, and Nadler suggests that 'it is fairly certain that Spinoza participated in [these] productions'. Pierre Bayle reports that a Jewish assailant tried to stab Spinoza one night when he was leaving the theatre. On Spinoza's theatrical interests, and the influence of Van den Enden during the late 1650s, see Rovere, 'Honors and Theater'.

8. There is an analogy here with Kant's enquiries into the nature of moral necessity—i.e., the 'ought' of moral obligation, which is neither a logical nor a physical (or 'natural') necessity—and into the nature of the necessity involved in aesthetic judgements: see Kant, *Critique of Practical Reason*, pp. 68-70, 120-21, and *Critique of Judgement*, pp. 39-41, 121-22.

9. Souriau, *The Different Modes*, p. 224.

10. Curley vol. 1, p. 7 / II 5 / TIE §1.

11. See Moreau, *Spinoza: L'expérience*, pp. 34-35, 42-47, 58-59. Moreau rightly points out that the opening pages of the TIE should not be read naively as a factual autobiography, and highlights their literary precedents.

12. See Curley vol. 1, p. xiii.

13. In the *Ethics*, Spinoza treats *devotio* as an affect, defining it as a kind of love directed towards another person: 'if we wonder at the prudence, diligence, etc. of a person whom we love, the love will thereby be greater, and this love joined to wonder, or veneration, we call devotion' (E3p52s); 'Devotion is a love of one whom we wonder at' (E3Def.Aff.10). The concept of devotion I am developing in this chapter may certainly be considered as a kind of love, though it has a wider scope—a philosopher may be devoted to the truth; a human being may be devoted to the ethical project of flourishing—and involves a practical expression. Devotion is not simply a feeling of love, but a lived love, which finds expression in a willingness to give one's time, effort, and attention to its object.

14. The devotional tone of Spinoza's *Treatise on the Emendation of the Intellect* can be compared with the following passage from Descartes's *Discourse on Method*: 'I came to the view that I could do no better than to ... devote my life to the cultivation of my reason and make such progress as I could in the knowledge of the truth following the method I had prescribed for myself. I had experienced such great joy since I began to employ this method that I did not believe that any sweeter or more innocent pleasures were to be had in this life; and as I discovered daily by its means a number of truths that seemed to me very important and generally unknown to other men, the satisfaction that I obtained from it filled my mind to such a degree that nothing else mattered to me'—Descartes, *A Discourse on the Method*, p. 24 / *Oeuvres complètes*, vol. 6, p. 27.

15. Souriau, *The Different Modes*, pp. 230-31.

16. For analysis of the spiritual labour of the modern subject—the idea of 'working on oneself'—see Sloterdijk, *You Must Change Your Life!*, and Khawaja, *The Religion of Existence*. For critiques of this modern (and perhaps largely Protestant) construal of

intellectual labour, see Pieper, *Leisure*, and Hitz, *Lost in Thought*: both these works emphasise leisure and enjoyment rather than labour and productivity.

17. Souriau, *The Different Modes*, pp. 230–31.

18. See Foucault, *The Hermeneutics of the Subject*, pp. 8–14. While both Foucault and his colleague Pierre Hadot tend to exclude the early modern period from their important analyses of what Hadot called 'philosophy as a way of life', Matthew Jones has shown how early seventeenth-century European culture 'was awash in possibilities, new and old, for simultaneously reforming oneself and one's knowledge. These sundry "spiritual exercises" offered different modes and ideals for cultivating the self: Ignatius of Loyola's *Spiritual Exercises*, a central reference in the period, and its various reformulations; François de Sales's *Introduction to the Devout Life*; Michel de Montaigne's *Essays*; Pierre Charon's *On Wisdom*; Eustachius a Sancto Paulo's *Spiritual Exercises*; Pierre Gassendi's spiritualized Epicureanism; Justus Lipsius's Stoicism; Cornelius Jansen's Augustinianism and its popularizations; popularized Scholasticism; and, finally, the frequently reprinted classics such as Seneca's *De vita beata* and Epictetus's *Manual*, to name but a few. . . . More than sets of doctrines, these spiritual exercises offered practices and objects of knowledge held to be intellectually appropriate for living well,'—see Jones, *The Good Life*, p. 6 and passim.

19. Foucault, *The Hermeneutics of the Subject*, pp. 26–27. In this second lecture, Foucault goes on to acknowledge that for Kant, followed by nineteenth-century German philosophers, 'the activity of knowing is . . . still linked to the requirements of spirituality' (p. 28).

20. Foucault, *The Hermeneutics of the Subject*, p. 27.

21. Foucault, *The Hermeneutics of the Subject*, p. 15.

22. Foucault, *The Hermeneutics of the Subject*, p. 15.

23. See Moreau, *Spinoza: L'expérience*, pp. 26–34.

24. Augustine, *On Free Choice of the Will*, p. 60 (Book 2 §16).

25. Curley vol. 1, pp. 7–8 / II 6 / TIE §3.

26. See Moreau, *Spinoza: L'expérience*, pp. 127–35. Moreau traces this trio of false goods from Aristotle to Cicero and Seneca, and also to Augustine and Boethius, and finally to Descartes.

27. In his response to Lambert de Velthuysen's hostile critique of the *Theologico-Political Treatise*, Spinoza cited his 'way of life' as a defence against the accusation of atheism: '[Velthuysen] says: it's not important to know what my nation is, or what way of life I follow. But of course if he had known, he would not so easily have persuaded himself that I teach atheism. For atheists are accustomed to seek honours and riches immoderately. But I have always scorned those things. Everyone who knows me knows that.'—Curley vol. 2, p. 386 / IV 219b / Letter 43 (Spinoza to Jacob Ostens, February 1671). Spinoza's claim that he 'always scorned' honour does not quite accord with the opening to the *Treatise on the Emendation of the Intellect*, where he describes himself struggling to relinquish the pursuit of honour.

28. Curley vol. 1, p. 8 / II 6 / TIE §§4, 5.

29. Curley vol. 1, p. 8 / II 6 / TIE §5.

30. Curley vol. 1, p. 7 / II 5 / TIE §§2, 3.

31. Curley vol. 1, p. 8 / II 6 / TIE §6.

32. Curley vol. 1, pp. 7–8 / II 5–6 / TIE §§2, 6, 7. See Moreau, *Spinoza: L'expérience*, pp. 65–103. Simone D'Agostino echoes Moreau's analysis of Spinoza's 'conversion' as a four-step process: see D'Agostino, *Esercizi spirituali*, pp. 181–92.

33. This is reminiscent of Augustine's account of how his habits kept him stuck in his former way of life after his conversion to true Christianity: 'I was held fast, not in fetters clamped upon me by another, but by my own will, which had the strength of iron chains. . . . [For desire had grown from my will] and when I gave in to desire habit was born, and when I did not resist the habit it became a necessity. . . . These two wills within me, one old, one new, one the servant of the flesh, the other of the spirit, were in conflict and between them they tore my soul apart'—see Augustine, *Confessions*, p. 164 (Book 8 §5). Here Augustine is offering a confessional gloss on Romans 7, where Paul describes an internal conflict between two different kinds of desire, two causal orders: the flesh and the spirit.

34. Curley vol. 1, pp. 8–10 / II 6–8 / TIE §§7, 10–11.

35. On the distinction between habit and practice, see Carlisle, 'Spiritual Desire'.

36. In 1645 Descartes wrote, in a letter to Princess Elisabeth of Bohemia, that 'besides knowledge of the truth, habituation is also required for being always disposed to judge well. For since we cannot always be attentive to the same thing—even though we have been convinced of some truth by reason of some clear and evident perceptions—we will be able to be turned, afterward, to believing false appearances, if we do not, after long and frequent meditation, imprint it sufficiently in our mind so that it turns into habit. In this sense, the Schools are right to say that the virtues are habits, for one rarely makes a mistake because one doesn't have theoretical knowledge of what to do, but only because one doesn't have practical knowledge, that is to say, because one doesn't have a firm habit of believing it'—Descartes, *The Correspondence*, pp. 113–14.

37. Curley vol. 1, p. 9 / II 6–7 / TIE §7.

38. Of course, pursuing 'those things people ordinarily strive for' might endanger bodily life: seeking pleasure by excessive eating or drinking could cause an early death; someone desperate for money might take a risk that leads to accidental death; a person pursuing honour might sacrifice his life fighting for his cause, perhaps (at least in the seventeenth century) enter into a disastrous duel. Yet we have no reason to believe that Spinoza ever considered his life to be in danger from immoderate pursuit of money or pleasure. It is true that others may have tried to harm him physically, even kill him, on account of his religious views—but dedicating himself to the pursuit of the true good would have been more likely to exacerbate this risk than to mitigate it.

39. Curley vol. 1, p. 9 / II 7 / TIE §9.

40. Curley vol. 1, p. 9 / II 7 / TIE §9.

41. *Animus*, unlike *mens*, can be translated as well by 'soul' as by 'mind'.

42. Curley vol. 1, p. 9 / II 7 / TIE §§9–10.

43. Curley vol. 1, p. 8 / II 6 / TIE §4.

44. On hope, see E3p18s2: 'Hope is nothing but an inconstant joy which has arisen from the image of a past or future thing whose outcome we doubt'; E3p50s: 'we easily believe the things we hope for, but believe only with difficulty those we fear. . . . This is the source of the superstitions by which men are everywhere troubled. For the rest,

I do not think it worth the trouble to show here the fluctuations of mind which arise from hope and fear, since it follows from the definitions of these affects that there is no hope without fear, and no fear without hope'; E4p47 and dem.: 'Affects of hope and fear cannot be good of themselves.... There are no affects of hope and fear without pain. For fear is a pain, and there is no hope without fear. Therefore these affects cannot be good of themselves, but only so far as they can restrain an excess of pleasure.' See also Curley vol. 2, pp. 65–66 / III 5 / TTP Preface.

45. Curley vol. 1, p. 10 / II 8 / TIE §12.

46. Curley vol. 1, p. 10 / II 8 / TIE §13.

47. On Spinoza's conception of the good, see Kisner, *Spinoza on Human Freedom*, pp. 87–111. Kisner argues that 'while Spinoza makes a bewildering number of claims about our good [within the *Ethics*], they are all ultimately reducible to the claim that our good is what promotes our power', and he calls this view 'subjectivism' (p. 110), which he traces to the *Treatise on the Emendation of the Intellect* (p. 96).

48. Curley vol. 1, pp. 10–11 / II 8 / TIE §13.

49. Curley vol. 1, p. 11 / II 8–9 / TIE §14. We can trace this idea to the *Ethics*, where Spinoza writes that 'there are many things outside ourselves which are useful to us, and are therefore to be sought. Of these, we can think of none more excellent than those which agree entirely with our nature. If, for example, two individuals of entirely the same nature are joined to one another, they compose an individual twice as powerful as each one. To man, then, there is nothing more useful than man. Man, I say, can wish for nothing more helpful to the preservation of his being, than that all should so agree in all things that the minds and bodies of all would compose, as it were, one mind and one body; that all should strive together, as far as they can, to preserve their being; and that all, together, should seek for themselves the common good of all. From this it follows that men who are governed by reason—that is, men who, from the guidance of reason, seek their own advantage—desire nothing for themselves which they do not desire for others also. Hence they are just, honest, and honourable' (E4p18s). This scholium follows a proposition about human desire, and read in light of the passage from the *Treatise on the Emendation of the Intellect* quoted above, being 'of the same nature' and 'agreeing in all things' can be glossed as a situation in which another's 'intellect and desire entirely agree with my intellect and desire'.

50. Curley vol. 1, pp. 7–8 / II 5–6 / TIE §§2, 5.

51. Curley vol. 1, p. 10 / II 8 / TIE §11.

52. Curley vol. 1, p. 12 / II 9 / TIE §17.

53. Curley vol. 1, p. 11 / II 9 / TIE §16.

54. Curley vol. 1, pp. 11–12 / II 9 / TIE §17.

55. Spinoza makes a similar point in the *Ethics*: 'so long as we do not have perfect knowledge of our affects, the best thing we can do is to conceive a correct principle of living, or sure maxims of life, to commit them to memory, and to apply them constantly to the particular cases frequently encountered in life' (E5p10s).

56. See Descartes, *A Discourse on the Method*, pp. 21–23 / *Oeuvres complètes*, vol. 6, pp. 22–26. Descartes outlines his maxims as follows: 'The first was to obey the laws and customs of my country, and to adhere to the religion in which God by His grace had me instructed from my childhood, and to govern myself in everything else

according to the most moderate and least extreme opinions, being those commonly received among the wisest of those with whom I should have to live. For, having begun already to discount my own opinions because I wished to subject them all to rigorous examination, I was certain that I could do no better than to follow those of the wisest. And although there may be as many wise people among the Persians and the Chinese as among ourselves, it seemed to me that the most useful thing to do would be to regulate my conduct by that of the people among whom I was to live. . . . My second maxim was to be as firm and resolute in my actions as I could, and to follow no less constantly the most doubtful opinions, once I had opted for them, than I would have if they had been the most certain ones. . . . My third maxim was to endeavour always to master myself rather than fortune, to try to change my desires rather than to change the order of the world, and in general to settle for the belief that there is nothing entirely in our power except our thoughts, and after we have tried, in respect of things external to us, to do our best, everything in which we do not succeed is absolutely impossible as far as we are concerned.' Descartes's second maxim, concerning resoluteness, is underscored by his remark that he formed his provisional moral code 'in order not to remain indecisive in my actions while my reason was forcing me to be so in my judgements'. Spinoza's first rule resembles Descartes's first maxim, but the other two are quite different. Descartes's third maxim suggests the influence of Stoic philosophy: see Olivo, '"Une patience sans espérance"?'; Mehl, 'Les Méditations stoïciennes'; Shapiro, 'Descartes on Human Nature'.

57. See Lear, *Wisdom Won from Illness*, pp. 206-43.

58. By 'faith' here I mean trust or confidence that what Spinoza calls 'the true good' is both real and attainable.

59. See my discussion of Spinoza's complex attitude to fear in Chapter 8.

60. Curley vol. 1, pp. 163-64 / IV 5-6 / Letter 1 (Henry Oldenburg to Spinoza, August 1661).

61. Curley vol. 1, p. 165 / IV 7 / Letter 2 (Spinoza to Henry Oldenburg, September 1661).

62. Curley vol. 1, p. 190 / IV 39 / Letter 8 (Simon de Vries to Spinoza, February 1663).

2. *What Is the* Ethics*?*

1. Pamela Smith's *The Body of the Artisan* traces a contrast between 'artisanal knowledge' and 'school knowledge' during the long Enlightenment period that encompasses Spinoza's lifetime. Smith's distinctions between the systematic, theoretical knowledge of the scholar, whose 'language was Latin', and artisanal 'processes of cognition' based on 'a carefully thought-out technology', are interesting in the case of Spinoza, who was both a scholar and a skilled artisan. Smith argues that until the seventeenth century, 'theory (*episteme* or *scientia*) was separate from practice. Theory was certain knowledge based on the logical syllogism and geometrical demonstration. Practice (*praxis* or *experientia*), on the other hand, could be of two kinds—things done and things made. . . . *Techne* . . . was the lowly knowledge of how to make things or produce effects, practiced by animals, slaves, and craftspeople. It was the only area of knowledge that was productive.' In the early modern period, Smith suggests,

'scientific knowledge came to include the production of effects, or productive knowledge. Thus the three areas of knowledge, *episteme*, *praxis* and *techne*, which had been separate in the Aristotelian scheme, became linked in an entirely new way' (see pp. 6-8, 17-20). Smith is interested in early modern science, or 'natural philosophy', rather than in the kind of enquiry pursued by Spinoza, but her remarks apply to the *Ethics* as it is interpreted in this chapter as both a theoretical and a practical system. On the link between knowledge and production in modernity, see also Funkenstein, *Theology and the Scientific Imagination* and Lachterman, *The Ethics of Geometry*; for a discussion of these ideas in relation to Descartes and, briefly, to Spinoza, see Smith, *Spinoza's Book of Life*, pp. 19-24.

2. Spinoza added two dialogues—one between 'The Intellect, Love, Reason and Lust', and the other between two characters named Erasmus and Theophilus—to his *Short Treatise on God, Man and His Well-Being*, composed in the early 1660s: see Curley vol. 1, pp. 73-79 / I 28-34. He wrote his exposition of Descartes's *Principles of Philosophy*, published in 1663, 'in the geometrical manner' which he would later employ in the *Ethics*. For a detailed discussion of the dates of composition of the *Ethics*, see Pierre-François Moreau and Piet Steenbakkers' Introduction to Moreau and Steenbakkers (eds), *Spinoza: Œuvres IV*, pp. 13-38; they show that Spinoza probably worked on the *Ethics* during 1662-65 and 1670-75.

3. For an in-depth study of Spinoza's method, see Garrett, *Meaning in Spinoza's Method*, and for an overview of different interpretations of Spinoza's use of the geometrical method, see Renz, *The Explainability of Experience*, pp. 20-21. The present chapter focuses on the way in which the *Ethics* offers a practical system, but insofar as it also presents a theoretical system (which, of course, it does), I think Renz makes an important point when she notes that 'the geometrical method, for Spinoza, is less *deductive* in nature than based on *systematic accumulation*' (p. 21).

4. Bayle, *Dictionnaire historique*, p. 423.

5. An anecdote about Hobbes's conversion to the geometrical method, recorded by his contemporary John Aubrey, illustrates this manner of reading: 'Being in a gentleman's library, Euclid's Elements lay open, and 'twas the 47th Element [of Book 1]. He read the proposition. "By G—", sayd he, "this is impossible!" So he read the demonstration of it, which referred him back to such a proposition; which proposition he read. That referred him back to another, which he also read. *Et sic deinceps*, that at last he was demonstratively convinced of that truethe. This made him in love with Geometry.' In his autobiography, Hobbes declared himself 'delighted by Euclid's method', and notes that he read the *Elements* 'not simply on account of its theorems, but also as a guide to the art of reasoning'—see Aubrey, *Brief Lives*, p. 332; Hobbes, *Examinatio et emendatio*, pp. 154-55. For a discussion of Hobbes's method, which invites interesting comparisons with Spinoza's *Ethics*, see Skinner, *Reason and Rhetoric*, especially Chapter 7 on 'Hobbes's Rejection of Eloquence'.

6. Steven B. Smith highlights the therapeutic or 'pedagogic' orientation of the *Ethics* in *Spinoza's Book of Life*: 'Its goal is to lessen emotional distress, or what Spinoza calls *fluctutatio animi*, vacillation of mind, which is the principal cause of so much misery and human conflict. The *Ethics* is intended as a work of moral therapy in which the reader is simultaneously analyst and patient' (p. 8). Smith suggests that there was a 'moral necessity' to Spinoza's use of the geometrical method, arguing that

this method was 'for Spinoza, Hobbes and Descartes strongly related not just to a model of knowledge but to their very ideas of the individual.... The mathematical method was not for these early moderns a mean of purging their philosophies of all personal touches or expressions of individuality, but was closely bound up with a vision of human beings as the products of their own making. Mathematics as a system of symbolization became the paradigm for the individual as, literally, something self-constructed' (p. 19; see also pp. 21–22, 199–200). These remarks echo Pamela Smith's reflections on 'productive knowledge' noted above.

7. Curley vol. 1, p. 190 / IV 39 / Letter 8 (Simon de Vries to Spinoza, February 1663). See also Nadler, *Spinoza: A Life*, p. 202.

8. See the passage on philosophy and spirituality from Foucault's *Hermeneutics of the Subject* quoted here on pp. 23–4.

9. See Hobbes, *Elements*, p. 349; Locke, *An Essay*, p. 293.

10. See Malebranche, *Search After Truth*, pp. 107–9, 134.

11. On early modern philosophies of habit and the concept of repetition, see Carlisle, *On Habit*, pp. 8–13, 41–58.

12. See E2p40s2: 'It is clear that we perceive many things and form universal notions: I. from singular things which have been represented to us through the senses in a way that is mutilated, confused, and without order for the intellect; for that reason I have been accustomed to call such perceptions knowledge from experience; II. from signs, e.g., from the fact that, having heard or read certain words, we recollect things, and form certain ideas of them, which are like them, and through which we imagine the things. These two ways of regarding things I shall henceforth call knowledge of the first kind, opinion or imagination. III. Finally, from the fact that we have common notions and adequate ideas of the properties of things (see E2p38c, p39, p39c, and p40). This I shall call reason and the second kind of knowledge. In addition to these two kinds of knowledge, there is . . . another, third kind, which we shall call intuitive knowledge. And this kind of knowing proceeds from an adequate idea of the formal essence of certain attributes of God to the adequate knowledge of the essence of things.' Spinoza defines the human mind as the idea (i.e., the consciousness) of the human body: see E3p11 and p13.

13. For an explanation of this point, see Maine de Biran, *The Influence of Habit*, p. 222; Carlisle, *On Habit*, p. 42.

14. Kant described Humean custom or habit (*Gewohnheit*) as a 'subjective necessity': see Kant, *Critique of Practical Reason*, p. 181. See also Carlisle, *On Habit*, pp. 46–52; 58–66.

15. Thomas Aquinas, *Summa Theologiae, Secunda secundae partis*, Q. 35, art. 3, ad 1.

16. Pieper, *Leisure*, pp. 33–34.

17. Pieper, *Leisure*, p. 35.

18. See Curley vol. 1, p. 167 / IV 9 / Letter 2 (Spinoza to Henry Oldenburg, September 1661). Here Spinoza lists three limitations imposed on the intellect by Bacon: 'first, [he] supposes that, besides the deceptions of the senses, the human intellect is fallible by its own nature . . . second, that the human intellect on account of its peculiar nature is prone to make abstractions, and imagines things to be stable which are in flux, etc. Thirdly, that the human understanding is unquiet, it cannot stop or rest.' In relation to this third point, Bacon's *Novum Organon* states, 'The human intellect is

active and cannot halt or rest, but even, though without effect, still presses forward . . . the human intellect, incapable of resting, seeks for something more intelligible'—see Bacon, *New Organon*, p. 44 (Book 1 §48). In *Advancement of Learning*, Bacon rejected a purely contemplative view of knowledge, 'as if there were to be sought in knowledge a couch, whereupon to rest a searching and restless spirit'; instead, knowledge should be industrious, oriented to 'use and action', continually adding to 'a rich store house, for the glory of the Creator and the relief of man's estate'. Bacon hoped that 'contemplation and action may be more nearly and straitly conjoined and united together than they have been; a conjunction like unto that of the two highest planets, Saturn, the planet of rest and contemplation, and Jupiter, the planet of civil society and action'—*Advancement of Learning*, Book 1, p. 13.

19. The attribute of thought is God's activity of understanding, God's 'power of thinking', and when I cognise my own activity of thinking, I know myself as sharing in this attribute, and thus I know myself in God. Spinoza remarks in E2p21s, that 'the idea of the mind and the mind itself are one and the same thing, which is conceived under one and the same attribute, viz. Thought. [In other words, the] idea of the mind, I say, and the mind itself follow in God from the same power of thinking and by the same necessity. For the idea of the mind, i.e., the idea of the idea, is nothing but the form of the idea insofar as this is considered as a mode of thinking without relation to the object'. This helps to explain his definition of *scientia intuitiva* at E2p40s2: 'this kind of knowing proceeds from an adequate idea of the formal essence of certain attributes of God to the adequate idea of the formal essence of things'. (It is interesting that this definition is more capacious than E2p21s, in that it does not specify the attribute of thought. Confined to the perimeters of E2p21s, Spinoza's definition of *scientia intuitiva* would read, 'This kind of knowing proceeds from an adequate idea of the formal essence of [the attribute of thought] to the adequate idea of the formal essence of [a mode of thinking].') E2p21s, with its focus on 'the form of the idea' and on the relation to God, also links to Spinoza's discussion of *scientia intuitiva* in Part Five: 'Insofar as our mind knows itself and the body under a species of eternity, it necessarily has knowledge of God, and knows that it is in God and is conceived through God' (E5p30); 'The third kind of knowledge depends on the mind, as on a formal cause, insofar as the mind itself is eternal' (E5p31). I am grateful to Kristin Primus for drawing my attention to the connection between E2p21s and *scientia intuitiva*, for Spinoza himself does not make this connection explicit.

20. See Marshall, *The Spiritual Automaton*, p. 186ff.

21. Curley vol. 1, pp. 11–12 / II 9 / TIE §17.

22. See Derrida, *Dissemination*, pp. 95–118; Carlisle, *On Habit*, p. 5. This parallels Daniel Garber's interesting suggestion that the passions of hope and fear function, similarly, as a means for eliminating such passions: 'the *Ethics* works on us not through its logical form alone: while its definitions, axioms and propositions may compel belief, they do not, by themselves, compel us to action. What compels us to action is the passion of hope, the hope that by following the regimen outlined in the *Ethics* we can eliminate the fear of death that paralyses us, along with all other passions that currently plague us, including the passion of hope. This strategy can work because even *after* having read the *Ethics* (and before successfully entering into the regimen of acquiring knowledge of the third kind), we *still* have passions, both the fear of death and the hope of overcoming that fear. In this way Spinoza is *using* our

passions to press us into the hope of *eliminating* our passions'—Garber, '"A Free Man"', p. 116.

23. See James, 'Spinoza the Stoic'; Miller, *Spinoza and the Stoics*.

24. Gilles Deleuze suggests that, for Spinoza, 'an individual is first of all a singular essence, which is to say, a degree of power'—see Deleuze, *Spinoza: Practical Philosophy*, p. 27. This interpretation rests in part on E3p7: 'The striving [*conatus*] by which each thing strives to persevere in its being is nothing but the actual essence of the thing.' In the demonstration of E5p9, Spinoza cites E3p7 to suggest an equivalence between essence and power: 'the Mind's essence, i.e., power [*potentia*] (by E3p7)'. In the 'General Definition of the Affects' at the end of Part Three, Spinoza writes that 'we understand by perfection the very essence of the thing'. The context indicates that he has in mind here a notion of degrees of perfection, which equates to degrees of power or 'reality' (see E2D6: 'By reality and perfection I understand the same thing') as he seems to use the phrases 'a greater or lesser perfection', 'more or less reality' and 'a greater or lesser force of existence' interchangeably. See also E4p26d: 'The striving to preserve itself is nothing but the essence of the thing itself (by E3p7), which insofar as it exists as it does, is conceived to have a force for persevering in existing (by E3p6) and for doing those things that necessarily follow from its given nature'; and the end of the Preface to Part Four: 'When I say that someone passes from a lesser to a greater perfection, and the opposite, I do not understand that he is changed from one essence, *or* form, to another.... Rather, we conceive that his power of acting [*agendi potentiam*], insofar as it is understood through his nature, is increased or diminished. Finally, by perfection in general I shall, as I have said, understand reality, i.e., the essence of each thing insofar as it exists and produces an effect, having no regard to its duration.'

25. Lowering the criterion for a super-proposition to nine citations roughly doubles the number of super-propositions in the *Ethics* as a whole.

26. See https://ethics.spinozism.org/ for a series of digital visualisations of the *Ethics*, created by Torin Doppelt.

27. See E1A4: 'The knowledge of an effect depends on, and involves, the knowledge of its cause.'

28. In the Preface to the *Theologico-Political Treatise*, Spinoza argues that 'because men vary greatly in their mentality, because one is content with these opinions, another with those, and because what moves one person to religion moves another laughter, from these considerations ... I conclude that each person must be allowed freedom of judgement and the power to interpret the foundations of faith according to his own mentality'—Curley vol. 2, p. 73 / III 11 / TTP Preface. For Jesus's prayer, also known as the Lord's Prayer, see Matthew 6:9–13.

3. Being-in-God

1. Discussing God's simplicity in the Appendix to his exposition of Descartes's *Principles of Philosophy*, Spinoza refers the reader to Descartes's claim (*Principles of Philosophy* 1 §§48, 49) 'that there is nothing in nature but substances and their modes'—Curley vol. 1, p. 323 / I 257 / CM II ch. 5.

2. Souriau, *The Different Modes*, pp. 190–91; Garrett, 'Representation and Consciousness'.

3. On the relation of 'being in', or inherence, see Garrett, 'Representation and Consciousness'; Nadler, '"Whatever Is, Is in God"'; Melamed, 'Inherence and the Immanent Cause'; 'Spinoza's Metaphysics of Substance'; 'Inherence, Causation '; *Spinoza's Metaphysics*, pp. 3–59; Garrett, *Nature and Necessity*, pp. 14–15, 90–91, 360–67; Della Rocca, 'Rationalism Run Amok', and 'Steps towards Eleaticism'. In this latter paper, Della Rocca makes two steps that have significant implications for Spinoza's metaphysics as a whole: first, he argues that modes can be 'in' one another just as modes can be 'in' God, thereby suggesting that mode–mode relations are essentially the same as mode–substance relations; and second, he argues that 'nothing limited can be or inhere in God' (p. 29), which suggests that modes, being limited, are not, in fact, in God, and do not exist—only substance is real, thus making Spinoza an Eleatic monist. For a counter-interpretation, see Melamed, 'Why Spinoza is not an Eleatic Monist'.

4. See Curley vol. 2, p. 406 / IV 239b–40b / Letter 50 (Spinoza to Jarig Jelles, June 1674), and Curley vol. 1, p. 312 / I 246 / CM I ch. 6. For discussion of these passages and the issues they raise, see Lærke, 'Spinoza's Monism?'; Della Rocca, 'The Elusiveness'.

5. Descartes, *Principles of Philosophy* 1 §51.

6. See Garrett, *Nature and Necessity*, pp. 365–66.

7. Ursula Renz's *The Explainability of Experience* offers an illuminating discussion of how the substance–mode relation has been treated in scholarly literature: see pp. 35–39. Renz argues that the relation between substance and modes 'is defined not by the modes' *ontological inherence* in the substance but by their *categorical difference*—which therefore also constitutes the key structural component of Spinoza's approach' (p. 44). This point about categorical difference is important— Spinoza insists that finite things in general, and human beings in particular, are not substances—but I do not see why this should be considered an alternative to ontological inherence, so long as this inherence, or being-in-God, is understood correctly. Renz is right to emphasise that 'a mode is by no means something that inheres in God in the manner of an accident' (p. 44) and to thereby deny that Spinoza is a pantheist. Though she acknowledges 'a mode's ontological dependency on the substance', i.e., on God, Renz seems to privilege a mode's dependency on other finite modes.

8. Della Rocca, 'Spinoza's Substance Monism', p. 15.

9. See Renz, *The Explainability of Experience*, pp. 29–34, which argues for Spinoza's 'radical *dissociation of the concept of substance from the concept of subject*' (p. 34, original italics).

10. See Cusa, *Directio speculantis*; Williams, *Not I*.

11. Curley vol. 1, p. 80 / I 35 / KV I ch. 3. In the *Short Treatise*, Spinoza also states that 'outside God, there is nothing, and [God] is an immanent cause'—Curley vol. 1, p. 72 / I 26 / KV I ch. 2. As Curley explains, the composition date of the *Short Treatise*—which was 'intended for circulation among friends', and was not published—is uncertain, and it is not known whether the original manuscript was in Latin or Dutch: see Curley vol. 1, pp. 46–53.

12. See Curley vol. 2, p. 467 / IV 307a / Letter 73 (Spinoza to Henry Oldenburg, December 1675). Spinoza's reference to Paul is an indirect citation of Acts 17:27–28: 'God . . . is not far from any one of us. "For in him we live and move and have our being."' Paul is citing a Greek source, thought to be the philosopher-poet Epimenides of Crete.

13. Michael Della Rocca regards 'being in' as 'co-extensive' with 'being caused by' and 'being conceived through', and thus he argues that all causal and conceptual relations are thereby in-relations: to the extent that mode A causes mode B, mode B is in mode A—see his 'Rationalism Run Amok' and 'Steps Towards Eleaticism'. When I asked Della Rocca why he would not apply Spinoza's distinction between immanent and transitive causation to distinguish between substance–mode causation and mode–mode causation, he replied that he thinks the idea of transitive causation—between modes as much as between substance and modes—is incoherent on Spinoza's own terms. Be that as it may, it seems that Spinoza meant his distinction between immanent and transitive causation to apply to modes: one of his super-propositions, the definition E3D2, states, 'I say that we act when something happens, in us or outside us, of which we are the adequate cause, i.e., when something in us or outside us follows from our nature, which can be clearly and distinctly understood through it alone.' This suggests that a mode can be either an immanent cause or a transitive cause, i.e., a cause of an effect either within us, or outside us. For a discussion of some of these issues, see Melamed, 'Inherence, Causation'; for a critique of the claim that causation and conception are co-extensive, see Morrison, 'The Relation between Conception and Causation'.

14. In another letter to Oldenburg, Spinoza wrote that 'I do not separate God from nature as everyone known to me has done'; see Curley vol. 1, p. 188 / IV 36 / Letter 6 (Spinoza to Henry Oldenburg, April 1662).

15. During the early 1640s, Gilbertus Voetius, Calvinist theologian and rector of the newly founded University of Utrecht, clashed with his Cartesian colleague Henricus Regius, a professor of medicine. See Verbeek, *Descartes and the Dutch*; James, *Spinoza on Philosophy*; Douglas, *Spinoza and Dutch Cartesianism*.

16. Calvin, *Institutes*, vol. 1, ch. 14 §5. Calvin was fond of citing Acts 17:27–28 (see *Institutes*, vol. 1, ch. 1 §1; ch. 5 §§3, 9, §14; ch. 16 §§1, 4), and he criticised 'the Anthropomorphites, who imagined God to be corporeal, because the Scripture frequently ascribes to him a mouth, ears, eyes, hands and feet' (ch. 13 §1); 'there is nothing more unreasonable than the thought of contracting the infinite and incomprehensible God within the compass of five feet' (ch. 11 §4). Calvin explains this figurative language in terms which somewhat anticipate Spinoza's *Theologico-Political Treatise*: 'such forms of expression do not clearly explain the nature of God, but accommodate the knowledge of him to our narrow capacity' (ch. 13 §1). However, Calvin's anthropomorphic descriptions of God's character make it difficult to avoid the image of a God presiding over and above the world. He attributes to God a strikingly punitive moral psychology, with particular emphasis on God's will, drawing on the portrayal of God in (what Calvin called) the Old Testament: 'In the law and in the prophets [God] frequently declares that whenever he moistens the earth with dew or with rain, he affords a testimony of his favour; and that, on the contrary, when at his command, heaven becomes hard as iron, when the crops of corn are blasted and otherwise destroyed, and when showers of hail and storms molest the fields, he gives a proof of a certain and specific vengeance' (ch. 16 §4); according to Calvin, inanimate things are 'no other than instruments into which God infuses as much efficacy as he pleases, bending and turning them to any actions, according to his will' (ch. 16 §2).

17. Descartes, *The Philosophical Writings*, vol. 3, p. 23.

18. The eighteenth-century sense of deism referred to here is different from the seventeenth-century sense, as articulated in Marin Mersenne's 1624 treatise *L'Impiété des Déistes, Athées, et Libertins, combattue et renversée*. In 1671, Lambert de Velthuysen associated Spinoza's views on religion with Mersenne's version of deism: '[Spinoza] doesn't rise above the religion of the Deists . . . [he] does not stay within the bounds of the Deists and leaves men an even narrower scope for worship'. Mersenne's seventeenth-century French deists denied that Christian scriptures were divinely revealed, and argued that following the moral law common to all monotheist religions was sufficient for salvation; Mersenne interpreted this view as a justification for 'libertine' conduct: see Curley vol. 2, p. 374.

19. See Melamed, 'Cohen, Spinoza'.

20. See Zachhuber, 'Transcendence and Immanence'; Westphal, 'Immanence and Transcendence'. The *Oxford English Dictionary* (*OED*) records the first use in English of 'transcendent' as a theological term in an article on 'Deism' in the 1877 *Encyclopedia Britannica*, where D. Patrick wrote that 'Shaftesbury vigorously protests against the notion of a wholly transcendent God'.

21. In his introduction to the Christian doctrine of creation, Simon Oliver explains that, for Aquinas, 'creation is not outside or alongside God as an alternative focus of being, as if God and creation were separate *things*. In an important sense, creation is 'in' God.'—see Oliver, *Creation*, pp. 89, 72.

22. Deleuze, *Spinoza: Practical Philosophy*, pp. 29, 88.

23. See Souriau, *The Different Modes*, pp. 190–91. Many of Deleuze's insights are recognizable, in embryo, in Souriau's note on these pages. Souriau argues that in the *Ethics* (as opposed to in the *Metaphysical Thoughts*), 'existence is certainly univocal, despite Axiom I [E1A1: Whatever is, is either in itself or in another], in which the *esse in alio* should be understood not as the fact of existing in a manner other than that of substance, but as the fact of being in the existence of the latter'.

24. Nadler, *Think Least of Death*, ch. 1. Similarly, Yovel claims that Spinoza's thought is characterised above all by 'the philosophy of immanence', or the idea that 'this-worldly existence is all there is, as the only actual being and the sole source of ethical value. God himself is identical with the totality of nature, and God's decrees are written not in the Bible but in the laws of nature and reason.'—see Yovel, *Spinoza and Other Heretics*, vol. 1, p. ix, and also vol. 2. Likewise, Steven B. Smith argues that Spinoza's God is 'not a divine or transcendent cause', and that the 'lesson' of the *Ethics* is 'to remove the prejudice that God is a transcendent creator'—see *Spinoza's Book of Life*, pp. 40, 48.

25. Latour, *An Inquiry*, p. 299.

26. Among exceptions to this tendency are Yitzhak Melamed, Sylvain Zac and Nancy Levene. For Levene, Spinoza advances 'a biblical concept of creation insofar as [his philosophy] maintains an absolute distinction between God and humankind while insisting that humankind transform itself into (because it is made from) the divine image. The crucial thing is to see that God's nonseparation from the world—a sore point for most theological readers—is at the center of Spinoza's understanding of the most valuable and difficult human project, which, as the Bible would put it, is to become holy as God is holy (Leviticus 19:2)—to become, in the words of Genesis, 'like' God (Genesis 3:22)'—*Spinoza's Revelation*, p. 57. Zac emphasises the difference

between Spinozist creation and Biblical creation, while also reading Spinoza as offering a 'spiritual path'; see Zac, 'On the Idea of Creation', p. 238.

27. See Gueroult, *Spinoza*, vol. 1: *Dieu*, pp. 220–39. Gueroult rightly argues that *panenthéisme* is the most accurate label for the position set out in E1p14 and E1p15, since 'les modes sont *en Dieu*, sans cependant être *Dieu* à la rigeur'—yet he understates the difference between pantheism and panentheism when he claims that 'par l'immanence des choses à Dieu est jeté le premier fondemont du panthéisme, ou, plus exactement, d'une certaine forme de panenthéisme' (p. 223). Gueroult argues (citing Letter 73) that Spinoza's panentheism differs from that of ancient Hebrews, antique philosophers, Saint Paul and Augustine insofar as, for Spinoza, 'les *substances de la Nature*, Etendue, Pensée, etc., *sont* Dieu même' (p. 223). Coupling these remarks with Gueroult's emphasis on immanence in his commentary on E1p15 (he identifies two forms of immanence in Ethics I: one which posits nature in God, and one which posits God, as immanent cause, in nature—see p. 222) we might place him among those readers who do not recognise the transcendence of Spinoza's God, and who see theological immanence and transcendence as contrary rather than as complementary. In his book *Spinoza*, Alan Donagan denies that Spinoza is a pantheist, because he affirms the ontological distinction between God and created things, and suggests that 'Spinoza is a "panentheist" in the sense in which process theologians understand that word'; however, he also insists that, for Spinoza, 'God is not a transcendent being' (pp. 90–91)—and the 'process theologians' Donagan aligns with Spinoza were twentieth-century Christian thinkers who tended to deny God's transcendence. For an outline of an interpretation of Spinozism as panentheism *and* a 'radical variant of transcendent theology', see Melamed, 'Cohen, Spinoza'.

For a valuable historical discussion of the Spinoza's association with pantheism, particularly in the German context, see Nadler, 'Benedictus Pantheissimus'. Nadler's own interpretation is that Spinoza was an atheist, not a pantheist: 'Novalis got it wrong. Spinoza did not elevate nature into the divine. On the contrary, he reduced the divine to nature—he naturalized God' (p. 253). The opposite view is put forward by the twentieth-century Catholic theologian Erich Przywara, who—following the 'acosmist' reading of Spinozism pioneered by Solomon Maimon—contrasts 'Spinoza's world-denying theopanism' with 'Schopenhauer-Nietzsche's God-denying pantheism': see Przywara, *Analogia Entis*, p. 52.

The view that Spinoza was an atheist is difficult to defend on the basis of the *Ethics*: in Part One we find a definition of God and a detailed account of God's nature and relation to everything that exists, and Part Five describes a 'wise person' who is 'conscious of himself, of God, and of things'. For a helpful note on the charge of atheism levelled against Spinoza by his contemporaries, see Curley vol. 2, pp. 47–49. Modern commentators who regard Spinoza as an atheist usually rely on the argument that his authentic views were entirely different from those expressed in his works and correspondence: see, for example, Strauss, 'Persecution'; Yovel, *Spinoza and Other Heretics*; Smith, *Spinoza's Book of Life*, pp. 41–44.

28. Toland, *Pantheisticon*, pp. 15–18. Toland envisaged pantheists as a 'Brotherhood' whose 'Religion is clear, simple, easy, without blemish, and freely bestowed, not painted over, not intricate, embarrassed, incomprehensible, or mercenary; not luring Minds with silly Fables, and ensnaring them by the Filth, Inhumanity or Ridicule

of Superstition ; not subservient, I say, to the private Advantage of any Family or Faction against the public Good; not scandalized or railing at, much less disturbing or tormenting any Person or Persons, so that they be honest and peaceable Men' (pp. 94–95). For a detailed discussion of Toland and his 'pantheism', see Jacob, *The Radical Enlightenment*; Champion, *The Pillars of Priestcraft Shaken* and 'John Toland'. Champion emphasises that Toland's pantheism was as much an intellectual (and moral) disposition, committed to toleration and free debate, as a philosophical or theological theory.

29. Coleridge, 'On the Prometheus', p. 1,261; Wilberforce, *The Doctrine of the Incarnation*, p. 151.

30. *OED* third edition (2005). The *OED* second edition (1989) offers the following definition of pantheism: 'The religious belief or philosophical theory that God and the universe are identical (implying a denial of the personality and transcendence of God); the doctrine that God is everything and everything is God.' See also Mander, 'Pantheism': 'at its most general, pantheism may be understood positively as the view that God is identical with the cosmos, the view that there exists nothing which is outside of God, or else negatively as the rejection of any view that considers God as distinct from the universe'. See also Mander, 'Omniscience and Pantheism', and Nadler, 'Benedictus Pantheissimus': 'in very general terms, pantheism is the view that rejects the transcendence of God' (pp. 243–44); Nadler goes on to distinguish two types of pantheism: a 'reductive pantheism' that regards God as 'identical with all that exists', thus refusing any distinction between God and the world, and a view (closer, Nadler points out, to Toland's pantheism) that recognises some distinction between God and the world and regards God as 'contained or immanent within' the natural world. Nadler argues that Spinoza is not a pantheist in either of these senses.

31. The *OED* third edition (2005) entry for 'panentheism' reads: 'The theory or belief that God encompasses and interpenetrates the universe but at the same time is greater than and independent of it. Frequently contrasted with *pantheism*.' The German *Panentheismus* appeared in 1828, in Carl C. F. Krause's *System der Philosophie*, and English and French versions of the term, drawn from Krause, were in circulation from the 1870s.

32. Spinoza does not offer a formal definition of 'Nature' in the *Ethics*. It does not appear in the eight Definitions at the beginning of Part One: this list of definitions comprises 'cause of itself', 'finite thing', 'substance', 'attribute', 'mode', 'God', 'free' and 'necessary' things and 'eternity.' The word 'nature' has many different meanings: the *OED* lists over thirty distinct uses of the noun, as well as transitive and intransitive verb forms. Given Spinoza's reluctance to define *natura* in the *Ethics*, it is wise to treat this word as a provisional placeholder, an open question—especially when it is associated with God—rather than as a determinate entity, to which 'God' can then be reduced. In a note in Chapter 6 of the *Theologico-Political Treatise*, Spinoza indicates that 'by Nature here I understand not only matter and its affections, but in addition to matter, infinite other things [*alia infinita*]' (Curley vol. 2, p. 154 / III 83 / TTP ch. 6), and this fits with his definition of *natura naturans* as 'such attributes of substance as express an eternal and infinite essence' in E1p29s, combined with his definition of God as 'a substance consisting of an infinity of attributes, of which each one expresses an external and infinite essence' (E1D6).

33. See Nadler, 'Benedictus Pantheissimus', p. 243; *Think Least of Death*, ch. 1. See also Smith, *Spinoza's Book of Life*, p. 42: '*Deus sive nature* [*sic*] is a formula for the atheism that Spinoza either could not or would not admit to. . . . God or nature is Spinoza's way of saying that nature is the ground of all things beyond which we need make no further inquiries.'

34. Taylor, *A Secular Age*, p. 543.

35. Deleuze, *Spinoza: Practical Philosophy*, pp. 110-11.

36. See E1p13.

37. See E3p3s, E4p2, E4p4, E4p57s, E4App1, E4App6, E4App7; see also Curley vol. 2, p. 14 / IV 166 / Letter 30 (Spinoza to Henry Oldenburg, October 1665); Curley vol. 2, p. 18 / IV 170a / Letter 32 (Spinoza to Henry Oldenburg, November 1665); Curley vol. 2, p. 113 / III 46 / TTP ch. 3; Curley vol. 2, p. 509 / III 277 / TP ch. 2 §5. In a note to E3p51s, Spinoza claims that 'the human mind is part of the divine intellect', the divine intellect being an infinite mode, not substance, i.e., not God *simpliciter*.

38. An alternative explanation for Spinoza's imprecision here, suggested to me by Michael Della Rocca, is that Spinoza *does* mean to identify God and Nature, and that he speaks loosely when he says that Nature has parts. This is possible, though Spinoza uses the phrase 'part of Nature' at least seven times in the *Ethics*, and never uses the phrase 'part of God'.

39. This view has been developed with respect to Platonism, drawing on the way Socrates affirms the 'presence' (*parousia*) or 'sharing' (*koinonia*) of the Form of Beauty in particular beautiful things (see *Phaedo* 100d5-7): see Perl, 'The Presence of the Paradigm'. Summarising Perl's argument, David Schindler explains how the 'coincidence' of immanence and transcendence follows from the 'logic of transcendence': 'radical [ontological] difference does not imply dualism, but is precisely what prevents it. The transcendence of forms in relation to the sensible images that participate in them would *exclude* their immanence in sensible things *only if* forms and images were relative to one another *within the same order of reality*[;] . . . it is precisely because the form transcends not only a particular sensible image, but in fact the very mode of existence of that image, that it can be present to it—and to every other. In other words, only partial transcendence—i.e., mere separation within the same order of reality—excludes immanence; true transcendence is coincident with immanence'—Schindler, 'What's the Difference?', pp. 5-7. Herbert McCabe makes a similar point, with respect to the Catholic tradition, when he writes that 'the God of Augustine and Aquinas, precisely by being wholly transcendent, *extra ordinem omnium entium existens*, is more intimately involved with each creature than any other creature could be'—*God Matters*, pp. 45-46.

40. This insight has been articulated with force and in detail by Michael Della Rocca, who identifies the 'principle of sufficient reason' as the core principle of Spinoza's metaphysics, drawing on E1p11d2, 'For each thing there must be assigned a cause or reason, both for its existence and for its non-existence.' See Della Rocca, *Spinoza*.

41. For a discussion of this idea (including a compelling argument to show that Spinoza was committed to God's infinite number of attributes), see Melamed, '"A Substance"'. Melamed points out that Descartes also asserts that God has 'countless' attributes beyond the ones we know: see Descartes's letter to Mersenne, July 1641 in *The Philosophical Writings*, vol. 3, p. 185. While 'Descartes' claim that there are

uncountable divine attributes which we cannot comprehend secures the transcendence of the Cartesian God,' Melamed argues, 'Spinoza's claim that *Deus sive Natura* has infinitely many attributes which are not accessible to us makes *Nature* (with capital N, i.e., as not restricted to extended and thinking nature) *just as transcendent to us as God is*. This is a bold and highly original view which is consistent with Spinoza's deep critique of anthropocentrism.' Michael Della Rocca, by contrast, questions the coherence of the claim that there are multiple attributes: see 'The Elusiveness'.

42. See Curley vol. 2, pp. 413–15 / IV 250–53 / Letter 54 (Spinoza to Hugo Boxel, October 1674). See also E1p17s.

43. For a discussion of the history of the concept of the infinite, which provides fascinating insight into the medieval background to Spinoza's use of this concept in the *Ethics*, see Lévy, *Figures de l'infini*, especially Chapter 3, on medieval Islamic thought; Chapter 4, on Christian scholastic theology; and Chapter 5, on Rabbinic Judaism, Kabbalism and debates between Crescas and Maimonides concerning the divine attributes.

44. See E2p11 and E2p13: 'The first thing that constitutes the actual being of a human Mind is nothing but the idea of a singular thing which actually exists' and 'The object of the idea constituting the human Mind is the body, or a certain mode of Extension which actually exists, and nothing else.' Ursula Renz provides a fine-grained analysis of these propositions in *The Explainability of Experience*, pp. 145–67.

45. See Biernacki and Clayton, *Panentheism*.

46. Augustine, *Eighty-Three Different Questions*, pp. 47–48; Thomas Aquinas, *Summa Theologiae, Prima pars*, Q8.

47. John of Damascus, *Writings*, p. 202.

48. Because this discipline developed in academic institutions that until very recently were closely linked to Christian churches, in Europe and North America 'philosophy of religion' still means, for the most part, the philosophy of the Christian religion. To situate Spinoza in this field of academic enquiry therefore risks Christianising his thought, but on the other hand his view of religion, which is the very opposite of parochial, is exactly what the philosophy of religion needs to help expand its cultural reach.

49. See Kant, *Critique of Pure Reason*, pp. 564–69.

50. Anselm, *Proslogion*, ch. 1.

51. Anselm, *Proslogion*, ch. 1.

52. Anselm, *Proslogion*, ch. 14.

53. Anselm, *Proslogion*, ch. 15.

54. Anselm, *Proslogion*, ch. 16.

55. Anselm, *Proslogion*, ch. 17. At the beginning of Chapter 8, I explore how Spinoza takes up this idea of the soul's senses, or intellectual feeling—including a conception of intuitive 'vision' by the 'eyes of the mind'.

56. God's existence is necessary: see Anselm, *Proslogion*, chs 3 and 22; God's existence is self-sufficient: see chs 12 and 22; God is 'unlimited and eternal . . . in a unique way': ch. 13; God is simple: ch. 18.

57. See Anselm, *Proslogion*, ch. 22.

58. Anselm, *Proslogion*, ch. 20.

59. Anselm, *Proslogion*, ch. 26.

60. Anselm, *Proslogion*, chs 24 and 19.

61. Anselm, *Proslogion*, ch. 26.
62. Anselm, *Proslogion*, ch. 26.
63. Anselm, *Proslogion*, ch. 26.
64. In a 1674 letter, Spinoza makes the suggestive, though ambiguous, remark that he knows 'some of' God's attributes, which might imply that his knowledge of God goes beyond thought and extension, the two attributes ordinarily accessible to us: 'I don't say that I know God completely, but only that I know some of his attributes, not all of them, not even most of them. Certainly, being ignorant of most of them, does not prevent my knowing some.'—Curley vol. 2, p. 423 / IV 261 / Letter 56 (Spinoza to Hugo Boxel, October or November 1674). For a discussion of this passage, see Melamed, '"A Substance"'.
65. See Curley vol. 2, p. 19 / IV 171a / Letter 32 (Spinoza to Henry Oldenburg, November 1665).
66. On the theological significance of analogy, see below, Chapter 5, note 44.
67. Curley vol. 1, p. 305 / I 239 / CM I ch. 1. See Melamed, 'Spinoza's Deification', p. 103.
68. See Heidegger, *Being and Time*, pp. 58–59, and the opening pages of the 1927 lecture 'Phenomenology and Theology'. Challenging Heidegger's classification of theology as 'ontic' as opposed to ontological helps to address the difficulties Ursula Renz encounters when she seeks, in reading the *Ethics*, to 'translate theological statements into ontological ones' (*The Explainability of Experience*, p. 40). Renz recognises that 'in most, if not all, cases in which Spinoza takes recourse to theological topoi, ontological questions are at stake', and if we grant that ontology and theology are, for Spinoza, either intertwined or identical, then we do not need to 'translate' his statements about God in order to grasp their ontological (and philosophical) import—since his conception of God is always already ontological.
69. See E1p8s2 and E1p11. For discussions of Spinoza, the ontological argument and God's necessity, see Earle, 'The Ontological Argument'; Garrett, *Nature and Necessity*, pp. 31–61; Lin, *Being and Reason*, pp. 53–73.
70. Étienne Souriau makes a complementary point, quoting the Russian theologian Lev Shestov: 'we cannot say of God that he exists. For, in saying "God exists," we necessarily lose him'—*The Different Modes*, p. 198.

4. *Whatever We Desire and Do*

1. On *animi commotiones* and *fluctuationes*, see E3p17s, E3p31, E3p35s, E3p50s, E3p56 and E3p59s (which also mentions *animi conflictus*), E4p17s, E5p2; on *animi acquiescentia*, see E4App4, E5p10s, E5p36s and E5p42s.
2. The verb *studere* means not only 'to strive for', but also 'to dedicate oneself' or 'to direct one's efforts and attention'.
3. See Aristotle, *Physics* 2: 3 and *Metaphysics* 5: 2. On the medieval and early modern appropriations of Aristotelian causation, see Van Ruler, *The Crisis of Causality*; J. K. McDonough, 'The Heyday of Teleology'; Harvey, 'Spinoza and Maimonides'; Pasnau, 'Teleology'; Melamed, 'Teleology in Jewish Philosophy'.
4. Spinoza ventures a critique of the doctrine of creation *ex nihilo* in the *Metaphysical Thoughts* appended to his 1663 exposition of Cartesian philosophy. See note 34 to Chapter 5 for a discussion of this.

5. Thomas Aquinas, *Compendium*, pp. 85-56 (Part 1 §§104-5).

6. Thomas Aquinas, *Summa Theologiae, Prima pars*, Q19 art.1, ads 1 and 3.

7. On Suárez and Descartes, see Flage and Bonnen, 'Descartes on Causation'; Schmaltz, *Descartes on Causation*. Schmaltz describes Suárez's 'main thesis' as 'the priority of efficient causes' and shows how he attributed agency to final causation only in the case of God, and here 'only because there is no real distinction between God's final and efficient causality' (pp. 34-35). Schmaltz explains how Descartes follows Suárez in prioritising efficient over final causation. Nevertheless, Descartes retains a conception of 'rational teleology' which underpins ethical action: 'Though Descartes denies that we can explain divine action in this way, he explicitly allows for this sort of explanation in the case of our own action. In the Second Replies, for instance, he cites as an axiom that "the will of a thinking thing is carried [*fertur*] voluntarily and freely (for this is the essence of the will), but nevertheless inevitably, toward a clearly known good" (AT 7:166)' (p. 64). Alison Simmons analyses Descartes's complex position on different kinds of teleology in 'Sensible Ends'.

8. Bacon, *New Organon*, pp. 102-3 (Book 2 §2).

9. Hobbes, *Leviathan*, p. 70 (First Part, ch. 11).

10. *Meditations* IV [AT 7: 55]; see also Fifth Replies [AT 7: 375]; *Principles of Philosophy* 1 §28; 3 §§2-3. See Pasnau, *Metaphysical Themes*, p. 603: 'Descartes repeatedly stresses our inability to grasp the true ends of nature.... All these passages take for granted that there are ends for which God created the world.' Pasnau disagrees with Alison Simmons's suggestion that in the Sixth Replies (AT7: 431) Descartes challenges the very notion of divine purposes. By contrast, in the *Metaphysical Thoughts*, Spinoza proposes that in divine creation 'no other causes concur beyond the efficient'—Curley vol. 1, p. 334 / I 268 / CM II ch. 10.

11. Descartes, *The Philosophical Writings*, vol. 3, pp. 261-62 / AT 4 :275-57.

12. Descartes, *The Philosophical Writings*, vol. 3, pp. 325-26 / AT 5: 83, 85. On free will, see also *Meditation* IV.

13. Thus Spinoza reflected on his view of moral responsibility in a letter to Henry Oldenburg: 'But, you insist, if men sin from a necessity of nature, then they are excusable. But you don't explain what you want to infer from that. Is it that God cannot become angry with them? Or that they are worthy of blessedness, i.e., of the knowledge and love of God? If the former, then I grant completely that God does not become angry, but that all things happen according to his decree. But I deny that for that reason all men ought be to blessed. Indeed, men can be excusable, and nevertheless lack blessedness and suffer in many ways.... [Someone] who cannot govern his desires, although he is to be excused because of his weakness, nevertheless cannot enjoy peace of mind, and the knowledge and love of God. He necessarily perishes.'—Curley vol. 2, pp. 480-81 / IV 327a (Letter 78, to Henry Oldenburg, February 1676). For a discussion of these issues, see Kisner, *Spinoza on Human Freedom*, pp. 63-70. Spinoza's view contrasts with that of Calvin, who emphasises blame, guilt and divine punishment: 'in saying that some fall into superstition through error, I would not insinuate that their ignorance excuses them from guilt, because their blindness is always connected with pride, vanity and contumacy'; 'no doubt can be entertained respecting [God's] punishment of flagitious crimes' (*Institutes*, vol. 1, ch. 4 §1; ch. 5 §7).

14. See Garrett, 'Teleology in Spinoza'; Carriero, 'Spinoza on Final Causality' and 'Conatus and Perfection'; Lin, 'Teleology and Human Action'. For an overview of

recent scholarly discussions of teleology in Spinoza, see Viljanen, *Spinoza's Geometry of Power*, pp. 112–25.

Yitzhak Melamed argues that 'for Spinoza, virtually all causation is efficient causation, though his notion of efficient causation is significantly expanded in order to cover the functions of the other Aristotelian causes ... he reduced final causation to the efficient causality of the *conatus*'—*Spinoza's Metaphysics*, p. 65. Melamed criticises arguments which propose Aristotle's formal cause as the model for Spinoza's concept of causation: see Carraud, *Causa sive ratio*; Viljanen, *Spinoza's Geometry of Power*, pp. 41–45.

15. Among the arguments that constitute the 'doctrine' Spinoza is discussing in this scholium are the following key passages: 'the infinite essence of God and his eternity are known to all. Now as all things are in God and are conceived through God, it follows that from this knowledge of the divine nature we can deduce many other adequate ideas, and thus form that third kind of cognition of which we spoke in E2p40s2, the pre-eminence and utility of which it will be our task to speak of in the Fifth Part. That, however, men have not so clear a knowledge of God as they have of common notions, arises from this, that they are able to *imagine* God as they do bodies, and that they have united the name *God* to images of things they are accustomed to see, which men can scarcely avoid, because they are continually affected by external bodies' (E2p47s); 'There is no absolute or free will in the mind, but [the mind] is determined to will this or that by a cause which is also determined by another cause, and this again by another, and so on *in infinitum*' (E2p48).

16. In translating E3p6, Curley notes that 'it is unclear whether *quantum in se est* should be regarded as an occurrence of the technical phrase used in the definition of substance or merely as an occurrence of an ordinary Latin idiom, which might be rendered *as far as it lies in itself* or *as far as it lies in its own power*'. Curley himself opts for 'as far as it can by its own power', but I have provided a more literal translation of *quantum in se est* to keep the resonance with E1D3 more explicit—see Curley vol. 2, pp. 498–99. Moreau translates *quantum in se est* more literally, as *autant qu'il est en elle*: see Moreau and Steenbakkers (eds), *Spinoza: Œuvres IV*, p. 255. Michael Della Rocca discusses the Cartesian background to Spinoza's use of *quantum in se est* in 'Spinoza's Metaphysical Psychology'. I discuss the interpretation of *quantum in se est* further here in Chapter 5.

For a persuasive account of Gersonides's influence on Spinoza's notion of *conatus*, which emphasises the role of God or Nature, see Harvey, 'Gersonides and Spinoza'. Harry Austryn Wolfson traces the history of the natural appetite for self-preservation through the Stoics, Cicero, Augustine, Thomas Aquinas, Duns Scotus, Dante, Telesius and 'other philosophers of the Renaissance', concluding that 'at the time of Spinoza the principle of self-preservation became a commonplace of popular wisdom, so much so that in the Hebrew collection of sermons by his teacher Rabbi Saul Levi Morteira one of the sermons begins with the statement that "Nature, mother of all created beings, has implanted in them a will and impulse to strive for their self-preservation [*Gibe' at Sha'ul*]"'—Wolfson, *The Philosophy of Spinoza*, vol. 2, pp. 195–96 and further to p. 208. More recently scholars have argued that the Cartesian principle of inertia is the key influence on Spinoza's concept of the *conatus*: see Della Rocca, 'Spinoza's Metaphysical Psychology' and 'Steps towards Eleaticism'; Renz, *The Explainability of*

Experience, pp. 211–13. Della Rocca identifies Descartes's *Principles of Philosophy* as Spinoza's key influence, while Renz argues that Johann Clauberg, a Dutch Cartesian, is a more proximate source.

17. On the concept of *conscientia*, see Balibar, 'A Note on "Consciousness/Conscience"'; Nadler, 'Spinoza on Consciousness'; Renz, *The Explainability of Experience*, pp. 214–16.

18. See Calvin's *Institutes*, vol. 1, ch. 2 §2; ch. 5 §10.

19. Spinoza thought that God's efficient causation was immanent, or that God is an 'internal cause' of things. Modes, however, can have transitive or 'external' causal relations to one another. On 'extrinsic causes' in Suárez, see Schmaltz, *Descartes on Causation*, pp. 29–33; on how this relates to Spinoza, see Melamed, *Spinoza's Metaphysics*, pp. 64–65. Melamed explains how early readers of Spinoza, including Pierre Bayle and Solomon Maimon, ascribed to him the view that God is the material cause of the universe, precisely because this kind of causation was characterised as intrinsic, or immanent, which fits the way Spinoza describes God as an immanent cause. However, this is an inaccurate interpretation of Spinoza's metaphysics, and as Melamed points out, 'Spinoza never claims that the substance (or the attributes) is the material cause (or the matter) of the modes'—see pp. 63–64.

20. On the identity of reality and activity, see E1p11s; E2Def.6; E5p40.

21. See Schelling, *On the History*, pp. 64–74.

22. See Anselm, *Monologion*, ch. 31.

23. Descartes, *The Philosophical Writings*, vol. 2, pp. 37–38 (Meditation IV). In his 1945 work *The Different Modes of Existence*, Étienne Souriau discusses the issue of degrees of being (or of existence) under the heading 'the intensive modes of existence', sketching a long philosophical history from the ancient Greeks onwards and situating this with respect to twentieth-century phenomenology and existentialism: see *The Different Modes*, pp. 109–31. Souriau returns to the question of degrees of existence in his 1959 lecture 'Du mode d'existence de l'oeuvre à faire', suggesting that 'in response to the question, "Does that being exist?" it is prudent to admit that we can hardly respond in accordance with the Yes–No couple, and that we must instead respond in accordance with that of the More and the Less'—ibid., pp. 220–21.

24. Curley vol. 1, p. 243 / I 154 / DPP, A4.

25. When these elements are combined with different trains of thought, and with different kinds of consciousness of external conditions, they produce more specific emotions. For example, if someone is aware of having done something wrong, which has been witnessed by another person, she will feel shame, which is a certain species of sadness.

26. Ursula Renz puts this point eloquently when she writes that 'by their very definition, affects are *transitional processes*. . . . [This] entails that God is, by definition, excluded from the circle of emotional beings. Spinoza clearly thinks that only finite things are capable of having affects and that having an emotion always has to do with a subject's finitude—or, more to the point, with its precarious existence'—*The Explainibility of Experience*, p. 210. The view that God does not, indeed cannot, have emotions is expressed in the traditional theological doctrine of divine impassibility. However, within this doctrine there is room to argue that since human consciousness is a reality which is—like all reality—known by God, i.e., part of God's infinite

intellect, then God knows whatever is happening within our consciousness, including affective experience, even though God does not *have* emotions. Perhaps there is a subtle distinction here between having an emotion, and seeing this emotion from the inside, which can be intuited within our own experience: it is possible, I think, to feel an emotion while seeing or knowing that one is feeling it (and knowing what it feels like), and this kind of seeing or knowing might be attributed to an impassive God.

5. Participating in Divine Nature

1. See Curley vol. 1, pp. 498–99. In his recent French translation of the *Ethics*, Pierre-François Moreau translates *quantum in se est* more literally, as *autant qu'il est en elle*. As Moreau and Steenbakkers observe, the formula *quantum in se est* occurs in Descartes's *Principles of Philosophy* (1 §37), and can be traced to Lucretius's *De rerum natura*: see Moreau and Steenbakkers (eds), *Spinoza: Œuvres IV*, pp. 255, 552–53. On the Cartesian background to Spinoza's use of *quantum in se est*, see Della Rocca, 'Spinoza's Metaphysical Psychology'. Don Garrett explores the implications of this phrase, as it occurs in E3p6, in *Nature and Necessity*, pp. 359–67, and suggests that this is an instance of Spinoza's view that 'finite things can have, *in varying degrees*, characteristics that only an infinite substance has absolutely' (p. 365).

2. See note 24 to Chapter 2.

3. Garrett, *Nature and Necessity*, p. 366.

4. Curley vol. 1, p. 360 / IV 94–95 / Letter 19 (Spinoza to Willem van Blyenbergh, 5 January 1665). In these reflections on service, Spinoza may have been alluding to 1 Corinthians 9:13: 'Do you not know that those who are employed in the temple get their food from the temple, and those who serve at the altar share in what is sacrificed on the altar?' In the Latin Vulgate, this verse includes the verb *participare*, translated here as 'share': 'Nescitis quoniam qui in sacrario operantur quæ de sacrario sunt, edunt: et qui altari deserviunt, de altari participant?'

5. Curley vol. 2, p. 77 / III 15 / TTP ch. 1.

6. Curley vol. 2, p. 78 / III 16 / TTP ch. 1.

7. See Curley vol. 2, p. 248–49 / III 158–59 / TTP ch. 12; p. 275 / III 182 / TTP ch. 15; Carlisle, 'Spinoza's Philosophy of Religious Life', pp. 214–15.

8. Curley vol. 2, pp. 127–28 / III 59 / TTP ch. 4.

9. Curley vol. 2, p. 128 / III 60 / TTP ch. 4.

10. Curley vol. 2, p. 266 / III 175 / TTP ch. 14.

11. Curley vol. 2, p. 266 /III 175 / TTP ch. 14.

12. Curley vol. 2, p. 266 / III 175–76 / TTP ch. 14.

13. Curley vol. 2, pp. 266–67 / III 176 / TTP ch. 14.

14. Divine love is discussed further here in Chapter 7. In an unpublished paper, John Heyderman has considered love as one of God's attributes, in parallel with thought and extension (and Spinoza does claim that our love of God arises necessarily alongside our knowledge of God, which suggests a parallel, and not a causal connection). On this basis, a greater degree of participation in God's nature might be conceived as a participation in a greater number of God's attributes—i.e., in extension, consciousness and love, rather than only in extension and consciousness—though at the same time this increase is also an increase of consciousness itself.

15. Curley vol. 2, p. 267 / III 176 / TTP ch. 14. As Dominic Erdozain has shown, Spinoza was one of a series of thinkers to invoke the ethics taught by Jesus and his apostles to protest against sectarian oppression and persecution. While religious authorities held doctrinal orthodoxy as their supreme principle, which sanctioned the use of force wherever deviation was detected, these critics (particularly Spinoza and Voltaire) appealed to neighbour-love, mercy and peace as the criteria of true faith—see Erdozain, *The Soul of Doubt*, pp. 69–117.

16. Curley vol. 2, p. 267 / III 176 / TTP ch. 14.

17. Curley vol. 2, p. 267 / III 176 / TTP ch. 14.

18. Following John's teaching that *Deus est charitas*, we can say that this divine love (*charitas*) is not an emotion; but insofar as we participate in this *charitas*, our love (*amor*) is an emotion. In the *Ethics*, Spinoza uses *amor* for both divine and human love, which produces some ambiguity: he wants to say that in one sense God cannot be said to love human beings, since God cannot be affected with emotions, which are transitions to greater or lesser perfection; yet in another sense God does love us, and our love is a participation in divine love. See Chapter 7 for further discussion of divine love.

19. Thomas Aquinas, *Summa Theologiae, Prima pars*, Q. 1, art. 3, ad. 3; Q. 44, art. 1. See Anselm's *Monologion*, chs 3, 5, 13 and 14 for a similar theological view, though without using the concept of participation: 'all existing beings exist through some one being, hence that being alone exists through itself, and others through another than themselves—by a like course of reasoning, I say, it can be proved that whatever things live, live through some one being; hence that being alone lives through itself, and others through another than themselves. . . . This Being is in all things, and throughout all; and all derive existence from it and exist through and in it [*Quod illa sit in omnibus et per omnia, et omnia sint ex illa et per illam et in illa*]' (*Monologion*, chs 13, 14).

20. Thomas Aquinas, *Compendium of Theology*, pp. 53–54 (Part 1 §68); see also *Summa Theologiae, Prima pars*, Q. 44, art. 1.

21. Cornelio Fabro and B. M. Bonansea suggest that Aquinas's doctrine of participation enables him to envisage a God who is 'at once both transcendent and immanent'—see 'The Intensive Hermeneutics', p. 487. Philipp Rosemann argues that Aquinas's God 'is *supra omnia* precisely *insofar as* he is *omnibus et intime*. Transcendence is the superlative mode of immanence'—see *Omne agens agit sibi simile*, p. 295. Rudi te Velde writes that 'the transcendence of the divine infinity is, in truth, a transcendence-in-immanence. As source of being, God is intimately present in each thing, causing and preserving it in its being', and argues, concerning Aquinas's philosophy of language, that 'the transcendence of God and the immanence of language are not allowed to fall apart; they must be kept together in terms of a semantic relation of transcendence-in-immanence, following the transcending immanence of God in his creatures'—Te Velde, *Aquinas on God*, pp. 83, 102. Simon Oliver elucidates Aquinas's participatory theology by reflecting on 'God's simultaneous immanence and transcendence with respect to creation'—Oliver, *Creation*, p. 89. Andrew Davison writes that Christian theology in general, and Thomist theology in particular, posits 'a certain interweaving of transcendence and immanence', which is integral to the doctrine of participation—Davison, *Participation in God*, p. 20.

22. Thomas Aquinas, *Compendium*, p. 106 (Part 1 §135). In Chapter 14 of the *Theologico-Political Treatise*, Spinoza might have been commenting on this Thomist doctrine (or on some version of it) when he argues that 'it doesn't matter, as far as faith is concerned, if someone believes that God is everywhere according to God's essence or according to God's power'—see Curley vol. 2, p. 269 / III 178 / TTP ch. 14.

23. See Te Velde, *Aquinas on God*, pp. 146, 175, 178. Fabro and Bonasea suggest that, for Aquinas, 'all things are in [God], from him and for him'—'The Intensive Hermeneutics', p. 488. Analyses concurring with this view include Turner, 'On Denying the Right God'; Oliver, *Creation*, pp. 72–73. On the other hand, Te Velde contrasts the procession of the Trinity in God with the procession of creation 'out of God' (*Aquinas on God*, p. 69), though he also writes that human life 'has its destination in God' (p. 27). Andrew Davison, more robustly, resists the language of being-in-God: see Davison, *Participation in God*, pp. 35–38, 180, and Carlisle, 'All Things in Relation to God'.

24. Thomas Aquinas, *Summa Theologiae, Prima pars*, Q. 8, art. 1, objection 2 and its response.

25. Thomas Aquinas, *Summa Theologiae, Prima secundae partis*), Q. 110, art. 3 and art. 4. For Aquinas, participation explains the goodness of creatures, just as it explains their being. Mirroring his analysis of the relation between divine and creaturely existence, Aquinas contrasts God's essential, self-sufficient goodness with the 'participated goodness of creatures': 'God alone is His own goodness, and God alone is essentially good. All other beings are said to be good according as they participate, to some extent, in God' (Solus igitur Deus est sua bonitas et essentialiter bonus; alia vero dicuntur bona secundum participationem aliquam ipsius)—*Compendium*, p. 88 (Part 1 §109); see also pp. 82–84 (Part 1 §103). Explaining 'the reasons for diversity in things', Aquinas claims that 'different things . . . participate in the divine goodness in varying degree', and that thus, 'the very order existing among diverse things issues in a certain beauty, which should call to mind the divine wisdom'—*Compendium*, pp. 81–82 (Part 1 §102). And to different degrees of participation correspond proportional degrees of 'likeness to God': 'the higher a thing is in the scale of being, the closer it draws to likeness with God. Thus we observe that some things, those pertaining to the lowest degree, such as lifeless beings, share in the divine likeness [*participare divinam similitudinem*] with respect to existence only; others, for example, plants, share in the divine likeness with respect to existence and life; yet others, such as animals, with respect to sense perception. But the highest degree, and that which makes us most like to God, is conferred by the intellect. Consequently the most excellent creatures are intellectual. Indeed, they are said to be fashioned in God's image for the very reason that among all creatures they approach most closely to likeness with God'—*Compendium*, p. 58 (Part 1 §75). In summary, Aquinas writes that 'all things are directed to the divine goodness as to their end, as we have shown. Among things ordained to this end, some are closer to the end than others, and so participate in the divine goodness [*plenius divinam bonitatem participant*] most abundantly'—*Compendium*, pp. 115–16 (Part 1 §148).

26. Thomas Aquinas, *Compendium*, p. 86 (Part 1 §106).

27. Thomas Aquinas, *Compendium*, p. 226 (Part 2 §9). John Carriero reads *Ethics* V alongside Aquinas's account of beatitude in 'The Highest Good'.

28. The dramas of Euripides and Aristophanes record a colloquial use of *methexis* and cognate words to denote communal sharing, and this is reflected by the suggestion in Plato's *Protagoras* that Prometheus's stolen fire gave human beings a 'share of the divine dispensation'—Plato, *Protagoras* 321d. The use of *methexis* becomes more metaphysical in Plato's later dialogues: in the *Phaedo*, for example, Socrates suggests that 'if anything is beautiful besides absolute beauty, it is beautiful for no other reason than because it shares in absolute beauty; and this applies to everything'; and in the *Cratylus* he equates 'what is' with 'what shares in being'—Plato, *Phaedo* 100c; *Cratylus* 401c. When Paul wrote to the Corinthians that 'we who are many are one body, for we all share [*metechomen*; Latin *participamus*] of the one bread', this may reflect either the colloquial or the metaphysical use of *methexis* in these older Greek texts.

29. See Aristotle, *Metaphysics* 1: 6 (987b 11–14).

30. Étienne Gilson argues that Platonic and Aristotelian philosophies represent 'two absolutely irreconcilable interpretations of the universe. Aristotle's universe, born of a mind which seeks the sufficient reason for things in the things themselves, detaches and separates the world from God. Plato's universe is the universe of images, the world wherein things are at once copies and symbols, with no autonomous nature belonging to themselves, essentially dependent, relative, leading thought to seek beyond things and even above itself for the reason of what they are'—see Gilson, *The Philosophy of Saint Bonaventure*, pp. 96–97. If we accept Gilson's account, Spinoza might be seen—like Aquinas, but in a different way—to mediate between Platonism and Aristotelianism: like Plato, he emphasises that finite things are 'essentially dependent', with 'no autonomous nature', and he resists Aristotle's effort to 'detach and separate the world from God'; yet he shares Aristotle's commitment to knowing particular things, which are the object of the highest kind of knowledge, *scientia intuitiva*.

31. See Gerson, *Aristotle and Other Platonists*, pp. 117–22. Fabro and Bonansea write that for Aquinas '[God] is immanent in the sense that he is the actuating, grounding principle of being, and not merely something accidentally contained in it. He is transcendent as the emerging incomparable act that is beyond all space, time, and measurement, for he is all in himself and all things are in him, from him and for him.'—'The Intensive Hermeneutics', pp. 487–88.

32. That said, some interpreters of Aquinas would argue that, despite his conceptual distinction between nature and grace, Thomist theology in fact refuses any duality between nature and grace, since nature is animated by a desire for grace, and this desire is itself a sign of grace: John Milbank, for example, following Henri de Lubac, advances such an interpretation.

33. It is difficult to determine the extent of Spinoza's acquaintance with Aquinas's thought. In Chapter 1 of his *Short Treatise*, he refers to Aquinas's *Summa Theologiae* in the course of discussing the possibility of proving God's existence: see Curley vol. 1, p. 65 / I 18 / KV I ch. 1. Other possible references occur in Curley vol. 1, pp. 88, 89, 320, 333, 334, 335, 336, 342, 344. Wolfson identifies Aquinas as the source of certain elements of the *Ethics*, including the distinction between *natura naturans* and *natura naturata*, and Spinoza's discussion of the virtues, or 'active affects': see Wolfson, *The Philosophy of Spinoza*, vol. 1, pp. 16, 254–55; vol. 2, pp. 218–19. Drawing on the work of Jacob Freudenthal on Spinoza and Scholasticism in the late nineteenth century, Curley discusses the influence on Spinoza of Aquinas as well as Maimonides,

Suárez and the seventeenth-century Dutch scholastics Burgersdijks and Heereboord, both professors of philosophy at the University of Leiden (Burgersdijk from 1620 to 1635, Heereboord from 1641 to 1661)—see Curley vol. 1, p. 223, and footnotes throughout the *Metaphysical Thoughts*: pp. 299–346.

34. See Thomas Aquinas, *Summa Theologiae, Prima pars*, Q. 75.

35. Spinoza argues that the grammatical construction '*ex nihilo*' erroneously projects an intra-worldly logic onto God. Because things in the world are produced 'from' or 'out of' something else, he suggests, theologians cling onto the preposition *ex* when describing divine creation, paradoxically reifying 'nothing' as the stuff out of which the universe was made, 'as if nothing was the matter from which things were produced. The reason why philosophers speak this way is that when things are generated, they customarily suppose something prior to the things, out of which the things are made; consequently they were not able to omit that particle *ex* in creation'—Curley vol. 1, p. 334 / I 268 / CM II ch. 10. So while Spinoza rejects the doctrine that God creates 'out of nothing', he endorses a different grammatical construction of the same thought: 'a created thing is that which presupposes nothing except God in order to exist' (ibid., and see Curley's note on this). For Spinoza, divine creation is not *ex nihilo* because it is not *ex* anything; on the contrary, creation is *in Deo*.

36. Spinoza briefly discusses angels in his *Metaphysical Thoughts*: he argues that 'their essence and existence are known only by revelation, and so pertain solely to Theology'—Curley vol. 1, pp. 340–41 / I 275 / CM II ch. 12.

37. Another intriguing parallel emerges in Rudi te Velde's study of Aquinas, which calls into question whether Aquinas's doctrine is 'theistic' in any conventional sense: '[Aquinas] does not, I think, argue that the theistic description of God corresponds to an independent reality, or that, in fact, a supreme being exists with the features attributed to God by the Christian religion. Interpreted in this way, the sense of Thomas's approach to God is fundamentally misunderstood, in my view. God is not an entity to which a description of any kind applies and which, as such, is an object of representational thought. Any description conceives its object as a determinate entity which can be identified by certain characteristics. Theism concerns, I think, in the first place, a representational form of thinking and imagining the divine; it characterizes the manner in which God is represented in the religious and theological way of talking about God in the Christian tradition. But Thomas certainly does not think that this theistic model is to be applied directly to the ontological reality it is meant to describe, however refined and purified it may be from anthropomorphic and metaphorical elements. We ought to distinguish between a theistic representation of God and an ontological account of that divine reality to which the representation is taken to refer as to its truth. As regards the latter, one should say that God, as the principle of the being of all things, must be understood in terms of self-subsistent being, which is not in any sense a description. I would not characterize what Thomas is engaged in as seeking for a rational justification and foundation of the (Christian) theistic concept of God. His approach to the truth of what Christian faith confesses of God is primarily ontological'—Te Velde, *Aquinas on God*, p. 177.

38. See Thomas Aquinas, *Summa Theologiae, Prima pars*, Q. 10, art. 2; Q. 7, art. 1; Q. 3, art. 7; Q. 9, art. 1. See *Metaphysical Thoughts*, Part 2 for a clear enumeration of God's qualities: Curley vol. 1, pp. 315–25 / I 249–60 / CM II chs 1–5.

39. On the name of God, see *Summa Theologiae, Prima pars*, Q. 13 art. 11; when Aquinas describes God as 'the infinite ocean of substance', he is citing John of Damascus.

40. See, for example, *Summa Theologiae, Prima pars*, Q. 3 art. 1; Q. 4, art. 3, ad 3; Gilson, *Being and Some Philosophers*, p. 90; Fabro and Bonansea, 'The Intensive Hermeneutics', p. 463. Étienne Souriau notes what is, I think, the other side of the same coin, when he writes that 'I am who I am' is 'equivalent to an outright refusal of any denomination of the divine', and connects this with negative theology—see Souriau, *The Different Modes*, p. 198.

41. Curley vol. 2, p. 259 / III 169 / TTP ch. 13. Curley translates *Jehova* as *Yahweh* but I have left the name in Latin, as it is in Spinoza's text. On the historical background to this passage, see Curley's helpful footnotes on p. 259, and Zac, *Spinoza et l'interprétation*, pp. 79–84.

42. See Thomas Aquinas, *Compendium*, p. 35 (Part 1 §36).

43. In 1277, shortly after his death, some of Aquinas's doctrines were condemned by the masters of Paris, the highest theological jurisdiction in the Church. Aquinas was canonised as a saint in 1323 (fifty years after his death), officially named a Doctor of the Church in 1567, and in 1879 Pope Leo XIII declared Aquinas's works to be an authoritative exposition of Christian doctrine.

44. Jacob Sherman acknowledges that 'Spinoza still uses the language of participation to convey the relationship between modes, attributes, and God—and in this one can hear echoes of [Neoplatonism and Thomism]—but Spinoza alters these traditions in a crucial manner so that there is no longer any distance between the modes and substances and that in which they participate. . . . Spinoza radicalizes participation by running it through the concepts of immanence and the univocity of being and refusing any doctrine of transcendence [and] by abolishing the distinction between Creator and creation'—Sherman, 'A Genealogy', pp. 95–98. While Sherman is right to stress Spinozist immanence, I think he is wrong about the refusal of transcendence, and also about the distinction between God and finite things, since the distinction between substance and modes is an ontological difference which preserves the asymmetry between God and the universe affirmed by Thomist participation, producing a synthesis of immanence and transcendence that echoes Thomist metaphysics.

The 'univocity of being' that Sherman attributes to Spinoza is borrowed from Deleuze's interpretation, which, like Deleuze's emphasis on the absolute immanence of Spinozism, should be called into question. Deleuze cites E1p25s to argue that 'God is said to be the cause of all things in the very sense [*eo sensu*] that he is said to be cause of himself'—*Expressionism in Philosophy*, p. 67. Read in context, Spinoza's remark in E1p25s is directed to the claim that God is the cause of both the essence and the existence of things (E1p24cor, E1p25). The line of argument Spinoza is pursuing here is that God causes the ongoing existence of things: God is not merely the cause of the essence of things, nor merely the cause of their beginning to exist, but the ground of their entire being. Spinoza then connects this point with the doctrine, which he shares with scholastic theologians, that God's essence and existence coincide: in Spinoza's terms, to say that God is *causa sui* is to say that God causes God's essence-and-existence. So when Spinoza insists that 'God must be called the cause of all things in the same sense in which he is called the cause of himself', his key point is that God causes both the essence and the existence of all things. By E1p25, Spinoza has already asserted the ontological difference and asymmetry between God, the self-causing substance, and the modes, and the simplicity of God's causal power asserted by the phrase *eo sensu* does not entail the claim that God exists in the same sense, and in the same way, that finite things exist. For Spinoza, our causal power is a participation in—and thereby an expression of—God's causal power. As with all participation, there is a relation of difference here, in that God is *causa sui* and we are not. Another way of putting this is to say that, for Spinoza, being caused by God means the same as being-in-God. Our being-in-God participates in God's own being-in-God. God's own being-in-God is a being *in se*, while our being-in-God is a being *in alio*.

While the *univocity of being* is proper to pantheism, with its identification of God and nature, the *analogy of being* is proper to panentheism, as expressing both difference and relation: the relation of being-in-God. According to some developments of Thomist theology, a doctrine of ontological analogy is inseparable from a metaphysics of participation—see Przywara, *Analogia Entis*. Spinoza does not propose a positive doctrine of analogy (whether ontological or epistemological), but it is striking that he consistently explains his three kinds of knowledge with a mathematical example concerning the analogy of proportion (A is to B as C is to D), suggesting that knowledge consists in grasping real relations. For an overview of the concept of analogy from Plato and Aristotle to Aquinas, Cajetan and Suárez, see John Betz's Introduction to Przywara's *Analogia Entis*, pp. 30–43; and for a seventeenth-century discussion of its philosophical and theological significance see Rodolphus Goclenius's *Lexicon Philosophicum*, pp. 96–103.

45. Suggesting that Aquinas's doctrine of participation occupies the 'theological middle ground', Andrew Davison describes how Aquinas charts a course between deism and pantheism: '[Thomism] does not imagine that the creature, once created, is in a state of indifferent independence when it comes to God. Yet ... such language of independence is not entirely false. Our sense of a creature's proper integrity and agency is not simply an illusion, as if the creature were but a phantom, on the one hand, or an extension of God, on the other. The creature is neither a pantheistic extension of God, nor a mere figment, nor independent of God. ... A creature does not subsist as God subsists, but it does subsist through a derived likeness to God's subsistence. Supposing otherwise, that subsistence applies to creatures as it applies to God, leads either to dualistic deism, or to pantheism. Dualism and deism, on the one hand, suppose that creatures are substances as God is; pantheism, on the other hand, and in the opposite direction, equates God and creatures'—Davison, *Participation in God*, pp. 59, 80. Unfortunately Davison adds that Spinoza is a pantheist because he argues 'that there is only one substance, namely god-or-nature'. He is right to discern a difference between Aquinas and Spinoza, who would not agree that creatures 'subsist through a derived likeness to God's subsistence', but the difference is far more subtle than Davison supposes. Both thinkers chart a course between deism and pantheism, but use different concepts to do so.

46. For claims that Jesus is the Son of God, see Mark 1:11, 3:11, 9:7, 15:39; Matthew 14:33, 27:43, 27:54; Luke 1:35, 4:41; John 1:34, 11:27; 20:31; Acts 9:20. On Christ as *logos*, see John 1:1–3.

47. CT §§214, 215.

48. Curley vol. 2, pp. 84–85 / III 21 / TTP ch. 1. Curley's translation reads, 'Christ was the way to salvation': there is no article in Latin, so a decision must be made

between 'the way' and 'a way'. Curley justifies his translation with the qualification that 'we understand this statement in a way which does not conflict with Spinoza's fundamental pluralism'. I think the best way to be faithful to this pluralism, and avoid assimilating Spinoza to the standard Christian view that Christ is the *only* way to salvation, is to opt for the indefinite article.

49. Curley vol. 2, pp. 132–33 / III 64 / TTP ch. 4.

50. Curley vol. 2, p. 137 / III 67 / TTP ch. 4. See also Curley vol. 2, p. 84 / III 21 / TTP ch. 1: 'I must warn here that I'm not speaking in any way about the things some of the Churches maintain about Christ. Not that I deny them. For I readily confess that I do not understand them.'

51. Curley vol. 2, p. 468 / IV 308a–309a / Letter 73 (Spinoza to Henry Oldenburg, December 1675). Curley notes an ambiguity in the Latin: Spinoza may be arguing that 'it is completely unnecessary for salvation to know Christ according to the flesh'; or he may be arguing that 'it is not completely necessary for salvation to know Christ according to the flesh'. Anselm describes Christ as 'the virtue of [God] the Father, and [God's] wisdom, and justice': 'the Son is the true Word, that is, the perfect intelligence, conceiving of the whole substance of the Father, or perfect cognition of that substance, and knowledge of it, and wisdom regarding it; that is, it understands, and conceives of, the very essence of the Father, and cognises it, and knows it, and is wise [*sapit*] regarding it'—see *Monologion*, chs 45–46.

52. Curley vol. 2, p. 473 / IV 316a /Letter 75 (Spinoza to Henry Oldenburg, January 1676).

53. Curley vol. 2, p. 133 / III 64 / TTP ch. 4.

54. Schlegel, *Philosophical Fragments*, p. 50.

6. Acquiescentia

1. Hobbes, *Leviathan*, p. 70 (First Part, ch. 11).

2. See Curley vol. 1, p. 167 / IV 9 / Letter 2 (Spinoza to Henry Oldenburg, September 1661). Bacon's *Novum Organon* states, 'The human intellect is active and cannot halt or rest [*Gliscit intellectus humanus, neque consistere aut acquiescere potis est*], but even, though without effect, still presses forward.... The human intellect, incapable of resting, seeks for something more intelligible [*intellectus humanus, nescius acquiescere, adhuc appetit notiora*]'—see Bacon, *New Organon*, p. 44 (Book 1 §48), and my note on Spinoza's critique of Bacon in Chapter 2. As mentioned there, Josef Pieper argues that conceiving knowledge as 'active intellectual effort' is a defining feature of modern philosophy, exemplified by Kant: see Pieper, *Leisure*, pp. 30–34.

3. See Frankfurt, *Taking Ourselves Seriously*, p. 17.

4. See Carlisle (ed.), *Spinoza's* Ethics, and Kisner (ed.), *Spinoza: Ethics*.

5. See translations by D.D.S. (New York, 1876), Elwes (London, 1883), William Hale White (1883), Henry Smith (Cincinnati, 1876), George Stuart Fullerton (New York, 1892) and Edwin Curley (Princeton, 1985). On the question of translation, see Curley vol. 1, p. 655. Although many modern scholars acknowledge that translating *acquiescentia in se ipso* as 'self-esteem' is questionable, most nevertheless follow Curley in adopting it: see especially Rutherford, 'Salvation as a State of Mind'; LeBuffe, *From Bondage*, pp. 194–208; Cooper, *Secular Powers*, pp. 91–104. Rutherford acknowledges that *acquiescentia in se ipso* 'carries the more literal meaning of "contentment

with oneself"', but argues for retaining Curley's translation on the grounds that '["self-esteem"] makes better sense of the conceptual relations Spinoza establishes in Parts II and IV between *acquiescentia in se ipso, humilitas, superbia,* and *gloria*'—see 'Salvation as a State of Mind' pp. 451–52, and especially note 8.

6. Curley vol. 2, p. 185 / III 111 / TTP ch. 7.

7. Julie Cooper highlights the 'polyvalence' of *acquiescentia* in the *Ethics* and explores Spinoza's 'ambivalence' towards this affect, which she explains in terms of a distinction between its passive and active variants: see *Secular Powers*, p. 91. Giuseppina Totaro suggests that we find 'an evolution, if not a real transformation' of *acquiescentia* from *Ethics* III to *Ethics* V, and she explains this 'semantic evolution' in terms of the distinction between 'reason' and 'the intellect'—that is to say, between the second and the third kinds of knowledge: see Totaro, '*Acquiescentia*', pp. 68–69. Developing Totaro's insight, we see that tracing the semantic evolution of *acquiescentia* through all three kinds of knowledge provides the link between Spinoza's critiques of free will, Cartesian philosophy and superstition, and his account of *acquiescentia* as the experiential, affective aspect of true understanding.

8. For a comparison of the French and Latin texts of Descartes's *Passions of the Soul*, see Totaro, '*Acquiescentia*', p. 68.

9. Desmarets's choice of *acquiescentia in se ipso* may be traced to Goclenius's 1613 *Lexicon Philosophicum*, a scholastic reference work which, as William Cox has shown in an unpublished paper, includes a verb construction close to *acquiescentia in se ipso*: *in se ipso acquiescens* (though Goclenius does not use the phrase *acquiescentia in se ipso*). Following Aquinas in distinguishing between God's independent goodness and the participated goodness of created or 'dependent' things, Goclenius states that God's independent goodness 'seeks nothing outside itself, but rests in itself [*in se ipso acquiescēns*]'—*Lexicon Philosophicum*, pp. 341–42. Goclenius also identifies a more psychological '*acquiescentia*' that he describes as 'peace of the will [*quies voluntatis*] in something it has, or has had' (p. 128; see also Goclenius's entry on *quies* and *quiescere*, pp. 942–47), which is closer to Descartes's concept of *la satisfaction de soi-même*. From these citations, we see that Spinoza's concept of *acquiescentia in se ipso* combines the theological and psychological senses of *acquiescentia* that remain separate in Goclenius's lexicon.

10. Descartes, *The Philosophical Writings*, vol. 1, p. 369 (*Passions of the Soul*, art. 190).

11. See Totaro, '*Acquiescentia*'; Voss, 'How Spinoza'. On the reception of Spinoza's account of the passions in relation to the Cartesian background, see Steenbakkers, *Spinoza's Ethica*, pp. 103–28. Desmarets's interpretative decision regarding *acquiescentia* puts a small but significant distance between Spinoza and Descartes. It is unlikely that Descartes, who died in 1650, read and authorised Desmarets's Latin translation of his text—see Voss, 'On the Authority'. Since it is unlikely that Spinoza read the original French text of the *Passions*, he probably did not know that *acquiescentia* translated *la satisfaction*, and indeed, he might never have wondered about the French original. He may well have taken *acquiescentia* at face value, as carrying connotations of stillness and rest, acceptance and obedience. He certainly exploits these connotations in responding to what he could have reasonably taken to be the Cartesian account of *acquiescentia in se ipso*.

12. This is partially obscured when Spinoza's *acquiescentia in se ipso* is translated into English as 'self-esteem', while the corresponding Cartesian passion is translated as 'self-satisfaction'—and further confusion follows from the fact that Descartes's *la satisfaction de soi-même* is a distinct passion from *l'estime*, which is coupled with and opposed to *le mépris* in Article 54.

13. See Descartes, *The Philosophical Writings*, vol. 1, pp. 351–52, 396–67 (*Passions of the Soul*, art. 63, art. 190).

14. Descartes, *The Philosophical Writings*, vol. 1, p. 379 (*Passions of the Soul*, art. 191).

15. Descartes, *The Philosophical Writings*, vol. 1, pp. 352, 396–97 (*Passions of the Soul*, art. 63, art. 191).

16. Descartes, *The Philosophical Writings*, vol. 1, p. 369 (*Passions of the Soul*, art. 190).

17. Descartes, *The Philosophical Writings*, vol. 1, p. 369 (*Passions of the Soul*, art. 190).

18. Descartes, *The Philosophical Writings*, vol. 1, p. 369 (*Passions of the Soul*, art. 190).

19. Descartes, *The Philosophical Writings*, vol. 1, p. 369 (*Passions of the Soul*, art. 190).

20. On the link between superstition and fear, see Curley vol. 2, pp. / III 5–6 / TTP Preface. See also James, *Spinoza on Philosophy*, pp. 15–17, 129–30, 194; Tosel, 'Superstition and Reading'; Nadler, *Spinoza's Heresy*, pp. 137–42.

21. Spinoza also emphasises the practical aspect of *acquiescentia in se ipso*: in the scholium to E5p10, which focuses on the cultivation and disciplining of the mind by a practice, at once imaginative and rational, of frequently attending to 'a correct principle of living, *or* sure maxim of life', he advises his reader to 'keep in mind that the highest satisfaction of mind [*summa acquiescentia animi*] stems from the right principle of living'.

22. Descartes, *The Philosophical Writings*, vol. 1, p. 384 (*Passions of the Soul*, art. 152). Spinoza criticises this view in E5 Preface. See Lloyd, *Part of Nature*, pp. 82–83; Cooper, *Secular Powers*, p. 81.

23. Descartes, *The Philosophical Writings*, vol. 1, p. 388 (*Passions of the Soul*, art. 161).

24. Descartes, *The Philosophical Writings*, vol. 1, p. 384 (*Passions of the Soul*, art. 153).

25. See also E2p35s.

26. See also E2p49 and scholia.

27. See Cooper, *Secular Powers*, pp. 95–96.

28. See Curley vol. 2, p. 155 / III 83–84 / TTP ch. 6.

29. See Wittich, *Anti-Spinoza*, p. 228; Cooper, *Secular Powers*, p. 94.

30. See E5 Preface, where Spinoza wonders at the views of Descartes—'so great a man'; 'that most distinguished man'; 'a philosopher of his caliber'—on the soul's power over the passions.

31. Hobbes, *De Cive*, ch. 17 §27: 'authoritati externae acquiescere, non constituere citvitatem per se, sed esse externi illius subditos'. Spinoza had the original Latin edition of this work in his library—see Servaas van Rooijen, *La Bibliothèque*, p. 188. The

1651 English translation of *De Cive* has 'acquiesce' for *acquiescere*: 'those subjects, who believe themselves bound to acquiesce to a foreign authority in those doctrines which are necessary to salvation, do not *per se* constitute a city, but are the subjects of that foreign power'—see Hobbes, *De Cive: The English Version*, ch. 17 §27.

32. Here we can recall Spinoza's remarks about two kinds of servitude in a letter to Blyenbergh, noted at the beginning of at the beginning of chapter 5: a person who does not know God is 'nothing but a tool ... that serves unknowingly and is consumed in serving', whereas the pious 'serve knowingly, and become more perfect by serving [*conscii servient, & serviendo perfectiores evadunt*]')—Curley vol. 1, p. 360 / IV 94–95 / Letter 19 (Spinoza to Blyenbergh, January 1665). In these reflections on service, Spinoza may have been alluding to 1 Corinthians 9:13: 'Do you not know that those who are employed in the temple get their food from the temple, and those who serve at the altar share in what is sacrificed on the altar?'

33. Levene, *Spinoza's Revelation*, p. 19; see also pp. 72–76.

34. Curley vol. 2, pp. 259–63 / III 168–72 / TTP ch. 13. On Spinoza's concept of obedience, see Balibar, *Spinoza and Politics*, pp. 88–95. Balibar's analysis differs from mine, not least in focusing more on Spinoza's political writings, but he does indicate a connection between divine necessity and an obedience which 'tends to cancel itself out through its own effects, as love and reason gradually gain the upper hand over fear and superstition' (p. 92).

35. Curley vol. 2, pp. 269–70 / III 178 / TTP ch. 14.

36. This insight is articulated by the theologian Herbert McCabe: see *God Matters*, pp. 10–24. McCabe writes that 'God brings about all my free actions, and this does not make them any the less free. ... A free action is one which *I* cause and which is not caused by anything else. It is caused by God ... [and] this is not the paradox it seems at first sight, for God is not *anything else*. God is not a separate and rival agent within the universe. The creative causal power of God does not operate on me from outside, as an alternative to me. ... It is, of course, our image-making that deceives us here. However hard we try, we cannot help picturing God as an individual existent, even an individual person, making the world or controlling it like the potter making a pot or as an artist makes a statue. But the pot is in the same world as the potter, the statue shares a studio with the sculptor. They interact with each other. Or, to put it another way, the potter is outside the pot he makes, the sculptor is outside the statue. But when we come to the creator of everything that has existence, none of that could be true. God cannot be outside, or alongside, what he has made. Everything only exists by being constantly held in being by him. I am free in fact, not because God withdraws from me and leaves me my independence—as with a man who frees his slaves, or good parents who let their children come to independence—but just the other way around. I am free because God is in a sense *more directly* the cause of my actions than he is of the behaviour of unfree things.'

37. See Pines, 'On Spinoza's Conception'; Kisner, *Spinoza on Human Freedom*, pp. 57–63, 229–35.

38. As Susan James shows, we can read this passage in light of Spinoza's remarks about 'corruption' in the Dutch Reformed Church in the Preface to the *Theologico-Political Treatise*: 'the love of propagating divine religion degenerated into sordid greed and ambition; and the temple itself became a theatre, where one hears, not learned ecclesiastics, but orators, each possessed by a longing, not to teach the people,

but to carry them away with admiration for himself'—Curley vol. 2, p. 70 / III 8 / TTP Preface; James, *Spinoza on Philosophy*, pp. 22–24.

39. See also E4p61.

40. See E4p35, p36, p37.

41. Curley vol. 2, p. 268 / III 176–77 / TTP ch. 14.

42. Laurent Bove couples *acquiescentia* with *hilaritas* to accentuate the bodily aspects of adequate knowledge, and its blessedness. He describes *hilaritas* as simultaneously restful and active: 'a kind of joy at rest [*une joie en quelque sorte en repos*] . . . but constitutive, active. . . . [T]he equilibrium in rest [*l'equilibre en repos*] of self-love is here immanent to the power of acting itself. . . . It is an active and creative [*féconde*] immobility.' In this way, *hilaritas* is the physical aspect of *acquiescentia* of the second kind: it is 'the adequate expression of . . . the *acquiescentia in se ipso* originating in reason, and of the essential equilibrium that Contentment encompasses'. For Bove, Spinoza's concept of *hilaritas* 'indicates that the ethical goal is the *acquiescentia in se ipso* of the human being as a whole, equally and positively affected in all the parts of his body and his spirit'—*La Stratégie*, pp. 111, 107–8. Bove's analysis differs from mine, however, insofar as he identifies *hilaritas* with the third, rather than the second, kind of knowledge.

43. See E2p44d; Yovel, 'The Third Kind of Knowledge'; Melamed, 'Mapping the Labyrinth'; Renz, *The Explainability of Experience*, pp. 249–55; Primus, '*Scientia Intuitiva*'. Spinoza's distinction between the second and third kinds of knowledge is prefigured in Thomas Aquinas's discussion of divine knowledge. Aquinas argues that 'to know a thing in general and not in particular is to have an imperfect knowledge', and God knows individual things in their particularity, specificity and distinctiveness; Aquinas calls this 'proper knowledge'. He links this divine knowledge of singular things to their being-in-God: 'We must say therefore that God not only knows that all things are in Himself; but by the fact that they are in Him [*sed per id quod in seipso continet res*], He knows them in their own nature and all the more perfectly, the more perfectly each one is in Him [*est unumquodque in ipso*]'—*Summa Theologiae, Prima pars*, Q. 14, art. 6. Aquinas suggests that human beings can participate in this divine knowledge: 'Although the knowledge which is most characteristic of the human soul occurs in the mode of *ratio*, nevertheless there is in it a sort of participation in the simple knowledge which is proper to higher things, of whom it is therefore said that they possess the faculty of spiritual vision' (Thomas Aquinas, *Quaestiones disputatae*, Q. 15, art. 1, *responsio*).

44. Curley vol. 2, pp. 280–81 / III 187–88 / TTP ch. 15. See Rutherford, 'Salvation as a State of Mind', p. 459: 'the third kind of knowledge . . . produces [the mind's] greatest contentment, because only with this kind of knowledge is the natural striving of the mind for understanding fully satisfied in an immediate apprehension of the necessary dependence of all things on the eternal and infinite essence of God'.

45. See Totaro, '*Acquiescentia*', p. 75: 'l'*acquiescentia animi* ne nait pas seulement de l'idée de soi mais de l'idée de Dieu comme principe et fondement de la connaissance en quoi consiste uniquement l'*essentia mentis*'.

46. Spinoza claims that 'we feel and know by experience that we are eternal' (E5p22s): see Chapter 8.

47. Spinoza illustrates this difference by the example of finding a fourth proportional number, given a sequence of three numbers: in the second kind of cognition,

the number is found by applying a Euclidian principle, whereas in the third kind of cognition the fourth proportional is seen 'in one glance' (E2p40s2). Intuitive thinking sees what 'follows' from God not as a sequence of effects, but as a simple, intelligible inherence or manifestation. Spinoza described this intuitive immediacy in his earliest works, including the *Treatise on the Emendation of the Intellect* and the *Short Treatise on God, Man and His Well-Being*, and in these texts he uses the same mathematical example. In the *Short Treatise*, he emphasises the immediacy of intuition: 'through his penetration he immediately sees the proportionality in all the calculations' (Curley vol. 1, p. 98 / I 55 / KV II ch. 1); in the *Treatise on the Emendation of the Intellect*, he suggests that when 'mathematicians ... see the adequate proportionality of the given numbers', they do so 'not by the force of that [Euclidean] proposition, but intuitively, without going through any procedure' (§24). See Melamed, 'Mapping the Labyrinth' for emphasis and explanation of this point: '[*scientia intuitiva*] is *not* a process that *takes time*. ... In [*scientia intuitiva*] the essence itself [of a thing] is perceived directly and not through any mediation. ... The inference involved in *scientia intuitiva* is clearly *not in time*' (pp. 104, 109, 111). For an illuminating discussion of the mathematical example Spinoza uses to illustrate the difference between his three kinds of knowledge, see Renz, *The Explainability of Experience*, pp. 252–53.

48. See E5p31s, E5p33s.

49. Poiret, *Cogitationes rationales*, p. 161. On Poiret's critique of Spinoza, see Israel, *Radical Enlightenment*, pp. 474–75; Cooper, *Secular Powers*, p. 77–94.

50. Julie Cooper reaches a similar conclusion, but with a different emphasis: 'Spinoza's enthusiasm for *acquiescentia* reflects a recognition of human interdependence and a commitment to egalitarian community—not, as Poiret complained, an aspiration to divine self-sufficiency'—Cooper, *Secular Powers*, p. 100. I agree with Cooper that Spinoza's radicalism lies in his attempt 'to reframe the question of human finitude, refusing the Augustinian demand to choose between humility and pride' (p. 104). But because her primary concern is to show that Spinoza's thought is 'consistent with egalitarian politics' (p. 102), she overlooks the important differences between *acquiescentia* of the second kind and that of the third kind. And her commitment to a secularising reading of Spinoza—albeit a nuanced and compelling version of such a reading—means that she does not recognise being-in-God as the fundamental principle of Spinoza's thought—see especially pp. 102–4. On the relationship between Spinoza's *acquiescentia* and Christian conceptions of self-love, see Bove, *La Stratégie*, pp. 87–88; Strauss, *Spinoza's Critique*, pp. 203–4.

51. Spinoza considers *humilitas* a sad passion, 'born of the fact that a man considers his own lack of power, or weakness'—E3Def.Aff.26; see also E3p55s.

7. *How to Love God*

1. Curley vol. 2, pp. 128–29 / III 60–61 / TTP ch. 4.

2. Curley vol. 1, p. 142 / I 104 / KV II ch. 24.

3. Curley vol. 1, p. 330 / I 264 / CM II ch. 8.

4. See Harvey, '*Ishq, ḥesheq*'. Harvey notes that Spinoza praised Gersonides as 'a most erudite man', and suggests that Gersonides's view that God passionately loves the world 'evidently had a strong impact on Spinoza' (p. 103).

5. The Catholic theologian Herbert McCabe offers a similar reflection on this point: 'God could not love creatures, it would make no sense.... God must be in no way passive with respect to the world and this must mean that God does not learn from or experience the world and cannot be affected by it.... [I]t does not follow that, if God is not affected by, say, human suffering, he is indifferent to it. In our case there are only two options open: we either feel with, sympathise with, have compassion for the sufferer, or else we cannot be present to the suffering, we must be callous, indifferent.... [Similarly] unless *we* learn, we are ignorant, but it is not the case with God that he would be ignorant if he did not learn.... Whatever the consciousness of the creator may be, it cannot be that of an experiencer confronted by what he experiences'—McCabe, *God Matters*, pp. 20, 44–45.

6. Curley vol. 1, p. 142 / I 104 / KV II ch. 24.

7. Curley vol. 1, pp. 104–5 / I 62 / KV I ch. 5.

8. Curley vol. 1, pp. 138–39 / I 100 / KV II ch. 22.

9. On *scientia intuitiva*, see Yovel, 'The Third Kind of Knowledge'; Melamed, 'Mapping the Labyrinth'; Garrett, *Nature and Necessity*, pp. 199–218; Renz, *The Explainability of Experience*, pp. 249–55. Spinoza's distinction between the second and third kinds of knowledge is prefigured in Thomas Aquinas's discussion of divine knowledge. Aquinas argues that 'to know a thing in general and not in particular is to have an imperfect knowledge', and that God knows individual things in their particularly, specificity and distinctiveness; Aquinas calls this 'proper knowledge', and links this divine knowledge of singular things to their being-in-God: 'We must say therefore that God not only knows that all things are in Himself; but by the fact that they are in Him [*sed per id quod in seipso continet res*], God knows them in their own nature and all the more perfectly, the more perfectly each one is in Him [*est unumquodque in ipso*]' (*Summa Theologiae, Prima pars*, Q. 14, art. 6).

10. See Curley vol. 2, pp. 292–93 / III 198 / TTP ch. 16, Addition 34.

11. See also E3Def.Aff.24exp. This concept of an 'internal cause' is closely connected to Spinoza's notion of immanent causation, which is integral to his principle of being-in-God. In his *Short Treatise*, Spinoza refers to an 'immanent or internal cause' (Curley vol. 1, p. 148 / I 110 / KV II ch. 26), and at E1p18d he states that 'God is the immanent, not the transitive, cause of all things. Dem.: Everything that is, is in God, and must be conceived through God (by P15), and so God is the cause of [all] things, which are in him.' On this idea of immanent causation, see Melamed, *Spinoza's Metaphysics*, pp. 61–66.

12. On the connection between *acquiescentia* and intellectual love of God, see Melamed, 'The Enigma'.

13. In an unpublished paper delivered to the London Spinoza Circle in 2019, John Heyderman traced the concept of glory, or *kavod*, through the Hebrew Bible and medieval Jewish sources, emphasising the ambiguity by which the concept can apply to God or to created beings. For example, Heyderman suggests that for Maimonides, glory, 'rather like Spinoza's intellectual love, is manifested at the same time in two movements: the downward expression of God's power in man and in Nature, and upward, in man and Nature's glorification of God'. See also Wolfson, *The Philosophy of Spinoza*, vol. 2, pp. 311–17; Efros, 'Holiness and Glory'.

14. Emphasis mine. See also E5p36d.

15. See E3p18s2, E3Def.Aff.12 and 13, E4p12d, E4p63s.
16. See also E3p58s.
17. See Augustine, *Confessions*, Book 4, ch. 10 §15; *The City of God*, Book 14, ch. 22.
18. See Matheron, *Individualité et relations*, pp. 583–602.
19. See Gallagher, 'Thomas Aquinas on Self-Love'.
20. Augustine, *On Christian Doctrine*, p. 45 (Book 1 §§76–77).

8. Eternal Life

1. Warren Zev Harvey notes parallels between *Ethics* V, propositions 21–42 and the conclusion of Maimonides's *Guide of the Perplexed*, III, 51: see '*Ishq, ḥesheq*'.
2. Curley, vol. 1, p. 7.
3. Moreau, *Spinoza: L'expérience*, p. 549.
4. See also E5p20s.
5. Kristin Primus made these remarks in a talk on Spinoza's *acquiescentia*, delivered to the London Spinoza Circle in June 2020.
6. E5p23s; Spinoza writes something very similar in the *Theologico-Political Treatise*: see Curley vol. 2, p. 260 / III 170 / TTP ch. 13. In both the *Ethics* and *Short Treatise*, Spinoza reserves the verb 'to see' for the highest kind of knowledge—see Curley vol. 1, p. 98 / I 55 / KV II ch. 1: 'a fourth [person], who has the clearest knowledge of all, has no need either of report, or of experience, or of the art of reasoning, because through his penetration he immediately sees the proportionality in all the calculations'. The *Short Treatise* suggests that the immediacy and directness of the highest kind of knowledge—the 'immediate manifestation of the object itself to the intellect'—can lead to the knower's union with what is known. 'If the object [of knowledge] is magnificent and good,' Spinoza writes here, 'the soul necessarily becomes united with it. . . . So if we come to know God in this way, then we must necessarily unite with him. . . . As we have already said, our blessedness consists only in this union with him'—Curley vol. 1, pp. 138–39 / I 100 / KV II ch. 22. He describes this condition in terms drawn from New Testament accounts of Christian conversion; for example, he takes up the distinction between flesh and spirit that recurs throughout Saint Paul's writings (see, e.g., Romans 8:6).

Spinoza's phrase 'eyes of the mind [*mentis oculi*]' echoes Maimonides's suggestion that immaterial forms 'are not visible to the eye, but are known by the eyes of the heart' (*Mishneh Torah* 4:7) and the Hebrew *lev*, translated here as 'heart', might also be translated 'mind' (which fits the context better); I am grateful to John Heyderman for this reference. Edwin Curley notes that the 'eyes of the mind' metaphor occurs in Leo Hebraeus's 1535 *Dialoghi d'amore* (Dialogues on love)—see Curley vol. 2, p. 260. Spinoza's language of seeing and feeling also echoes a Christian-Platonic conception of 'intellectual vision or intellectual intuition', understood as 'a non-discursive mental act involving a direct cognitive contact with the object of contemplation'—see Gavrilyuk and Coakley's Introduction to *The Spiritual Senses*, p. 7. Moreau likewise refers to the 'long history' of the metaphor of 'eyes of the mind' (or soul), mentioning Plato's *Republic* and *Sophist*, yet suggests that the Augustinian reference is 'more important for Spinoza': see Moreau, *Spinoza: L'expérience*, p. 548; Augustine, *Soliloquies* I, especially §13. Gavrilyuk and Coakley suggest that the early Christian idea of 'a diachronic spectrum of possibilities in human responses to God ... is doubtless why it has been so hard for the modern philosophic mind either to comprehend or to approve [the language of spiritual senses]. Here is no flat, universalistic account of human reason and affect, but rather an invitation to ongoing epistemic and spiritual transformation, in which some are necessarily more advanced than others. It was the much later secular philosophy of the Enlightenment which was to prise epistemology and spirituality apart'—Gavrilyuk and Coakley (eds), *The Spiritual Senses*, p. 13. The idea of direct cognitive contact, unmediated by concepts and explanations, is included in the description of intuitive knowledge in the *Short Treatise*: 'we call that clear knowledge which comes not from being convinced by reasons, but from being aware of and enjoying the thing itself'—Curley vol. 1, p. 99 / I 55 / KV II ch. 1.

7. Yovel points to the transformative effects of the third kind of knowledge, arguing that these '*ethical effects* ... make it count as salvation': 'These salvational effects are of two kinds, psychological and metaphysical: (a) psychologically, the third kind of knowledge is supposed to produce vigour, joy, love, and an intense sense of liberation capable of transforming the whole personality to the point of 'rebirth'; and (b) metaphysically it is said to overcome the mind's finitude and endow it with immortality—or rather (to express Spinoza's meaning more accurately), with eternity'—Yovel, 'The Third Kind of Knowledge', pp. 168–69. See also Primus, '*Scientia Intuitiva*'.

8. This raises the question of whether it is possible to fully grasp what Spinoza says about human eternity in the rationalistic terms normative for modern scholarly discourse. Understandably, much commentary on the *Ethics* is confined to the perspective of Spinoza's 'second kind of knowledge': this applies equally to 'analytic' readings in the Anglo-American style (whether hostile or sympathetic to the claims of *Ethics* V): see, e.g., Bennett, *A Study of Spinoza's Ethics*, pp. 357–75; Donagan, *Spinoza*, pp 190–207; Nadler, *Spinoza's Heresy*, pp. 105-8; to more politicised 'continental' interpretations: see, e.g., Balibar's *Spinoza and Politics*; and to 'religious' studies of Spinoza's thought that accentuate its affinities with Jewish, Christian, Buddhist or Hindu traditions: see, e.g., Wetlesen, *The Sage*; Wienpahl, *The Radical Spinoza*; Hunter, *Radical Protestantism*.

9. See Lord, *Spinoza's* Ethics, p. 153; Deleuze, *Expressionism in Philosophy*, p. 296.

10. Hallett, 'Spinoza's Conception'.

11. See Garber, '"A Free Man"', p. 106: 'in addition to [the] kind of minimal eternal existence [that holds throughout nature], Spinoza appears to recognise a further sense in which the human mind ... can be eternal, indeed a sense in which the more rational we are, the more eternal we are'. Similarly, Moreau distinguishes between 'une perspective absolue et une perspective différentielle' on eternity—see *Spinoza: L'expérience*, pp. 532–49; and Mogens Lærke distinguishes between 'absolute' and 'scalar' eternity—see Lærke, 'Spinoza on the Eternity of the Mind'. This is a specific instance of Don Garrett's general point that 'it is common for Spinoza to hold that finite things can have, in *varying degrees*, characteristics that only an infinite substance possesses *absolutely*'—Garrett, *Nature and Necessity*, p. 365.

12. For an alternative reading, situating Spinoza's views on eternity in the tradition of Jewish thought, see Nadler, *Spinoza's Heresy*.

13. Spinoza's denial of personal immorality is a contested issue, but most commentators seem to share this view: see, for example, Garrett, *Nature and Necessity*, pp. 243-62; Moreau, *Spinoza: L'expérience*, p. 534-36. However, Donagan argues for a robust doctrine of personal immortality in *Spinoza*, pp 190-207.

14. See, however, Lærke, 'Spinoza on the Eternity of the Mind', which argues that Spinoza attributes both eternity *and* sempiternity to the human mind, on the basis that 'Spinoza's distinction between eternity and duration does not involve two distinct levels of existence, or two distinct kinds of existence, but that they refer to two really distinct and, therefore, compatible aspects of one and the same existence,' so that 'we need not choose between eternity and sempiternity of the mind and . . . both can, and do exist within Spinoza's account in EV' (pp. 266-67).

15. Calvin, *Institutes*, vol. 1, ch. 5 §10.

16. Garber, '"A Free Man"', p. 113. For further exploration of these themes, see Nadler, *Think Least of Death*.

17. Curley vol. 2, p. 387 / IV 220-21b / Letter 43 (Spinoza to Jacob Ostens, February 1671). On this point that virtue is its own reward, see E4p18s, TTP ch. 4, and Chapter 4 above.

18. See James, *Spinoza on Philosophy*, pp. 194, 263. Theo Verbeek notes the ambiguity of Spinoza's philosophical project that arises from the tension between his deep concern for freedom, on the one hand, and for order and stability in a political situation of conflict and unrest, on the other—see Verbeek, *Spinoza's Theologico-Political Treatise*, p. 7. On the historical background to Spinoza's positive evaluation of fear, see Van Bunge, *Spinoza Past and Present*, pp. 68-71.

19. This raises the question of the ethical and the metaphysical or eschatological aspects of both doctrines. To put it simplistically for a moment: it may seem that eternal life is primarily a metaphysical or eschatological issue, while sin is primarily an ethical category. But the close connection between sin and eternal life in Christian theology suggests that both doctrines have ethical and eschatological aspects. I will return to this question at the end of this chapter—for it seems to me that Spinoza is insisting quite forcefully that ethics and metaphysics or eschatology are inseparable, and that they are both at heart ontological matters.

20. See also 2 Corinthians 5:17, Romans 6:4, Galatians 6:15 and Ephesians 4:22-24.

21. See also Romans 5:14. In January 1676 Spinoza wrote to Henry Oldenburg, in response to the latter's questions about his position on tenets of Christian faith, that he believed that 'the resurrection of Christ from the dead was really spiritual', adding that 'only on this hypothesis can 1 Corinthians 15 be explained, and the arguments of Paul understood'—Curley vol. 2, p. 472 / IV 314a / Letter 75 (Spinoza to Henry Oldenburgh, January 1676).

22. On the Stoic background to Spinoza's discussion of the fear of death, see Pines, 'On Spinoza's Conception', pp. 147-50. On the Epicurean background, see Strauss, *Spinoza's Critique*, pp. 40-47. On the Christian doctrine of sin, see also Spinoza's correspondence with Blyenbergh in Curley vol. 1, pp. 354-92 / IV 79-157 / Letters 18-24 (December 1664 to March 1665); Zac, *Philosophie, théologie, politique*, pp. 215-27.

23. Curley vol. 2, pp. 134-35 / III 65-66 / TTP ch. 4.

24. See Curley vol. 2, pp. 66-67 / III 5-6 / TTP Preface; James, *Spinoza on Philosophy*, pp. 15-17, 129-30, 194; Tosel, 'Superstition and Reading'; Nadler, *Spinoza's Heresy*, pp. 137-42.

25. See James, *Spinoza on Philosophy*, pp. 14–27; Levene, *Spinoza's Revelation*, pp. 16–32.

26. Curley vol. 2, p. 247 / III 158 / TTP ch. 11. In Letter 73, Spinoza emphasises the distinction between religion and superstition: 'I regard it as the chief difference between Religion and Superstition, that the latter has ignorance, the former has wisdom, for its foundation.' Van Bunge notes that when in the *Theologico-Political Treatise* Spinoza begins to consider 'true religion', his attention turns from the Hebrew Bible to the New Testament: see Van Bunge, *Spinoza Past and Present*, p. 109.

27. Many modern scholars challenge the traditional view that the Gospel of John was written by a single author. On the authorship of 1 John, see Marshall, *The Epistles of John*, pp. 31–42; Brown, *The Epistles of John*, pp. 19–29; Wahlde, *The Gospel and Letters*, pp. 6–11. On the influence of Greek philosophy on John's writings, see Engberg-Pedersen, *John and Philosophy*; Van Kooten, 'The Last Days', and his inaugural lecture at the University of Cambridge in 2019: https://sms.cam.ac.uk/media/2925842.

28. ζωη αιωνιος—5:20; την ζωην την αιωνιον—1:2; ζωην αιωνιον—3:15, 5:11, 5:13.

29. Wahlde, *The Gospel and Letters*, p. 460. See also Brown, *The Epistles of John*, which argues that *zoe*, as distinct from *psyche*, always signifies eternal life for the Johannine writers: see pp. 168, 472; Coetzee, 'Life (Eternal Life)'.

30. Although the Christian idea of eternal life has a background in the Hebrew Bible, particularly in the Wisdom of Solomon, the 'realised eschatology' view is specifically Christian. See Wahlde, *The Gospel and Letters*, pp. 324–26, 463–70: 'a distinctive aspect of the treatment of eternal life [in 1 John] is that it affirms both a present and a future dimension of that life' (p. 470).

31. See Brown, *The Epistles of John*, p. 472; Wahlde, *The Gospel and Letters*: 'the reception of eternal life is equivalent to a new birth that transforms and "divinises" the individual. . . . For the Johannine believer "eternal life" was *not* something symbolic. It was understood as a radical transformation resulting in a new level of existence that was literally a reception of the life of God himself' (pp. 460–62).

In the *Short Treatise* Spinoza's references to a 'second birth' echo John 3, where Jesus talks to Nicodemus of the need to be 'born from above', 'born of the spirit': 'When we become aware of [the] effects [arising from our union with God], we can truly say that we have been born again. For our first birth was when we were united with the body. From this union have arisen the effects and motions of the [animal] spirits. But our other, or second, birth will occur when we become aware in ourselves of the completely different effects of love produced by knowledge of this incorporeal object. This [love of God] is as different from [love of the body] as the incorporeal is from the corporeal, the spirit from the flesh. This, therefore, may the more rightly and truly be called Rebirth, because . . . an eternal and immutable constancy comes only from this Love and Union'—Curley vol. 1, p. 140 / I 102 / KV II ch. 22. Spinoza proceeds directly from here to a doctrine of immortality, asserting that if the 'Soul' is united only with the body, then it will perish when the body perishes, but if it unites with what is immutable, then 'it will have to remain immutable also. For through what would it then be possible that it should be able to perish?'—Curley vol. 1, p. 141 / I 103 / KV II ch. 23. Although the *Ethics* no longer employs the biblical vocabulary of the *Short Treatise*, Spinoza's position on these issues does not seem to change substantially during the 1660s and 1670s.

32. See Marshall, *The Epistles of John*, pp. 102–3.

33. On the opposition between fear and love, see Strauss, *Spinoza's Critique*, pp. 208–9: 'To the 'carnal' attitude of *fear* Spinoza opposes the 'spiritual' attitude of love.' However, Strauss views this opposition in terms of the Christian critique of Judaism, and not, as I do, in terms of a critique of the superstitious form of Christianity.

34. See also E4p24: 'Acting absolutely from virtue is nothing else in us but acting, living and preserving our being (these three signify the same thing) by the guidance of reason, from the foundation of seeking one's own advantage.' These references to living echo Spinoza's definition of 'life' in the *Metaphysical Thoughts* appended to his 1663 text on Descartes's philosophy: 'we understand by *life* the *force through which things persevere in their being*'. What is in question here is the distinction between divine and human life: 'because that force is different from the things themselves, we say properly that the things themselves have life. But the power by which God perseveres in his being is nothing but his essence. So they speak best who call God life'—Curley vol. 1, p. 326 / I 260 / CM II ch. 6. This echoes an earlier chapter of the *Metaphysical Thoughts*, 'Of God's Eternity', where Spinoza indicates that 'the created thing can be said to enjoy existence, because existence is not of its essence; but God cannot be said to enjoy existence, for the existence of God is God himself'—Curley vol. 1, pp. 317–18 / I 252 / CM II ch. 1. In the *Ethics*, Spinoza for the most part drops the term 'life', preferring the notion of a 'force through which things persevere in their being' that, in the earlier text, is offered as a definition of 'life'.

Sylvain Zac argues that 'even if the phrase *vita dei* is not to be found in the first two books of the *Ethics*, what this phrase denotes is found constantly. When Spinoza affirms, using a scholastic term, that God is cause of the being of things, not only in the sense that s/he gives them existence, but also insofar as s/he is the cause which makes them persevere in existence, he is in fact repeating, albeit with a different terminology, the thesis which he argued in [*Metaphysical Thoughts*], i.e., that God is life because s/he is the force which causes all beings to persevere in their existence [E1p24c]. When Spinoza adds [in E2p14s] that "the force by which each singular thing perseveres in its existence follows from the eternal necessity of God's nature", he is reasserting, in another form, the notion that the *conatus* proper to each thing is an expression of the life of God'—see Zac, 'Life in the Philosophy'. Here Zac repeats his earlier argument that, for Spinoza, 'to depend on God . . . is to live in God, and the more perfection a thing has, the more it acts and lives and, in consequence, the better it expresses the life of God. The life of men, by reason of their superior capacities—both physical and intellectual—expresses the life of God more than that of all other things, and consequently depends on this [divine life] more and better'—Zac, *Philosophie, théologie, politique*, p. 217 (Zac here cites Spinoza's letter to Blyenbergh, although the text in question does not use the term 'life'). On the concept of life in Spinoza's philosophy, see also Vatter, 'Eternal Life and Biopower'.

35. Curley vol. 1, p. 9.

36. See E4p2–p4; E4App7.

37. See Yovel, 'The Third Kind of Knowledge', pp. 162–63, 171.

38. On the transformation of the body, see Harris, 'Spinoza's Theory'.

39. See also E5p10s.

40. See E5p12d, referring to E2p18.

41. See E2p14; Negri, *Subversive Spinoza*, p. 110.

42. See Zac, 'Life in the Philosophy', p. 258: 'To speak of liberation or salvation is to speak of a 'true life,' an eternal life. But eternity for Spinoza is not defined as a function of duration; and the road to eternal life does not pass through death. How then could I be conscious of the eternity of my own life through a union with God by way of *scientia intuitiva* if the eternity of God itself was not one 'of life'?' See also Yovel, 'The Third Kind of Knowledge', pp. 170-72.

43. Yovel takes a similar view in identifying the 'moral' and 'metaphysical' dimensions of Spinoza's account of salvation (see note 7 to this chapter). However, he regards Spinoza's version of immortality as the metaphysical dimension, rather than as combining the moral and the metaphysical. His interpretation also differs from mine in placing Spinoza's account of immortality in a Marrano context, and in insisting that Spinoza is presenting a 'secular form of salvation'—see Yovel, 'The Third Kind of Knowledge', pp. 168-72.

9. Spinoza's Religion

1. Thomas Aquinas, *Summa Theologiae, Secunda secundae partis*, Q. 81, art. 1, *responsio*.

2. Aquinas clarifies that superstition deviates from the virtue of religion 'not because it offers more of the divine worship than true religion, but because it offers divine worship either to whom it ought not, or in a manner it ought not'—*Summa Theologiae, Secunda secundae partis*, Q. 92, art. 1.

3. Thomas Aquinas, *Summa Theologiae, Secunda secundae partis*, Q. 81, art. 2, *responsio*.

4. Thomas Aquinas, *Summa Theologiae, Secunda secundae partis*, Q. 81, art. 6.

5. Thomas Aquinas, *Summa Theologiae, Secunda secundae partis*, Q. 81, art. 7.

6. Another echo of Aquinas's analysis of *religio* can be discerned in the way Spinoza often couples *religio* and *pietas*, as he does in E4p37s1. For Aquinas, *religio* concerns a relationship to God, while *pietas* concerns a relation to other human beings; *religio* means giving due honour to God, while *pietas* means honouring one's parents and one's country—see *Summa Theologiae, Secunda secundae partis*, Q. 101, art. 1 and art. 3; Aquinas considers these two virtues consecutively. In E4p37s1, Spinoza's definition of *religio* is followed by a definition of *pietas*: 'whatever we desire or do, or cause to be done, in virtue of our having the idea of God, or of knowing God, I relate to religion. The desire of acting rightly which is dependent on our living according to reason, I call piety.' Calvin discusses the relationship between *religio* and interpersonal, social morality (to which he assigns the virtue of *charitas*, or love of neighbour) in *Institutes*, vol. 2, ch. 8 §11, and it is interesting to compare this discussion with Spinoza's account of faith in the *Theologico-Political Treatise*, which refuses to separate *charitas* from religion or faith.

7. Curley vol. 2, p. 467 / IV 307a / Letter 73 (Henry Oldenburg to Spinoza, December 1675); Curley vol. 2, p. 469 / IV 309 / Letter 74 (Spinoza to Henry Oldenburg, December 1675).

8. Harrison, *The Territories*, p. 84.

9. See Israel, *Enlightenment Contested*, pp. 135-63; Taylor, *A Secular Age*; Milbank, *Theology and Social Theory*.

10. See Mill, *On Liberty*, ch. 3: 'Those who first broke the yoke of what called itself the Universal Church, were in general as little willing to permit difference of religious opinion as that church itself. But when the heat of the conflict was over, without giving a complete victory to any party, and each church or sect was reduced to limit its hopes to retaining possession of the ground it already occupied; minorities, seeing that they had no chance of becoming majorities, were under the necessity of pleading to those whom they could not convert, for permission to differ. It is accordingly on this battle-field, almost solely, that the rights of the individual against society have been asserted on broad grounds of principle, and the claim of society to exercise authority over dissentients, openly controverted. The great writers to whom the world owes what religious liberty it possesses, have mostly asserted freedom of conscience as an indefeasible right, and denied absolutely that a human being is accountable to others for his religious belief. Yet so natural to mankind is intolerance in whatever they really care about, that religious freedom has hardly anywhere been practically realised.' For an influential analysis of how religious conflict and reconciliation formed seventeenth-century intellectual life (with particular reference to Descartes and Leibniz, though not to Spinoza), see Toulmin, *Cosmopolis*, pp. 89–117.

11. Harrison, *The Territories*, p. 97.

12. Calvin, for example, associated *religio* with *pietas*, and emphasised 'sincerity of heart': 'pure and genuine religion . . . consists in faith, united with a serious fear of God, comprehending a voluntary reverence, and producing legitimate worship agreeable to the injunctions of the law. And this requires to be the more carefully remarked, because men in general render to God a formal worship, but very few truly reverence him; while great ostentation in ceremonies is universally displayed, but sincerity of heart is rarely to be found.'—*Institutes*, vol. 1, ch. 2 §2.

13. Harrison, *The Territories*, p. 84.

14. See, for example, Talal Asad's essay 'The Construction of Religion as an Anthropological Category' in his *Genealogies of Religion*. Here Asad seeks to 'problematize the idea of an anthropological definition of religion by assigning that endeavour to a particular history of knowledge and power' (p. 54). He criticises Clifford Geertz's 'universal' definition of religion, applicable to different traditions, as '(1) a system of symbols which act to (2) establish powerful, pervasive and long-lasting moods in men by (3) formulating conceptions of a general order of existence and (4) clothing these conceptions with such an aura of factuality that (5) the moods and motivations seem uniquely realistic' (pp. 29–30; see Geertz's 1966 article 'Religion as a Cultural System'). Asad argues that the concept of religion 'is itself the historical product of discursive processes' emerging from the Christian tradition (p. 29), and traces the attempt to produce a universal definition of religion to seventeenth-century Christianity (see pp. 40–43). While he argues, against Geertz, that 'religious belief' is 'a constituting activity in the world', rather than 'a state of mind', Asad accepts the category of belief, along with authority, as a defining feature of religion—and rather anachronistically projects this modern concept of religion onto the medieval period (see pp. 37–39).

15. On the connection between Herbert of Cherbury's 'common notions' of religion and Spinoza's analysis of faith in the *Theologico-Political Treatise*, see Lagrée, *Le Salut de laïc*, pp. 79–95, 108–16; Lærke, *Spinoza on the Freedom*, pp. 173–75.

16. Turner, *The History of All Religions*, title page; see Harrison, *The Territories*, pp. 99–101.

17. See Harrison, *The Territories*, pp. 10-11, 92-94. Edwin Curley discusses this translation issue with respect to Spinoza's use of the term *religio*: see Curley vol. 2, p. 522, and 'Spinoza's Exchange'.

18. See Marion, *Sur l'ontologie grise* for an influential account of changing conceptions of intellectual virtue during the seventeenth century, and in particular the Cartesian critique of the concept of *habitus*.

19. See Van Ruler, *The Crisis of Causality*, pp. 309-10; Harrison, *The Territories*, pp. 91-92.

20. Calvin, *Institutes*, vol. 1, ch. 1 §2.

21. See Carlisle, 'The Question of Habit' and *On Habit*. See also Harrison, *The Territories*, pp. 85-86.

22. Harrison, *The Territories*, p. 92.

23. Spinoza did insist that human beings, like everything else, are subject to laws of nature—so much so, however, that he refused to carve out a separate domain for spontaneous action, or free will. He argued that our thoughts, our emotions, our moral activity and our philosophical work are as much a part of nature as our embodied life—a thought that was revived by his post-Kantian readers, the German idealists. While Kant thought that autonomy, and thus morality itself, is incommensurable with our subjection to the laws of nature, Spinoza refused to recognise anything outside or beyond natural laws: human power, and liberty, and virtue, have to be achieved *within* nature. In the *Ethics*, he introduces his account of human affect and activity by disagreeing with those who wrote on these subjects 'as if they were not treating of natural things which follow from the common laws of nature, but of things which lie beyond the domain of nature; they appear, indeed, to regard man in nature as a dominium within a dominion [*imperium in imperio*]. For they believe that man disturbs rather than follows the order of nature, that he has absolute power over his actions, and that he is determined by nothing besides himself' (E3 Preface). This passage addresses Descartes's notion of free will in particular, while offering a more general critique of the dualistic thinking of his time.

When Spinoza defines virtue, he makes it clear that this signifies human power, and connects it closely with the concept of natural law: 'By virtue and power I understand the same thing: i.e., virtue is the very essence or nature of man, insofar as he has the power of doing certain things which can be understood by the laws of his nature alone' (E4D8). This Spinozist conception of autonomy is not a matter of willing, or choosing, but of understanding: 'To act absolutely from virtue is nothing else than to act according to the laws of our own nature. But we act thus only so far as we understand [*intelligimus*].... Therefore to act from virtue is nothing else in us than to act, and to preserve our being, according to the guidance of reason' (E4p24d).

24. Curley vol. 2, pp. 386-87 / IV 220b-221b / Letter 43 (Spinoza to Jacob Ostens, February 1671). For a discussion of Lambert van Velthuysen's 'ambiguous' critique of the *Theologico-Political Treatise* in the context of other contemporary responses, see Israel, 'The Early Dutch and German Reaction', pp. 89-90.

25. Curley vol. 2, pp. 475-76 / IV 320a / Letter 76 (Spinoza to Albert Burgh, December 1675 or January 1676).

26. Curley vol. 2, p. 474 / IV 318a / Letter 76 (Spinoza to Albert Burgh, December 1675 or January 1676), translation modified; Curley's translation reads 'sign of the true Universal faith'. Spinoza had made a similar point in the Jewish context in

Chapter 3 of the TTP, where he discusses the idea that the Hebrews are God's chosen people: see Harvey, 'Spinoza's Counterfactual Zionism'.

27. Curley vol 2, p. 333 / III 229 / TTP ch. 19.

28. Curley vol. 2, p. 137 / III 68 / TTP ch. 4.

29. See Curley vol. 2, pp. 332-44 / III 228-38 / TTP ch. 19. Spinoza's opponents on this issue are those who 'claim to separate sacred right from civil right, and claim that the supreme power possesses only the latter, whereas the universal church possesses the former' (p. 339 / III 234), and he insists that his own view 'is conducive, in no small measure, to the increase of religion and piety' (p. 341 / III 236). He attributes the disputes within Christianity over the distribution of power over secular and sacred laws partly to the fact that Christianity originated not as a national religion, but in communities of 'private men' who gathered 'in private Churches'; and partly to the fact that by the time Christianity did become a state religion (presumably under the emperor Constantine), ecclesial leaders 'had increased the doctrines of Religion to such a great number, and confused them so much with Philosophy, that the supreme interpreter of Religion had to be a supreme Philosopher and Theologian' (p. 342 / III 237).

In his unfinished *Political Treatise*, Spinoza spells out in more detail the kind of command that sovereigns should exercise over external religion, and asserts as a general principle that 'everyone . . . can worship God in accordance with true Religion, and look out for himself, which is a duty of a private man'—Curley vol. 2, p. 522 / III 289 / TP ch. 3; by 'true Religion' here he seems to have in mind internal religion. Spinoza's analysis of the forms of external religion is complex: he considers it in the context of three forms of political organisation—monarchy, aristocracy and democracy—and since his treatise is incomplete it only discusses religion in the context of monarchy and aristocracy, both flawed in different ways, so we cannot necessarily take his remarks as prescriptive; whereas we do not know what he thought about external religion within with a democracy, which was (under the right historical conditions) his preferred form of government. See pp. 543, 587.

30. Curley vol. 2, pp. 294-95 / III 199 / TTP ch. 16; p. 521 / III 288 / TP ch. 3.

31. Curley vol. 2, p. 271 / III 180 / TTP ch. 14.

32. Curley vol. 2, p. 271 / III 180 / TTP ch. 14.

33. Curley vol. 2, pp. 257-58 / III 167 / TTP ch. 13.

34. Curley vol. 2, pp. 258-59 / III 168 / TTP ch. 13.

35. Curley vol. 2, pp. 260-61 / III 170 / TTP ch. 13.

36. Curley vol. 2, pp. 261-62 / III 170-71 / TTP ch. 13.

37. Curley vol. 2, p. 263 / III 172 / TTP ch. 13.

38. Curley vol. 2, p. 264 / III 173 / TTP ch. 14.

39. For a comprehensive and compelling interpretation of Spinoza's views on the freedom to philosophise, see Lærke, *Spinoza and the Freedom*.

40. James shows how Spinoza's strategy here follows others in the Dutch Republics, including the jurist Hugo Grotius, who argued in 1613 that the Church should 'define only the absolute minimum and leave to the individual his own free judgement on many questions, because many things are very obscure', and shows that, for similar reasons, Velthuysen produced 'his own list of religious fundamentals'—see James, *Spinoza on Philosophy*, pp. 189-91. See also Israel, *The Dutch Republic*, pp. 428-32.

41. Curley vol. 2, p. 266 / III 175 / TTP ch. 14, translation modified—see following note.

42. Spinoza's definition of *fides* reads as follows: 'nempe quod nihil aliud sit, quam de Deo talia sentire, quibus ignoratis tollitur erga Deum obedientia, et hac obedientia posita, necessario ponuntur'. Among various English translations of this difficult sentence, Michael Silverthorne's is probably the most precise, and he translates *sentire* as 'acknowledging', which is softer than the 'knowing' or 'knowledge' preferred by other translators: 'faith can only be defined by, indeed can be nothing other than, acknowledging certain things about God, ignorance of which makes obedience impossible and which are necessarily found wherever obedience is met with'—Israel (ed.), *Spinoza: Theological-Political Treatise*, p. 180. R.H.M. Elwes's translation is succinct and clear: 'faith consists in a knowledge of God, without which obedience to him would be impossible, and which the mere fact of obedience to him implies'. Curley's translation is overly cognitive, choosing 'thinking' for *sentire*, and inserting 'thoughts', which has no corresponding word in the Latin: '[Faith is] thinking such things about God that if you had no knowledge of them, obedience to God would be destroyed, whereas if you are obedient to God, you necessarily have these thoughts' (p. 266).

43. Curley vol. 2, pp. 266–67 / III 175–76 / TTP ch. 14.

44. James, *Spinoza on Philosophy*, pp. 207–8, 213. This is, James suggests, a functional conception of faith: 'What makes the belief that God is just a significant one is not its truth, but rather its function—its capacity to motivate us to live together cooperatively or love our neighbours. . . . Like the prophets, philosophers trade on a functional relationship between a certain conception of God and the ability to live cooperatively, though each articulates it in terms of their own beliefs' (pp. 198–99). This emphasis on functionality is illuminating, though identifying cooperation with neighbour-love, and even with religion—James writes of 'a cooperative or religious way of life' (p. 299)—lies at the humanist end of the interpretative spectrum opened up by Spinoza's concept of *religio*. This raises the question of how *religio* differs in practice from *pietas*, which is a more explicitly humanist virtue—and whether conflating *religio* and *pietas* would flatten Spinoza's concept of *religio* as a distinctive form of virtue. Cooperation seems rather behaviourist and procedural, in comparison with *charitas*, loving-kindness. We can cooperate with other people without loving them, and perhaps even without kindness, and surely we can be cooperative without being religious (in either the medieval or the modern sense of 'religion').

45. Lærke, *Spinoza and the Freedom*, pp. 177–78.

46. Curley vol. 2, p. 270 / III 179 / TTP ch. 14.

47. Curley vol. 2, p. 266 / III 175 / TTP ch. 14.

48. Curley vol. 2, pp. 268–70 / III 177–78 / TTP ch. 14. Spinoza lists first his seven tenets, followed by the corresponding list of seven points that 'do not matter as far as faith is concerned'. I have rearranged them here, to make the correspondence between each tenet, and its negation, more clear.

49. Calvin, *Institutes*, Dedication.

50. Lærke points out that Spinoza generally uses the adjective 'universal' to qualify '*faith, religion*, or *divine law*, all of which are related to the practical side [of religion], i.e., to the exercise of justice and charity. But he never uses 'universal' to qualify *doctrines*'—Lærke, *Spinoza and the Freedom*, p. 176. See Curley vol. 2, p. 72 / III 10 /

TTP Preface; p. 190 / III 116 / TTP ch. 7; p. 252 / III 162 / TTP ch. 12; p. 365 / III 174 / TTP ch. 14; p. 268 / III 177 / TTP ch. 14; p. 389 / IV 226 / Letter 43 (Spinoza to Jacob Ostens, February 1671); p. 474 / IV 318 / Letter 76 (Spinoza to Albert Burgh, December 1675 or January 1676).

51. See Laursen, 'Spinoza, Strauss'; Fraenkel, 'Spinoza's Philosophy of Religion'.

52. Curley vol. 2, p. 270 / III 17 / TTP ch. 14.

53. Lærke argues that, in insisting on personal 'accommodation' of faith's basic tenets, Spinoza 'diagnosed a serious weakness in the minimalist programme [that others recommended as a strategy to combat sectarianism], namely, a curious blindness to the fact that religious doctrines should not only guide our actions but also provide sufficient motivation for embracing them'. Spinoza realised, suggests Lærke, that 'if the minimal structure of universal faith was *necessary* for any authentic religious narrative to serve its practical purpose, it would never be *sufficient*. In order to gain practical efficacy, doctrine had to be dressed up in a fuller attire of narratives and ceremonial practices'—Lærke, *Spinoza and the Freedom*, pp. 184–85.

54. Rosenthal, 'Spinoza's Dogmas', pp. 65, 68. Rosenthal argues that the *dogmata* set out in Chapter 14 of the *Theologico-Political Treatise* 'do not lead to the abolition of traditional religion, as some have claimed, but rather support the toleration of diverse religious practices' (p. 53), and he concludes that 'the complex structure and function of the dogmas should complicate any answer to Spinoza's ultimate position on religion[;] . . . he was not a believer in the abolition of revealed religion, for either the masses or the philosopher. Both, as finite beings enmeshed in the imagination and passions, must find ways to regulate their composite nature, and the long-standing practices of religious traditions are useful in that regard. On the other hand, because of the enormous conflict [Spinoza] witnessed due to religious strife, he thought that religion had to be internally reformed and regulated by the goals of the state' (p. 69).

55. Among the most boldly (and interestingly) nostalgic Christian theologians are Catherine Pickstock and John Milbank, who describe their position as 'radical orthodoxy.' Echoing Victor Cousin's eclectic approach to the history of philosophy, their work constructs a critical grand narrative of modernity anchored in Platonism and Thomism. See, for example, Milbank, *Theology and Social Theory*; Milbank and Pickstock, *Truth in Aquinas*; Pickstock, *Aspects of Truth*.

Afterword: 'The path to these things'

1. See, however, Rosenthal, 'Why Spinoza is Intolerant', which makes important qualifications to this claim.

2. Michael Della Rocca has explored Spinoza's commitment to intelligibility by identifying the 'principle of sufficient reason' as the bedrock of Spinoza's philosophy: see, e.g., Della Rocca, *Spinoza*, pp. 1–31, and also Lin, 'The Principle of Sufficient Reason'.

3. Souriau, *The Different Modes*, p. 232.

4. On Kierkegaard's question of existence, see Carlisle, *Philosopher of the Heart*, pp. 3–14.

5. Rahner, *Foundations*, pp. 46, 54.

6. Bruno Latour, echoing Kierkegaard, writes that 'the impetus of religion is lost every time someone asks: "But, finally, what does it say?" It is immediately transmuted into a primordial monstrosity. For the religious mode informs about nothing whatsoever. It does something better: it converts, it saves, it transports transformations, it arouses persons anew.'—Latour, *An Inquiry*, p. 319.

7. Latour, *An Inquiry*, p. 300.

8. Curley vol. 1, p. 9 / II 7 / TIE §10.

WORKS CITED

Spinoza's works

Translations from Spinoza's works are based on those by Edwin Curley, with occasional modifications. References to the *Ethics* use Spinoza's own number system; references to other texts refer to Curley's *Collected Works*, followed by Gebhardt's *Opera*, followed by the abbreviated title of the text, as set out below. The different editions of Spinoza's text consulted in this book are listed by editor rather than by author.

Curley, Edwin (ed.). *The Collected Works of Spinoza*, vol. 1. Princeton: Princeton University Press, 1985.
———. *The Collected Works of Spinoza*, vol. 2. Princeton: Princeton University Press, 2016.
Carlisle, Clare (ed.). *Spinoza's* Ethics, *Translated by George Eliot*. Princeton: Princeton University Press, 2020.
Gebhardt, Carl (ed.). *Spinoza Opera*, vols 1–4. Heidelberg: Carl Winters, 1925.
Israel, Jonathan (ed.). *Spinoza: Theological-Political Treatise*, trans. Michael Silverthorne and Jonathan Israel. Cambridge: Cambridge University Press, 2007.
Kisner, Matthew J. (ed.). *Spinoza: Ethics Demonstrated in Geometrical Order*, trans. Michael Silverthorne and Matthew J. Kisner. Cambridge: Cambridge University Press, 2018.
Moreau, Pierre-François and Piet Steenbakkers (eds). *Spinoza: Œuvres IV: Ethica/Éthique*, trans. Pierre-François Moreau; text established by Fokke Akkerman and Piet Steenbakkers. Paris: Presses Universitaires de France, 2020.

ABBREVIATIONS

E   *Ethica / Ethics*
KV *Korte Verhandeling / Short Treatise on God, Man and His Well-Being*
CM *Cogitata Metaphysica / Metaphysical Thoughts*
TTP *Tractatus Theologico-Politicus / Theologico-Political Treatise*
TP *Tractatus Politicus / Political Treatise*

Other works

Anselm, *Monologion*, in *Monologion and Proslogion*, trans. Thomas Williams. Indianapolis: Hackett, 1995.
———. *Proslogion*, in ibid.
Aristotle, *Metaphysics*, vol. 1, Books 1–9, trans. Hugh Tredennick. Cambridge, MA: Harvard University Press, 1933.
———. *Physics*, trans. Robin Waterfield. Oxford: Oxford University Press, 1996.

Asad, Talal. 'The Construction of Religion as an Anthropological Category', in Asad, *Genealogies of Religion: Discipline and Reasons of Power in Christianity and Islam*, pp. 27–54. Baltimore: Johns Hopkins University Press, 1993.
Aubrey, John. *Brief Lives*, vol. 1, ed. Andrew Clark. Oxford: Clarendon Press, 1898.
Augustine, *Confessions*, trans. Henry Chadwick. London: Penguin, 1961.
——. *Eighty-Three Different Questions*, trans. David L. Mosher. Washington, DC: Catholic University of America Press, 1977.
——. *On Christian Doctrine*. Oxford: Oxford University Press, 1995.
——. *On Free Choice of the Will*, trans. Thomas Williams. Indianapolis: Hackett, 1993.
——. *Soliloquies and Immortality of the Soul*, ed. and trans. Gerard Watson. Warminster: Aris and Phillips, 1990.
——. *The City of God against the Pagans*, ed. and trans. R. W. Dyson. Cambridge: Cambridge University Press, 1998.
Bacon, Francis. 'Of Superstition', in *Francis Bacon*, ed. Brian Vickers. Oxford: Oxford University Press, 1996.
——. *The Advancement of Learning*, Book 1, in *The Works of Lord Bacon*, vol. 1. London: Henry Bohn, 1854.
——. *New Organon*, ed. Lisa Jardine and Michael Silverthorne. Cambridge: Cambridge University Press, 2000.
Balibar, Étienne. 'A Note on "Consciousness/Conscience" in the *Ethics*', *Studia Spinozana* 8 (1992), pp. 37–53.
——. *Spinoza and Politics*. London: Verso. 1998.
Bayle, Pierre. *Dictionnaire historique et critique*, new edition, vol. 13. Paris: 1820.
Bennett, Jonathan. *A Study of Spinoza's Ethics*. Indianapolis: Hackett, 1984.
Biernacki, L. and P. Clayton (eds) *Panentheism across the World's Traditions*. Oxford: Oxford University Press, 2014.
Bove, Laurent. *La Stratégie du conatus: Affirmation et résistance chez Spinoza*. Paris: Vrin, 1996.
Brown, Raymond E. *The Epistles of John*. London: Geoffrey Chapman, 1982.
Brykman, Geneviève. *La Judéité de Spinoza*. Paris: Vrin, 1972.
Calvin, Jean. *Institutes of the Christian Religion*, trans. John Allen. Philadelphia: 1813.
Cameron, Evan. *Enchanted Europe: Superstition, Reason and Religion, 1250–1750*. Oxford: Oxford University Press, 2010.
Carlisle, Clare. 'All Things in Relation to God', *TLS* 5 June 2020.
——. *On Habit*. London: Routledge, 2014.
——. *Philosopher of the Heart: The Restless Life of Søren Kierkegaard*. London: Allen Lane, 2019.
——. 'Spinoza's Philosophy of Religious Life', in *Renewing Philosophy of Religion*, ed. P. Draper and J. Schellenberger, pp. 208–22. Oxford: Oxford University Press, 2017.
——. 'Spiritual Desire and Religious Practice', *Religious Studies* 55, no. 3 (2019), pp. 429–46.
——. 'The Question of Habit in Philosophy and Theology: From Hexis to Plasticity', *Body & Society* 19, nos 2–3 (2013), pp. 30–57.
——. 'The Self and the Good Life', in *The Oxford Handbook of Theology and Modern European Thought*, ed. Nicholas Adams, George Pattison and Graham Ward, pp. 19–39. Oxford: Oxford University Press, 2013.

Carlisle, Clare and Yitzhak Y. Melamed, 'God-Intoxicated Man', *TLS* 15 May 2020.
Carraud, Vincent. *Causa sive ratio: La raison de la cause, de Suárez a Leibniz*. Paris: PUF, 2002.
Carriero, John. 'Conatus and Perfection in Spinoza', *Midwest Studies in Philosophy* 35 (2011), pp. 69–92.
———'Spinoza on Final Causality', *Oxford Studies in Early Modern Philosophy* 2 (2005), pp. 105–47.
———. 'The Highest Good and Perfection in Spinoza', in *The Oxford Handbook of Spinoza*, ed. Michael Della Rocca, pp. 240–72. Oxford: Oxford University Press, 2017.
Chalier, Catherine. *Spinoza lecteur de Maimonide: La question theologico-politique*. Paris: Cerf, 2006.
Champion, Justin A. I. 'John Toland: The Politics of Pantheism', *Revue de synthèse* 116, nos 2–3 (1995), pp. 259–80.
———. *The Pillars of Priestcraft Shaken: The Church of England and Its Enemies, 1660–1730*. Cambridge: Cambridge University Press, 1992.
Coetzee, J. C. 'Life (Eternal Life) in John's Writings and the Qumran Scrolls', *Neotestamentica* 6 (1972), pp. 46–66.
Coleridge, S. T. 'On the Prometheus of Aeschylus', in *The Collected Works of Samuel Taylor Coleridge*, vol. 11, part 2: *Shorter Works and Fragments*, ed. H. J. Jackson and J. R. de J. Jackson. Princeton: Princeton University Press, 2019.
Colerus, Johannes. *The Life of Benedict de Spinosa*. London: 1706
Cooper, Julie. *Secular Powers: Humility in Modern Political Thought*. Chicago: University of Chicago Press, 2013.
Curley, Edwin. 'Spinoza's Exchange with Albert Burgh', in *Spinoza's Theological Political Treatise: A Critical Guide*, ed. Yitzhak Melamed and Michael Rosenthal, pp. 11–28. Cambridge: Cambridge University Press, 2010.
Cusa, Nicolas de. *Directio speculantis, seu, De non aliud*, in *Nicolai de Cusa Opera Omnia*, vol. 13, ed. Ludwig Bauer and Paul Wilpert. Leipzig: Meiner, 1944.
D'Agostino, Simone. *Esercizi spirituali e filosofia moderna: Bacon, Descartes, Spinoza*. Pisa: Edizioni ETS, 2017.
Davison, Andrew. *Participation in God*. Cambridge: Cambridge University Press, 2019.
Deleuze, Gilles. *Expressionism in Philosophy: Spinoza*, trans. Martin Joughin. New York: Zone Books, 1992.
———. *Spinoza: Practical Philosophy*, trans. Robert Hurley. San Francisco: City Lights Books, 1988.
Della Rocca, Michael. 'Rationalism Run Amok: Representation and the Reality of the Emotions in Spinoza', in *Interpreting Spinoza: Critical Essays*, ed. Charlie Huenemann, pp. 53–70. Cambridge: Cambridge University Press, 2008.
———. *Spinoza*. London: Routledge, 2008.
———. 'Spinoza's Metaphysical Psychology', in *The Cambridge Companion to Spinoza*, ed. Don Garrett, pp. 192–266. Cambridge: Cambridge University Press, 1996.
———. 'Spinoza's Substance Monism', in *Spinoza: Metaphysical Themes*, ed. Olli Koistinen and J. I. Biro, pp. 11–37. Oxford: Oxford University Press, 2002.
———. 'Steps Towards Eleaticism in Spinoza's Philosophy of Action', in *Freedom, Action and Motivation in Spinoza's 'Ethics'*, ed. Noa Naaman-Zauderer, pp. 15–36. London: Routledge 2019.

―――. 'The Elusiveness of the One and the Many in Spinoza: Substance, Attribute, and Mode', in *Spinoza in Twenty-First-Century American and French Philosophy*, ed. Jack Stetter and Charles Ramond, pp. 59-86. London: Bloomsbury, 2019.

Derrida, Jacques. *Dissemination*, trans. Barbara Johnson. Chicago: University of Chicago Press, 1983.

Descartes, René. *A Discourse on the Method of Rightly Conducting One's Reason and Seeking Truth in the Sciences*, trans. and ed. Ian Maclean. Oxford: Oxford University Press, 2006.

―――. *Oeuvres complètes*, vol. 6, ed. Charles Adam and Paul Tannery. Paris: Vrin, 1996

―――. *The Correspondence between Princess Elisabeth of Bohemia and René Descartes*, trans. Lisa Shapiro. Chicago: University of Chicago Press, 2007.

―――. *The Philosophical Writings of Descartes*, vols 1 and 2, trans. John Cottingham, Robert Stoothoff and Dugald Murdoch. Cambridge: Cambridge University Press, 1985.

―――. *The Philosophical Writings of Descartes*, vol. 3: *The Correspondence*, ed. and trans. John Cottingham, Robert Stoothoff, Dugald Murdoch and Anthony Kenny. Cambridge: Cambridge University Press, 1991.

Donagan, Alan. *Spinoza*. Chicago: University of Chicago Press, 1989.

Douglas, Alexander. *Spinoza and Dutch Cartesianism: Philosophy and Theology*. Oxford: Oxford University Press, 2015.

Earle, William A. 'The Ontological Argument in Spinoza', *Philosophy and Phenomenological Research* 11, no. 3 (1950), pp. 549-54.

Efros, I. 'Holiness and Glory in the Bible: An Approach to the History of Jewish Thought', *The Jewish Quarterly Review* 41, no. 4 (1951), pp. 363-77.

Engberg-Pedersen, Troels. *John and Philosophy: A New Reading of the Fourth Gospel*. Oxford: Oxford University Press, 2017.

Erdozain, Dominic. *The Soul of Doubt: The Religious Roots of Unbelief from Luther to Marx*. Oxford: Oxford University Press, 2015.

Fabro, Cornelio and B. M. Bonansea. 'The Intensive Hermeneutics of Thomistic Philosophy: The Notion of Participation', *The Review of Metaphysics* 27, no. 3 (1974), pp. 449-91.

Feld, Edward. 'Spinoza the Jew', *Modern Judaism* 9, no. 1 (1989), pp. 101-19.

Felski, Rita. 'Critique and the Hermeneutics of Suspicion', *M/C Journal* 15, no. 1 (2012).

―――. *The Limits of Critique*. Chicago: University of Chicago Press, 2015.

Flage, Daniel E. and Clarence A. Bonnen, 'Descartes on Causation', *The Review of Metaphysics* 50, no. 4 (1997), pp. 841-72.

Foucault, Michel. *The Hermeneutics of the Subject: Lectures at the Collège de France, 1981-82*, ed. Frédéric Gros, trans. Graham Burchell. Basingstoke: Palgrave Macmillan, 2005.

Fraenkel, Carlos. 'Maimonides's God and Spinoza's *Deus sive Natura*', *Journal of the History of Philosophy* 44 (2006), pp. 169-215.

―――. *Philosophical Religions from Plato to Spinoza*. Cambridge: Cambridge University Press, 2012.

―――. 'Spinoza's Philosophy of Religion', in *The Oxford Handbook of Spinoza*, ed. Michael Della Rocca, pp. 377-407. Oxford: Oxford University Press, 2017.

Frankfurt, Harry. *Taking Ourselves Seriously and Getting It Right*, ed. Debra Satz. Stanford: Stanford University Press, 2006.

Froude, J. A. 'Spinoza' (*Westminster Review* 64, July 1855), in *Short Studies on Great Subjects*, vol. 1. London: 1873.

Funkenstein, Amos. *Theology and the Scientific Imagination: From the Middle Ages to the Seventeenth Century*. Princeton: Princeton University Press, 1986.

Gallagher, David M. 'Thomas Aquinas on Self-Love as the Basis for Love of Others', *Acta Philosophica* 8 (1999), pp. 23-44.

Garber, Daniel. '"A Free Man Thinks of Nothing Less Than of Death": Spinoza on the Eternity of the Mind', in *Early Modern Philosophy: Mind, Matter, and Metaphysics*, ed. Christia Mercer and Eileen O'Neill, pp. 104-17. Oxford: Oxford University Press, 2005.

Garrett, Aaron V. *Meaning in Spinoza's Method*. Cambridge: Cambridge University Press, 2003.

Garrett, Don. *Nature and Necessity in Spinoza's Philosophy*. Oxford: Oxford University Press, 2019.

———. Representation and Consciousness in Spinoza's Naturalistic Theory of the Imagination', in *Interpreting Spinoza: Critical Essays*, ed. Charlie Huenemann. Cambridge: Cambridge University Press, 2008.

———. 'Teleology in Spinoza and Early Modern Rationalism', in *New Essays on the Rationalists*, ed. R. J. Gennaro and C. Huenemann, pp. 310-35. Oxford: Oxford University Press, 1999.

Gavrilyuk, Paul L. and Sarah Coakley (eds). *The Spiritual Senses: Perceiving God in Western Christianity*. Cambridge: Cambridge University Press, 2012.

Geertz, Clifford. 'Religion as a Cultural System', in *Anthropological Approaches to the Study of Religion*, ed. Michael Banton, pp. 1-46. London: Tavistock Publications, 1966.

Gerson, Lloyd. *Aristotle and Other Platonists*. Ithaca, NY: Cornell University Press, 2005.

Gilson, Étienne. *Being and Some Philosophers*, second edition. Toronto: Pontifical Institute of Medieval Studies, 1952.

———. *The Philosophy of Saint Bonaventure*, trans. I. Trethowan and F. J. Sheed. London: Sheed and Ward, 1938.

Goclenius, Rodolphus. *Lexicon Philosophicum*. Frankfurt: 1613.

Gueroult, Martial. *Spinoza*, vol 1: *Dieu*. Hildesheim: Georg Olms, 1968.

Haight, Gordon S. (ed.). *The George Eliot Letters*. New York: Oxford University Press, 1954.

Hallett, H. F. 'Spinoza's Conception of Eternity', *Mind* 37, no. 147 (1928), pp. 283-303.

Harris, Errol E. 'Spinoza's Theory of Human Immortality', in *Spinoza: Essays in Interpretation*, ed. Maurice Mandelbaum and Eugene Freeman, pp. 245-62. LaSalle, IL: Open Court, 1975.

Harrison, Peter. *The Territories of Science and Religion*. Oxford: Oxford University Press, 2015.

Harvey, Warren Zev. 'A Portrait of Spinoza as a Maimonidean', *Journal of the History of Philosophy* 19 (1981), pp. 151-72.

———. 'Du mysticisme au-delà de la philosophie: Maïmonide et Spinoza', in *Mystique et philosophie dans les trois monothéismes*, ed. Danielle Cohen-Levinas et al. Paris: Hermann, 2015.

———. 'Gersonides and Spinoza on Conatus', *Aleph* 12, no. 2 (2012), pp. 273-297.

———. '*Ishq*, *ḥesheq*, and *amor Dei intellectualis*', in *Spinoza and Medieval Jewish Philosophy*, ed. Steven Nadler, pp. 96-107. Cambridge: Cambridge University Press, 2014.

———. 'Spinoza and Maimonides on Teleology and Anthropocentrism' in *Spinoza's Ethics: A Critical Guide*, ed. Yitzhak Melamed, pp. 43–55. Cambridge: Cambridge University Press, 2017.

———. 'Spinoza's Counterfactual Zionism', *Iyyun: The Jewish Philosophical Quarterly* 62 (2013), pp. 235–44.

———. 'The Judeo-Christian Tradition's Five Others', in *Is There a Judeo-Christian Tradition? A European Perspective*, ed. Emmanuel Nathan and Anya Topolski, pp. 211–24. Berlin: De Gruyter, 2016.

Hatfield, Gary. 'Descartes's *Meditations* as Cognitive Exercises', *Philosophy and Literature* 9, no. 11 (1985), pp. 41–58.

Heidegger, Martin. *Being and Time*, trans. John Macquarrie and Edward Robinson. Oxford: Blackwell, 1978.

———. 'Phenomenology and Theology', in *Pathmarks*, ed. William McNeil, pp. 39–62. Cambridge: Cambridge University Press, 1998.

Hitz, Zina. *Lost in Thought: The Hidden Pleasures of an Intellectual Life*. Princeton: Princeton University Press, 2020.

Hobbes, Thomas. *De Cive*. Paris: 1642.

———. *De Cive: The English Version Entitled, in the First Edition, Philosophicall Rudiments Concerning Government and Society*, ed. Howard Warrender. Oxford: Clarendon Press, 1983.

———. *Elements of Philosophy, The First Section: Concerning Body* (*The English Works of Thomas Hobbes of Malmesbury*, vol. 1), ed. William Molesworth. London: 1839.

———. *Examinatio et emendatio mathematicae hodiernae qualis explicatur in libris Johannis Wallisii*. London: 1660.

———. *Leviathan*, ed. Richard Tuck, revised edition. Cambridge: Cambridge University Press, 1996.

Huenemann, Charlie. *Spinoza's Radical Theology: The Metaphysics of the Infinite*. Durham (UK): Acumen, 2014.

Hunter, Graeme. *Radical Protestantism in Spinoza's Thought*. Aldershot: Ashgate, 2005.

Israel, Jonathan. *Enlightenment Contested: Philosophy, Modernity and the Emancipation of Man 1670–1752*. Oxford: Oxford University Press, 2006.

———. 'Meyer, Koerbagh and the Radical Enlightenment Critique of Socinianism', *Geschiedenis van de wijsbegeerte in Nederland* 14 (2003), pp. 197–208.

———. *Radical Enlightenment: Philosophy and the Making of Modernity, 1650–1750*. Oxford: Oxford University Press, 2001.

———. *The Dutch Republic: Its Rise, Greatness, and Fall, 1477–1806*. Oxford: Clarendon Press, 1995.

———. 'The Early Dutch and German Reaction to the *Tractatus Theologico-Politicus*: Foreshadowing the Enlightenment's More General Spinoza Reception?', in *Spinoza's Theological Political Treatise: A Critical Guide*, ed. Yitzhak Melamed and Michael Rosenthal, pp. 72–100. Cambridge: Cambridge University Press, 2010.

Jacob, Margaret. *The Radical Enlightenment: Pantheists, Freemasons and Republicans*. London: Allen and Unwin, 1981.

James, Susan. *Spinoza on Philosophy, Religion, and Politics: The Theologico-Political Treatise*. Oxford: Oxford University Press, 2012.

———. 'Spinoza the Stoic', in *The Rise of Modern Philosophy*, ed. Tom Sorrell, pp. 289–316. Oxford: Clarendon Press, 1993.

———. 'The Interdependence of Hope and Fear', in *Spinoza: Thoughts on Hope in Our Political Present*, ed. Moira Gatens, *Contemporary Critical Theory* special issue (2020).

John of Damascus, *Writings*, trans. Frederic H. Chase. Washington, DC: Catholic University of America Press, 1958.

Jones, Matthew L. 'Descartes's Geometry as Spiritual Exercise', *Critical Inquiry* 28, no. 1 (2001), pp. 40–71.

———. *The Good Life in the Scientific Revolution: Descartes, Pascal, Leibniz, and the Cultivation of Virtue*. Chicago: University of Chicago Press, 2006.

Kant, Immanuel. *Critique of Judgement*, trans. Paul Guyer and Eric Matthews. Cambridge: Cambridge University Press, 2000.

———. *Critique of Practical Reason*, trans. Mary Gregor. Cambridge: Cambridge University Press, 1997.

———. *The Conflict of the Faculties*, trans. Mary Gregor. Lincoln, NE: University of Nebraska Press, 1992.

Khawaja, Noreen. *The Religion of Existence: Asceticism in Philosophy from Kierkegaard to Sartre*. Chicago: University of Chicago Press, 2016.

Kierkegaard, Søren. *Concluding Unscientific Postscript*, vols 1 and 2, trans. Howard V. Hong and Edna H. Hong. Princeton: Princeton University Press, 1992.

———. *Fear and Trembling*, trans. Edna H. Hong and Howard V. Hong. Princeton: Princeton University Press, 1983.

Kisner, Matthew. *Spinoza on Human Freedom*. Cambridge: Cambridge University Press, 2011.

Kneller, Jane. 'Early German Romanticism: The Challenge of Philosophizing', in *The Routledge Companion to Nineteenth-Century Philosophy*, ed. Dean Moyar. London: Routledge, 2010.

Kołakowski, Leszek. *Chrétiens sans église: La conscience religieuse et le lien confessional au XVIIe siècle*. Paris: Gallimard, 1987.

Lachterman, David. *The Ethics of Geometry: A Genealogy of Modernity*. London: Routledge, 1989.

Lærke, Mogens. *Spinoza and the Freedom of Philosophising*. Oxford: Oxford University Press, 2021.

———. 'Spinoza on the Eternity of the Mind', *Dialogue* 55 (2016), pp. 265–86.

———. 'Spinoza's Monism? What Monism?', in *Spinoza on Monism*, ed. Philip Goff, pp. 244–61. Basingstoke: Palgrave Macmillan, 2010.

Lagrée, Jacqueline. *'Le Salut de laïc', Edward Herbert of Cherbury: Étude et traduction du 'De religione laïci'*. Paris: Vrin, 1989.

Latour, Bruno. *An Inquiry into Modes of Existence: An Anthropology of the Moderns*, trans. Catherine Porter. Cambridge, MA: Harvard University Press, 2013.

Laursen, John. 'Spinoza, Strauss and the Morality of Lying for Safety and Peace', in *Reading between the Lines: Leo Strauss and the History of Early Modern Philosophy*, ed. Winifried Schröder, pp. 171–92. Berlin: De Gruyter, 2015.

Lear, Jonathan. *Wisdom Won from Illness*. Cambridge, MA: Harvard University Press, 2017.

LeBuffe, Michael. *From Bondage to Freedom: Spinoza on the Human Good*. Oxford: Oxford University Press, 2010.

Levene, Nancy. *Spinoza's Revelation: Religion, Democracy and Reason*. Cambridge: Cambridge University Press, 2004.

Lévy, Tony. *Figures de l'infini: Les mathematiques au miroir des cultures*. Paris: Éditions Seuil, 1985.

Lin, Martin. *Being and Reason: An Essay on Spinoza's Metaphysics*. Oxford: Oxford University Press, 2019.

———. 'Teleology and Human Action in Spinoza', *Philosophical Review* 115 (2006), pp. 317–54.

———. 'The Principle of Sufficient Reason', in *The Oxford Handbook of Spinoza*, ed. Michael Della Rocca, pp. 133–54. Oxford: Oxford University Press, 2017.

Lloyd, Genevieve. *Part of Nature: Self-Knowledge in Spinoza's Ethics*. Ithaca, NY: Cornell University Press, 1994.

Locke, John. *An Essay Concerning Human Understanding*, ed. P. H. Nidditch. Oxford: Clarendon Press, 1975.

Lord, Beth. *Spinoza's Ethics: An Edinburgh Philosophical Guide*. Edinburgh University Press, 2010.

MacPhail, Eric. 'Montaigne, Hobbes and Bayle on the Archaeology of Religion', *Early Modern French Studies* 36, no. 2 (2016), pp. 111–20

Maine de Biran, Pierre. *The Influence of Habit on the Faculty of Thinking*, trans. Margaret Donaldson Boehm. Westport, CT: Greenwood Press, 1970.

Malebranche, Nicolas. *Search after Truth*, trans. Thomas M. Lennon and Paul J. Olscamp. Cambridge: Cambridge University Press, 1997.

Mander, William J. 'Omniscience and Pantheism', *Heythrop Journal* 61 (2000), pp. 199–208.

———. 'Pantheism', *Stanford Encyclopedia of Philosophy* (Spring 2020 edition).

Marion, Jean-Luc. *Sur l'ontologie grise de Descartes: Science cartésienne et savoir Aristotelicien dans les 'Regulae'*, fourth edition. Paris: Vrin, 2000.

Marshall, Eugene. *The Spiritual Automaton: Spinoza's Science of the Mind*. Oxford: Oxford University Press, 2013.

Marshall, I. Howard. *The Epistles of John*. Grand Rapids, MI: Eerdmans, 1978.

Matheron, Alexandre. *Individualité et relations interhumaines chez Spinoza*. Paris: Éditions de Minuit, 1969.

McCabe, Herbert. *God Matters*. London: Geoffrey Chapman, 1987.

McDonough, J. K. 'The Heyday of Teleology and Early Modern Philosophy', in *Early Modern Philosophy Reconsidered*, ed. John Carriero, *Midwest Studies in Philosophy* 35 (2011), pp. 179–204.

Mehl, É. 'Les Méditations stoïciennes de Descartes: Hypothèses sur l'influence du stoïcisme dans la constitution de la pensée cartésienne', in *Le Stoïcisme au XVIe et au XVIIe siècle*, ed. Pierre-François Moreau, pp. 251–80. Paris: Albin Michel, 1999.

Melamed, Yitzhak Y. '"A Substance Consisting of an Infinity of Attributes": Spinoza on the Infinity of Attributes', in *Infinity in Early Modern Philosophy*, ed. Ohad Nachtomy and Reed Winegar, pp. 63–75. New York: Springer, 2018.

———. 'Cohen, Spinoza and the Nature of Pantheism', *Jewish Studies Quarterly* 25, no. 2 (2018), pp. 171–80.

———. 'Inherence and the Immanent Cause in Spinoza', *The Leibniz Review* 16 (2006), pp. 43–52.

———. 'Inherence, Causation and Conception in Spinoza', *Journal of the History of Philosophy* 50 (2012), pp. 365–86.

———. 'Mapping the Labyrinth of Spinoza's *Scientia Intuitiva*', in *Übergänge— diskursiv oder intuitiv? Essays zu Eckart Försters 'Die 25 Jahre der Philosophie'*, ed. Johannes Haag and Markus Wild, pp. 99–116. Frankfurt: Klostermann, 2013.

———. 'Spinoza's Deification of Existence', *Oxford Studies in Early Modern Philosophy* 6 (2012) (ed. Daniel Garber and Donald Rutherford), pp. 75–104.

———. 'Spinoza's Metaphysics of Substance: The Substance–Mode Relation as a Relation of Inherence and Predication', *Philosophy and Phenomenological Research* 78, no. 1 (2009), pp. 17–82.

———. *Spinoza's Metaphysics: Substance and Thought*. Oxford: Oxford University Press, 2013.

———. 'Teleology in Jewish Philosophy: Early Talmudists to Spinoza', in *Teleology: A History*, ed. J. K. McDonough. Oxford: Oxford University Press, 2020.

———. 'The Enigma of Spinoza's *Amor Dei Intellectualis*', in *Freedom, Action and Motivation in Spinoza's 'Ethics'*, ed. Noa Naaman-Zauderer, pp. 222–38. London: Routledge, 2019.

———. 'Why Spinoza is not an Eleatic Monist (or Why Diversity Exists)', in *Spinoza on Monism*, ed. Philip Goff, pp. 206–22. Basingstoke: Palgrave Macmillan, 2010.

Milbank, John. *The Word Made Strange*. Oxford: Blackwell, 1997.

———. *Theology and Social Theory: Beyond Secular Reason*, second edition. Oxford: Blackwell, 2006.

Milbank, John and Catherine Pickstock. *Truth in Aquinas*. London: Routledge, 2001.

Mill, J. S. *On Liberty*, ed. Stefan Collini. Cambridge: Cambridge University Press, 1989.

Miller, Jon. *Spinoza and the Stoics*. Cambridge: Cambridge University Press, 2015.

Moreau, Pierre-François. *Spinoza: L'expérience et l'éternité*. Paris: PUF, 1994.

Morrison, John. 'The Relation between Conception and Causation in Spinoza's Metaphysics', *Philosophers' Imprint* 13, no. 3 (2013).

Nadler, Steven. 'Benedictus Pantheissimus', in *Insiders and Outsiders in Seventeenth-Century Philosophy*, ed. G.A.J. Rogers, Tom Sorrell and Gill Kray, pp. 238–55. London: Routledge, 2010.

———. *Spinoza: A Life*. Cambridge: Cambridge University Press, 1999.

———. 'Spinoza on Consciousness', *Mind* 117, no. 467 (2008), pp. 575–601.

———. *Spinoza's Heresy: Immortality and the Jewish Mind*. Oxford: Oxford University Press, 2001.

———. 'The Jewish Spinoza', *Journal of the History of Ideas* 70, no. 3 (2009), pp. 491–510.

———. *Think Least of Death: Spinoza on How to Live and How to Die*. Princeton: Princeton University Press, 2020.

———. '"Whatever Is, Is in God"': Substance and Things in Spinoza's Metaphysics', in *Interpreting Spinoza: Critical Essays*, ed. Charlie Huenemann. Cambridge: Cambridge University Press, 2008.

Negri, Antonio. *Subversive Spinoza*, ed. Timothy S. Murphy. Manchester: Manchester University Press 2004.

Oliver, Simon. *Creation*. London: Bloomsbury, 2017.
Olivo, G. '"Une patience sans espérance"? Descartes et le stoïcisme', in *Le Stoïcisme au XVIe et au XVIIe siècle*, ed. Pierre-François Moreau, pp. 234–50. Paris: Albin Michel, 1999.
Parkinson, G.H.R. '"Truth Is Its Own Standard": Aspects of Spinoza's Theory of Truth', *Southwestern Journal of Philosophy* 8, no. 3 (1977), pp. 35–55.
Pasnau, Robert. *Metaphysical Themes 1271–1671*. Oxford: Oxford University Press, 2013.
———. 'Teleology in the Later Middle Ages', in *Teleology: A History*, ed. J. K. McDonough. Oxford: Oxford University Press, 2020.
Perl, Eric. 'The Presence of the Paradigm: Immanence and Transcendence in Plato's Theory of Forms', *Review of Metaphysics* 53 (1999), pp. 339–62.
Pickstock, Catherine. *Aspects of Truth: A New Religious Metaphysics*. Cambridge: Cambridge University Press, 2020.
———. *Repetition and Identity*. Oxford: Oxford University Press, 2014..
Pieper, Josef. *Leisure: The Basis of Culture*, trans. Alexander Dru with an introduction by T. S. Eliot. London: Faber and Faber, 1952.
Pines, S. 'On Spinoza's Conception of Human Freedom and of Good and Evil', in *Spinoza: His Thought and Work*, ed. Nathan Rotenstreich and Norma Schneider. Jerusalem: The Israel Academy of Sciences and Humanities, 1983.
Plato, *Cratylus*, in *Cratylus. Parmenides. Greater Hippias. Lesser Hippias*, trans. Harold North Fowler. Cambridge, MA: Harvard University Press, 1926.
———. *Phaedo*, in *Euthyphro. Apology. Crito. Phaedo. Phaedrus*, trans. Harold North Fowler. Cambridge, MA: Harvard University Press, 1914.
———. *Protagoras*, in *Laches. Protagoras. Meno. Euthydemus*, trans. W.R.M. Lamb. Cambridge, MA: Harvard University Press, 1924.
Poiret, Pierre. *Cogitationes rationales de Deo, anima et malo*. Amsterdam: 1685.
Popkin, Richard. 'Spinoza, Neoplatonist Kabbalist?', in *Neoplatonism in Jewish Thought*, ed. Lenn E. Goodman, pp. 387–409. Albany: State University of New York Press, 1992.
Primus, Kristin. '*Scientia Intuitiva* in the *Ethics*', in *Spinoza's* Ethics*: A Critical Guide*, ed. Yitzhak Melamed, pp. 169–86. Cambridge: Cambridge University Press, 2017.
Przywara, Erich. *Analogia Entis*, trans. John Betz and David Bentley Hart. Grand Rapids, MI: Eerdmans, 2014.
Rahner, Karl. *Foundations of Christian Faith: An Introduction to the Idea of Christianity*, trans. William V. Dych. New York: Crossroad, 2016.
Ravven, Heidi. 'Some Thoughts on What Spinoza Learned from Maimonides about the Prophetic Imagination': Part One: 'Maimonides on Prophecy and the Imagination; Part Two: 'Spinoza's Maimonideanism', *Journal of the History of Philosophy* 39 (2001), pp. 193–214; 385–406.
Ravven, Heidi and. Goodman, Lenn E. (eds). *Jewish Themes in Spinoza's Philosophy*. Albany: State University of New York Press, 2002.
Renz, Ursula. *The Explainability of Experience: Realism and Subjectivity in Spinoza's Theory of the Human Mind*. Oxford: Oxford University Press, 2018.
Ricoeur, Paul. *Freud and Philosophy*, trans. Denis Savage. New Haven, CT: Yale University Press, 1970.

Rosemann, Philipp W. *Omne agens agit sibi simile: A 'Repetition' of Scholastic Metaphysics*. Leuven: Leuven University Press, 1996.

Rosenthal, Michael A. 'Persuasive Passions: Rhetoric and the Interpretation of Spinoza's Theological-Political Treatise', *Archiv für Geschichte der Philosophie* 85 (2003), pp. 249–68.

——. 'Spinoza's Dogmas of the Universal Faith and the Problem of Religion', *Philosophy and Theology* 13, no. 1 (2001), pp. 53–73.

——. 'Why Spinoza is Intolerant of Atheists: God and the Limits of Early Modern Liberalism', *Review of Metaphysics* 65 (2012), pp. 813–39.

Roth, Leon. *Spinoza, Descartes, and Maimonides*. Oxford: Oxford University Press, 1924.

Rovere, Maxime. 'Honors and Theater: Spinoza's Pedagogical Experience and his Relation to F. Van den Enden', *Educational Philosophy and Theory* 50, no. 9 (2018), pp. 809–18.

Rutherford, Donald. 'Salvation as a State of Mind: The Place of *Acquiescentia* in Spinoza's Ethics', *British Journal for the History of Philosophy* 7 (1999), pp. 447–73.

Schelling, F.W.J. *On the History of Modern Philosophy*, trans. Andrew Bowie. Cambridge: Cambridge University Press, 1994.

Schindler, David C. 'What's the Difference? On the Metaphysics of Participation in a Christian Context', *Saint Anselm Journal* 3, no. 1 (2005), pp. 1–27.

Schlegel, Friedrich. *Philosophical Fragments*, trans. Peter Firchow. Minneapolis: University of Minnesota Press, 1991.

Schmaltz, Tad M. *Descartes on Causation*. Oxford: Oxford University Press, 2007.

Seeskin, Kenneth. 'From Maimonides to Spinoza: Three Versions of an Intellectual Tradition', in *The Oxford Handbook of Spinoza*, ed. Michael Della Rocca, pp. 45–62. Oxford: Oxford University Press, 2017.

Servaas van Rooijen, A. J. (ed.). *La Bibliothèque de Bénédict de Spinoza*. La Haye: 1889.

Shapiro, Lisa. 'Descartes on Human Nature and the Human Good', in *The Rationalists: Between Tradition and Innovation*, ed. C. Fraenkel, D. Perinetti and J.E.H. Smith, pp. 13–26. Dordrecht: Springer, 2011.

Sherman, Jacob H. 'A Genealogy of Participation', in *The Participatory Turn: Spirituality, Mysticism, Religious Studies*, ed. Jorge N. Ferrer and Jacob H. Sherman, pp. 81–112. Albany: State University of New York Press, 2008.

Simmons, Alison. 'Sensible Ends: Latent Teleology in Descartes's Account of Sensation', *Journal of the History of Philosophy* 39, no. 1 (2001), pp. 49–75.

Skinner, Quentin. *Reason and Rhetoric in the Philosophy of Hobbes*. Cambridge: Cambridge University Press, 1996.

Sloterdijk, Peter. *You Must Change Your Life!*, trans. Wieland Hoban. Cambridge: Polity Press, 2013.

Smith, Pamela. *The Body of the Artisan: Art and Experience in the Scientific Revolution*. Chicago: University of Chicago Press, 2004.

Smith, Steven B. *Spinoza, Liberalism, and the Question of Jewish Identity*. New Haven, CT: Yale University Press, 1997.

——. *Spinoza's Book of Life: Freedom and Redemption in the Ethics*. New Haven, CT: Yale University Press, 2003.

Souriau, Étienne. *The Different Modes of Existence*, trans. Erik Beranek and Tim Howles. Minneapolis: Univocal, 2015.

Steenbakkers, Piet. *Spinoza's Ethica from Manuscript to Print*. Assen: Van Gorcum, 1994.
Strauss, Leo. 'Persecution and the Art of Writing', *Social Research* 8, no. 4 (1941), pp. 488–504.
——. *Persecution and the Art of Writing*. Glencoe, IL: Free Press, 1952.
——. *Spinoza's Critique of Religion*, trans. Elsa Sinclair. Chicago: University of Chicago Press, 1997.
Taylor, Charles. *A Secular Age*. Cambridge, MA: Harvard University Press, 2007.
Te Velde, Rudi. *Aquinas on God: The 'Divine Science' of the Summa Theologiae*. Aldershot: Ashgate, 2006.
Thomas Aquinas. *Compendium of Theology*, trans. Richard J. Regan. Oxford: Oxford University Press, 2009.
——. *Quaestiones disputatae de veritate*. Aquinas Institute bilingual edition available online at https://aquinas.cc/la/la/~QDeVer.
——. *Summa Theologiae*. Aquinas Institute bilingual edition available online at https://aquinas.cc/la/en/~ST.I.
Toland, John. *Pantheisticon: Or, the Form of Celebrating the Socratic-Society*. London: 1751.
Topolski, Anya. 'Spinoza's True Religion: The Modern Origins of a Contemporary Floating Signifier', *Societate și Politică* 8, no. 1 (2014), pp. 41–59.
Tosel, André. 'Superstition and Reading', in *The New Spinoza*, ed. Warren Montag and Ted Stolze. Minneapolis: University of Minnesota Press, 1997.
Totaro, Giuseppina. '*Acquiescentia* dans la cinquième partie de l'*Éthique* de Spinoza', *Revue philosophique de la France et de l'étranger* 184 (1994), pp. 65–79.
——. 'On the Recently Discovered Vatican Manuscript of Spinoza's *Ethics*', *Journal of the History of Philosophy* 51, no. 3 (2013), pp. 465–76.
Toulmin, Stephen. *Cosmopolis: The Hidden Agenda of Modernity*. Chicago: University of Chicago Press, 1990.
Turner, Denys. 'On Denying the Right God: Aquinas on Atheism and Idolatry', in *Aquinas in Dialogue: Thomas for the Twenty-First Century*, ed. J. Fodor and F. C. Bauerschmidt, pp. 137–58. Oxford: Blackwell, 2004.
Turner, William. *The History of All Religions of the World*. London: 1695.
Van Bunge, Wiep. *From Stevin to Spinoza: An Essay on Philosophy in the Seventeenth-Century Dutch Republic*. Leiden: Brill, 2001.
——. *Spinoza Past and Present: Essays on Spinoza, Spinozism and Spinoza Scholarship*. Leiden: Brill, 2012.
——. 'Spinoza's Jewish Identity and the Use of Context', *Studia Spinozana* 13 (1997), pp. 100–118.
Van Bunge, Wiep, Henri Krop, Piet Steenbakkers and Jeroen van de Ven (eds). *The Continuum Companion to Spinoza*. London: Bloomsbury, 2011.
Van Kooten, George. 'The Last Days of Socrates and Christ: *Euthyphro*, *Apology*, *Crito*, and *Phaedo* Read in Counterpoint with John's Gospel', in *Religio-Philosophical Discourses in the Mediterranean World: From Plato, through Jesus, to Late Antiquity*, ed. Anders Klostergaard Petersen and George van Kooten. Leiden: Brill, 2017.
Van Ruler, J. A. *The Crisis of Causality: Voetius and Descartes on God, Nature and Change*. Leiden: Brill, 1995.

Vatter, Miguel. 'Eternal Life and Biopower', *The New Centennial Review* 10, no. 3 (2011), pp. 217–50.
Verbeek, Theo. *Descartes and the Dutch Early Reactions to Cartesian Philosophy*. Carbondale, IL: Southern Illinois University Press, 1992.
———. *Spinoza's Theologico-Political Treatise: Exploring 'The Will of God'*. Aldershot: Ashgate, 2003.
Viljanen, Valtteri. *Spinoza's Geometry of Power*. Cambridge: Cambridge University Press, 2011.
Voss, Stephen H. 'How Spinoza Enumerated the Affects', *Archiv für Geschichte der Philosophie* 63 (1981), pp. 167–79.
———. 'On the Authority of the *Passiones Animae*', *Archiv für Geschichte der Philosophie* 75 (1993), pp. 160–78.
Wahlde, Urban C. von. *The Gospel and Letters of John*, vol. 1. Grand Rapids, MI: Eerdmans, 2010.
Weber, Max. *The Protestant Ethic and the Spirit of Capitalism*, trans. Talcott Parsons. London: Routledge, 2002.
Webster, Charles. *The Great Instauration: Science, Medicine and Reform, 1626–1660*. London: Duckworth, 1975.
Westphal, Merold. 'Immanence and Transcendence', in *The Oxford Handbook of Nineteenth-Century Christian Thought*, ed. Joel Rasmussen, Judith Wolfe and Johannes Zachhuber, pp. 111–26. Oxford: Oxford University Press, 2017.
Wetlesen, Jon. *The Sage and the Way*. Assen: Van Gorcum, 1979.
Wienpahl, Paul. *The Radical Spinoza*. New York: New York University Press, 1979.
Wilberforce, Robert Isaac. *The Doctrine of the Incarnation of Our Lord Jesus Christ*. London: 1848.
Williams, Russel. *Not I, Not other than I*, ed. Steve Taylor. Ropley, Hants: O-Books, 2015.
Wittich, Christoph. *Anti-Spinoza; sive examen Ethices B. de Spinoza et Commentarius de Deo et ejus attributis. Epistolæ*. Amsterdam: 1690.
Wolfson, Henry Austryn. *The Philosophy of Spinoza*. Cambridge, MA: Harvard University Press, 1934.
Yovel, Yirmiyahu. *Spinoza and Other Heretics*, vol. 1: *The Marrano of Reason*; vol. 2: *The Adventures of Immanence*. Princeton: Princeton University Press, 1989.
———. 'The Third Kind of Knowledge as Alternative Salvation', in *Spinoza: Issues and Directions: The Proceedings of the Chicago Spinoza Conference, 1986*, ed. Edwin Curley and Pierre-François Moreau, pp. 157–75. Leiden: Brill, 1990.
Zac, Sylvain. 'Life in the Philosophy of Spinoza', *Philosophy and Theology* 1, no. 3 (1987), pp. 255–66.
———. 'On the Idea of Creation in Spinoza's Philosophy', in *God and Nature: Spinoza's Metaphysics*, ed. Y. Yovel, pp. 231–41. Leiden: Brill, 1991.
———. *Philosophie, théologie, politique dans l'œuvre de Spinoza*. Paris: Vrin, 1979.
———. *Spinoza et l'interprétation de l'Écriture*. Paris: PUF, 1965.
Zachhuber, Johannes. 'Transcendence and Immanence', in *The Edinburgh Critical History of Nineteenth-Century Thought*, ed. Daniel Whistler, pp. 164–81. Edinburgh: Edinburgh University Press, 2018.

INDEX

acquiescentia in se ipso, 16, 112–33; *amor Dei intellectualis* and, 129, 137, 139–41, 145; conceptual history of, 112; cooperatively relating to other people and, 146; first kind of cognition and, 114, 125–27, 131, 132, 143; freedom and, 113, 115, 118, 124; as highest thing we can hope for, 112, 113, 116, 127, 132; hope and fear about death and, 153; necessity and, 121–24; participation in divine nature and, 107, 133; practical aspect of, 225n21; as resting in oneself, not in God, 112; second kind of cognition and, 114, 117, 122, 127–29, 130–31, 132, 143, 227n42; Spinoza's definition of, 112; striving to be *in se* and, 94; third kind of cognition and, 41, 114, 117, 129–31, 132, 143; threefold meaning of, 112–13; translation of, 113–14, 223n5; vain, empty, or false form of, 117, 118, 122, 126–27. *See also* resting in God

action: Spinoza's definition of, 53, 94, 122; in Spinoza's definition of *religio*, 166, 183

activity: degrees of, 89, 132, 133; desire and, 86

Adam's Fall, 156–58

adequate knowledge, 75, 77, 79, 202n12, 214n15

affects, 8; *acquiescentia in se ipso* as, 112, 113, 114–15, 124–25; central to Spinoza's discussion of religion, 142–44; cognition intimately tied to, 185; degrees of being and, 90; grounded in God, 188; instability of, 125; only possessed by finite things, 215n26; three elemental affects, 54, 90, 215n25. *See also* emotions

afterlife: Aquinas on, 102, 104; Spinoza on Christian doctrines of, 143, 152, 157. *See also* eternal life; fear of death

amor Dei intellectualis (intellectual love of God), 134–46; *acquiescentia in se ipso* and, 129, 137, 139–41, 145; *animi acquiescentia* and, 141–42; empowering character of true religion and, 143–44; encompassing our love for God and God's love for us, 134–35, 137; eternal character of, 152; greatest human perfection and, 107, 137; as joy accompanied by idea of God as cause, 130, 138; loving other people most purely and, 145–46; *scientia intuitiva* and, 129, 138, 140, 145; three components of, 137–39; three kinds of cognition and, 137–38. *See also* divine love

Amsterdam's Jewish community: aware of secular and Christian learning, 194n36; casting out Spinoza at age twenty-three, 1, 13, 19, 191n1; complex relations to Christianity, 13; extreme diversity of, 195n40

angels, 105, 220n36

animi acquiescentia (satisfaction of mind): *amor Dei intellectualis* and, 141–42; glory and, 130, 141; highest, 122, 129, 139, 225n21; intuitive knowledge of God and, 79; as resting-place of being-in-God, 79. *See also* peace of mind

animi commotiones, 28, 29, 79, 125, 128

animi fluctuationes: caused by love and hate, 125, 128; distinction between contentment and, 138; the *Ethics* intended to lessen, 201n6; oscillating between hope and fear, 4, 21; Spinoza's painful emotions and, 21–22, 28, 29; Spinoza's view of human condition and, 79

animus (mind or soul), 28, 198n41. *See also* mind

Anselm, 71–75, 78, 88, 89, 112, 217n19, 223n51

anthropomorphic God: of Calvinism and Cartesianism, 60, 206n16; divine love and, 135, 137, 139; inversion of teleological thinking about, 87;

anthropomorphic God (*continued*)
natura naturans freeing concept of God from, 66; Part One of the *Ethics* as radical critique of, 59; punishment after death attributed to, 159; resisted by substance-mode distinction, 58; spiritual exercise of the *Ethics* and, 49; superstitious faith and, 4–5; teleological confusions and, 82. *See also* superstitious religion

apophatic theology, 12, 73, 75, 78. *See also* negative theology

appetite, and desire, 54, 85–86, 87, 90, 128

Aquinas, Thomas: Anselm's apophatic appeal to faith and, 74, 75; arguing that God cannot have extrinsic purposes, 87; controversial in his own time, 106, 221n43; Davison on course between deism and pantheism of, 221n45; degrees of reality and, 89; on divine knowledge of singular things, 227n43; Foucault on break between philosophy and spirituality and, 23; on God as first cause, 80–81, 82; on God's independent goodness, 224n9; on God's knowledge of particular things, 229n9; God's transcendence and, 61, 62, 207n21, 210n39; on grace, 102, 104, 107–8, 219n32; on the mind resting in God, 41, 112; name of God in theology of, 105, 221nn39–40; ontological, not theistic, representation of God and, 220n37; on participation in divine nature, 101–8; on *religio*, 6, 164–65, 166, 167, 235n2, 235n6; on self-love as basis of love for others, 146; Spinoza's concept of *religio* and, 172; Spinoza's engagement with, 15; Spinoza's theology compared to, 104–8, 219n33; synthesising Platonic transcendence and Aristotelian immanence, 103; theology not distinguished from ontology for, 78

Aristotle: on causation, 80, 213n14; on *mimesis* vs. *methexis*, 103; Spinoza mediating between Plato's philosophy and, 219n30; virtue and, 164, 167, 169, 170, 171, 172

Arndt, Johann, 171

Asad, Talal, 236n14

association: habitual thinking and, 38, 39, 40, 44, 45; retraining the mind by following, 40, 45; super-proposition on, 52

atheism, accusation or attribution of: accommodated by the *Ethics*, 186; by Bayle, 19; as doctrinal or metaphysical interpretation, 10; by Nadler, 193n29; by Poiret, 132; by Protestants and Catholics of the time, 6, 61; by Smith quoting 'Deus sive nature,' 210n33; suspicious reading of the *Ethics* and, 10–11, 13, 193nn30–31, 208n27; by Velthuysen, 5, 197n27

atheism, nineteenth-century, 60

attributes of God: infinite, 69–70, 137, 210n41; *natura naturata* and, 64; Spinoza's claim to know some of, 212n64. *See also* extension, attribute of; thought, attribute of

Augustine: being-in-God and, 70, 79, 102; *Confessions*, 22, 24–25, 79, 198n33; on etymology of *religio*, 164; on evil as non-being, 89; God's transcendence and, 62, 210n39; on humility vs. pride, 228n50; on joyful communion with others, 147; metaphor of 'eyes of the mind' and, 230n6; on misdirected love, 144; as possible influence on Spinoza, 14, 15; on resting in God, 81, 112; on striving to be wise, 24–25; turning from the transient to the eternal, 28

Bacon, Francis: denial of final causation, 81; knowledge as effortful work, 41, 202n18, 223n2; modern pursuit of scientific knowledge, 3, 192n9; replacing teleology with laws, 169–70, 172; Spinoza's criticism of, 41, 112, 202n18; on superstition vs. true religion, 4

Balibar, Étienne, 226n34

Bayle, Pierre: on attempted assassination of Spinoza, 196n7; God as immanent cause, 215n19; on Spinoza's desire to inquire into truth, 18, 33, 71; on Spinoza's precision in writing, 35–36; on Spinoza's way of life, 18–19, 21; on superstition vs. true religion, 4

beatitude: Aquinas on, 102–3; Spinoza on, 100, 104–5, 113. *See also* blessedness 'being in,' 57–58, 205n3; expressing both difference and identity, 59, 64

being-in-God, 56–78; Anselm and, 71–75, 78, 88, 102, 217n19; Aquinas on divine knowledge of singular things and, 227n43; Aquinas's concept of participation and, 101, 106, 218n22; Augustine and, 70, 102; being caused by God and, 221n44; blessedness and, 91, 137; Christian context of *Theologico-Political Treatise* and, 99; Christian doctrines in conflict with, 172; Christian writers before Aquinas and, 102; consequences for task of philosophy, 70; as core of Spinoza's thought, 4, 184, 186; criticism of Calvinism and Cartesianism and, 61; degrees of, 89; deism and pantheism compared to, 68, 106; dependence of created beings on God and, 62; desire as feeling of, 79, 80, 86; in dialogue with Christian theologians, 15; as ethical or spiritual task, 56, 88, 91, 163, 184; freedom and, 91, 137, 184, 226n36; God's knowledge of particular things and, 229n9; God's love and, 136; as heavily-cited proposition, 57; immanent causation and, 229n11; immanent obedience and, 121, 132; inadequacy of our language for, 58, 59; intensification of consciousness as growth of, 149; John of Damascus and, 70, 102; knowledge of, 78; love and joy in experience of, 100; love for God and, 139; loving oneself and others in light of, 147; modern issues and, 10; natural propensity to error and, 75; as ontological principle, 56, 57, 88; as open question with regard to meaning, 58–59; as our source and our telos, 88; pantheism vs. panentheism and, 63, 67; participation in God and, 94, 98, 103–4, 145; philosophy made inseparable from theology by, 8; resting-place constituted by, 79; *scientia intuitiva* and, 77, 129, 130, 138, 140, 185; of singular things, 145, 227n43; substance-mode relation and, 57–59, 68–69, 88–89, 94; superproposition on, 50; virtue cultivated through understanding of, 182

belief: as defining feature of religion for Asad, 236n14; *religio* in the *Ethics* never a matter of, 6; Spinoza on knowledge vs., 176; Spinoza's different kind of religion and, 7

Bible: participation in divine nature and, 97–99, 100, 103, 217n18; Spinoza's discussion of virtue and, 176–77; Spinoza's use of, 14; as word of God for Calvin, 9. *See also* 1 Corinthians; Exodus; Genesis; James, Letter of; John, First Letter of; John's Gospel; Paul; Peter, Second Letter of

blessedness: *acquiescentia in se ipso* and, 113, 114, 115, 118; Aquinas on, 102–3; being-in-God and, 91, 137; consisting in knowledge and love of God, 10; knowledge of God and, 96–97, 134; as remedy for fear of death, 158–59. *See also* beatitude

Blyenbergh, Willem van, 95
Bonansea, B. M., 217n21, 217n23, 219n31
Bourignon, Antoinette, 132
Bove, Laurent, 227n42
Boxel, Hugo, 69
Burgersdijck, Francis, 14
Burgh, Albert, 1–2, 4, 173–74, 191n4

Calvin, John: on Bible as the word of God, 9; on *charitas*, 235n6; on importance of doctrine, 181; *Institutes of Christian Religion*, 26–27, 181; on reward or punishment in afterlife, 86, 153, 213n13; Spinoza's familiarity with ideas of, 14; on superstition, 4; on virtue, 86, 170

Calvinism: separating God from nature, 60, 104; as target of the *Ethics*, 60, 61; of Velthuysen, 5; voluntarist and anthropomorphic conception of God, 60, 206n16. *See also* Dutch Reformed Church

Cartesianism: separating God from nature, 60, 104; separating philosophy and theology, 193n26; Spinoza's critique of, 115; as target of the *Ethics*, 60, 61; voluntarist and anthropomorphic conception of God, 60. *See also* Descartes, René causation: Aquinas on God and, 101, 104; Aristotelian causes in Spinoza's metaphysics and, 213n14; Aristotle's fourfold analysis of, 80; being-in-God and, 57, 68; knowledge of a thing depending on knowledge of, 47; love involving the idea of, 138; order and connection of ideas and, 40. *See also* efficient causation; external causes; final causes; first causes; immanent causation; internal cause; transitive causation

charitas, 97, 99, 178, 217n18, 235n6, 239n44

Christ: on loving your enemies, echoed by Spinoza, 146; Paul on new life through, 156, 158; resurrection of, 14, 109, 111, 156, 232n21; returning from retreat in the wilderness, 32; Spinoza and, 107–11, 222n48, 223nn50–51; Spinoza's tenets of universal faith and, 180, 181

Christianity: attributed to Spinoza, 6; conquering hate with love in, 45; as context of *Theologico-Political Treatise*, 33, 97–99; direct cognitive contact and, 230n6; disputes over secular vs. sacred laws and, 238n29; early modern moral philosophy and, 170; faculty of will in, 83; panentheistic tendency in, 70; Spinoza's influence on thinkers of, 14; Spinoza's openmindedness about, 111; Spinoza's refusal to convert to, 1, 15, 191n2; Spinoza's tenets of universal faith and, 181; Spinoza's thought in dialogue between Judaism and, 13, 15; Spinoza's thought in dialogue with theology of, 70–71

Christianity, Spinoza's critique of: on brutal dogmatism, 99, 100, 111, 217n15; on distinction between grace and nature, 172; on doctrines of an afterlife, 143, 152–61; on ideas about virtue, 86; on moralising ethic, 92; on moral schema, 132–33

Cicero, 22, 164, 170

Coakley, Sarah, 230n6

cognition, three kinds of, 37–44, 202n12; *amor Dei intellectualis* and, 137–38; mathematical example to explain, 42–43, 76–77, 78, 227n47; *religio* based on any one of, 183; super-proposition explaining, 52–53; theological knowing and, 75; three different modes of obedience and, 122, 124, 132; threefold taxonomy of love and, 138. *See also* imagination; opinion; reason (*ratio*); *scientia intuitiva* (intuitive knowledge)

Coleridge, S. T., 63

Colerus, Johannes, 19–21, 71, 191n2, 195n6

conatus (striving), 8, 84–85; Cartesian principle of inertia and, 214n16; desire and, 84, 86; efficient causality of, 213n14; as essence of a thing, 53; expressing the life of God, 234n34; highest good attained by human effort and, 172; influences on Spinoza's concept of, 214n16. *See also* self-preservation

Cooper, Julie, 224n7, 228n50

1 Corinthians, 100, 226n32

cosmotheism, 63

Cox, William, 224n9

creation *ex nihilo*, 80, 104, 212n4, 220n35

Curley, Edwin: on Spinoza's religion, 7; translating *acquiescentia in se ipso*, 113, 223n5; translating *dare operam* as 'devote,' 22; translating *institutum*, 26; translating *quantum in se est*, 93

Cusa, Nicolas of, 59

Davison, Andrew, 217n21, 217n23, 221n45

deism: concept of, 60; natural theology and, 96; privileging transcendence over immanence, 74; seventeenth- vs. eighteenth-century sense of, 207n18; Spinoza and Aquinas charting a course between pantheism and, 221n45; Spinoza's rejection of, 68, 106

Deleuze, Gilles, 61–62, 150–51, 204n24, 221n44

Della Rocca, Michael, 59, 205n3, 206n13, 210n38, 210nn40–41

democracy, preferred by Spinoza, 238n29

Derrida, Jacques, 45

Descartes, René: *acquiescentia in se ipso* and, 115–20, 124, 224n9, 225n12; on degrees of being, 90; Foucault on spirituality and, 23; on free will, 81–82,

83, 118, 124, 237n23; on habit, 198n36; importance for modern philosophy, 10; influence on Velthuysen, 5; intellectual eclecticism of the seventeenth century and, 13; on provisional moral code, 31, 199n56; on religious bigotry and violence, 117, 118, 119; on role of repetition, 37; self-preservation and, 84, 214n16; Spinoza's guide to *Principles of Philosophy* by, 135, 234n34; Spinoza's metaphysics and, 14, 58; Spinoza's *Treatise on the Emendation of the Intellect* and, 22, 31, 196n14; on substances and modes, 204n1; teleology and, 81–82, 169–70, 172, 213n7, 213n10; on uncountable divine attributes, 210n41; on virtue as moral concept, 167; on virtue in relation to happiness, 86. *See also* Cartesianism

desire: for adequate knowledge, 79; appetite and, 54, 85–86, 87, 90, 128; arising from reason, 128; as basis of Spinoza's religion, 80; being-in-God and, 79, 80, 86; as elemental affect, 90; faculty of will and, 83, 84; fortitude and, 165; resting-place for, 188; Spinoza's conversion as a matter of, 27, 28; Spinoza's definition of, 85; in Spinoza's definition of religion, 7, 80, 142, 166, 182, 183

Desmarets, Henri, 115, 124, 224n9, 224n11

Deus sive Natura, 11–12, 64–67, 104, 186

devotio, 22, 196n13

devotion, 21, 22, 23, 24, 34

de Vries, Simon, 34, 36–37

divine impassibility, 215n26

divine love, 134–36; in anthropomorphic theology, 135, 137, 139; differences from human love, 135–36, 229n5; as identity, not reciprocity, 135, 141; Spinoza on salvation and, 134–35, 143–44; Spinoza's early texts on, 135–36; Spinoza's questioning of 'joy' when writing of, 141–42. See also *amor Dei intellectualis* (intellectual love of God)

divine nature, 92. *See also* participation in divine nature

Donagan, Alan, 208n27

dualism: body–mind, 44; deism, 222n45; pantheism and panentheism contrary to, 63; Spinoza's philosophy offering resistance to, 183

duration: of adopting a new practice, 26–27; ontological distinction between eternity and, 29, 138, 152–53

Dutch Reformed Church: doctrinal minimalism in, 238n40; Spinoza on corruption in, 226n38; superstitious popular religion ascribed to, 4, 14, 142–43, 159. *See also* Calvinism

efficient causation: Descartes and, 81, 213n7; natural philosophy and, 81; Spinoza on, 213n10, 213n14; Spinoza on final causation and, 87, 88; Spinoza on God's immanent causation and, 215n19

Eleatic monism, 205n3

Eliot, George, 14, 16, 113

emotions: cannot be had by God, 215n26; misguided conceptions of, 49; rational understanding of, 45; Spinoza as brilliant theorist of, 10. *See also* affects

empathy, super-proposition on, 54

Enlightenment thought: concept of autonomy in, 124, 170; distinction between habit and reason in, 44; on separating philosophy from theology, 8–9, 193n26; Smith on artisanal knowledge vs. school knowledge in, 200n1; waning of churches' intellectual influence due to, 61

Erdozain, Dominic, 217n15

eternal life: Christian theology on sinfulness and, 156, 161, 232n19; ethical and eschatological aspects of, 161; as ethical principle, 163; John on, 160–61, 233nn30–31; as knowledge we have by experience, 188; mind's intuition of its own eternity and, 150; Spinoza's engagement with scriptural tradition and, 156–58; Spinoza's ontology about participation in God and, 161; through union with God, 235n42. *See also* afterlife; fear of death; realised eschatology

eternity: *amor Dei intellectualis* and, 138; having no relation to time, 148; metaphysical distinction between duration and, 29, 138, 152–53 eternity of the mind: Christian teachings about personal immortality and, 152–54; feeling of, 148–49, 150, 163, 185; intensification of consciousness and, 149; overcoming the fear of death and, 153–54, 159; *ratio* in Spinoza's account of, 151–52; *scientia intuitiva* and, 149–50, 151–52, 203n19, 231n7; sempiternity and, 232n14; as transformation involving eternal life of God, 162–63; twofold structure of, 152, 231n11

ethical task: to become eternal, 162; to become what we are, 88, 204n24; being-in-God as, 56, 88, 91, 163, 184; loving oneself and others in, 147; of the mind to become eternal, 152; of participating more fully in the divine nature, 100; Spinoza's summary of, 79

Ethics: accomplishing Anselm's task in *Proslogion*, 74; ambiguous on the question of religion, 11–12, 186; as dynamic text unfolding in act of reading, 35, 36–37, 44, 46; geometrical method of, 35, 201n3, 201n6; in Latinate lineage of Christian thought, 14; manuscript confiscated by Vatican, 5; metaphysical and ethical aspects of, 184; as a practical system, 36–37; prepared for publication by Spinoza's friends after his death, 34; primarily about how to live a good life, 4; produced in more than eight years of labour, 35; profound inclusivity of, 186; publication arranged by Spinoza for after his death, 32; repetition in, 36, 40, 46; as spiritual exercise, 37, 48–49; as static theoretical system, 35–36; studied together by group of students, 36–37; *Theologico-Political Treatise* in relation to, 182; unconstrained by doctrinal orthodoxy, 1; written over many years without extrinsic reward, 185–86

Euclid's *Elements*, 35, 40

evil: degrees of perfection and, 95; hatred and, 55; as non-being according to Augustine, 89; punished naturally, 182

Exodus 3:14, 105

experience, thinking ordered by, 44, 202n12

extension, attribute of, 50, 51, 66, 69–70, 75, 78, 104, 137, 144, 212n64, 216n14

external causes: affects and, 125, 127, 162; inadequate self-image and, 122, 127; joy and sadness associated with, 85; love and, 54, 130, 136, 140–41; *scientia intuitiva* and, 140–41

eyes of the mind, 150, 230n6

Fabro, Cornelio, 217n21, 217n23, 219n31

faith (*fides*): Anselm on, 71, 74; Aquinas on, 102, 106; in Christ's special status, 107; Spinoza on, 97, 98, 99, 106, 121, 177–78, 182, 239n42; Spinoza's dogmata of universal faith, 6–7, 110, 179–82, 239n44, 240nn53–54; superstitious, 21, 158; works and, 97, 170, 179

fear: conquered with repetition, 45; 1 John on love casting out, 161; repeatedly linked with death by Spinoza, 161; Spinoza's philosophical quest and, 21–22; superstitious religion and, 21, 117–18, 161. *See also* hope and fear

fear of death: blessedness as remedy for, 158–59; Christian belief in personal immortality and, 153, 155–56; eternity of the mind and, 153–54, 162–63; free man thinking of life instead of, 156–57, 158; replaced by conversion of passive to active affect, 159; resisted by love, 162; Spinoza's interpretation of the Fall and, 156–57; superstitious religion and, 4. *See also* eternal life

Feld, Edward, 194n36

final causes: in medieval thought, 4; seventeenth-century thinkers arguing against, 81, 213n7; Spinoza on, 82, 87, 88, 104, 213n14

first causes: Aquinas on God as, 81; genuine knowledge through idea of God and, 48; logical order of ideas and, 40

first kind of cognition: *acquiescentia in se ipso* and, 114, 125–27, 131, 132, 143. *See also* imagination; opinion

fortitude, 165

Foucault, Michel: on spirituality, 23–24, 26, 28, 33, 37, 187, 197nn18–19

Francis de Sales, 171

freedom, human: *acquiescentia in se ipso* and, 113, 115, 118, 124; being-in-God and, 91, 137, 184, 226n36; bondage to the fear of death and, 156–57, 158, 159; in contemplation of life, not death, 162; fortitude and, 165; identical to necessity, 124; immanent teleology and, 88; love of God and, 134; natural philosophies of seventeenth century and, 170; service to God and, 121, 226n32; Spinoza's concern for political stability and, 232n18; strength of character and, 146–47; virtue as, 84

free will, Descartes on, 81–82, 83, 118, 124, 237n23

free will, Spinoza's denial of, 83–84; *acquiescentia in se ipso* and, 115, 118–20, 124–25; attribution to dependent beings and, 75; causation and, 214n15; Christian doctrines and, 172; desire for good way to live and, 79–80; as a fiction exacerbating love and hate, 122–23; forcefully expressed in the *Ethics*, 49; as a kind of superstition, 3; laws of nature and, 237n23; recognition that we are in God and, 139; for refusing to accept divine necessity, 122. *See also* freedom, human

Froude, J. A., 6

Garber, Daniel, 153–54, 203n22, 231n11
Garrett, Don: on 'being in,' 57; on finite things having some characteristics of a substance, 58, 231n11; on meaning of *quantum in se est*, 93–94, 216n1
Gavrilyuk, Paul L., 230n6
Geertz, Clifford, 236n14
generosity, 29, 146, 154, 165, 166
Genesis 2:17, Spinoza's exegesis of, 157–58
geometrical method: of Descartes, 201n6; of the *Ethics*, 35, 44, 201n3, 201n6; of Hobbes, 201n5, 201n6
Gersonides, 84, 214n16, 228n4
Gilson, Étienne, 219n30
gloria: as *kavod* in Hebrew, 141, 229n13; as love of esteem, 126; love of God and, 130, 141, 188
Goclenius, Rudolph, 224n9
God: Anselm's ontological argument for existence of, 71, 78; name of, 105, 186–87, 221nn39–40. *See also* anthropomorphic God; being-in-God; deism; panentheism; pantheism

God in the *Ethics*: as *causa sui*, 221n44; as cause of essence and existence of all things, 221n44; characteristics of, 137; definition of, 9, 47, 48, 50; hiddenness of, 70; as immanent, not transitive, cause, 59–60; infinite attributes of, 69–70, 137, 210n41; as ontological ground, 188; practice of relating 'all images of things' to idea of, 48, 163; as substance, not subject, 59, 205n9; union with, 151, 230n6, 235n42; virtue of giving honour to, 187; Zac on life of, 234n34. *See also* being-in-God

God's love for us, 134–35. See also *amor Dei intellectualis* (intellectual love of God); divine love

good. *See* highest good; true good

grace: Aquinas on, 102, 104, 107–8, 219n32; Luther on, 170; Spinoza's unwillingness to distinguish nature from, 102, 172

Grotius, Hugo, 14, 238n40

Gueroult, Martial, 208n27

habit: Aquinas on virtue as, 167; Descartes on, 198n36; repetition and, 37, 40, 44; Spinoza on *institutum* and, 26–27

habitual thinking of imagination, 37–39; to connect images with idea of God, 163; converted to rational thinking, 40, 44; retrained to change patterns of thinking, 45

habitus, scholastic ideas of, 169–70

Hadot, Pierre, 197n18

Hallett, H. F., 151

happiness, Descartes on free will and, 82, 86

happiness, Spinoza on: empowerment from rational thinking and, 44; erroneous attitudes and, 49; eternal, 25; intuitive knowledge of God and, 79, 84; in knowledge, not competitive success, 3; in virtue, 3–4

Harrison, Peter, 167–69, 171–72

Harvey, Warren Zev, 13, 135, 228n4, 230n1

hatred: love as response or replacement for, 29, 45, 146–47, 161, 165, 166; repeatedly linked with death, 161; as sadness with idea of external cause, 54
Hebraeus, Leo, 230n6
Heereboord, Adriaan, 14
Hegel, G. W. F., 35, 171
Heidegger, Martin, 56, 78, 212n68
Herbert, Edward, 168
Herder, Johann Gottfried, 6
hermeneutic of credulity, 11, 193n31
hermeneutic of suspicion, 11, 193n31
'The Hermeneutics of the Subject' (Foucault), 23–24, 197nn18–19
Heyderman, John, 216n14, 229n13, 230n6
highest good: attained by human effort, 172; desire and action in relation to, 80, 87–88; as knowledge and love of God, 12, 96–97, 134; knowledge of God and, 96; path in pursuit of, 89, 184; social nature of, 29–30, 31–32, 34, 199n49. *See also* true good
hilaritas (cheerfulness), 90, 128–29, 130, 227n42
Hinduism, panentheistic tendency in, 70
Hobbes, Thomas: denial of final causation by, 81; on habit, 37; replacing teleology with laws, 169–70, 172; on restless desire of power, 112; on submission to an external authority, 121, 225n31; on superstition, 4; Velthuysen influenced by, 5
honour: virtue of giving honour to God, 187, 235n6. *See also* wealth, honour and sensual pleasure
hope and fear: as agitating emotions, 29; Christian doctrines of an afterlife and, 143, 153, 154–55; as means for eliminating hope and fear, 203n22; pain associated with, 198n44; superstitious religion and, 4, 21. *See also* fear
human body, super-propositions on, 51–52
Hume, David: on habitual thinking, 39, 202n14; on role of repetition, 37; Spinoza on order and connection of ideas and, 40
humility, 116, 119, 120, 132, 133, 143, 155, 228nn50–51

Ignatius of Loyola, 13, 197n18
imagination, 37–41, 44, 45, 202n12; *acquiescentia* based on, 114, 125, 126–27, 131, 132; as basis of superstitious religion, 132; intuitive knowledge drowned out by, 77–78; obedience to God of superstitious religion and, 124; path of spiritual transformation leading through, 163; super-proposition on, 52; theological knowing and, 75
immanence, Aristotelian, 103
immanence of God, and transcendence: Anselm's *Proslogion* and, 73, 74; Aquinas's concept of participation and, 101, 106, 217n21, 219n31; God of Augustine and Aquinas and, 210n39; inseparable for Spinoza, 68, 70; misunderstandings of Spinoza's thought and, 61–62; Platonism and, 210n39; Sherman's refusal of transcendence and, 221n44. *See also* transcendence of God
immanent causation, 59–60, 61–62; of effects within ourselves, 94, 206n13; God as substance and, 69; internal causation and, 215n19, 229n11; Spinoza's reconfiguring of, 88
immanent obedience, 120–21, 122, 124, 132, 133
immortality. *See* eternal life
'in,' 57–58, 59
in se, 94, 104; God's own being-in-God and, 221n44
intellectus, 41
internal cause, 139, 215n19, 229n11
Islam, 1, 70
Israel, Jonathan, 2, 239n42

James, biblical Letter of, 97–98
James, Susan, 7–8, 179, 193n26, 226n38, 238n40, 239n44
John, First Letter of, 97–98, 100, 160–61, 162, 178, 217n18, 233nn30
John of Damascus: Aquinas's description of God and, 221n39; being-in-God and, 70, 102
John's Gospel: distinctive theology of, 160; on loving-kindness, 176–77; second birth in, 233n31; Spinoza on Christ's divinity and, 109
Jones, Matthew, 197n18

joy: *acquiescentia in se ipso* and, 112, 114, 116, 120, 125, 128–30, 131; *amor Dei intellectualis* and, 137; Anselm's reflections on, 73–74, 88; becoming acquainted with our feelings of, 185; communitarian ethic and, 147; eternal, 26; with idea of its external cause, as love, 99–100, 112, 136, 138, 140; love toward the eternal and, 28; participating in divine nature and, 92, 99–100; sadness and, 28, 29, 47, 85, 86, 90; *scientia intuitiva* and, 129–30; threefold taxonomy of cognition and, 138; transition in degree of perfection and, 47, 54, 88, 90

Judaism: panentheistic tendency in, 70; Spinoza's critique of scriptures in, 33; Spinoza's philosophy developed in dialogue with Christianity and, 13; Spinoza's rejection of dogmatic, sectarian religion and, 1, 2. *See also* Amsterdam's Jewish community

Judeo-Christian tradition, 13

justice, 7, 164, 165, 166, 176, 178, 179, 180, 182, 183

Kabbalistic authors, 89

Kant, Immanuel: autonomy in moral philosophy of, 170, 237n23; Foucault on spirituality and, 197n19; on Humean custom, 202n14; importance for modern philosophy, 10; on knowledge as active intellectual effort, 223n2; on moral necessity, 196n8; on religion as ethical life, 98; three *Critiques* by, 35

Kierkegaard, Søren, 12, 35, 171, 187, 241n6

knowing-in-God, 75

knowledge: adequate, 75, 77, 79, 202n12, 214n15; error as privation of, 75; of our being-in-God, 78; Spinoza on nature of religion and, 176; union with object of, 230n6

knowledge and love of God: *amor Dei intellectualis* and, 137–38; blessedness consisting in, 10; as highest human good, 12, 96–97, 134; intensification of consciousness and, 149; participation and, 95–98; as union with God in Spinoza's early texts, 136

knowledge of God: desire for the good and, 80; desiring the good for others and, 55, 146, 165; excluded from first kind of cognition, 143; faith and, 178, 239n42; happiness consisting in, 84; inadequate due to imagining, 214n15; intuitive, 79, 80; requiring sustained attention, 185; resulting from Spinoza's philosophical enquiries, 182; Spinoza on Christ and, 108–9, 110; *Theologico-Political Treatise* on, 96–97

Lærke, Mogens, 179, 232n14, 239n50, 240n53

landlady of Spinoza, 19–20, 32, 33, 186

Latour, Bruno, 6, 62, 241n6

laws, natural and moral, 169–70, 172, 237n23

Levene, Nancy, 121, 207n26

life, 234n34

Locke, John, 37

Lord, Beth, 150

love, 144–47; damaging if misdirected, 144–45; divine, 134–39, 141–42, 143–44, 229n5; external and internal objects of, 138–39; as joy with idea of its external cause, 54, 99–100, 112, 136, 138, 140; participation in God's nature and, 99, 217n18; to resist death, 162; as response or replacement for hatred, 29, 45, 146–47, 161, 165, 166; Spinoza's reordering of, 28; striving to benefit someone who is loved, 55; suggested as one of God's attributes, 216n14; threefold taxonomy of, 138; toward the eternal and infinite thing, 28; toward the eternal rather than what perishes, 188; as transforming power in 1 John, 160–61, 233n31. *See also* self-love

love of God. See *amor Dei intellectualis* (intellectual love of God); knowledge and love of God

loving-kindness, 7, 97–99, 121, 173–75, 176, 178, 179, 180, 182, 183

Luther, Martin, 153, 170

Lutheranism, 168, 171

Maimon, Solomon, 215n19

Maimonides, Moses, 13, 80, 135, 229n13, 230n1, 230n6

Malebranche, Nicolas, 37
McCabe, Herbert, 210n39, 226n36, 229n5
Melamed, Yitzhak, 140–41, 207n26, 210n41, 213n14, 215n19
mercy, 176, 177, 178, 180, 181, 217n15
mereology, 67
Mersenne, Marin, 207n18
Metaphysical Thoughts, 220n36, 234n34
methexis: Platonic participation and, 103, 219n28; Spinoza's being-in-God and, 103–4
Milbank, John, 192n7, 219n32, 240n55
Mill, J. S., 167–68, 236n10
mimesis, 103, 104
mind: as *animus*, 28, 198n41; as idea of the human body, 51–52, 69–70, 202n12, 211n44; as *mens*, in union with nature, 29; sensing itself immediately, 149; super-propositions on, 50–52; visual metaphor of, 150, 230n6. *See also* eternity of the mind
miracles, belief in, 3, 4, 96
modernity: *acquiescentia in se ipso* and, 112; conceptual shift about religion and, 165, 167–69; grammatical shift in translations about religion and, 169; nostalgic contemporary theologians and, 183, 240n55; Spinoza's ambivalent relation to, 2–4, 192n8; Spinoza's alternative version of, 3–4, 10; Spinozism offering resistance to diseases of, 183
modes: being-in-God and, 57, 58; following necessarily from God, 50; as immanent or transitive causes, 206n13; metaphysics of substance and, 8; our language applying only to, 58; possessing substance characteristics to some degree, 58, 93–94; to some degree eternal, 94; traditional theological view and, 3; transitive causation by, 215n19. *See also* substance-mode relation
Monologion (Anselm), 217n19
Montaigne, Michel de, 4
moralism, grounded on illusion of free will, 120–21
moral law. *See* laws, natural and moral
moral responsibility, Spinoza on, 213n13

Moreau, Pierre-François, 24, 149, 197n26, 230n6, 231n11
Morteira, Saul Levi, 194n36, 214n16

Nadler, Steven: asserting identity between God and nature, 64–65, 193n29; on transcendence, 62; on Spinoza as atheist, 193n29, 208n27; on Spinoza and pantheism, 208n27, 209n30; on Spinoza's participation in theatre, 196n7; on variety of Spinoza's sources and influences, 14
natural philosophy, 169–70, 172
natural theology, 96
natura naturans, 63–66, 68; Aquinas on, 219n33; elusive nature of, 76; as ontological ground of Spinoza's metaphysics, 186, 188; Spinoza's definition of, 209n32
natura naturata, 63–65, 68; Aquinas on, 219n33; wholes and parts in, 76
nature: Della Rocca on identification of God with, 210n38; *Deus sive Natura* and, 11–12, 64–67, 104, 186; knowledge according to reason and, 40; Melamed on transcendence of, 210n41; modern tendency to separate God and, 3, 60, 61, 104; not formally defined by Spinoza, 209n32; Spinoza's idea of God and, 3, 60; union of the mind with, 29
necessary existence of God, 50, 78
necessity: *acquiescentia in se ipso*, 121–24; freedom identical to, 124; Kant on, 196n8; obedience and, 121–22, 123–24, 226n34; Spinoza's alternative ethics grounded on, 121
negative theology, 59, 221n40. *See also* apophatic theology
Neoplatonism: concepts of participation of, 103; degrees of being and, 90. *See also* Platonism
New Testament. *See* 1 Corinthians; James, Letter of; John, First Letter of; John's Gospel; Paul; Peter, Second Letter of
Nicolas of Cusa, 59
nihilism, 10, 183
nostalgic contemporary theologians, 183, 240n55
Novalis, 6, 193n29, 208n27

obedience: divine necessity and, 121–22, 123–24, 226n34; to God of superstitious religion, 124, 133; immanent, 120–21, 122, 124, 132, 133; practical, 121; to scriptural or 'revealed' religion, 176; Spinoza on faith and, 178, 180, 239n42; Spinoza on piety and, 177; three different modes of, 122, 124, 132

objectification of *religio*: concept of *fides* connected to, 178; resistance to, 171, 172–73, 175–76, 186; in terms of belief and belonging, 2, 7, 169

Oldenburg, Henry, 34, 41, 60, 75–76, 109, 166, 213n13, 232n21

Oliver, Simon, 207n21, 217n21

ontological asymmetry, 59, 67, 73, 101, 142, 221n44; denied by deism and pantheism, 68

ontology: Spinoza's core principle of, 88; theology and, 78, 212n68

opinion: in first kind of cognition, 125–27, 131; second kind of cognition and, 128

panentheism: analogy of being and, 221n44; Anselm's *Proslogion* and, 73; being-in-God and, 67; defined, 63, 209n31; diversity of opinion on Spinoza's ontology and, 208n27; expressing both difference and relation, 221n44; pantheism and, 62; Spinoza's theological knowing and, 75; as tendency within theistic traditions, 70

pantheism, 62–68, 208nn27–28, 209n30; historical differences in concept of, 62–63; privileging immanence over transcendence, 74; Spinoza and Aquinas charting a course between deism and, 221n45; Spinoza's rejection of, 106; today's common understanding of, 63; univocity of being and, 221n44

participation in divine nature, 92–111; *acquiescentia in se ipso* and, 107, 133; advancing towards greater perfection and, 100; Aquinas on, 101–3, 104, 106, 218n25; Aquinas on Christ and, 107–8; biblical context of, 97–99, 100, 103, 217n18; combining difference and identity, 104, 106; difficulty of becoming conscious of, 75; English translations of *participare* and, 92–93, 102; joyful, 92, 94; long history of concept of, 103, 107; love and, 99, 217n18; as matter of degree, 95; the more we are in ourselves, 94; as normative ethical principle, 137; Platonic philosophical tradition and, 103, 219n28; significance of verb *participare* and, 95, 100; Spinoza's treatment of Christ and, 110; *Theologico-Political Treatise* on, 95–100

Pascal, Blaise, 171

path in pursuit of highest good, 89, 184

Paul: Augustine's gloss on, 198n33; 1 Corinthians, 100, 226n32; distinction between flesh and spirit, 230n6; living and moving in God and, 98, 106; participation and, 100, 219n28; on salvation from sin through Christ, 156, 232n21; on setting the mind toward life and peace, 162; Spinoza's citation of, 13, 14, 60, 100, 109, 129, 205n12; Spinoza's mirroring of, on bondage and freedom, 156, 158

peace of mind: *acquiescentia in se ipso* and, 113, 114, 132; connection to God and, 185; echoing ideal of contemplation, 3; intuitive knowledge of God and, 79; Spinoza's conversion in way of life and, 28–29; of wise person, 3, 33–34, 113, 116, 127, 131, 144, 162. See also *animi acquiescentia* (satisfaction of mind)

perfection: *amor Dei intellectualis* and, 107, 137; degrees of, 89, 90, 94, 95, 204n24; degrees of, as applied to Christ, 110; of human actions, 88; participation in divine nature and, 100; as reality, 204n24; *scientia intuitiva* and, 129; transitions in degree of, 47; as we are affected with joy, 92, 94

Perl, Eric, 210n39

Peter, Second Letter of, 100, 102

pharmakon, 45

philosophy: break between spirituality and, 23–24; connection between theology and, 8–9, 193n26; as a form of religion according to James, 8; importance of Spinoza to, 10, 14; tradition about living in the world while reaching for truth in, 32

philosophy of religion: academic discipline of, 211n48; Anselm's *Proslogion* and, 71

Pickstock, Catherine, 240n55
Pieper, Josef, 41, 223n2
pietists, 171
piety and *religio*, 165, 166, 171, 235n6; Calvin and, 236n12; external practice vs. internal worship and, 174; Spinoza on behavior as opposed to beliefs and, 177, 239n44
Plato: extensive writings of, 35; metaphor of 'eyes of the mind' and, 230n6; parable of the cave, 32; participation vs. imitation in works of, 103, 219n28; on virtue synonymous with happiness, 3–4, 86
Platonism: coincidence of immanence and transcendence in, 210n39; degrees of being and, 89, 90; Spinoza's philosophy and, 219n30. *See also* Neoplatonism
Plotinus, 89
Poiret, Pierre, 132, 228n50
Political Treatise, 238n29
porous self, vs. individualism in modernity, 3, 192n8
power: *acquiescentia in se ipso* and, 120; being and, 93; degrees of, 89, 132, 133, 204n24; diminished by puritanical teachings, 92; diminished by superstitious religion, 143; enhanced when recognising our ontological dependence, 139; enlightened self-love and, 143; increased by knowing, 138; love and joy related to increase in, 99, 138; Luther's polemic on virtue and, 170; perfection and, 204n24; virtue as, 167, 172, 237n23
practice: as adoption of new habit, 27; of relating 'all images of things' to idea of God, 48, 163; vs. theory until the seventeenth century, 200n1
pragmatism of Spinoza: mitigating critique of superstitious religion, 33, 155, 158; sovereign rule over external religion and, 175
Primus, Kristin, 149–50
principle of sufficient reason, 210n40
Proslogion (Anselm), 71–75, 78, 88
Protestant neo-scholasticism, 14
Protestant Reformation, 168, 171; plural creeds emerging from, 181; politicised sectarianism and, 169
Protestant theologies, and capitalist culture, 3
Przywara, Erich, 208n27

quantum in se est, 85, 93–95, 214n16, 216n1
quies, 113, 132, 138. *See also* peace of mind; rest

Rahner, Karl, 187
realised eschatology, 160, 233n30
reality: degrees of, 89–90; perfection as, 204n24
reason (*ratio*), 44, 202n12; *acquiescentia in se ipso* and, 114, 117, 122, 127–29, 130–31, 132, 143, 227n42; acting from necessity of our nature and, 122; being-in-God and, 77; desire arising from, 128; desiring the good for others and, 161, 165; happiness achieved through, 79; laws of man's nature and, 237n23; less powerful than *scientia intuitiva*, 144; medieval thinkers contrasting *intellectus* with, 41; repetition and, 37, 40; Spinoza on piety and, 235n6; Spinoza's insistence on third kind of knowing and, 41–42; Spinoza's thought on eternity in terms of, 231n8; striving for understanding, 55; theological knowing and, 75; transition from imagination to, 39–41, 44
Reid, Thomas, 37
religio (religion): Aquinas on, 6, 164–65, 166, 167, 235n2, 235n6; conceptual shift to modern understanding of, 165, 167–69, 171; conventional, Spinoza's ambivalence toward, 2, 33; external vs. internal, 174–75; forms of devotion or attention to, 187–88; meaning a binding in Latin, 21; modern category of, 2, 7; as a question, 187, 241n6; Spinoza on form and content of, 165–67; Spinoza on freedom of judgment about, 204n28; Spinoza on virtues comprising, 176; Spinoza's definition of, 7–8, 80, 142, 165–66, 182–83; Spinoza's non-sectarian understanding of, 172–73; *Theologico-Political Treatise* on nature and scope of, 175–82; as virtue, 6–7, 12, 164, 166–67; as virtue

of giving honour to God, 187. *See also* objectification of *religio*; piety and *religio*; Spinoza's religion; superstitious religion
religious diversity, 10
religious liberty, 167–68
religious rituals, 48–49
Renz, Ursula, 205n7, 212n68, 215n26
repentance, 116, 118, 119, 120, 125, 132, 155, 180
repetition: in act of reading the *Ethics*, 56–57; in bringing our emotions into harmony with reason, 45; early modern philosophers' fascination with, 37; the *Ethics* on habitual thinking and, 37–38, 40, 45; intuitive, 43–44; in many religious practices, 48–49; rationality entrenched by, 44; as remedy for what it helped produce, 45; in structure of the *Ethics*, 36, 40, 46
rest: Bacon on human intellect and, 202n18; distinction between fluctuation and, 138; finding in the true good, 32; grounded in God, 188; highest human good and, 23; intuitive knowledge and, 41–42, 132; of the mind in the good, 28–29; path of freedom leading to, 184. See also *quies*
resting in God: Anselm's aspiration for, 71–72; being-in-God and, 79; as highest human good, 3; loving God and, 16; obedience to oneself and to God as, 124; *scientia intuitiva* and, 41. See also *acquiescentia in se ipso*
resurrection of Christ, 14, 109, 111, 156, 232n21
Ricoeur, Paul, 193n31
rituals, religious, 48–49
Roman Catholic Church: Protestant Reformation and, 168; Spinoza's letter to Burgh on, 2, 4, 173–74, 191n4; superstitious popular religion ascribed to, 142–43, 159
Romanticism, and Spinozism, 6, 111, 171
Rosemann, Philipp, 217n21
Rosenthal, Michael, 182, 240n54
Rutherford, Donald, 223n5, 227n44

sadness: becoming acquainted with our feelings of, 185; humility as kind of, 120; joy and, 28, 29, 47, 85, 86, 90; promoted by superstitious religion, 142; repentance as kind of, 116, 119, 120; shame as specific type of, 215n25; transition to a lesser perfection and, 54
salvation: Calvinist emphasis on damnation and, 4; Christian disputes over means of, 169–70; Paul on salvation from sin through Christ, 156, 232n21; seventeenth-century French deists and, 207n18; Spinoza on Christ and, 107–9, 222n48, 223n51; Spinoza on claims of Christian churches and, 110–11, 153; Spinoza on divine love and, 134–35, 143–44; Spinoza on peace of mind and, 114; Spinoza on turn from death to life and, 153; Yovel on Spinoza's 'secular form of,' 235n43; Yovel on third kind of knowledge and, 231n7
Schelling, Friedrich, 89
Schindler, David, 210n39
Schlegel, Friedrich, 111
Schleiermacher, Friedrich, 6, 171
Schmaltz, Tad M., 213n7
scholasticism: Descartes' metaphysics shaped by, 14; Protestant neo-scholasticism, 14. See also Aquinas, Thomas
scientia intuitiva (intuitive knowledge), 37, 41–44, 202n12, 203n19; *acquiescentia in se ipso* and, 41, 114, 117, 129–31, 132, 143; *amor Dei intellectualis* and, 129, 138, 140, 145; Aquinas on knowledge of singular things and, 227n43; Aristotelian philosophy and, 219n30; being-in-God and, 77, 129, 130, 138, 140, 185; Christ's knowledge of God and, 110; desire and, 80; disagreement about attributing it to Spinoza, 150–51; dynamic text of the *Ethics* and, 44; enlightened self-love and, 143; eternity of the mind and, 149–50, 151–52, 203n19, 231n7; of God's essence-and-existence, 77–78; immediacy of, 42–43; mental peace arising from, 129, 227n44; more powerful than *ratio*, 144; rest and, 80; Spinoza's mathematical example of, 42–43, 76–77, 78, 227n47; theological knowing and, 75

scientific knowledge: Bacon and, 3, 192n9; benefit of the *Ethics* for theologians and, 10; Spinoza's interest in, 3

second kind of cognition. *See* reason (*ratio*)

secular interpretations of the *Ethics*, 5, 11–12, 186, 228n50

secularism: modern concept of religion and, 2; Spinoza's theological orientation and, 15, 70; Taylor on Nature identical with God and, 65

self-contentment, 107, 113, 133, 138

self-esteem, 113, 223n5, 225n12

self-knowledge, 45, 115, 140, 185

self-love: *acquiescentia in se ipso* and, 112, 113, 114; *amor Dei intellectualis* and, 139, 145–46; anxiety associated with, 126; Aquinas on love for other people and, 146; different kinds of cognition and, 143; love of God and, 140, 141; pride and, 117

self-preservation, 84–86; appetite and, 85–86, 87, 90; desire and, 90, 161–62, 165; history of concept of, 214n16; medieval conception of *virtus* and, 172; *quantum in se est* and, 93–94; Spinoza's definition of life and, 234n34. See also *conatus* (striving)

self-satisfaction, 113, 115, 116, 117, 118, 225n12

Seneca, 22

Sherman, Jacob, 221n44

Shestov, Lev, 212n70

Short Treatise, 60, 135–36, 205n11, 230n6, 233n31

Silverthorne, Michael, 239n42

sin: Anselm on, 73; eternal life in Christian theology and, 161, 232n19; Luther's view of, 170; Paul's Christ releasing humans from, 156, 158; Spinoza on peace of mind and, 213n13; Spinoza's dogmata of universal faith and, 180; Spinoza's rejection of concept of, 75, 82, 156–57, 172

Smith, Pamela, 200n1

Smith, Steven B., 201n6, 207n24, 210n33

Souriau, Étienne: on degrees of being, 215n23; on devotion, 21, 23, 24; on existence as univocal in the *Ethics*, 207n23; on meaning of *in*, 57; name of God and, 221n40; on the existence of God, 212n70; on a questioning situation, 187; on significance of expression in Spinozism, 62

Spinoza, Benedict de: attempted assassination of, 19, 191n1, 196n7; biographical writings about, 18–21, 32, 71 (*see also* Nadler, Steven); Christian associates and influences of, 14–15, 195n42; conversion to new way of life, 24–32, 197n27; excommunication of, 1, 13, 19, 191n1; importance for modern philosophy, 10, 14; influence on Christian thinkers, 14; inspiring devotion in his friends, 34; intellectual influences on, 13–14, 194n36; landlady of, 19–20, 32, 33, 186; making his living as a lens-grinder, 35; meditating, 18, 26, 32; outsider perspective of, 15; reclusive quietude in later years of, 71; suffering from hope and fear, 21–22; as unusual seventeenth-century freethinker, 1, 70

Spinoza's religion, 5–8; ambiguity of the *Ethics* on, 11–12, 186; Curley's judgement on, 7; described in his reply to Velthuysen, 5; his definition of religion and, 7–8, 80, 142, 165–66, 182–83; modern category of religion and, 2, 7; as open question, 6, 13; our grasping of, 12–13. See also *religio* (religion); true religion, Spinozist

spiritual exercises: early seventeenth-century, 13, 197n18; the *Ethics* as, 37, 48–49

spirituality, Foucault on, 23–24, 26, 28, 33, 37, 197nn18–19

Stoicism: on bondage to the passions, 156; on desire restrained by reason, 128; ideal of tranquillity in, 41; Spinoza's retraining of the mind and, 45; of texts recovered during Renaissance, 13

Strauss, Leo, 234n33

striving. See *conatus* (striving)

Suárez, Francisco, 81, 88, 169, 213n7

substance: Aquinas on individual beings as, 104; Descartes on application to God and to other things, 58; Renz on dissociation from concept of subject, 205n9

substance-mode relation, 3; Aquinas's metaphysics and, 101; being-in-God and, 57–59, 68–69, 88–89, 94; as categorical distinction, 58, 205n7; distinguishing Spinoza's theology from pantheism, 67–68; incarnation of Christ and, 109–10; *quantum in se est* and, 93–94; as Spinoza's innovation, 106. *See also* modes

super-propositions, 46–49; correcting readers' darkest errors, 49; on degrees of perfection of the mind, 89; desire for the good and, 80; list of twenty-six in the *Ethics*, 50–55; lowering the criterion for, 204n25; on striving and desire, 84

superstition, as vice according to Aquinas, 164, 235n2

superstitious religion, 3–5; *acquiescentia in se ipso* and, 115, 117–18, 132; affects promoted by, 4, 142–43; Calvinism and, 4, 14; causing conflict in Dutch Republic, 158, 161; fear of punishment in afterlife and, 4, 157; hope and fear as source of, 198n44; illusion of free will and, 120; misleading doctrines of immortality in, 150; obedience to God of, 124; prohibition of enjoyment in, 92; religious rituals causing troublesome emotions and, 49; Spinoza's pragmatism mitigating critique of, 33, 155, 158; Spinoza's proposal of porous self and, 192n8; Spinoza's students acquiring defense against, 36–37; subject to rigorous critique in *Theologico-Political Treatise*, 33. *See also* anthropomorphic God

Tauler, Johannes, 171
Taylor, Charles, 65, 192nn7–8
teleological thinking: Descartes and, 81–82, 169–70, 172, 213n7, 213n10; of medieval philosophers, 80–81, 169; seventeenth-century shift in, 81–82; Spinoza on causation and, 87–88, 213n14; Spinoza on divine purposes and, 82–83; Spinoza on good way to live and, 79–80; Spinoza on virtue and, 86–87, 172
tenets of universal faith, 6–7, 110, 179–82, 239n44, 240nn53–54
tetragrammaton (YHWH), 105, 186
te Velde, Rudi, 217n21, 217n23, 220n37

theologians: nostalgic, 183, 240n55; paying little attention to the *Ethics*, 9, 62, 207n26; Spinoza as marginal figure for, 10

Theologico-Political Treatise: *acquiescentia* in, 114; Bayle on 'Atheism' in, 19; on beliefs being less important than ethical conduct, 33; on Christ's connection to God, 108–9; conception of religion in, 5; criticism of theology and theologians in, 78; as critique of Judaism and Christianity, 13; definition of Nature in, 209n32; distinguishing between superstition and true religion, 4, 192n11; echoing Aquinas on name of God, 105; idea of God's chosen people and, 2; James on relationship between philosophy and religion and, 7–8; on knowledge and love of God, 134; on nature and scope of *religio*, 175–82; on obedience, 121; *participare* in, 95–100; on relationship between philosophy and theology, 9, 193n26; *religio* in relation to faith and, 182; on social and political aspect of religious questions, 33; tenets (dogmata) of universal faith in, 6–7, 110, 179–82, 239n44, 240nn53–54; Velthuysen's critique of, 5, 173, 197n27

theology: apophatic, 12, 73, 75, 78 (*see also* negative theology); broad and literal sense of, 8; connection between philosophy and, 8–9, 193n26; ontology and, 78, 212n68; Spinoza's critique of, 8–9, 78

third kind of cognition. See *scientia intuitiva* (intuitive knowledge)

Thomas à Kempis, 171
thought, attribute of, 42, 50, 69, 70, 75, 78, 137, 150, 203n19, 212n64, 216n14
Toland, John, 62–63, 208n28
Totaro, Giuseppina, 224n7
transcendence, Platonic, 103
transcendence of God: deism in relation to, 68; for Descartes, 210n41; God's infinite attributes and, 69; for modern theologians, 68; panentheism in relation to, 63; pantheism in relation to, 63, 68. *See also* immanence of God, and transcendence
transitive causation, 59–61, 69, 206n13, 215n19

Treatise on the Emendation of the Intellect: cognitive conversion and, 44; on conversion in way of life, 24–33, 197n27; Descartes' tone compared to, 196n14; Foucault on spirituality and, 23–24; influences on, 13, 22; on joy of love for the eternal thing, 188; on minds disturbed by love for what can perish, 188; on seeking a remedy for suffering, 162; on seeking the greatest joy, to eternity, 148–49; Spinoza's suffering from unstable emotions and, 21–22, 29; three rules of living in, 31–32, 45, 199n55

true good: importance of pursuing, 29; not necessarily hindered by worldly pursuits, 30–31; returning to the world after pursuit of, 32–33, 200n58; Spinoza's pursuit of, 25–27, 28, 29–30, 198n38; state of being at peace in, 28–29. *See also* highest good

true idea, 42–43

true knowledge, 75; love proceeding from, 138. *See also* adequate knowledge

true religion, Spinozist: empowering character of, 143–44; explained to Velthuysen, 5; knowledge of God and, 143; practical obedience and, 121; sovereign rule over external religion and, 175, 238n29; Spinoza's attention to New Testament sources and, 161, 233n26; superstition and, 4, 159, 192n11; tenets of universal faith and, 179, 182; as a virtue, 183. *See also* Spinoza's religion

truth: difference between Spinoza's two great works and, 33; the *Ethics* inspiring readers' devotion to, 34; Foucault on spirituality and, 23–24; *scientia intuitiva* and, 42–43; as self-evident, 1, 191n3; Spinoza's desire of inquiring into, 18, 33; Spinoza's devotion to pursuit of, 23

Tschirnhaus, 5

Turner, William, 168

union with God: in the *Ethics*, 151, 230n6, 235n42; in the *Short Treatise*, 136; Zac on eternal life through, 235n42

universal images, 38–39

univocity of being, 221n44

Van Bunge, Wiep, 233n26
van den Enden, Franciscus, 13, 196n7
Velthuysen, Lambert van, 5, 154, 173, 193n26, 197n27, 207n18, 238n40
Verbeek, Theo, 232n18
virtue: *acquiescentia in se ipso* and, 113; Aristotelian understanding of, 164, 167, 169, 170, 171, 172; Calvin on, 86, 170; Christian doctrine of eternal life and, 154–55; consisting in justice, loving kindness, and mercy, 176–77; Descartes on free will and, 118; desiring the good for others and, 55; external vs. internal, 174–75; faith and, 178; false religion linked to lack of, 166; fortitude as, 165; as habit according to Descartes, 198n36; as its own reward, 84, 86–87, 133, 154; joy as experience of, 91; requiring knowledge, 182; motivated by love of the good, not fear of evil, 157; not peculiar to any religion, 2; as power, 167, 172, 237n23; regarded as burden by most people, 159; *religio as*, 6–7, 12, 164, 166–67; replaced in modernity by concept of law, 169–70; in Spinoza's alternative modernity, 3–4; Spinoza's tenets of universal faith and, 179; teleological thinking and, 86–87, 172; transformation of lived body and, 163

Voetius, Gisbert, 170
Voltaire, 217n15

Wahlde, Urban C. von, 233nn30–31
wealth, honour and sensual pleasure, 25–26, 27, 28, 30–31, 197nn26–27
Weber, Max, 3, 192n9
Webster, Charles, 192n9
Wilberforce, Robert, 63
wise person: free from bondage of Christian superstition, 158; peace of mind of, 3, 33–34, 113, 116, 127, 131, 144, 162
Wolfson, Harry Austryn, 214n16
worm in the blood, metaphor of, 75–76

Yovel, Yirmiyahu, 193n30, 207n24, 231n7, 235n43

Zac, Sylvain, 207n26, 234n34, 235n42

A NOTE ON THE TYPE

THIS BOOK has been composed in Miller, a Scotch Roman typeface designed by Matthew Carter and first released by Font Bureau in 1997. It resembles Monticello, the typeface developed for The Papers of Thomas Jefferson in the 1940s by C. H. Griffith and P. J. Conkwright and reinterpreted in digital form by Carter in 2003.

Pleasant Jefferson ("P. J.") Conkwright (1905–1986) was Typographer at Princeton University Press from 1939 to 1970. He was an acclaimed book designer and AIGA Medalist.

The ornament used throughout this book was designed by Pierre Simon Fournier (1712–1768) and was a favorite of Conkwright's, used in his design of the *Princeton University Library Chronicle*.

Ingram Content Group UK Ltd.
Milton Keynes UK
UKHW010855210523
422080UK00003B/118